The Development and Reform of Financial Systems in Central and Eastern Europe

To Hélène, Corinne and Jennifer
in appreciation for your support and understanding of the
demands of my professional life.

To Éva, Andrea and Gábor

The Development and Reform of Financial Systems in Central and Eastern Europe

Edited by
John P. Bonin
and
István P. Székely

Edward Elgar

Published by

Edward Elgar Publishing Limited
Gower House
Croft Road
Aldershot
Hants GU11 3HR
England

Edward Elgar Publishing Company
Old Post Road
Brookfield
Vermont 05036
USA

British Library Cataloguing in Publication Data

Development and Reform of Financial
Systems in Central and Eastern Europe
    I. Bonin, John P. II. Szekely, Istvan P.
    332.094

Library of Congress Cataloguing in Publication Data

The development and reform of financial systems in Central and Eastern
    Europe / edited by John P. Bonin and István P. Székely.
        p.   cm.
    1. Financial institutions—Europe, Eastern. 2. Financial
institutions—Central Europe. 3. Europe, Eastern—Economic
policy—1989–   4. Central Europe—Economic policy. 5. Europe,
Eastern—Economic conditions—1989–   6. Central Europe—Economic
conditions. I. Bonin, John. II. Székely, István P., 1959–
HG186.E82D48   1994
332.1'0947–dc20

94–25519
CIP

ISBN 1 85898 024 0

Printed and bound in Great Britain by
Hartnolls Limited, Bodmin, Cornwall

Contents

Figures

Tables

Contributors

István Ábel, *Budapest Bank, Budapest University of Economics, and CEPR, London*
Peter Backé, *Oesterreichische Nationalbank, Vienna*
John P. Bonin, *Wesleyan University, Middletown, CT*
Peter Dittus, *Bank for International Settlements, Basle*
Rumen Dobrinsky, *Centre for Strategic Business and Political Studies, Sofia*
Lyubomir Filipov, *Bulgarian National Bank, Sofia*
Heinz Glück, *Oesterreichische Nationalbank, Vienna*
Richard A. Golden, *Creditanstalt Investment AG, Vienna*
Eduard Hochreiter, *Oesterreichische Nationalbank, Vienna*
Miroslav Hrnčíř, *Institute of Economics of the Czech National Bank, Prague*
David M. Kemme, *Wichita State University, Wichita, KS*
Christian Kirchner, *Humboldt University, Berlin*
Ryszard Kokoszczyński, *National Bank of Poland, Warsaw*
Douglas Kruse, *Institute for EastWest Studies Banking and Finance Assistance Center, Budapest*
Kálmán Mizsei, *Institute for EastWest Studies, New York*
John Michael Montias, *Yale University, New Haven, CT*
Peter Mooslechner, *Austrian Institute of Economic Research, Vienna*
Rosemary Piper, *Hudson Institute, Indianapolis, IN*
Jouko Rautava, *Bank of Finland, Helsinki*
György Sándor, *National Bank of Hungary, Budapest*
Mark E. Schaffer, *Centre for Economic Performance, London School of Economics*
Aurel Schubert, *Oesterreichische Nationalbank, Vienna*
Pierre L. Siklos, *Wilfrid Laurier University, Waterloo, Ontario*
István P. Székely, *United Nations Secretariat, New York, Budapest University of Economics, and CEPR, London*
Werner Varga, *Creditanstalt, Vienna*
Éva Várhegyi, *Financial Research Ltd., Budapest*
Paweł Wyczański, *National Bank of Poland, Warsaw*

1 Introduction

John P. Bonin, Heinz Glück, and István P. Székely

'If capital is at the heart of capitalism, then well-functioning capital markets are at the heart of a well-functioning capitalist economy' (Stiglitz, 1992). Since capital markets are both transaction intensive (the payments settlement function) and highly dependent on information (the credit allocation function), commercial banks are at the heart of capital markets. However, commercial banks in the Central and Eastern European (CEE) economies in transition are financially weak, state-owned institutions burdened with the legacy of bad loans inherited from discredited political regimes. Consequently, they do not function like real banks so that these countries find themselves trapped in a bad equilibrium with a distressed financial sector coupled with a weak real sector. The challenge is to find the appropriate policies to transform these economies and put them on the road to the good equilibrium consisting of a healthy financial sector linked with a strong, vibrant, growing real sector.

'Enterprise restructuring, privatization and banking reform must go forward together' (Brainard, 1991). Enterprise privatization without banking reform will not ensure that credit is allocated to its most productive uses. Similarly, banking reform without enterprise privatization is likely to perpetuate the bad allocation of credit. Privatization of enterprises must be a natural *consequence* of the restructuring banks so that cleaning up the balance sheets of both banks and enterprises goes hand in hand. Privatization cannot be relied upon to solve the problems of the financial sector. This interdependency raises a 'chicken-egg' type of dilemma. What should be done first?

To address this issue, it is crucial to understand the root of financial distress in the CEE countries. In the traditional planning system, the state directed the allocation of investment and provided the liquidity necessary to carry out the plan directly through the fiscal budget. As the CEE countries reformed their financial sectors, the state withdrew from capital markets leaving behind a significant void (Ábel and Bonin, 1994). The banking system consisted of an underdeveloped technical infrastructure (a technologically backward payment settlements system) employing underdeveloped human capital (weak corporate governance due to the drastic change in economic cultures). In all CEE countries, state-owned

1

commercial banks (SOCBs) were created by dividing up the commercial division of the national bank without regard to the strength of the resulting loan portfolios. Hence, these nascent institutions with virtually no branch system inherited concentrated loan portfolios of dubious quality with little opportunity in the short term to improve their situation. Consequently, the cause of financial distress in the CEE countries is significantly different from that in developed countries in that it is not due to 'overly' aggressive market activities but rather to past state-directed decisions for which current actors accept no responsibility.

The problems caused by the state's desertion of its commercial banks was compounded by the proliferation of well-meaning legislation. Banking Acts adopted Western-style prudential rules requiring the accumulation of loan-loss reserves against the qualified portion of the portfolio and the achievement of minimum risk-adjusted capital adequacy ratios according to Bank of International Settlements (BIS) standards. Taken together with the financially weak positions of the commercial banks, these requirements led to a severe credit crunch in the real productive sector. Banks maintain high spreads on business loans so that 'good' companies that are servicing their loans provide the necessary cash flow to provision against the non-performing part of the portfolio. This perverse 'Robin Hood' policy resembles the financial levelling practised under the traditional system (Kornai, 1986) and forces the financial sector to bear the burden of the state's industrial policy. From the customer's perspective, such a policy encourages the good clients to seek financing outside the domestic commercial banking system leading to disintermediation. The banking legislation also induces banks to seek out safe assets with a reasonable rate of return. Hence, short-term, highly liquid government securities with an attractive risk/return profile are purchased by commercial bankers seeking both to improve the quality of their portfolios and to accumulate sufficient reserves to satisfy provisioning requirements.

Although household savings have increased dramatically in the CEE countries during the early stages of the transition, the financial sector is not effectively intermediating this savings to business investment. Rather, the network of national savings bank branches collects these deposits and transfers them on the interbank market to SOCBs which, in turn, use them to purchase government securities. Increasing fiscal deficits are financed through the issue of mainly short-term securities purchased by the commercial banks. Hence, business investment is stunted as little or no bank financing is available to the new (risky) firms entering the emerging private sector or for the necessary restructuring of state-owned enterprises. The needs of fiscal financing crowd out business investment as financially weak SOCBs attempt to satisfy prudential regulations without any assistance. Hence, the bad equilibrium of a weak financial sector coupled with a feeble real sector prevails currently in the CEE countries.

Although there is virtual agreement among academics, policy makers, and business analysts that properly designed and sequenced financial reforms are crucial for the success of the transformation, actual policy prescriptions differ significantly and are often based on politically motivated decisions. The financial sector is the segment of the economy in which central planning and the planners' mentality have survived for the longest period of time. The liberalization of the goods market is almost completed thanks in part to a significant degree of openness in the product markets of many CEE countries, but the liberalization of capital markets is lagging behind. The complexity of the issues and the interdependencies of policies make separation and sequencing of financial sector reforms difficult. Add to these the extreme changes in economic culture required and the degree of institution building necessary to support these reforms and the task becomes herculean. The contributors to this volume have made significant progress in identifying the problems, posing the appropriate questions, and discussing policy alternatives.

In Part One, Montias (Chapter 2) and Kemme (Chapter 3) provide probing overviews of the financial distress in the CEE countries by comparing problems and issues across countries. They highlight the financial aspects peculiar to the economies in transition so as to differentiate the situation in the CEE countries from the financial distress typical of market economies. In Part Two, the banking system is considered as the foundation for emerging financial markets. Siklos (Chapter 4) discusses the crucial role of central bank independence, both de jure and de facto. Ábel and Bonin (Chapter 5) consider the interrelationships between policies dealing with bad loan consolidation, bank recapitalization and enterprise restructuring and, thus, develop the preconditions for bank privatization. Mizsei (Chapter 6) analyses the relationship between bankruptcy legislation and the overall health of the banking system. In the first two parts, the contributors stress that the move toward the good equilibrium requires the creation of banks that will act like real banks and take on their rightful position at the heart of capital markets. As both repositories of financial information on existing companies and the institutions primarily responsible for payment settlements, these authors support the salvaging of the SOCBs. Eventually of course, the state should divest itself of its ownership claims in SOCBs by privatizing the banks but the brides must be first endowed. Hence, the state must first take responsibility for designing an interim period policy in which the credit gridlock is broken and the SOCBs' behaviour is modified and monitored on the way toward bank privatization. Otherwise, there may be no escaping the bad equilibrium.

Unfortunately, the CEE countries have few examples on which to rely to orchestrate this financial liberalization. As Sándor points out (Chapter 7), the time period must necessarily be telescoped in that CEE countries do not have the luxury of transforming their commercial banking sector gradually over several decades. He argues that an increased degree of convertibility of the national currencies cannot be obtained without further liberalization of domestic financial markets. In looking to other countries for lessons in financial reform, we chose two market countries, Austria and Finland, with characteristics similar to those found in the CEE countries. For example, their size, degree of openness, factor endowments, geographical locations, and cultures make them good twins. However, these two countries began the process of financial liberalization before World War II and took a significant amount of time to complete their reforms. The long and complicated process in Austria is described by Glück (Chapter 8). Policy makers must avoid the transition trap in which expectations and the lack of credible policies encourage actors to engage in a stalling strategy as experienced in Finland according to Rautava (Chapter 9). The necessary coordination of financial liberalization with fiscal and monetary policy on the one hand, and legislation and supervision on the other, stands out as an important lesson from these two market economies. That the process took more than 50 years in Austria may not augur well for financial reform in the CEE countries.

While direct measures are underway to ensure proper governance of the SOCBs, a new economic culture appropriate to the market environment must be created and nurtured. In the final part, the progress made toward financial liberalization in four CEE countries, namely, the Czech Republic, Poland, Hungary, and Bulgaria is reviewed. Hrnčíř (Chapter 10) discusses the relationship between financial sector reform and the voucher privatization scheme in the Czech Republic. Since the large banks were major participants in acquiring enterprise shares through investment funds, a new situation of cross-ownership has arisen. Poland has taken a different, slower route to privatization but the Polish capital market has been developing a broader array of financial instruments as Kokoszczyński (Chapter 11) points out. The money market and the capital market have developed rapidly and are positioned to be important foundations of financial liberalization. In Hungary, the focus has been on reforming the banking system both from above and below. Ábel and Székely (Chapter 12) focus on the emerging new Hungarian financial institutions that are gaining a significant market share from the SOCBs. They argue that competition from new banks should not be constrained but rather encouraged to facilitate the development of new financial instruments which might otherwise be hindered by the legacies of the planning system. Várhegyi (Chapter 13) examines critically the attempts to reform the Hungarian banking system from above by a recapitalization of the large SOCBs that has yet to yield the desired outcome. In contrast to these three countries, financial deregulation in Bulgaria resulted initially in a plethora of small SOCBs. Dobrinsky (Chapter 14) describes the legislation and the yet-to-be-completed process of state-orchestrated consolidation toward a smaller number of larger SOCBs. The significantly different experiences of these four CEE countries in attempting to liberalize their financial sectors on the road to developing the capital markets capable of supporting a strong market economy indicate that there are still 'miles to go before they reap' the fruits of the good equilibrium.

Drafts of the papers in this volume were presented at a conference on the Development and Reform of Financial Systems in Central and Eastern Europe held in Vienna, Austria from 28 October through 30 October 1993. We are extremely grateful to the following organizations for financial support for this project. The Austrian National Bank, one of our hosts for the conference, provided considerable financial support and local organizational support. Creditanstalt, our other conference host, provided the comfortable and functional venue for the conference as well as financial support. We wish to thank the Soros Foundation for the financial support both to pay the travel expenses of some of the Eastern European participants and to help defray the costs of preparing this volume. We are extremely grateful to the United Nations Department for Economic and Social Information and Policy Analysis for providing continuing support for this project from the preparations for the conference through the production of this volume. Finally, but by no means least, we thank Ms. Clare Meiklejohn for her meticulous copy editing and skilful word processing. Without her and the support we received from the above four organizations, the conference and this volume would have been impossible.

References

Ábel, I. and Bonin, J.P. (1994), 'State desertion and credit market failure in the Hungarian transition', *Acta Oeconomica*, (forthcoming).

Brainard, L. (1991), 'Strategies for economic transformation in Central and Eastern Europe: the role of financial market reform', in Blommenstein, H. and Marrese, M. (eds), *Transformation of Planned Economies: Property Rights Reform and Macroeconomic Stability*, Paris, OECD.

Kornai, J. (1986), 'The Hungarian reform process: visions, hopes and reality', *Journal of Economic Literature* 24(4), 1687—1737.

Stiglitz, J.E. (1992), 'The design of financial systems for the newly emerging democracies of Eastern Europe', in Clague, C. and Rausser, G. (eds), *The Emergence of Market Economies in Eastern Europe*, Cambridge, MA., Blackwell.

PART ONE

Financial Distress in Central and Eastern
Europe: An Overview

2 Financial and Fiscal Aspects of System Change in Eastern Europe

John Michael Montias

1 System rules[1]

Economists are much more apt to speculate about good and bad macroeconomic policies than about the system rules that constrain the range of policies that can be put into effect and what their impact will be. Decisions and policies affecting macroeconomic variables such as money supply and demand and budget incomes and outlays are framed by laws, regulations, and customary ways of doing things, the formal and informal rules and procedures that may be said to constitute an economy's system.[2] It is useful to distinguish among these rules those that make up the decision-making structure of the system (who decides about what), the information structure (what information is collected, by and to whom it is transmitted), and the motivation structure (how the economy's gains and losses are shared among its participants and how the prospects of these gains and losses affect their decisions). Changes in all three of these subsystems have paved the way to a market economy in Eastern Europe.

Broadly speaking, an economy's outcomes, such as its current level of GNP per capita, the distribution of incomes among its participants, and the stability of these incomes, depend on its system, the policies that are open to decision makers under that system, and exogenous factors that constitute the environment in which it operates during the period when the outcomes are observed. This environment in turn may be divided into sets of initial and contemporary states. The initial environment contains the preferences and values of participants, the demographic characteristics of its population, and the level of development achieved prior to the period of observation (as measured by its capital stock, the proven reserves of minerals available to the economy, the skills of its workforce etc.). If the system is known to have undergone change during the period of observation, then the previous system may also be included in the initial environment. The contemporary environment is made up of the exogenous events that occurred during the period of observation that affected outcomes in the period (external political events, terms of trade, temperature, rainfall, etc.).

In this chapter, I will try to apply these categories with regard to post-communist developments in Eastern Europe. I will focus on the organizations responsible for macroeconomic policies (government bureaus, banks) and on their interaction with consumers and producing firms. A large number of the statistics and many of the examples I will be citing are drawn from recent Polish sources, for which I have the best documentation, but I will also refer from time to time to the other economies of Eastern Europe, particularly that of Romania, which offers an interesting contrast to the Polish experience.

My main themes concern the informational and motivational components of the pre- and post-reform fiscal and banking systems. I will show that the ability to conduct successful reforms is constrained by the initial environment in which the economy is embedded. Sometimes a new system variant may be created that will 'substitute' for a missing precondition (Gerschenkron, 1962a). This was the case for the institutions set up in Bulgaria, the Czech Republic, and Hungary to deal with non-performing credits, where the missing precondition was the lack of a market for accounts receivable. But in general the lack of information and of rating experience are real obstacles that can only be remedied over time.[3] It will also be seen that one system change frequently necessitates another. The succession of such linked changes will cease only when a new, internally coherent private-enterprise system will have been put into place.

2   The initial environment of the post-communist nations

The year 1989, when most of the nations of Eastern Europe went through their 'velvet revolutions', is of course the watershed between the old and the new environment. Nevertheless, the system reforms that took place in Hungary and Poland starting in the 1960s had already begun to transform the formal and informal rules by which business was conducted; by the late 1980s, a quasi-new environment in these countries had been created that facilitated the transition to market relations in the post-communist period.

It is fair to say that the fiscal and financial structure of the communist systems was poorly articulated, as compared to developed market economies. This low level of articulation reflected the subordination of the macroeconomic system to the overall system for guiding the economy through production and distribution orders expressed in physical terms.

About all that was expected of the macroeconomic system was that it provide a viable framework within which policies aimed at macroeconomic stability could be implemented. A successful macroeconomic policy was one that enabled consumers, given their disposable incomes, to find enough goods and services available in government outlets to effect their desired purchases at prevailing (government-determined) prices. If this requirement of 'consumer's choice' was perfectly realized, which it rarely was, consumers would have no more income left after each period's purchases than the amounts of currency or savings deposits they might desire to keep for transaction or precautionary purposes. In periods of social and political stress, such as all the Eastern European nations experienced in the 1980s, budgetary deficits and credit expansion, coupled with the inflexibility of government-administered prices for consumer goods, created conditions of excess aggregate demand and repressed inflation. In these conditions of limited consumer's choice, consumers were induced (or 'forced') to save a greater part of their incomes than they would have if more goods and services had been available. Nevertheless, because living standards were low in all the countries of the region and because savings were eaten away by inflation, the ratio of the total stock of household savings to the national wealth, most of which was government-owned, was small. This became a problem when the time came to sell off government-owned assets to private citizens. I shall come back to the choices faced by households in making their saving and investment decisions in the previous system presently.

The fiscal systems were relatively simple. Indirect taxes and levies on the profits of government-owned firms (henceforth abbreviated GOFs) were the principal instruments available to the government for mopping up excess disbursements by government organs and GOFs in the form of wages and transfer payments. The levies on profits of GOFs were, by and large, arbitrary and confiscatory. Direct taxes on individuals were generally of minor significance. Central and local government budgets were closely interconnected. Local government organs, which received a fixed percentage of central budget receipts or had to remit to the central budget a fixed percentage of their own receipts, had little financial autonomy. The central government could draw on the household savings deposited in the savings banks or borrow from the national bank to cover its budget deficits. Only government-owned 'foreign-trade enterprises' and the specialized bank on foreign trade were permitted to deal in foreign exchange; purchases of goods for export by producing GOFs and sales of imports by distributing GOFs were all carried out in domestic currency. Differences between purchase prices of exported goods and the value of the proceeds in foreign exchange converted into domestic currency were settled in special budget accounts, as were equivalent differences on imports.

Households had few options open to them other than spending their incomes on consumer goods and services. They could keep some cash on hand in the national currency in which they were paid. They could save a part of their income in a savings bank, which was in fact if not in name a branch of the unique bank which monopolized the banking business of the country. The interest on these savings was exceedingly low (2—3 per cent);

in the decade of the 1980s when all the Eastern European nations suffered, to some degree, from open inflation, real rates of interest were negative. On the other hand, all such household deposits in the savings bank were guaranteed, in nominal terms, by the government.[4]

Households could also buy and hold foreign convertible currencies (in the more repressive regimes, such as Romania, at a risk premium). This form of zero-interest saving, given the depreciation of Western currencies, was only partially successful in preserving the purchasing value of the money savers laid by. Poland, incidentally, was the only country in the region which offered households the opportunity of opening interest-bearing accounts denominated in a foreign convertible currency, an option that was extremely popular among private savers.[5]

Households could buy life insurance, but, if we consider this decision from a saving rather than an actuarial point of view, the payment of premiums did not differ very much from depositing money in a savings account since government-owned insurance companies themselves had no other choice than to deposit their receipts in a branch of the savings bank.[6] A Polish citizen could also deposit money in a savings bank with a view to buying a cooperative apartment or a domestically produced car. The depositor would obtain the apartment or the car at some indefinite time in the future when he or she reached the head of the line in the lengthy queue for these highly coveted items.[7]

The last option was to buy goods or other physical assets in the expectation that their value would increase at least in line with the rate of inflation. But the purchase of durable goods, such as housing or cars, from government sources was subject to strict rationing, even in periods when consumers' choice prevailed for most non-durable goods. If the durable goods were bought from other citizens, then the problem of securing one's savings from the erosion due to inflation was merely transferred from the buyers to the sellers. The long-run advantage of investing savings in durable goods and other physical assets was also limited by the fact that markets for private transactions were highly imperfect (if they were not illegal).

It is hardly necessary to recall that neither the treasury nor local government organs, let alone private firms, issued bonds for households to invest in;[8] there was of course no stock market in which households might have bought shares of private firms or, for that matter, of GOFs.

Besides serving as a receptacle for household savings, the banking system had two other functions connected with the operation of the nationalized economy. First, specialized banks, which were also *de facto* branches of the national bank, were used as conduits to channel budget grants to finance the expenditures of GOFs carrying out investments and to finance foreign trade. Second, the main business of the regional branches of the monobank was to provide short-term credit to GOFs to finance their inventories, tide them over while they waited for payment from their customers, and otherwise meet their seasonal or other above-norm working-capital needs. The branches of the national bank held assets in the form of these short-term loans (along with limited amounts of currency), while their liabilities consisted chiefly of the deposits of GOFs and of government and non-government organizations (including the ruling party and trade unions). The government drew on household savings, to the extent that it did not need them to cover its own deficits, to finance short-term credit to GOFs. In principle, GOF deposits could only be converted into currency via approved wage and salary payments. Otherwise they could be expended on goods and services sold by other GOFs, meet tax obligations, and effect other transactions restricted to the sphere of firms and bureaus under government ownership and control. However, for reasons that are not entirely clear, the separation between 'cash' and 'non-cash' money seems not to have been as strict in Eastern Europe as in the Soviet Union where the system originated.

The managers of the national bank's branches normally extended credit to GOFs, provided the applicant was able to submit documents justifying the request (to carry inventories that were in line with the GOF's plan or for other sanctioned purposes). If the bank manager rejected the application, because he judged the loan to be unjustified or because it was subject to credit rationing (which frequently happened during periods of inflationary pressure),[9] the firm had nowhere else to go: its only source of finance was the branch of the national bank to which it was assigned (Wyczański, 1993, p. 12). In general, risk assessment played little or no role in the crediting decision. The guiding idea of credit policy was that 'money must not interfere with production' (Balcerowicz, 1992). Owing to this neglect of risk factors,[10] many credits could not be reimbursed in time or could not be reimbursed at all. Such credits were then more or less automatically renewed. The only disadvantages of the failure to return loans on time, from the debtor's point of view, was that the firm might have to pay penalty interest rates on the amount outstanding (several times higher than the nominal rates charged on loans) and, if such delays were repeated, that it could be brought under the special surveillance of the Ministry of Finance. This last eventuality must have had some nuisance value in deterring non-performing loans, but penalty rates had little effect so long as firms were subject to weak budget constraints. In principle, liquidity-constrained GOFs were barred from seeking relief from the debts they owed to supplying firms by getting trade credits from them. Although inter-firm credits were formally prohibited (Balcerowicz, 1992, p. 8), they were frequently extended, particularly in periods of budget or credit restraint. The portfolios of banks were full of non-performing loans; yet banks held virtually no reserves against the risk of default. The lack of prudential reserves was of course a reflection of the banks' lack of autonomy *vis-à-vis* the government budget, which could always be depended on to reinforce their financial position in case of need.

In Poland, where communist rule had been shaken by repeated strikes and social upheavals, the 1970s and 1980s were marked by the loosening of the links of subordination in the economic hierarchy, especially in the financial realm. Bargaining between officials at different echelons, bank managers and GOFs became increasingly common. Firms put pressure on local branches of the national bank; local branches on regional ('wojewodship') branches; and regional branches on central organs. The pressures to extend easy and inexpensive credits were 'incredibly difficult to resist' (Wyczański, 1993, p. 13).

In Eastern Europe, in general, the information about the financial conditions of GOFs that was developed under the pre-1989 system was very limited. Some of it, generally in aggregated form, travelled up the hierarchy to higher bureaus of the Ministry of Finance. But otherwise it remained impacted in the branches of the National Bank where it originated. There were no pools of financial information for other branches or producing firms to tap into. Indeed, there was little demand for such information. The diffused demand for financial information only manifested itself when the post-communist economies became more decentralized and market-oriented.

In all systems, decision makers accumulate information through education and training, both of which naturally emphasize the acquisition of information that will be useful in the prevailing environment and under given system rules. Very few lawyers, financial analysts, risk-oriented managers and qualified accountants who would have been capable of coping with the problems raised by the post-communist system were trained under the old dispensation. Here the Hungarian economy was in a superior starting position by virtue of the longer experience that it had with the quasi-market conditions that emerged in the course of its lengthy reform process.

In general, differences in the initial environments of the Eastern European economies (dated as of 1989) also had an impact on subsequent outcomes. Among the significant differences that should be cited are the level of development achieved (two or three times higher in a country such as Czechoslovakia than in Romania), the degree of repressed inflation (high in Poland, Romania, and Bulgaria, relatively low in Czechoslovakia and Hungary), the highly disparate levels of foreign indebtedness (from virtually zero in Romania to over USD 40 bn in Poland), the unequal extent of dependence on trade with fellow members of CMEA (roughly 50 per cent of Polish and Romanian and nearly 80 per cent of Bulgarian foreign trade), and the different degree to which the capital stock of industry and the transportation and communication infrastructure of the various Eastern European economies were worn out and technologically obsolete, due to stagnation or decline in net investments in the 1980s (at least in Bulgaria, Poland, and Romania).

3   The contemporary environment

The velvet revolutions of 1989 put into power individuals in the legislative and executive branches of government whose values in most respects radically diverged from those of the communists who had preceded them. Almost all of them were committed to the reform of the economic system, including the privatization of *some* GOFs and the liberalization of prices for *some* goods. But the balance of power between those who were intent on more far-reaching and rapid changes and those who wanted less sweeping and slower changes differed from country to country and, within each country, from one period to the next.

The successive governments of Poland, for instance, from the premiership of Mazowiecki to that of Suchocka,[11] appear to have been more energetic in promoting system change than the various Romanian governments presided over by former communist-party member Ion Iliescu.[12] There were also some notable differences among groups of members of parliament in the newly-democratized states (whose power rose and ebbed as the political climate changed), between parliament and the executive branches of government, and, within the government, among officials belonging to various administrations. There was, for instance, a striking divergence of attitudes and 'mentalities' between officials belonging to the Ministry of Industry and Trade (or whatever the administration supervising most GOFs has been renamed) and those belonging to the Ministry of Finance or the National Bank. One may cite similar statements emanating from the former in countries such as Poland and Romania calling for cheaper credits and subsidies to government-owned firms, in contrast to the fiscal and financial restraint generally advocated by officials in the Ministry of Finance and, especially, in the National Bank.[13] One common element in the contemporary environments of the post-communist economies, which helps to explain the convergence of views of officials responsible for the fiscal and financial state of their economy, is the presence of international agencies, such as the World Bank, the International Monetary Fund and the European Bank for Reconstruction and Development, which all put pressure on these officials to exercise fiscal and financial restraint (and threaten the withdrawal of multilateral aid if they don't). So the outcomes of interest to us (rate of inflation, level of unemployment, growth of GNP, and so forth)[14] will at least in part depend on the political support various ministries, representing divergent interests, receive.

The economies of Eastern Europe differ in the extent to which the representatives of workers and other employees of government-owned firms have been able to influence economic reform. In Poland, Solidarity has parlayed its critical contribution to the defeat of the communist regime into lasting political power and influence. No reform can be brought about without some measure of its support. But workers' councils at the firm level, which may or may not be under Solidarity's stamp, also have a greater say in privatization decisions and in other strategic matters than they do elsewhere. In Romania, trade unions have successfully exerted pressure on the government to raise wages, reduce working hours, and prevent firms from shedding labour.[15] In Bulgaria, the government has been successful in negotiating a social compact limiting wage increases, somewhat in the Swedish tradition (Thorne, 1992, p. 25).

One exogenous event that has been part of the contemporary environment of all the post-communist European states has been the collapse of the Soviet market (of far greater importance than the decline in trade among the Eastern European nations). The former Soviet Union supplied cheap energy and raw materials and provided a virtually unlimited market for the middling-quality manufactures of Eastern Europe. The branches of heavy industry and the armaments manufactures that had been developed in Eastern Europe under these favourable supply and demand conditions have suffered grievously from their virtual disappearance.

Some decline in domestic demand was also experienced in Poland by GOFs producing consumer goods, such as textiles and shoes, in 1990 and 1991. This decline was more or less inevitable in the new environment for the following reasons. (1) There had been little or no specialization in the production of consumer goods within CMEA and imports of such goods from developed market economies were kept to a minimum; domestic manufactures were produced at high cost and were widely discredited for their low quality and poor packaging; any opening up of the country to foreign trade was likely to cause some shift of purchases from domestic to imported goods; and widespread, competitive smuggling, by making available imported goods at low cost reinforced this trend. (2) In some branches of light industry, private handicraft or other small-scale production, which, in pre-communist times, had accounted for the bulk of output, particularly in the less developed countries in the region, began to pull consumers away from government-produced goods soon after more liberal conditions were created for their existence. (3) GOFs producing consumer goods were not as adaptable to meeting consumers' requirements as they developed under the new conditions as they might have been.

Whether exports of both producer and consumer goods to developed market economies could have picked up the slack in demand from former CMEA partners and from domestic consumers and a substantial fall in output could have been averted is a complex question which cannot be answered within the system-oriented confines of this paper. My own guess, for what it is worth, is that declines in industrial output were inevitable, although perhaps not as deep as those that were actually experienced (typically in the 30 to 50 per cent range from 1990 to 1992, with Poland, Romania, and Bulgaria closer to the upper limit and Czechoslovakia and Hungary closer to the lower).[16]

4   System change in the macroeconomic sphere

In the first months after the overthrow of the communist regimes, the new governments began to loosen the system constraints to which their citizens had been subject. They were encouraged to open small businesses ('small privatization'), to separate their holdings from the agricultural cooperatives in which they or their predecessors had been forcefully enrolled in the 1960s (in Eastern European countries other than Poland, where agriculture had remained primarily in private hands throughout the communist period), to open accounts in foreign currencies where they had not been allowed to hold such accounts previously,[17] and so forth.

The changes that were introduced after 1989 in the fiscal and financial systems, on which this chapter is focused, were generally meant to reinforce the price-liberalization and stabilization policies that were put into effect throughout Eastern Europe.[18] This was particularly the case for reforms in the taxation system that were intended to plug the gaps in the receipts of central government that had been depleted as a result of the declining profitability of GOFs. As I pointed out earlier, the bulk of government revenue in the old system had come from the profit levies and turnover taxes on GOFs. The first effect of price liberalization had been an increase in enterprise profits and in government revenue (in the first half of 1990 in Poland, in the first months of 1991 in Czechoslovakia), which was in part due to a lag of wage costs behind the increases in retail prices. But the collapse of the CMEA market in 1991, together with the uneven pace of price liberalization, which caught many firms in a profit squeeze, and the catching up of wages caused profits to shrink (or turn into losses, particularly in heavy industry) with a negative impact on government revenue, to the extent that the budget depended on GOF profits as a source of taxation.[19] At the same time the government transfers required to protect the most vulnerable elements in the population (pensioners, the newly unemployed, handicapped persons, and so forth) from the freeing of consumer goods prices had to be vastly increased.[20] The result was widening budget deficits (3.8 per cent of GDP in Poland in 1991, 7.1 per cent in 1992, closer to 10 per cent in Romania) that could not be stanched without resorting to new sources of taxation (Kołodko, 1992, p.31). The response, throughout Eastern Europe, was to put into place new and improved methods of collecting direct taxes on individuals and taxes on the profits of private firms and to institute value-added taxes (VAT).

Before the new taxes could be introduced, the old taxes on GOFs were fine-tuned and adapted to the policy of maintaining the tightest possible controls on wage increases — a common element of the stabilization policies of the nations in the region. Already in the pre-1989 period, Hungary had experimented with a tax on wage increases. In Poland a tax of this sort, popularly known, from its initials in Polish, as the 'popiwek' (gratuity or 'pourboire'), was introduced at the beginning of 1990 to bolster the government's attempt to maintain, or slow down, increases in nominal wages (one of the two 'anchors', along with the nominal exchange rate, of the official stabilization policy). This new tax absorbed nearly 7 per cent of profits in state industry in 1990 and 23 per cent in 1991. A similar tax was adopted in Romania in mid-1991 to slow down the cost-push inflation which had begun to wind its way upwards. The tax could go as high as 500 per cent of wage increases above 20 per cent.[21] But many GOFs, both in Poland and Romania, still preferred to pay these taxes than to do without the labour they needed. They could, alternatively, disguise wage increases in the form of bonuses, on which they did not have to pay the special tax. Finally, as Rosati (1993, p. 251) has pointed out, private firms in Poland did not have to pay the 'popiwek' on wage increases; their resulting ability to pay higher wages created distortions in the labour market. Another fiscal measure adopted in Poland was to reinforce an old tax on capital (called the 'dividend tax'). It absorbed 5 per cent of the profits in state industry in 1989, 9 per cent in 1990, and 32 per cent in 1991 (Glikman, 1993, p. 14).

By 1991, Hungary had a Personal Income Tax and a VAT in place. It took Poland and Romania three years, until mid-1993, to set up a VAT.[22] The VAT, beside the advantages that are usually ascribed to it (ease of collection, less distorting effects on the product-mix of industry), has a virtue that is associated with the contemporary environments of Eastern European economies. It is well suited to combating smuggling and tax evasion at earlier stages of production, which have been widespread in recent years. Anyone buying a product for further processing or for resale must pay the full tax on it (i.e., he cannot deduct the taxes or tariffs that have already been imposed on it at earlier stages of production), unless he can show that taxes or tariffs have already been levied on the product.[23]

Exchange-rate policies, which were also part of the package of liberalization measures that were introduced after 1989, were accompanied by system changes as well. Exchange-rate regulations had already been liberalized to a moderate extent in Hungary and Poland in the 1980s. After 1989, progress was made in all Eastern European countries toward instituting internal convertibility. The first steps toward this goal was to reduce the enormous gap between official and black- or parallel-market rates of exchange. As early as July 1989 the Mazowiecki government in Poland had succeeded in curtailing the ratio of the zloty-to-USD rates in the two markets from 6 to 1.5 to 1. By January 1990, the two rates had been unified and internal convertibility had been achieved. Anyone henceforth could purchase foreign exchange with the purpose of paying for any current-account transaction at a rate of 9500 zloty (zl) per USD. This was the rate at which, omitting a small service charge, exporters sold their foreign exchange proceeds to the National Bank (Kokoszczyński and Kondratowicz, 1991, p. 19). It should be noted, however, that any exporter or supplier of services earning foreign exchange must turn it over to the Bank at the pegged rate (which is in fact virtually the same as the free-market rate available at exchange counters). A similar system operates in Hungary, the Czech Republic, and Slovakia.

In Romania, an interbank foreign exchange market was set up in February 1991, where transactions holding foreign currencies and potential importers were conducted. Transactions at the free-market rates on the new market were initially at a low level because exporters were only allowed to keep 30 per cent of their earnings in foreign exchange. The volume of transactions on the interbank market expanded when, two months later, exporters were allowed to keep 50 per cent of their foreign-exchange proceeds (National Bank of Romania, 1993a, p. 10). The partial retention of export earnings introduced a fully-fledged dual market for foreign currency. The portion of the funds that exporters were compelled to hand over to the National Bank was resold (at rates that were significantly lower than the interbank rate) to importers of 'essential' goods, including most fuels and raw materials. According to a recent report of the National Bank of Romania, the dual-exchange rate system was instituted 'to prevent major disturbances to enterprises using imported raw materials' in an economy that was said to depend more on such imports than any other in Eastern Europe (National Bank of Romania, 1993b, p. 11). According to this same report, Romania was the only country in Eastern Europe where the IMF supported this duality (ibid.). As it turned out, the dual rate was unsustainable. The gap increased between the two rates as the domestic inflation unravelled.[24] An attempt to unify the two rates in November 1991 foundered. In June 1992, external multilateral credits made it possible to unify the two rates. The initially beneficial results, including a temporary appreciation of the Lei, were soon dissipated as inflation accelerated in the summer and fall.[25] By the end of the year the interbank auction rate had fallen by 25 per cent behind the free rate (transacted in the Forex bureaus). Since then the auction rate in the interbank market has been maintained below the free rate by limiting the access of bidders to those clients whose foreign-currency needs are approved by the government. The excess demand for foreign exchange is either satisfied by paying premium rates on the parallel market or is not satisfied at all.[26] Preferred sectors, including agriculture, continue to obtain their imported inputs at privileged rates (National Bank of Romania, 1993b, p. 17). As a result, 'corruption increased, imbalances [were] aggravated, and the transition process was jeopardized' (National Bank of Romania, 1992a).

In one significant respect, however, the Romanian (as well as the Bulgarian) foreign-exchange system is more liberal than elsewhere in Eastern Europe. While, as in Poland, exporters must *transfer* their earnings abroad to domestic banks, they need not *surrender* them to the National Bank (National Bank of Romania, 1993b, p. 14). They may keep the proceeds in USD or DM accounts and use them for their own importing needs. This of course impedes the intermediating role that the market could play in making foreign exchange available to those agents who need it most.

Financial intermediation, as we have seen, had been kept at a primitive level in the pre-1989 systems. Reforms were sorely needed in this domain if a fully-fledged market economy, primarily based on private enterprise, was to be created. In the new decision-making structure, private firms, GOFs, and 'corporatized' government firms (joint-stock corporations with limited liability, with majority government ownership) were all to be made financially responsible for the consequences of their decisions. Firms that were not viable on the market, whatever the nature of their ownership, would be reorganized, forced into bankruptcy, or liquidated. The liability for risky decisions would be transferred from the participants in the economy as a whole to the decision makers themselves (or at least to the organizations in which they were employed). New financial instruments had to be created that would enable individuals and profit-oriented organizations that were willing and able to take risks to satisfy the demand for risk capital. The first steps taken toward reform were in the realm of banking.

In 1989—1990, all the Eastern European nations proceeded to divest their national banks from commercial banking functions. Henceforth, each national bank was expected to act as a central bank responsible for monetary stability, using exclusively indirect instruments (interest rates, reserve requirements, open-market operations) to achieve this goal. Although resort to direct controls was in principle abjured (on the volume and allocation of credits, in particular), there was much backsliding in this area, as we shall see subsequently.

In each nation, the loans to government enterprises in the portfolio of the national bank were transferred to newly-created government-owned commercial banks and to previously existing specialized banks (for savings, foreign trade, and so forth).[27] In Poland, nine commercial regional banks were hived off the national bank in February 1989. Polish firms, whether government-owned or private, as well as private citizens could, in principle, choose which bank they wanted to be affiliated with. To preserve some measure of competition among banks, it was decided that while each bank would be concentrated in a given region (such as Silesia), it could open branches in other regions as well, although this apparently happened only on a small scale. Like the commercial banks, the specialized banks were allowed to accept deposits and to make loans to all applicants. The rationale given for creating commercial banks that would be mainly confined to a single region is that the alternative system of country-wide banking 'would quickly have run against obstacles due to the underdevelopment of tele-communications in Poland' (Wyczański, 1993, p. 14). This is a good example of a desirable system change hampered by the initial environment.

In Bulgaria, in contrast to Poland, 59 government-owned commercial banks were created in 1990, with 160 places of business and 114 branches. None of these banks, which were generally small and undercapitalized, could meet the needs of an entire region. In an attempt to ensure that the commercial banks would not act as pliant subordinates of the National Bank of Bulgaria, the government decided to set up these banks as joint-stock corporations and to sell some of their shares to GOFs and other banks. As it turned out, the GOFs that bought shares in commercial banks were also major borrowers from these banks. Many of them had problem loans, which they hoped to alleviate by exerting partial ownership rights over the banks. Banks also bought shares from each other to reduce their dependence on the National Bank (Thorne, 1992, p. 7). These 'pocket banks' became cooperatives in all but name. The inevitable consequence was gradual decapitalization, much as in Yugoslavia and present-day Russia.[28] In 1992, this system was discontinued. A new institution, the Bank Consolidation Company (BCC), was created to help consolidate the state banking system and to eliminate the interlocking relationship between banks and their clients. GOFs owning shares of banks were to exchange these shares for shares issued by the BCC. The large number of small banks were merged into 10 medium-sized banks.

In Romania, a single government-owned commercial bank was set up with regional branches, along with specialized banks in foreign trade, investments, and agriculture, which could also extend ordinary commercial loans. Except possibly in Bucharest, where two private banks compete with the government banks in the extension of credit, both GOFs and private enterprises are still more or less obliged to deal with the branch of the Romanian Commercial Bank in their locality.

Elsewhere, in the new spirit of post-communism, the government encouraged the creation of private banks. In Poland the minimum capital to found a private bank in 1990 was set at only USD 2 mn (USD 6 mn if it was founded in part or in whole with foreign capital).[29] By the end of

1990, there were 75 country-wide private banks, of which 30 had a majority of foreign capital. In October 1991, nine government-owned commercial banks which had been founded in 1989, were converted to joint-stock corporations with government-held shares with a view to subsequent privatization. In June 1993, the majority of the shares of one of these banks — the Wielkopolski Bank Kredytowy — was successfully offered to investors on the Warsaw stock market, which itself had begun to function in April 1991. The privatization of the WBK was facilitated by the acquisition of 1.8 mn shares (28.7 per cent of the total value of shares outstanding) by the European Bank for Reconstruction and Development.[30]

Private banks throughout Eastern Europe have specialized in financing private enterprises, even though government banks have also played a role in this domain.[31] In spite of the official encouragement to domestic and foreign investors to found private banks, government discrimination in the treatment of these banks, as compared to government-owned banks, has not ceased. In Poland, for example, savings deposits are guaranteed by the government in its own banks but not in private banks. Individual depositors pay no taxes on the interest paid by government savings banks, whereas dividends paid by private firms are included in income and fully taxed. Private banks are excluded from the clearing system (Krajowa Izba Rozrachunkowa), which was set up in 1992 to facilitate bank transfers. They cannot benefit from the restructuring loans that the government extends, in large part with the aid of multilateral institutions, to government banks in need of aid (*Jaworski*, No. 2, 1993, p. 13). On the other hand, they are not subject to the credit ceilings to which government-owned banks must abide.[32]

Formal and informal system rules determine who (or what organization) has the right or the power to set interest rates on bank loans. It may make a good deal of difference to the volume and the allocation of credits whether the Ministry of Finance or the National Bank arbitrarily sets the basic rate to which commercial banks add a margin to determine their lending rates or whether basic rates are set as a result of a market process (supply and demand for interbank funds or whatever). If rates are administratively set by a government bureau, it also matters whether they are pegged above or below the inflation. Since 1989, all the Eastern European central banks have raised interest rates, which were initially very low, to levels that kept up at least to some extent with the rate of inflation, but not all have succeeded in generating rates in excess of price increases.

The contrast between Poland and Romania in this respect is instructive. In 1990, the National Bank of Poland, which was still dominated by the Ministry of Finance, pursued a policy aimed at stimulating the economy. The refinancing rate, on which 80 per cent of credits extended by government banks depended as a source of finance, was set below the rate of inflation. From the first months of 1991 on, the Bank set its refinancing rate at a level approximately equal to the expected rate of inflation. From then on, with short and temporary exceptions, the banks' lending rates, including the 20—30 per cent margin charged above the refinancing rate,[33] exceeded the rate of inflation (Wyczański, 1993, pp. 59—60). Such subsidization of favoured sectors as occurred took the form of government guarantees on loans, which I will discuss below.

In Romania, it took some time for the National Bank to raise its refinancing rate above the traditional 3 per cent per year. In December 1990, both short- and long-term lending was still pegged at that level, even though prices were already rising at a rapid rate. The short-term lending rate of the bank rose to 18 per cent per year in September 1991, compared to a rate of increase of retail prices of 10 per cent *per month* in the next three months. In the first quarter of 1993, the refinancing rate on lines of credit was pegged at 71 per cent, compared to a yearly inflation rate of about 100—120 per cent (National Bank of Romania, 1993a, pp. 7—8). While progress has been achieved in aligning the National Bank's lending rate on the rate of inflation,[34] the objective of matching the two rates was never achieved. Worse yet, in the first quarter of 1993, 'favoured lines of credit', principally extended to finance agriculture, exports, and GOFs in difficulties in heavy industry, increased to 89 per cent of all credits granted by the Bank (compared to 68 per cent in the preceding quarter). As a result, the average effective rate of interest on refinancing credits has been reduced to 30.6 per cent, or about one fourth of the inflation rate (ibid., p. 11). Refinancing credits earmarked for the agricultural sector were set as low as 15 per cent per year.[35] These subsidized credits were, of course, de facto, guaranteed by the government.

In Poland, the National Bank began issuing guarantees in the form of insurance to private firms in 1990. The guarantees, which were issued mainly for small establishments in trade and services, covered 60 per cent of the exposure (Wyczański, 1993, p. 53). But the majority of government guarantees applied to short-term credits that were essentially meant to stave off the cessation of payments of unprofitable GOFs. It is the policy of the Bank to gradually reduce the guarantees on loans to GOFs. The Bank recently stated that in 1993 guarantees would only be given to insure investment credits (earmarked for infrastructure, ecological ventures, the expansion of export capacity, technological progress, or projects located in high-unemployment regions). As in the case of private firms, the National Bank's guarantee covers only 60 per cent of the credit. The risk for the remainder is born by the bank financing the credit. A budget reserve equivalent to USD 100 mn was set in the central budget to cover the risks of non-reimbursement of these credits. It is said that about 100 GOFs are likely to apply for the guarantees, of which only a small proportion will be successful (*Gazeta bankowa*, no. 23, 4 June 1993, p. 40). These guarantees, which have some of the earmarks of subsidies (in addition to the interest that the government will have to pay in case the credits are not repaid), must be seen in the context of the near-collapse of long-term investments and of the pressures exerted by the industrial sector for a minimum level of investments. The Polish system, by letting the budget share the risk with banks (a measure that at least reduces the arbitrariness of bureaucratic decision making) and by severely limiting the number of projects selected, partially closes the sluices; the Romanian system of subsidized credits, by all appearances, keeps them wide open.

Interest rates on current account and savings deposits in domestic currency lagged behind the inflation in both Poland and Romania even more than the two National Banks' lending rates. In Poland, they have typically hovered around 50 per cent of the refinancing rate; in Romania the average effective rate on deposits was 31 per cent per year, which was just about equal to the average rate on refinancing (National Bank of Romania, 1993a, p. 8). Thus in the two countries, private and enterprise savings are subject to an inflation tax, which is used chiefly to finance the budget deficit and the credit needs of GOFs.[36] One important difference between the two countries is that, in Poland, the treasury has eased the burden of financing the budget deficit by issuing bonds and other interest-bearing obligations that allow the banks to decide on what terms they wish to acquire government debt. This innovation widens the autonomy of, and the strategic choices open to, commercial banks at the expense of a one-time increase in government expenditures (to pay for the interest). In Poland, growing competition among banks, including private ones, has put pressure on the margins between the cost of acquiring money and the interest on loans. As a result, banks have become less profitable (particularly in 1992). The rate squeeze has also induced them to increase the share of government obligations in their portfolios at the expense of loans to public and private enterprises because these obligations are safer and do not require them to make provisions for bad loans (*Gazeta bankowa*, 18 June 1993). In Romania, the low intensity of competition among banks has kept margins high between the interest paid on deposits and the interest obtained on loans — too high by some accounts — and government-owned banks have remained solvent despite the high percentage of the non-performing loans they have had to cope with (McKinsey *et al.*, 1993, vol. 2, p. 3).

It has been widely reported in the West that inter-enterprise credits (IEC) in Russia and Eastern Europe have risen from very low levels under communism when they were strenuously resisted[37] to very high levels in recent years. Here again the decision-making component of the system has been affected: supplying firms decide whether or not they wish to extend credit to their clients rather than bank officers. The terms on which credits are extended also differ. Banks charge interest; suppliers charge zero nominal interest but are likely to demand higher prices than if they were paid in cash.

However, the importance of the IEC problem, as Begg and Portes (1992) have argued, should not be exaggerated. In low-inflation countries, such as the Czech Republic, where IEC amounted to about one fifth of total bank credit outstanding at the end of 1991, arrears in paying suppliers were normal by the standards of developed Western economies. Even in Poland, where arrears were equal to 87 per cent of total bank credits outstanding in mid-1992, the situation was not too grave, especially if we take into consideration the precipitous decline in this percentage ratio, which had reached a peak of 168 per cent in March 1990 when shock therapy was first applied (Rostowski, 1993, p. 50). But in Russia and Romania, the IEC problem was significantly aggravated by government attempts to solve the 'payments blockage' by the arbitrary cancellation of mutually held debts and by occasional massive infusions of credits, with evident inflationary effect.

In Russia, the level of IEC had risen to over 200 per cent of bank credits outstanding in June 1992 and then was reduced to 52 per cent one month later as a result of the clearing of debts and the extension of government credits, via the National Bank, to settle net creditor positions (ibid., p. 49). This was only a temporary remedy. Fortified by the repeated experience of government bail-outs, credit-extending firms had no reason to fear a liquidity crunch that would leave them high and dry. Supplying firms continued to let their customers delay payment, as they delayed payment to their own suppliers.

Similarly, in Romania, the government initiated a 'global compensation scheme' at the end of 1991 and injected Lei 400 bn (USD 0.5 bn) of bank credits into the system to clear the remaining debts. Six months later IEC had risen again to nearly the level of total bank credit outstanding (Lei 1.1 trillion). The government had to lend firms another Lei 200 bn in March 1993 to alleviate the problem (World Bank, 1993, pp. 3, 9; National Bank of Romania, 1992b, p. 10).[38] The Polish solution of minimizing the government's role in solving the problem — based on the theory that supplying firms should, if possible, collect the debts owed to them and, if not, should stop deliveries to recalcitrant payers, sell their accounts receivable to specialized intermediaries, or bring suit to recover their claims — has much to recommend it (Begg and Portes, 1992). The National Bank of Poland's high-interest policy (high, in real terms, by Romanian or Russian standards) has also helped to inhibit IEC by increasing the opportunity costs to would-be lenders of extending supplier's credit.

One common theme in Eastern Europe is that payments arrears of all sorts are provoked by the instability of the environment in which firms operate. Hungary offers an interesting example. As late as 1991, the

National Bank of Hungary was hardly concerned with bad and doubtful loans, which amounted to only 4—5 per cent of loans outstanding. Since about half the bad and doubtful loans were guaranteed by the government and since banks could make a provision for their anticipated losses *before* taxes, it was thought the problem would easily be resolved in a matter of two or three years without having to clean up the portfolio of banks before they were privatized (Balassa, 1993, p. 26).[39] But in 1991—1992, the receipts of firms dropped unexpectedly and their financial results worsened markedly. By 30 September 1992, the proportion of bad and doubtful credits had risen to 15 per cent. The reserves the banks were obliged to create in anticipation of the losses on non-performing loans reduced their profitability. As a result they became less attractive to private investors and their privatization had to be delayed. To protect themselves against losses, the banks had to raise their margins,[40] with unfavourable consequences for the development of the economy.

In late 1992, the government decided to help the banks in which it held shares (as well as some privately held banks with a very low ratio of owned capital to assets) clean up their portfolio. These banks were encouraged to sell at market prices the bad and doubtful credits they were owed by non-financial firms. They could also transfer their claims to specialized firms (created by banks or other firms with a small participation of the government) to manage these assets. To cover the difference between the nominal and the market value of the claims (but only to the extent of 50 per cent of their nominal value and of 50 per cent of the total of a bank's non-performing loans), the government offered the banks three-year bonds yielding interest. Banks accepting these bonds committed themselves to pay for them over the course of the next ten years by earmarking a fixed share of their profits for that purpose. Since market firms equipped to transact in bad debts were not yet in existence, the government had to create a special institution, the Hungarian Development-Investment Corporation, to which banks could temporarily sell their claims in exchange for government bonds covering 50 per cent of their value. This corporation was expected to sell its holdings to newly-formed market intermediaries in due time (ibid., pp. 26—27). The entire operation was said to be 'for one time only', although there is no guarantee that it will not have to be repeated if the profitability of firms deteriorates again. The bad-debts problem in Hungary has been exacerbated by the self-imposed constraint that banks must not own shares in non-financial firms. This rules out debt-for-equity swaps which are expected to play a major role in the restructuring of debtor firms elsewhere. It is not clear why the equivalent of the American Glass-Steagall Act[41] has been adopted in Hungary in preference to the 'continental model' of banking, which would seem especially attractive in a situation where most firms are too small and lack the reputation that would enable them to secure investment funds by issuing bonds or tradeable shares. Another peculiarity of the Hungarian system is its uniquely severe bankruptcy law. Debtors unable to pay their debts during a period of 90 days must declare bankruptcy. This law, which came into effect in early 1993, has led to a spate of bankruptcies which are bottling up the courts.

In Poland, the debts of 'economic units [non-governmental and non-financial firms] having lost their credit-worthiness' amounted to 14 per cent of total credits to economic units at the end of 1991 and 19 per cent at the end of 1992 (Pietruszynska, 1993, p. 24).[42] Due to the high volatility of economic conditions (an important aspect of the contemporary environment), the population of debtor firms has undergone rapid change. In 1992 alone, for instance, 3526 firms lost their credit capacity, but 1958 firms regained it (ibid., p. 23). Of the 4448 economic units that were not credit-worthy in the fourth quarter of 1992, 517 were in a state of liquidation and 354 were bankrupt. The rest were undergoing restructuring or other financial sanitization (ibid., p. 26). It may be remarked in passing that 50 per cent of the firms that were not credit-worthy were still getting new credits in 1992 (ibid., p. 24).

The system for dealing with the non-performing credits of government-owned banks that has been adopted in Poland vests the responsibility for these credits squarely in 'Departments of Difficult Credits' (DTK, to use the Polish abbreviation), which will be set up in the headquarters ('centrale') of these banks. The idea behind the segregation of bad and doubtful debts and their removal from the control of branch managers is that the latter, many of whom have dealt with the same clients for years on end, have a reputation for treating bad debtors too leniently. They are too often apt to accept their clients' claim that the difficulties they are going through are only temporary when in fact only a serious restructuring could save them (Parfinewicz and Zebrowski, 1993, p. 26).[43] Other critics have pointed out that the banks do not have the competent cadres to restructure firms in difficulty. To do so requires an evaluation of the chances of a firm's survival in the market and a calculation of the long-run risks in financing its continued operation, which bank officers are not qualified to make (Wesołek, 1993, p. 24). As this experience accumulates through trial and error, however, the DTKs may develop the expertise needed for the assessment of investment projects. If they are successful, they may become the nuclei of the investment departments of commercial banks.

As in Hungary, the cleaning up of the bad debts in the portfolios of Polish banks will have to be supported by the treasury. Government-owned banks will be given additional capital in the form of bonds to finance the postponement of reimbursements, the writing down of loans, the sale of debt at below-nominal prices, and other operations that will have the effect of reducing the realistic value of banks' assets (Wyczański, 1993, p.58).

The restructuring reform has given rise to a good deal of controversy in the Polish financial press. Several commentators have pointed to the contradictory pressures to which the banks are subject (cf. *Gazeta bankowa*, 11 June 1993, p. 2). On the one hand, the government administration would like them to be the main reconstructing agent for the GOFs, in part by acquiring shares in them, with a view to supporting the economy and providing cheap credits to firms. (In Poland, unlike in Hungary, the law permits a bank to acquire shares in commercial firms, with a governmental or private majority, provided that its maximum exposure per investment be no larger than 10 per cent of its owned capital and that its total investments in commercial paper not exceed 25 per cent of its owned capital) (Groszek, 1993, p. 20).[44] On the other hand, the National Bank of Poland has been applying pressure on banks to adopt prudential rules which have the effect of forcing them to reduce credits and to get rid of shares in debtor-firms. The prudential rules that went into effect in 1993 increased the level of obligatory reserves. They also raised the capital-adequacy index (the ratio of owned capital to the sum of risk-weighted assets) to 8 per cent,[45] the minimum-liquidity index (ratio of 90-day loans to three-month term deposits) to 0.8—1.0, and the minimum level of capital for founded banks to zl 70 bn (USD 4.2 mn at June 1993 rate). These enhanced requirements have placed the banks, which were already faced with declining levels of profitability, in a very difficult position. They have had little choice but to reduce their exposure and earmark a larger part of their assets in government bonds and other obligations. The National Bank of Poland had set a *ceiling* of zl 80 bn on bank credits for 1992, but only zl 50 bn were actually lent. In real terms, credits declined by 14.5 per cent from the previous year. At the end of 1992, in 29 out of 85 banks for which data were available, the value of commercial paper held as assets exceeded the level of loans outstanding (*Gazeta bankowa*, 18 June 1993, p.7).

In Romania, the Parliament has not yet promulgated a law to deal with the bad-debts problem and the restructuring of debtor-firms, but there are good chances that the main recommendations of McKinsey *et al.* will be adopted. This auditing firm has recommended the segregation of the GOFs that are chiefly responsible for the bad-debts problem in a separate restructuring institution, much as in the Czech Republic and Hungary (McKinsey *et al.*, 1993). In 1992, about half of all outstanding bank loans (two thirds of the Romanian Commercial Bank's loans) were to firms that were 'in trouble'. To clean up the banks' portfolios, a write-off of almost Lei 500 bn (USD 580 mn at June 1993 exchange rate) would be necessary, which would exceed the aggregate value of the banks' owned capital (ibid., p. 20).[46] Three sectors — petroleum-processing, metallurgy, and machine-building — account for 45 per cent of the 'bad assets'. Of the 229 firms in the troubled sectors that would be segregated under the structuring institution's aegis, 35 are large (with over 5000 employees) and 193 are middle-sized (500 to 5000 employees). These 'white elephants' were built up in the course of 40 years of semi-autarkic industrialization concentrated on heavy industry. Few of them are likely to undergo successful restructuring and achieve viability in the market place in the absence of significant protection and/or subsidies. Most should probably be stripped of their productive assets and liquidated. Whether the restructuring institution created to deal with these debtor firms would be able to resist the pressures from Parliament, from local authorities, from managers and from trade unions to keep them going at the cost of massive infusions of capital was a controversial question in Bucharest in the summer of 1993.[47]

Much of this chapter has been devoted to the difficult adaptation of GOFs, burdened with problems inherited from the old system, to a new market environment fraught with uncertainty. This particular focus is due in part to the relative importance of these firms, which still dominate the industrial landscape, but also that so much more is known about them than about the newly-emergent private firms, including banks. A recent Polish study covering most 'large' (mainly government-owned)[48] and 'small' (private or cooperative) banks revealed significant differences between the two types (Boguszewski, 1992). It is only very generally true that government banks have been lending primarily to GOFs and private banks to private firms. In fact, as of June 1992, only 53.8 per cent of the credits of the 'large banks' were extended to GOFs. Cooperatives received 27 per cent and private businesses of all sorts 10.8 per cent. Of the credit extended by small banks, 53.7 per cent had gone to private business and 2.7 per cent to cooperatives, but that still left 29.3 per cent of these banks' credit outstanding that was owed by GOFs (ibid., p. 5).[49] Large banks lent 61.5 per cent of their credits for 'production activities' (presumably, for the most part, industrial); small firms divided their credits almost equally between production activities (41.6 per cent) and trade and services (46 per cent). The study noted that, in addition to the official banks (government-owned or private), there was also a third sector of small quasi-banks, not captured in the survey, that specialized in lending capital for risky ventures. Due to their low costs of operation, these lenders were able to reduce the spread between the interest rates they paid on deposits and the rates they collected on loans (in spite of the greater risk to which they were exposed). Their existence was justified by the 'lack of institutions specializing in servicing the risk capital sector' (ibid., p. 3). From an informational perspective, it is worthy of note that large banks dealt mainly with 'old clients' (half their loans were made out to clients they had known over two years) and small banks with new clients (56 per cent of their credits were lent to clients they had known less than one quarter.) One might have expected that small private banks, disposing of minimal capital resources, would be more risk-averse than large banks with larger resources and *de jure* or *de facto* government guarantees. This does not seem to have been the case. About the same proportion of small and large banks (18—20 per cent) held portfolios containing at least 30 per cent of non-performing loans. It was the smallest banks, whose share of total credits was only 0.01 per cent, that held most (60 per cent) of these risk-fraught portfolios.[50] Whereas 66 per cent of the large banks reported that credit risks were rising, only 22 per cent of the small banks did so (ibid., p. 6). This seeming evidence of a lack of sensitivity to risk on the part of small private banks may reflect the inexperience of these new institutions. It would be a more serious portent of trouble to come if it were the result of moral hazard: bankers with a small, and possibly diminishing stake, going for broke.

5   In the guise of conclusions

It is difficult enough, under any circumstances, to reform an entire system: to reassign decision-making power by altering property relations; to rebuild information and incentive structures to make them compatible with the new property relations; in short, to achieve system coherence with a new set of rules. But it is doubly difficult to do so when the authorities that have acceded to power also wish to make radical changes in economic policy: to correct the severe distortions in the economy brought about by excessive investment in heavy industry for a period of 40 years or more; to reorient trade from East to West. And to carry out these policies while protecting the more vulnerable elements of the population (the old, the very young, the handicapped, the unemployable). The new authorities must recognize the fact that the individuals who made decisions in the old structures — the government-owned firms and banks, the government bureaus that have become used to regulate every aspect of economic life — will resist change, especially of the kind that may threaten their livelihood. They will form coalitions with like-minded politicians and government officials to undermine the reforms. If the old channels of communication are still open, they will use them to influence, or put pressure on, decision makers at neuralgic points in the new system. It is not enough just to hive off a number of government-owned commercial banks from the national bank if the directors of these banks still respond to the national bank's pressures or those of the Ministry of Finance and the Ministry of Industry and Trade, to finance the 'troubled sectors' of industry with low-interest credits. It is not enough to set up auctions for foreign exchange under the aegis of the national bank or of a specialized bank for foreign trade if these auctions are going to be rigged in favour of industrial GOFs and against struggling private businesses. Informational channels must be cut off or redirected if they transmit the wrong messages.[51] The choice between (1) letting banks deal with firms that owe them money as best they can (selling their accounts receivable, swapping debt for shares, or driving them into bankruptcy) and (2) creating special government-owned and -controlled institutions to cope with these firms must be seen in this light. I am inclined to prefer the first solution, chiefly because the second sets up an additional channel of influence through which entrenched bureaucrats can press their case for support of 'white elephant' industries.

I have tried to show in this essay that the more radical reforms carried out in Poland have been more effective in breaking the influence of the old vested interests on the new decision makers than in Romania. System reforms and policy changes have jointly given rise to superior outcomes in the former than in the latter. Poland's lower rate of inflation, its smaller loss of real wages, the more rapid elimination of distortions in its allocation of resources, and the resurgence of industrial output that it was able to bring about a full year earlier than in Romania — in spite of the initial disadvantage of a heavy foreign debt — testify to the merits of a decisive and trenchant approach as opposed to the more hesitant and tentative initiatives of the successive Romanian governments. (I write this with explicit knowledge of the recent electoral shift toward the left in Poland, which suggests that 'shock therapy' was unacceptable to most voters.)

From a system perspective, privatization is not only apt to change the rules of organization in such a way as to provide stronger incentives for firms to make efficient decisions. By breaking lines of hierarchic subordination — of firms subject to the dictates of their ministerial superiors, of commercial banks under the influence of the central bank and the ministry of finance — privatization restricts or nullifies the opportunities for undermining government policy open to individuals who might oppose them. But privatization, especially in the realm of banking that is our main concern here, is very difficult to carry out in countries where few citizens have had a chance to accumulate wealth (Marx's primitive capitalist accumulation)[52] and where such savings as individuals were able to build up have been depleted by inflation. In Poland, which has gone farther on the road to capitalism than Romania or Bulgaria, only one large government bank (WBK) has so far been privatized. One important reason is that the other banks are undercapitalized and financially weak — too weak presumably to compete effectively in a free market without government support — and it has not been possible so far to find them foreign partners who would supply the capital to strengthen them. Those private banks that have been formed *ab ovo* tend to be even smaller and weaker. They seem to take greater risks than government-owned banks. Many of them will undoubtedly fail. The dilemma faced by the liberal administration of the National Bank of Poland is that if the banks do not merge into a few conglomerates or trusts, the weaker ones are likely to fail. But if they do so merge, competition will suffer. (In Romania, there are too few private banks for mergers to take place.)

Thin and incomplete markets are the bane of economies in transition. Take as a conspicuous example the market for investment funds. In Poland firms may, theoretically, (1) get long-term loans from banks, (2) issue stock or bonds, or (3) tap into the unorganized money market. But banks facing the risks associated with a high and uncertain rate of inflation are hesitant to lend long-term without full and expensive collateralization (or other securitization). The stock market so far has been limited to 16 firms, including banks. The government has set demanding rules for the issue of stock and bonds that very few firms can meet. (These rules are probably necessary precisely because markets are thin, information is poorly diffused, and investors may easily be cheated). So the third option, the unorganized money market (quasi-banks operating 'out of a valise') may be the only one open to firms wishing to invest. But then the risk premiums these money-lenders demand are so high that they restrict investments to a few high-return projects. The situation is even worse in Romania where long-term investments have sunk to minimal levels.

In the long run, the prospects for efficient markets are good, provided the governments in power are willing to nurture them and ensure the minimum macroeconomic stability to enable them to work. Privatization, via auction sales of government property, manager-employment buy-outs, and voucher schemes, will increase the number of participants in markets. Successful firms and individuals will gradually accumulate the financial resources necessary to cope with uncertainty and volatility. As a result of this evolution, markets will become 'thicker'. The asymmetry of information will also diminish as data banks (especially on credit-worthiness) are created and circulated. But it will take quite a few years to complete this transformation.

Notes

1.   Research for this paper was supported by a grant from the International Research & Exchanges Board, with funds provided by the US Department of State (Title VIII) and the National Endowment for the Humanities. None of these organizations is responsible for the views expressed. I am grateful to Avner Ben-Ner and John Bonin for their very helpful comments and suggestions on the first version of this paper.
2.   I follow here the concepts and definitions developed in *Comparative Economics* (J.M. Montias, A. Ben-Ner, and E. Neuberger), Fundamentals of Pure and Applied Economics, Harwood Academic Publishers, 1994.

3. Murrell (1993) places much emphasis on the need for continuity between the old and the new system (informational channels, personnel, routine ways of doing things). I shall try to show in the paper that this continuity may be dysfunctional if it helps perpetuate inefficient system traits or makes it possible for old bureaucrats to conduct policies at variance with those of the new élites.

4. In October 1950, the Polish government instituted a monetary reform which had the effect of confiscating two thirds of the currency holdings of the population. However, savings deposited in the country's savings banks were spared from this imposition. This undoubtedly helped to reinforce the notion that these banks were 'safe'.

5. In 1988, the value of these foreign-currency accounts expressed in zloty came to nearly 75 per cent of the value of domestic-currency savings accounts (Głowny urząd, 1992, p.146)

6. Recently released Polish data show that the premiums paid to life insurance companies amounted to a very small part of national saving.

7. Between 23 March and 22 April 1981, at the time when special savings accounts to buy cars were first made available, 1.5 mn Polish citizens made deposits in them. Polmozbytu, the car-distribution agency that had contracted with the banks eventually to supply cars to depositors, is no longer in existence. The Supreme Court of Poland will soon decide precisely what responsibility the government, which had 'guaranteed' the deposits, bears with respect to honouring the agency's commitment to supply cars. So far the government's principal concession has been to exempt holders of deposits from payment of the tariff on imported cars (*Gazeta Bankowa*, 28 June 1993, p.29). A similar question has risen with regard to deposit accounts for cooperative apartments (*Gazeta Bankowa*, 28 May 1993, p.2). The long-term open-ended contracts for future delivery of cars and apartments that citizens entered into in the 1980s created special problems in the 1990s by reason of the far-reaching system changes that had occurred between the two periods.

8. In the Soviet Union, during the period of Stalin's rule, government bonds were sold to the population. However, the purchase of these bonds was not voluntary; it can hardly have been considered a desirable option for savers.

9. It was gradually recognized that the 'real-bills' doctrine, according to which the extension of short-term credits to 'cover' increases in inventories required for plan-approved production could be expected to preserve financial equilibrium, was invalid. To prevent an excessive amount of liquidity from being injected into the system, increases in net amounts of credit outstanding had to be financed at least in part by a budget surplus (Montias, 1971).

10. It should, nevertheless, be remarked that a bank officer could be held criminally responsible for making an injudicious loan. This provision of the criminal code was still in force in Poland in June 1993 (*Gazeta Bankowa*, 11 June 1993, p.2). It has been invoked in a few cases, where irregularities were suspected, since 1989.

11. With the possible exception of the brief-lived government of Jan Olszewski. It was too early, at the time when the conference for which this paper was prepared took place, to discern what sort of economic policy the left-of-centre government appointed in October 1993 by the newly-elected Parliament would conduct.

12. The elections of October 1992 led to the formation of a majority in Parliament that was less favourable to full-fledged reforms. The Vacaroiu government that was formed after the elections reflects this trend.

13. In June 1993 the Polish Minister of Industry submitted a set of recommendations
     to the Economic Committee of the Council of Ministers, which included (1)
     devaluation of the zloty to encourage exports and discourage imports, (2) the
     annulment of debts contracted by government-owned enterprises before 1990, (3)
     cheaper credit for enterprises, and (4) the elimination of certain taxes on
     enterprises. It is very doubtful whether the government will accept these proposals
     (*Rzeczpospolita*, 22 June 1993, p.1). On the other hand, the officials of the
     National Bank of Poland, from its president down, have advocated fiscal and
     financial prudence (minimum budget deficits, positive real interest rates, the
     creation of financial reserves against non-performing loans, and bankruptcy or
     liquidation for government-owned enterprises incapable of eliminating losses in the
     foreseeable future.) (For a typical instance, see the speech by the president of the
     National Bank of Poland in *Bank*, No. 1, 1992, 12—13.) In Romania, the journal
     of the association of Romanian economists, *Economistul*, edited by the former
     editor of the communist paper *Scinteia*, systematically gives voice to the views of
     the pro-industry lobby, in opposition to the views of the representatives of the
     National Bank of Romania (see, in particular, F. Magereanu's violent attack on the
     report of the National Bank on foreign-exchange problems and the value of the Lei
     in *Economistul*, 25 June 1993) (Magereanu, 1993). The Romanian government, if
     we may judge by the interest-rate policy favouring large industrial debtors that it
     has imposed on the National Bank, seems to lend a more sympathetic ear to the
     industrial lobby than any of the post-1989 Polish governments have done.
14. These outcomes contribute directly or indirectly to the ultimate outcomes (GNP per
     capita, distribution and stability of incomes, national strength, and so forth) that
     were referred to at the beginning of this paper.
15. The miners of the Jiu Valley were used by the government to help repress liberal
     opposition, in June 1990 and again in 1991, in part by violent means. It is said that
     the wage concessions that they received were a reward for their political
     contribution. At the time of this writing (early August 1993), a strike of the Jiu
     Valley miners had broken out, which, if it is successful in raising wages, will
     accelerate inflation (presently running at about 15 per cent per month).
16. Among the many economists who blame the 'recession' on errors in economic
     policy (in particular, on excessive fiscal and financial restraint), see, for the case
     of Czechoslovakia, Vintrova (1993), for that of Poland, Kołodko (1992) and
     Poznanski (1993) and, with some nuances, Rosati (1993). For a more positive
     assessment of Polish developments, see Gomulka (1993).
17. In Bulgaria, as early as January 1990, citizens were allowed to open accounts in
     USD and DM. USD accounts earned 5.75 per cent for short-term deposits and
     6.25 per cent for deposits held at least a year. These rates were substantially
     higher than the rate of inflation in USD-denominated prices in world markets
     (Thorne, 1992, p.17).
18. The liberalization of prices was more thorough and more rapid in Poland than in
     Romania (or Bulgaria). In Poland, as early as 1990, 23 per cent of transactions in
     intermediate inputs and 27 per cent of those in consumer goods sold to the
     population were effected at administered (controlled) market prices. By 1992, these
     percentages had decreased to 12 and 15 per cent respectively (Gomulka, 1993, p.
     197). In Romania, as late as May 1993, prices of a wide variety of products were
     still subject to some degree of control or surveillance, including electricity, coal,
     petroleum, iron ore, metallurgical products, trucks, lumber, bread, milk, meat,
     and pharmaceuticals, which, in the aggregate, must have represented a substantially

higher percentage of sales than those cited above for Poland (see Government Decision No. 18. 206 of 7 May 1993, *Adevarul*, Economic Supplement, 18—24 July 1993).

19. According to McKinnon (1991) and Bruno (1993), the 'unexpectedly large price shock' in Poland initially caused an 'unanticipated drop in real wages', which resulted in larger profits and taxes thereon than had been counted on. When real wages rebounded, enterprise profits were squeezed, and so were budgetary receipts. The financial pressure on enterprises was aggravated by the introduction of taxes on capital gains on inventories and foreign currency deposits.

20. In Poland, for instance, social security payments to wage and salary recipients (expressed in real terms), fell by 14 per cent in 1990 then rose by 29.8 per cent in 1991. The share of social security payments in the wages and salaries of the bottom quintile of the recipients rose from 25 per cent in 1985 to 30 per cent in 1990 and 32 per cent in 1991. It also rose for the top quintile. In the total income of retired people, the share of social security payments went up from 59 per cent to 84 per cent. Its share of peasants' incomes rose from 7 per cent to 15 per cent. Peasants represented the group who were most adversely affected by shock therapy, in part because they were less protected by the social-security system (*Zycie gospodarcze*, No. 2, 1993).

21. The base above which taxes on wage increases were levied differed over time. It has at different times been defined as the total wage fund, the average wage of all employees, and the wages of individual employees.

22. Bruno (1993) points out that it took at least three years for Western nations to put into place a VAT system, even when enterprise accounting was already geared up for it. In Romania, when the VAT was introduced during the summer of 1993, there were complaints that there had been inadequate preparation for the reform, particularly for the collection of the tax at the border in lieu of tariffs (*Capital*, No. 25, 23 June 1993).

23. This system sometimes leads to unexpected consequences. In Romania, small cooperatives that give work to handicapped people have been exempted from the VAT. This has discouraged buyers of their products wishing to process them further or resell them because they cannot deduct from *their* VAT the taxes already paid by their suppliers (*Capital*, No. 29, 23 July 1993).

24. From November 1990 to May 1992 wholesale prices in Romania increased 7.7-fold while the official exchange rate with the USD depreciated by 6.45-fold (National Bank of Romania, 1992a, p.12). During this protracted period, there were times when the official exchange rate lagged much more significantly behind increases in prices.

25. The budget deficit of the government and the policy of extending credits to GOFs at highly negative real rates were chiefly responsible for the continued inflation. On interest-rate policy, see below.

26. There were also said to be secondary auctions where successful bidders in the primary auction resold foreign exchange to the highest bidders. On the problem of unifying the rates, see *Adevarul economic*, 2 August 1993.

27. In Bulgaria in the course of 1990, for example, the National Bank transferred to the newly-created commercial banks assets in the form of credits to government enterprises evaluated at 40 per cent of GDP. As a result, this type of credits disappeared from the balance sheet of the National Bank (Thorne, 1992, p.3).

28.   In Poland, where this cross-ownership system was barred in the case of government-owned banks, a far-flung network of cooperative banks was allowed to develop which served mainly the agricultural and food-processing sectors. The bankruptcy of the large Srem cooperative bank in 1991 sent repercussions throughout the system.

29.   The minimum level of owned capital was raised to nearly USD 5 mn in 1992, but banks were given some time to build up their capital to this level.

30.   The public sale of shares of the WBK and the Bank Śląski, which was also slated for privatization, would have occurred at least a year earlier if a suitable foreign partner could have been found for either of the banks. But, owing to the problems raised by Poland's enormous foreign debt and to the negative attitude of the Western creditors associated with the London Club, no willing investors had come forward. This adverse feature of the initial environment was specific to Poland. On the privatization of the WBK, see *Rzeczpospolita*, 22 June 1993.

31.   For details on the credits extended by 'large' (mainly government-owned) and 'small' (mainly private banks), see below.

32.   Note, however, that government banks subject to a credit ceiling may not circumvent it by lending above-ceiling funds to private banks (Wyczański, 1993, p. 620).

33.   The Polish government for a brief period in the first half of 1990 capped the lending rate of government banks at 130 per cent of the refinancing rate, but since that time the margin has been set freely by the banks' management (Wyczański, 1993, p. 60).

34.   The National Bank of Romania was strenuously attacked by pro-industry economists for raising interest rates as much as it did. Magereanu (1993), for instance, objected that rates of interest were now several times higher than GOFs' rates of profit. Rates as high as those that had been set by the bank could only finance 'speculative operations'. This objection raises an interesting theoretical point. Is the risk faced by the lending banks greater when they raise their lending rate? Is there adverse selection, as low-return, low-risk borrowers are forced to withdraw from the market? This depends on whether the average expected rate of return on loans is positively correlated with their expected variance. This is likely to be the case in equilibrium in a perfect market where intermediaries are free to trade debts with different degrees of risk and return. It is not so clear that this situation obtains before trade takes place or in a highly imperfect market.

35.   Interview information, National Bank of Romania (4 August 1993).

36.   In Poland and Romania, some of the credits extended by government banks go to private firms, but at least 80 per cent are earmarked for the use of GOFs.

37.   Rostowski (1993, p. 49) argues persuasively that in a centrally planned system the extension of credit by supplying firms gives both creditors and debtors more freedom of decision making than the planning hierarchy desires. On the wide literature on IEC, both in English and in Eastern European languages, see the bibliography for Rostowski's article.

38.   During 1991, when payments arrears rose at a rapid level in Romania, inventories increased to unprecedented levels (to 23.4 per cent of GDP at the end of the year). Some of these inventories were held for 'speculative purposes' — i.e., for resale at much higher prices (National Bank of Romania, 1992a, p.7).

39.   The high ratio of non-performing loans to the equity of banks (Ábel and Bonin, 1992, p.7), already noticeable in 1990, should have given pause to the optimists.

40. Were the banks' margins formerly lower than they might have been to ensure the maximization of profits? The fact that they could raise these margins with impunity suggests that the banks were not competitive to begin with.

41. The Glass-Steagall Act does permit banks to hold equity in defaulting firms for a period of time and provides for other exceptions that reduce the differences between the American and the continental models.

42. It is not clear to me whether the Polish definition of the debts of firms in arrears in their payments to banks corresponds to the 'doubtful and bad loans' of the National Bank of Hungary.

43. Ábel and Bonin (1992) also refer to the 'old-boy' linkages between loan officers and clients of long standing which make it possible for inefficient firms to conduct business as usual. Alexandrowicz and Paprot (1993), on the other hand, argue that setting up separate DTKs will sever the link between bank officials and debtors and lead to an 'impersonal approach'. This argument is consonant with Peter Murrell's call for 'organic reforms' that disturb as little as possible the personal links and the information channels that existed before (Murrell, 1993). In my view, Murrell does not sufficiently distinguish between personal links (and the information interacting agents possess) that should be preserved because these channels will promote efficient decision making in the reformed system and those that will not contribute to higher efficiency. The latter may even, if Parfinewicz and Zebrowski are right, detract from the purposes of the reform.

44. Groszek (1993) is of the opinion that these limits will seriously hamper the debt-for-swap initiatives contemplated in the restructuring reforms, this owing to the undercapitalization of banks and to the massive capital requirements of firms undergoing restructuring.

45. At the end of 1992, 19 banks (22 per cent of the total number of Polish banks) did not meet this criterion (*Gazeta bankowa*, 18 June 1993, p.10).

46. The estimates of bad loans are based on the auditing of banks in 1991 and the anticipated growth in lending in 1992. The 50 per cent estimate makes allowance for the sale value of the collateral on non-performing loans. According to the banks' own estimates, the value of bad loans amounted to only 37 per cent of loans outstanding.

47. In the Czech Republic, where the problem is much less severe than in Romania, the management of bad debts has also been vested in a special institution, the Konsolidačni Banka. This bank, unlike the proposed Romanian institution that would be expected to manage the assets of only debtor-firms in troubled sectors, has the obligation to buy out the debts of all companies for which bankruptcy has been declared. The government is also organizing a massive process of clearing mutual debts. It has made participation in this debt-clearing process a requirement for firms wishing to benefit from an out-of-court alternative to bankruptcy. Creditors generally have an incentive not to press their debtors into bankruptcy because they expect that it will take years to get their money and because they are unlikely to recover more than about 15 per cent of the amounts they are owed (*The Prague Post*, 23—29 June 1993).

48. Of the nine large government-owned banks that were created in 1989, one, the Wielkopolski Bank Kreditowy, Poznań, has been privatized. None of the large specialized banks, including the savings bank Pekao and the Development Bank, has been privatized. All the government-owned banks, however, have been 'corporatized', in the sense that they are now autonomous units with limited liability and independent governing boards. The owned capital of the WBK

Poznań, which amounted to zl 712 bn (USD 42 mn) in March 1993, placed it in the fourteenth rank of Polish banks (*Gazeta bankowa*, 4 June 1993, p.41).

49.   A credit officer of Dacia Felix, a private Romanian bank, informed me that this bank also regularly lent to government-owned commercial firms.

50.   The association between risk-taking and non-performing loans emerges from the answers of respondents in the survey about their willingness to take occasional 'large risks'. Only 23 per cent of banks with a low percentage of non-performing loans but 56 per cent of those with a portfolio containing more than 30 per cent of such loans stated that they occasionally took large risks.

51.   Here again I mark my disagreement with Murrell (1993) who pleads for the preservation of the information and of the 'organic links' generated under the old system.

52.   Alexander Gerschenkron was one of the few economic historians to understand the significance of 'primitive accumulation' for successful capitalist development. See, for example, Gerschenkron 1962b.

References

Ábel, I. and Bonin, J.P. (1992), 'Non-performing loans: Hungarian banks as shaky pillars', (mimeo), Wesleyan University.

Alexandrowicz, A. and Paprot, D. (1993), 'Trudne kredity: amerykanskie doswiadczenia i polskie realia', (in Polish), *Bank* 1(5), 28—35.

Balassa, Á. (1993), 'Konsolidacja kredytów na Wgrzech', (in Polish), *Bank* 2(5), 26—27.

Balcerowicz, L. (1992), 'Pieniadz jest dobrym wspolnym', (in Polish), *Bank* 2(3), 8—11.

Begg, D. and Portes, R. (1992), 'Enterprise debt and economic transformation: financial restructuring in the state sector in Central and Eastern Europe', Discussion Paper Series No. 695, Centre for Economic Policy Research, London.

Boguszewski, P. (1992), 'Wybrane problemy działalnosci kredytowej banków w okresie transformacji gospodarki', (in Polish), *Bank i kredyt* 23(10—12), 1—8.

Bruno, M. (1993), 'Stabilization and the macroeconomics of transition — how different is Eastern Europe?', *Economics of Transition* 1(1), 5—19.

Gerschenkron, A. (1962a), 'Russia: patterns and problems of development, 1861—1958', in *Economic Backwardness in Historical Perspective*, Cambridge, MA., Harvard University Press.

Gerschenkron, A. (1962b), 'Rosario Romeo and the original accumulation of capital', in *Economic Backwardness in Historical Perspective*, Cambridge, MA., Harvard University Press.

Glikman, P. (1993), 'Recession, stagnation, and ways out', *Eastern European Economics* 31(3), 4—77.

Głowny urząd statystyczny (1993), *Rocznik statystyczny*, (in Polish).

Gomulka, S. (1993), 'Poland: glass half full', in Portes, R. (ed.), *Economic Transformation in Central Europe: A Progress Report*, London, Centre for Economic Policy Research.

Groszek, M. (1993), 'Banki i restrukturyzacja przedsiębiórstw', (in Polish), *Bank* 3, 20—22.

Kokoszczyński, R. and Kondratowicz, A. (1991), 'Monetary and credit policy in Poland', PPRG Discussion Papers no.10, Warsaw University.

Kołodko, G. (1992), 'From output collapse to sustainable growth in transition economies: the fiscal implications', (mimeo), International Monetary Fund, Washington, D.C.

Magereanu, F. (1993), 'Raportul BNR, fuga de responsibilita' (in Romanian), *Economistul*, 25 June 1993.

McKinnon, R.I. (1991), 'Financial control in the transition from classical socialism to a market economy', Working Paper Series, Institute for Policy Reform.

McKinsey, R. *et al.* (1993), 'An integrated solution to the restructuring of the Romanian banking sector', vol. 1, Final Report of the Restructuring Committee, Bucharest, February 1993; Final Presentation, June 1993.

Montias, J.M. (1971), 'Bank lending and fiscal policy in Eastern Europe', in G. Grossman (ed.), *Money and Plan; Financial Aspects of East European Reforms*, Berkeley, University of California Press.

Murrell, P. (1993), 'Evolutionary and radical approaches to economic reform', in Poznanski, K. (ed.), *Stabilization and Privatization in Poland: An Economic Evaluation of the Shock Theory Program*, Boston, Dordrecht and London, Kluwer Academic Publishers.

National Bank of Romania (1992a), 'Monetary policy during the transition period'.

National Bank of Romania (1992b), *Quarterly Bulletin* 3.

National Bank of Romania (1993a), *Bulletin trimestrial* 1 (preliminary printed version).

National Bank of Romania (1993b), 'Report concerning the Romanian foreign exchange system and measures needed to stabilize the exchange rate of the Lei', English translation of official National Bank report.

Parfinewicz, A. and Zebrowski, J. (1993), 'Rola banków w wdrazanie programu restrukturyzacji finansowej', (in Polish), *Bank* 1(5), 26—27.

Pietruszynska, K. (1993), 'Zdolność kredytowa podmiotów gospodarczych, przyczyny jej utraty i odzyskiwania (okres 1990—1992)', (in Polish), *Bank i kredyt* 24(4), 22—26.

Poznanski, K. (1993), 'Poland's transition to capitalism: shock and therapy', in Poznanski, K. (ed.), *Stabilization and Privatization in Poland; An Economic Evaluation of the Shock Therapy Program*, Boston, Dordrecht and London, Kluwer Academic Publishers.

Rosati, D.K. (1993), 'Poland: glass half empty', in R. Portes (ed.), *Economic Transformation in Central Europe: A Progress Report*, London, Centre for Economic Policy Research.

Rostowski, J. (1993), 'Zadłuzenie między przedsiębiorstwami', (in Polish), *Bank* 2(5), 49—53.

Thorne, A. (1992), 'Issues in reforming financial systems in Eastern Europe: the case of Bulgaria', Working Papers, Technical Department, The World Bank, Washington, D.C.

Vintrova, R. (1993), 'Macroeconomic analysis of transformation in the CSFR', Forschungsberichte No. 188, The Vienna Institute for Comparative Economic Studies.

Wesołek, S. (1993), 'Z drugiej strony barykady; Wokół restrukturyzacji finansowej przedsiębiórstw i banków', (in Polish), *Bank* 2(5), 24—25.

World Bank (1993), 'Financial and enterprise sector adjustment loan (FESAL); Initiating memorandum', Country Operations Division, The World Bank, Washington, D.C.

Wyczański, P. (1993), 'Polish banking system 1990—1992', Economic and Social Policy Series No. 32, Friedrich Ebert Stiftung, Warsaw.

3 Banking in Central Europe during the Protomarket Period: Developments and Emerging Issues

David M. Kemme

1 Introduction[1]

Historically, banking activity in the planned economies of Eastern Europe and the Soviet Union was designed and carried out principally as a means of monitoring and enforcing the planned production activity of enterprises on the one hand, and maintaining monetary balance at the macroeconomic level on the other. As such the allocation and distribution of financial resources was not left to the market place with banking and financial institutions as intermediaries, but left to the exact dictates of the appropriate central planning agency and the national bank. The revolutions of 1989—1990 throughout the socialist world initiated the transition from centrally planned economies to market-oriented economies with private property. If central planning was to be abandoned then it was no longer necessary for the banking system to serve solely as controller/auditor for the state. Further, an alternative market-oriented means of intermediating between households with excess liquidity and the enterprises demanding liquidity for investment purposes had to be developed.

A simple reform of the existing financial system was not sufficient.[2] The creation of an entirely new institutional structure and the introduction of financial markets was required. Further, with the creation of new institutions and instruments, a new relationship between monetary authorities and the private sector had to be developed to allow appropriate control of monetary aggregates and management of the macroeconomy. New policies at both the micro and macro level had to be developed quickly. The period from 1990 to mid-1993 has been characterized by: (1) the creation of new institutions, *inter alia*, a functional central bank and commercial banks, predominately state owned, but also some privately owned; (2) the creation of new financial instruments, both for intermediation and monetary control; (3) the development of monetary policy to utilize the newly-created instruments for macroeconomic management, which has, for the most part, succumbed to the temptation to use the predominately state-owned banking system to finance irresponsible fiscal policies; and (4) a regulatory policy which may be termed 'ignorant forbearance' allowing the state-owned commercial banks to continue lending to state-owned enterprises which are not likely to be creditworthy at all. Only the simplest financial markets were created, in part in response to the needs of the nascent business community. The markets remain thin, illiquid and function irregularly. As a result I label 1990—1993 the protomarket period in Eastern Europe.

While the creation of the fundamental institutions and instruments has taken place, an evaluation of the actual policies implemented with the use of the new instruments indicates much is to be done. During the remainder of this century policy makers will continue to be challenged in two areas. The first strikes at the heart of monetary policy formulation and implementation, the second at commercial bank management. In each country the parliaments continue to whittle away at the limited central bank independence which prevailed early in the transition period. The inability of legislatures to finance fiscal appropriations with new taxes has forced monetary policies to accommodate government budget deficits, and this trend will continue. With respect to commercial bank management it is likely that we will see: (1) an increase in investment banking relative to commercial banking;[3] (2) unyielding pressures for the abandonment of ignorant forbearance on the part of commercial bankers and replacement of this policy with selective forbearance at the direction of the Ministries of Privatization and Finance and support of the Treasury; (3) the ingenious creation of fictitious capital on the part of banks to meet capital/asset requirements, while at the same time regulators continuously efface existing fictitious capital; and (4) new evasive institutional structures, also to avoid capital/asset requirements, which will require greater regulatory vigilance or legislation to ban the financial subterfuge pioneered by many institutions in market economies in the West.

While other financial intermediaries prevalent in Western market economies play an important role in the intermediation process, they are not well developed or are non-existent in the transition economies. The commercial banking system lies at the heart of intermediation and the central bank lies at the heart of macroeconomic management. As a result, in this chapter I will focus on the creation of the central banking institutions and the monetary policy instruments created during 1990—1993 in the CSFR (focusing solely on the Czech Republic since the dissolution), Hungary and Poland.[4]

2   The role and creation of central banks

The banking system in a market economy serves to mobilize domestic savings from households, allocates those savings among competing uses and provides a means of payments clearing. All of these functions were subsumed by the annual plan and price controls which allocated both physical and financial resources in the socialist economy. The transition to a market economy requires the rapid development of the commercial banking system in order to allocate resources efficiently. A corollary to commercial banking is the development of the central bank.[5]

For successful transition it is argued that three critical areas of central bank operations must be resolved.[6] First, the central bank must be independent of the government, both the legislature and the administration. Second, there must be a means of providing liquidity to the economy as a whole and the means of doing so must be neutral in terms of allocating liquidity among competing uses — the market place should be the decision maker in terms of allocation details. And third, a system of supervisory and prudential regulations to oversee commercial banking activities must be developed.

Price stability is essential to building public confidence in new monetary institutions and also contributes to the establishment of long-term capital markets. In countries with weak governments legislatures lack fiscal discipline and are prone to deficit spending financed via an inflation tax. An independent central bank provides an additional check on the inflationary process and enhances fiscal discipline. The central bank's principal task becomes provision of sufficient liquidity to finance non-inflationary growth. The exact allocation of liquidity then remains at the discretion of the market place. This requires a new set of market-oriented instruments for the creation and distribution of liquidity. With these instruments come financial sector institutions, predominately commercial banks, serving as intermediaries. To ensure public confidence in financial institutions the monetary authorities must implement a supervisory and prudential system to oversee their operation. The principle tasks of the supervisory authorities are promoting competition and efficiency in the commercial banking industry, assuring the safety and soundness of the banking system, and providing consumer protection for both deposit and loan activities. Supervisory agencies in Western market-type economies are often found under the jurisdiction of the central bank, but not necessarily. All of these fundamental issues have been addressed, but in slightly different ways in each of the three Central European countries.

In the *Czech Republic* (CR) the central bank, the Czech National Bank (CNB) was created from the State Bank of the CSFR (SBC) on 1 January 1993.[7] The SBC itself was created only three years earlier.[8] The managing body of the CNB is the Bank Board which consists of seven members: the Governor, two Vice Governors and four senior bank officers. All are appointed and recallable by the President of the Republic. The legislation creating the CNB states that in 'providing for its primary objective the CNB shall be independent of any instructions given by the government' (CNB, 1993a, p. 4). Because the government and parliament have put major emphasis on price stability and have been fiscally responsible, the CNB has not been forced to finance an inordinate amount of government debt — its independence has not been tested in that sense.

Instruments for the creation and management of liquidity have been developed relatively quickly. Table 3.1 provides the basic instruments created by the SBC which also remain available for the CNB. While all of the traditional instruments available to Western central banks have been created (a system of reserve requirements, discounting, and securities for open market operations), the most effective means of controlling liquidity creation has been direct quotas or ceilings on bank credits. In part this is a necessity — neither institutions nor personnel were capable of the sophisticated management of market instruments, nor were securities markets sufficiently developed for open market operations. Nonetheless, monetary authorities actively employed the instruments to attempt to manage liquidity. Table 3.2 provides a calendar of monetary policy changes in 1992 in the CSFR. The monetary authorities clearly were active during the year with every instrument except open market operations.

Finally, the issue of bank supervision and prudential regulation has been addressed with the creation of the Banking Supervision Department within the SBC. In 1992 independent banking supervision departments for each republic were created within the SBC in preparation for the split of the nation and they have become the supervisory agencies for each of the new central banks. The Departments were organized in three sections: Methods, responsible for determining banking principles and procedures; Banking Activities, responsible for banking and foreign exchange trading licences; and Financial Analysis and Inspection, responsible for organizing bank inspections, monitoring the activities of banks and analysing regular bank reports. In addition to the creation of the Banking Supervision Department, capital adequacy standards (BIS standards) and bank liquidity regulations have been adopted. Of all the reforms enacted, the development of the regulatory and supervisory system is the most recent and probably the least prepared to perform as in a market economy. The dissemination of information regarding new standards, training of personnel, both at the central bank and at individual commercial banks, and the implementation of the new standards has been problematic. To alleviate some of these problems the Banking Supervision Department of the CNB re-drafted rules governing prudential requirements for bank activity taking into account recent experiences, the division of the country and the new Bankruptcy Act. The new regulations went into effect on 1 June 1993 (CNB, 1993b, p. 7). This area, including the classification of the creditworthiness of loans in the commercial banks' portfolios, will likely remain troublesome.

In *Hungary* the reform of the banking system began somewhat earlier than in the rest of Central Europe. In 1987 the National Bank of Hungary (NBH) no longer served as 'monetary controller' for the national economic plans. Legislation in 1990, almost continuously amended and fine-tuned by legal decrees, gave the NBH formal independence from the government. The amount of lending to the government is restricted to a percentage of government revenues, but the ceiling may vary from year to year by legislation and according to the fiscal needs of the budget. Direct lending to the government has been reduced though, as the Treasury has begun to issue Treasury bills and bonds.

The NBH is obligated by law to support the overall economic programme developed by the government and Parliament. It is emphasized by the NBH, however, that the programme should be consistent with the Bank's responsibility for price stability and the overall monetary policy determined by the NBH. Fundamental monetary policy objectives are developed by the NBH Council, consisting of the President of the Bank, the Vice-Presidents of the Bank and a number of outside members equal to the number of Vice Presidents. There has been disagreement between the need for the NBH to maintain price stability and the needs of legislative programmes. The record on inflation indicates that this has become a serious problem.

While the NBH has struggled to maintain the independence and firmness of monetary policy, the NBH, Ministry of Finance and Treasury have made remarkable progress in the creation of new monetary instruments and securities for implementation of monetary control. As Table 3.3 indicates, the whole range of policy instruments available in the Western market-type economy has been created. As Table 3.4 indicates, through 1992 the monetary authorities did not hesitate to adjust interest rates (slowly lowering them) and the Treasury and NBH were quick to begin issuing bonds. Of the former socialist planned economies of Eastern Europe, Hungary clearly leads in the development of securities markets. Nonetheless, the market is still too thin to conduct significant open market operations for monetary policy purposes.

Also in 1987 the State Bank Supervisory Agency was established within the Ministry of Finance. Since 1990 it has functioned as a free-standing agency and is responsible for licensing financial institutions, and since 1991 the Agency is empowered to regulate and oversee bank operations.[9] The Agency enforces rules on ownership, provisions for capital adequacy, liquidity and loan set-asides, rules governing the assumption of risk and procedures for liquidation in cases of insolvency. Capital adequacy standards and loan provisions were also adopted.[10]

In *Poland* legislation in 1982 gave the National Bank of Poland (NBP) greater authority in determining monetary policy. However, it wasn't until 1989 that the monobank was transformed into a two-tier system. Increased independence of the Bank resulted from continuing legislative changes: in 1990 (giving the bank authority to formulate and conduct monetary policy without parliamentary approval of detailed credit plans) and September 1991 (strengthening the position of the President and giving the Bank greater supervisory authority).[11] The highest policy-making body of the bank is the Monetary Policy Committee which annually presents the 'monetary policy outline' to the Council of Ministers and Parliament. Unlike the policy council of the NBH, which has outside members, the Monetary Policy Committee of the NBP is composed of Bank staff, including all of the Deputy Presidents. As in Hungary the amount of government debt the NBP must finance is restricted and the restrictions are specified as part of the economic legislation approved by the Parliament each year.

The instruments for the provision and allocation of liquidity necessary for the smooth functioning of the financial system in a market economy have also been created by the monetary authorities in Poland. These are detailed in Table 3.5. However, Poland, unlike the CSFR and Hungary, began the transition in a hyperinflationary environment. The monetary authorities maintained credit ceilings, set high reserve requirements and high interest rates. As inflation subsided from inflationary levels, credit ceilings were soon abandoned and the Polish monetary authorities turned to market instruments for the allocation of credit. Early 1990 and 1991 saw numerous changes in policies — reserve requirements, refinancing rates and discount rates in particular — in an attempt to fine-tune monetary performance, but with mixed results (see Kemme, 1993). At the same time debt instruments were being developed and the secondary market was being promoted. No serious open market operations were undertaken, however. Table 3.6 details monetary policy changes through mid-1993.

On the regulatory front the General Inspectorate for Bank Supervision was established in 1990 within the NBP and the 1991 Banking law strengthened its authority for bank supervision. It is empowered to examine and supervise commercial banks and is charged with ensuring capital adequacy, the quality of the commercial bank's portfolio and deposit safety. Loan classifications (pass, watch, substandard, doubtful and loss) have been adopted and set aside provisions specified (2, 5, 20, 50, and 100 per cent respectively). Only recently have these specifications been implemented, but it is clear that the loan portfolios of commercial banks as a group have deteriorated through 1993, and the bad loan problem is severe.

3   Unresolved issues and future prospects

In all of the Central European countries remarkable progress has been made in terms of institutional change and the creation of new financial instruments. Of concern, however, has been the development of monetary policy and the central bank's ability to carry out the desired policy. While the issue of central bank independence appears (nominally) to be resolved, in fact in each country the link between the government budget and money creation by the central bank is apparent. Only in the CSFR, and now the CR, where the Parliament and government have so far proven to be fiscally responsible, has the central bank been able to maintain a strong record of price stability. For 1993 the approved CR budget was a balanced budget of CK 342.2 bn in revenues and expenditures. However, at the end of the first quarter of 1993 there was a government budget surplus of CK 10.4 bn and a decline in outstanding government debt and lending by the CNB to the government (CNB, 1993b, p. 11). It should also be noted that the composition of lending by commercial banks has changed dramatically in the CR. In December 1991 state firms and cooperatives accounted for 76.89 per cent of total bank credits and the private sector accounted for 9.78 per cent. By June 1993 these proportions were 42.53 per cent for the state sector and 40.10 per cent for the private sector (cf. Table 10.6 in Chapter 10).

In Hungary inflationary tendencies worsened from 1990 to 1991 and improved slightly in 1992. In 1990, CPI inflation was 28.9 per cent. In 1991 it was 35.0, and in 1992 23.0 per cent (NBH, 1992, p. 8). No doubt budgetary pressures played a role in excess money creation. In 1992 Parliament approved a government budget deficit of HUF 69.8 bn (or USD 883 mn), but the actual deficit reached HUF 197.1 bn (or USD 2.494 bn), 7 per cent of GDP. For 1993 the budget deficit was projected to be HUF 185.4 bn, but by June it had already reached HUF 119.4 bn and the planned annual budget deficit was increased to HUF 213.3 bn (NBH, 1993, p. 5). As government budget deficits have expanded beyond Parliamentary approved levels for implementation each year there has been crowding out of the private, entrepreneurial sector as well. The proportion of lending of commercial banks to the entrepreneurial sector fell from 73.8 per cent on 1 January 1992 to 52.6 per cent on 1 January 1993 at the same time the share of lending to general government increased from 7.2 per cent on 1 January 1992 to 26.5 per cent on 1 January 1993 (NBH, 1993, p. 67). Thus, excessive government spending may have not only an inflationary effect if financed via money creation, but also a detrimental impact on the composition of commercial bank lending. Clearly the NBH's ability to check the government's deficit spending is limited and the commercial banking sector's desire to replace private sector lending with lending to the government sector remains a problem to be resolved.[12]

In Poland the government budget deficit has been large, but generally within IMF negotiated targets (generally around 5 or 6 per cent of GDP). For 1992 the budget deficit reached (zloty) zl 71 900 bn. Lending from the central bank to the government and the resulting inflationary impact remains a problem, but the amount of direct lending and the inflationary impact appears to be declining.

The most important issue with respect to the transition of industry in each country is how to resolve the issue of non-performing loans to state-owned enterprises. While the central banks and appropriate prudential agencies have implemented appropriate loan classification and monitoring mechanisms, the fundamental questions have not been resolved. In the CR the Consolidation Bank has been the recipient of the 'perpetual loans' on the books of the commercial banks at the beginning of the privatization process. Through 1992, the government provided CSK 170 bn, or 30 per cent of enterprise loans outstanding at the end of 1991, for bank recapitalization. It is estimated, however, that the commercial banks held another CSK 145 bn in non-performing loans. This began the cleansing of the balance sheets of the large state-owned commercial banks. However, the new bankruptcy law has not been implemented aggressively and the overall quality of commercial bank balance sheets is still somewhat ambiguous.

A similar problem exists in Hungary, although the latest official data indicate the problem is less severe. Table 3.7 reports outstanding debts of the banking sector by risk using recently adopted criteria. On 31 December 1992 loans graded below standard amounted to HUF 179.8 bn or 11 per cent of total lending, while on 31 March 1993 this amount was HUF 194.3 bn or 11.5 per cent of total lending. Of these qualified loans the proportion that were non-performing or 'bad' loans was 4.8 and 5.2 per cent, respectively. This was in March 1993. The new Hungarian bankruptcy law has probably worsened the situation as the automatic triggering mechanism has caused nearly a third of all Hungarian enterprises to enter bankruptcy proceedings.[13] It is informally estimated that the percentage of qualified loans is actually now in the 15 to 25 per cent range.[14]

In Poland the problem is more apparent and more severe. At the end of December 1991 the number of enterprises in default was 2880 and the total amount of loans from the largest 12 commercial banks was zl 25 452 982 mn. The total debts of these defaulting enterprises accounted for 18.1 per cent of the total lending by these banks (Kemme, 1993, p. 85). By December 1992 there were 4448 enterprises in default to the largest 12 banks (NBP 1992b, p. 4). And by February 1993 there were 4666 enterprises in default to the largest 14 banks and this amounted to 23.8 per cent of total lending of these banks and 19.1 per cent of total lending of the entire banking system.[15] Recent World Bank programmes for bank recapitalization will address the commercial bank solvency problem, but whether or not the behaviour of the banks and the borrowing enterprises improve is an open question. Polish banks began the transition in a relatively good position since the hyperinflation of late 1989 greatly reduced the real value of enterprise debts. The current high levels of bad debt are the result of continued lending during the transition period. Only if new commercial bank lending policies are in place and staff are appropriately trained to implement the new lending policies will the bad debt problem be resolved. If commercial banks continue to lend haphazardly, expecting yet another bail-out, the moral hazard problem will be magnified. How the prudential authorities move from ignorant forbearance to selective forbearance depends on how bankruptcy legislation is interpreted and applied. This is an issue beyond the scope of this paper.

4   Summary

Overall, the countries under investigation have made great strides in developing the institutions and instruments necessary to manage the monetary sector for the development of a market economy. The problems confronting the countries is now one of actual macroeconomic management on the one hand — implementation of monetary policy with the existing tools and maintenance of central bank independence — and continued enhancement of commercial bank management skills on the other hand. The last is of great difficulty since it requires the additional training of hundreds of bank managers, and provision of incentives to apply strict management policies in an atmosphere where doing so may have harsh social consequences. In addition there is no historical precedent for applying new standards and forcing firms into bankruptcy. In fact recent recapitalization schemes increase the moral hazard problem rather than eliminate it. Moving from ignorant forbearance to selective forbearance will be most difficult.

There are significant risks associated with the failure to address these issues. First is the risk of early crises due to financial panics. The public faith in the financial and banking systems in each country varies and is not to be taken for granted. A run on a bank or the banking system would be disastrous. There is also a significant risk of a wave of bankruptcies; perhaps appropriate, but if mismanaged they will bring about very high social costs.[16] These costs are not only the layoffs of employees, but also the obstacle bankruptcy proceedings pose to the installation of new plant and equipment at viable enterprises, the decline in research and develop-ment expenditures and activities toward new product development. Finally, there is the risk that negative monetary developments continue to spill over into the real sector of the economy and are magnified, not just slowing the rate of recovery but causing a more serious economic contraction.

Notes

1. I would like to thank my colleagues at the central banks in the Czech Republic, the Slovak Republic, Hungary and Poland, many of whom are authors of this book, for their helpful discussions over the past two years on the development of banking in each of their countries.
2. See Nuti (1989) for a discussion of the financial systems prior to the revolutions of 1989—1990.
3. This is not necessarily by choice, however. Essentially, as Richard Golden pointed out in the conference discussions, in many cases the Central European commercial banks are acquiring unwanted equity positions which must be disposed of. It is safe to say that bank work-out departments dealing with problem loans and enterprise restructuring are likely to be active for the rest of the decade.
4. For more country-specific details see Part Four.
5. I note central banking as a corollary to commercial banking because there are alternative methods of regulating both commercial bank activity and macroeconomic activity. For example, a currency board and monetary rules may be utilized for monetary policy. Or alternatively free banking with only minimal regulatory interference may promote commercial banking activity most quickly. Historically, a central bank is a relatively new phenomenon and is generally not necessary for financial intermediation.
6. A fourth area of concern is the payments system itself. The payments system under central planning was designed to verify that payment was made for a particular item, as specified in the annual plan. Timeliness of payment was not a primary concern. The payments system in a market-type economy emphasizes timeliness and accuracy and is generally not at all concerned with what originated the payment. I don't discuss this function of central banking below because it seems to be primarily a technological issue which has already been solved. For example, in Poland the payments clearing system was fully in place by the first quarter of 1993 allowing overnight deposit transactions.
7. On 8 October 1992 the Federal Assembly amended the Constitutional Act on the Czechoslovak Federation allowing the republics to establish new banks of issue by partitioning the SBC. This proceeded on the basis of legislation on the division of the property of the CSFR between the two successor states (see CNB, 1993a).
8. While the break up of the SBC into a central bank and commercial banks occurred in 1990, the two laws which govern most banking activity were passed/amended later: the Act on the SBC and the Act on Banks (20 December 1991) which came into effect on 1 February 1992 (see Kemme, 1993 for further details).
9. Act No. LXIX of 1991 on Financial Institutions and Financial Institution Activities.
10. Loan classifications are standard, substandard, doubtful and bad with mandatory set asides of 20 per cent for sub-standard, 50 per cent for doubtful and 100 per cent for bad loans. Only after these risk reserves are set aside and commercial banks become adept at loan classification and portfolio management will the full extent of the bad loan problem be revealed.
11. See Wyczański and Nowinski (1991) and Wyczański (1993) for details.
12. It may be too early to tell if the changed composition of lending will have a long-term detrimental impact on the Hungarian economy. During the discussion Peter Dittus suggested that this definition of crowding out may be too simple and the government may be 'crowding in' economic activities that otherwise may not take

place. This may be true, but the changes in the state vs. private sector composition in lending by Hungarian commercial banks contrast sharply with the changes evidenced in the Czech Republic (see Chapter 10).

13.   See Chapter 6 on bankruptcy for further specifics.
14.   One unofficial source estimates that bad loans amount to 20 per cent of the total and a one time recapitalization would amount to two times the current government budget deficit.
15.   Note that the NBP is now reporting for the 14 largest banks (NBP, 1993, p. 5.)
16.   The issue is not whether or not bankruptcies benefit the economy as a whole. They clearly do since resources are moved from non-viable enterprises to other areas of the economy. Further, the financial discipline imposed by the threat of bankruptcy provides hard financial incentives forcing efficient management of the firm's resources. The issue to be considered here is how best to manage the process in a macroeconomic sense. The bad debt issue is in essence a residual systemic characteristic which must be dealt with carefully.

References

CNB (1993a), 'Report on the establishment of the Czech National Bank', Czech National Bank, Prague.

CNB (1993b), 'Report on monetary development in the Czech Republic, for the period from January to March 1993', Czech National Bank, Prague.

Kemme, D.M. (1993), *The Reform of the System of Money, Banking and Credit in Central Europe*, New York, Institute for EastWest Studies, (forthcoming).

NBH (1992), *Annual Report 1992*, Budapest, National Bank of Hungary.

NBH (1993), *Monthly Report* No. 5—6, Budapest, National Bank of Hungary.

NBP (1992a), *Annual Report 1992*, Warsaw, National Bank of Poland.

NBP (1992b), *Information Bulletin* No. 13, Warsaw, National Bank of Poland.

NBP (1993), *Information Bulletin* No. 2, Warsaw, National Bank of Poland.

Nuti, D.M. (1989), 'Feasible financial innovation under market socialism', in Kessides, C. *et al.* (eds), *Financial Reform in Socialist Economies*, Washington, D.C., The World Bank.

SBC (1992), *Annual Report 1992*, Prague, State Bank of CSFR.

Wyczański, P. (1993), 'Polish banking system, 1990—1992', Economic and Social Policy Series No. 32, Freidrich Ebert Stiftung, Warsaw.

Wyczański, P. and Nowinski, K. (1991), 'Poland's banking system: current developments and prospects', Economic and Social Policy Series No. 4, Freidrich Ebert Stiftung, Warsaw.

Table 3.1 Monetary policy instruments of the State Bank of the CSFR

1.	Credit limits for commercial banks	Determined on the basis of the monetary programme. No limits as of April, 1992.
2.	Discount rate	Has varied through 1991—1992, 9.5% end of year 1992.
3.	Maximum deviation from the Discount Rate (for the granting of credits by commercial banks)	Was 7.5% through 1992 (while the discount was 9.5%).
4.	Limits of refinancing credits (auction refinancing credits and advance credits for refinancing the credit market)	Determined on the basis of the monetary programme.
5.	Minimum reserve requirements of commercial banks (with SBCS)	3% on time deposits, 9% on demand deposits, end of 1992.
6.	Liquidity and capital adequacy principles — Obligatory ratio of the volume of medium-term and long-term CSK credits extended, loans and capital investments and the medium- and long-term resources of the bank	125% max.
	— Obligatory ratio of own capital and the total volume of assets; based on length of time of operation, for banks:	
	- established after 1 January 1990	8% (by 31/12/1991)
	- established before 1 January 1990	1.5%—2% (by 31/12/1991)
	- Savings Banks	1%
7.	Exchange Rate (end of period) Exchange Rate (annual average)	27.84 CSK/USD 29.49 CSK/USD
8.	Maximum Allowable Foreign Exchange Purchase by individuals for private use)	CSK 5000 per year
9.	Import Surcharge	15%, 10% as of 1/1/92
10.	Payment Conditions for Imports	Varies (binding rules for the postponement of payments for imports).

Source: Report of the SBC on Economic and Monetary Developments of the CSFR in the fourth quarter of 1991, p.13.

Table 3.2   Monetary changes in the CSFR in 1992

Date	Policy change
Discount rate policy	
1 January	Discount rate is 9.5%
25 March	Discount rate lowered to 9.0%
1 April	Removal of discount ceilings
26 August	Discount rate lowered to 8.0%, Lombard rate to 11.5%
30 December	Discount rate raised to 9.5%, Lombard rate to 14%
Foreign exchange and exchange rate policy	
1 January	Drawing limits for forex by individuals was increased to CSK 7500
2 January	British Pound replaced by the French Franc in currency basket
1 September	liquidity rules liberalized
1 January — 31 December	No change in value of CSK
Reserve requirements	
1 February	Elimination of payment of interest on reserves Foreign deposits included in reserves Min. Reserve Requirements (MRR) set at 2% for time, 8% for demand deposits.
1 November	Increase in reserve requirements to 3% for time deposits, 9% for demand deposits.
1 December	Change in methodology for calculating reserves: now based on average of three positions during ten-day reporting period.
Credit limits	
1 January	Credit limits are set quarterly on the basis of the monetary programme.
July	Credit limits removed for all banks except five largest banks (Comm. Bank Prague, Gen. Credit Bank Bratislava, Invest. Bank Prague, IRZ Bratislava, and CSOB).
October	Credit limits removed for five largest banks.
Refinancing system	
1 January	Max. limits on quantity of refinancing credits adjusted.
1 February	Weekly auctions of refinancing credits with one week maturity and at least once a month auctions of refin. credits with one month and three month maturities. Treasury Bills issued by Federal Ministry of Finance and both Czech and Slovak Ministries of Finance.
1 April	Maximum limits on quantity of refinancing credits removed. Weekly auctions of refinancing credits with one month and three month maturities.
25 May	Lombard credit for selected securities and rediscounting of bills.
July	SBC issues own treasury bills.

Source: SBC (1992), p. 32.

Table 3.3   Monetary policy instruments of the National Bank of Hungary

1.	NBH refinancing rates	Rate varies by term to maturity and use of funds. January 1993 base rate is 21%.
2.	NBH interest on commercial bank reserves	Rate varies by length of term, whether reserves are required or excess, and whether reserves are set aside for foreign exchange liabilities.
3.	Interest rates on deposits in commercial banks and lending rates of commercial banks	Market determined. Limit on household deposits eliminated at year end 1991.
4.	Mandatory reserve requirements	Uniform for all deposit institutions, 14% as of Jan. 1993.
5.	NBH daily liquidity reserves	Sets amount of total assets which must be held in liquid assets.
6.	Open market operations	Regularly participates in the market for discounted treasury bills and NBH CDs. Currently markets are thin. Participation in market for Hungarian Government Bonds possible.
7.	Foreign exchange rate	Controlled. Based on market basket of currencies, 50% ECU, 50% USD. Interbank market developing. Devalued 3 times in 1992, twice in 1st quarter 1993, from 1.6% to 2.9% in each case.
8.	Capital adequacy principles	8% of risk weighted assets by January 1993.
9.	Import surcharge	Varies.

Source: NBH

Table 3.4   *Monetary policy calendar for Hungary 1992*

Date	Policy change

Discount rate policy (interest rate measures)

16 March	Refinancing rate for loans maturing in less than one year reduced from 29% to 28%. Rediscounting of bills limited to maturities of less than 90 days and rate reduced to 26%. Rate on HUF refinancing of foreign exchange deposits reduced from 32.2% to 28%. Rate on voluntary deposits placed at the NBH reduced to 22%. Rate on mandatory reserves against household liabilities reduced from 29% to 11%. Rate paid on HUF provisions for foreign exchange liabilities reduced from 29% to 22%.
16 April	Refinancing rate reduced to 27%. Rediscount rate on bills reduced to 25.3%. Rate on refinancing of foreign exchange deposits reduced to 27%.
27 May	Refinancing rate reduced to 26%. Rediscount rate reduced to 24.5%. Rate on refinancing of foreign exchange deposits reduced to 26%. Rate on voluntary deposits at the NBH reduced to 21%. Rate on mandatory reserves on HUF liabilities decreased to 9%. Rate on HUF reserves on foreign exchange liabilities reduced to 20%.
24 June	Refinancing rate reduced to 24%. Rediscount rate reduced to 22.7%. Rate on refinancing foreign exchange deposits reduced to 24%. Rate on voluntary deposits at the NBH reduced to 14.5%. Rate on mandatory reserves decreased to 8%. Rate on HUF reserves on foreign exchange liabilities reduced to 18%.
10 August	Rate on refinancing loans reduced to 23%. Rate on rediscounts reduced to 21.8%. Rate on refinancing of foreign exchange deposits reduced to 23%. Rate on mandatory reserves decreased to 6%, rate on HUF reserves against foreign exchange liabilities reduced to 14%.
11 Sept.	Rate on refinancing loans reduced to 22%. Rate on rediscounts reduced to 20.9%. Rate on refinancing of foreign exchange deposits reduced to 22%. Rate on voluntary deposits at the NBH reduced to 14%. Rate on mandatory reserves decreased to 4%, rate on HUF reserves against exchange liabilities reduced to 13%.

Table 3.4   Monetary policy calendar for Hungary 1992 (continued)

Date	Policy change

Discount rate policy (continued)

5 Oct.   Rate on refinancing loans reduced to 21%.
            Rate on rediscounts reduced to 20%.
            Rate on refinancing of foreign exchange deposits reduced to 21%.
            Termination of interest paid on voluntary deposits of financial institutions at the NBH.
            Rate on mandatory reserves decreased to 3%.
            Rate on HUF reserves against foreign exchange liabilities reduced to 12%.
15 Oct.   NBH base rate reduced from 22% to 21% (key rate for financing government budget deficit, existence loans, start loans).

Foreign exchange and exchange rate policy

23 June   NBH devalued HUF by 1.6% against market basket of currencies.
1 July   Start of operation of interbank foreign exchange market.
9 Nov.   NBH devalued HUF by 1.9% against market basket of currencies.

Open market operations (issuance of new securities)

31 Jan.   Issuance of series 1992/I liquid Treasury bills.
30 April   First 180 day discounted Treasury bill auction.
18 May   180-day Treasury bills trade on Stock Exchange.
29 June   Issue of Series II liquidity Treasury bill at auction.
3 July   First 360-day discounted Treasury bill auction.
22 July   360-day discounted Treasury Bills listed on the Stock Exchange.
6 Oct.   Issue of 3-year government bonds (1995/A).
12 Nov.   Issue of 3-year government bonds (1995/B).
4 Dec.   Issue of 5-year government bonds (1997/A-B).
18 Dec.   Issue of 2-year government bonds (1994/B).
28 Dec.   Issue of 4-year government bonds (1996/A).

Source: NBH (1992), p. 167—169.

Table 3.5   Monetary policy instruments of the National Bank of Poland

1. Credit ceilings	Determined in accordance with performance criteria set with the IMF separately for each state-owned bank (commercial banks are excluded), on the basis of capital and total assets figures.
2. Refinancing credit rate	Reference rate for commercial banks especially in 1990, 1991. Applicable to short-term loans to commercial banks and central investment loans, the latter being phased out. Was 38% end year 1992.
3. Rediscount credit rate	Reference rate for commercial banks, rediscounting gradually replacing refinancing. This is becoming measure of commercial banks' cost of funds. It was 32% at the end of 1992.
4. Lombard credit rate	37%, end year 1992.
5. Reserve requirements*	10% time deposits, 23% demand deposits, 0% savings deposits end year 1992.
6. Capital adequacy ratio*	8%, by the end of 1995 (starting from January 1993 applicable to all chartered banks).
7. Rediscount credit limit	Set separately for each interested bank on a discretionary basis
8. Exchange rate	Pegged to a basket of five currencies (USD 45%, DM 35%, L 10%, FF 5%, ChF 5%), may be revalued 5 days a week at a maximum rate of 12 Zlotys per day. Was 15 767 zl/USD end of year 1992.
9. Subsidized credit rate	20% (refinancing of loans extended to farmers mainly via cooperative banks reporting to the Bank for Food Economy).

Notes: *   Set according to the requirements of the Banking Law of 1989 (amended in 1992).
Source: NBP (1992a)

Table 3.6   Monetary policy calendar for Poland 1989—1993

Date	Policy change

Discount policy

1989	February	NBP refinancing is automatic; refin. rate is 44% p.a.
	August	Refinancing rate is 56% p.a.
	September	Refinancing rate is 72% p.a.
	November	Refinancing rate is 100% p.a.
	December	Refinancing rate is 140% p.a.
		Introduction of rediscount credits at 26%.
1990	January	Refinancing rate is 36% p.m.
	February	Refinancing rate is 20% p.m.
	March	Refinancing rate is 10% p.m.
	April	Refinancing rate is 8% p.m.
	May	Refinancing rate is 5.5% p.m.
	June	Refinancing rate is 4% p.m.
	July	Refinancing rate is 34% p.a.
	August	Refinancing credits converted into long-term credit payable by end of 1995.
	October	Refinancing rate is 43%.
	November	Refinancing rate is 55% (Note: redisc. credit rate is lower than and changed in parallel with refin. rate.)
1991	February	Refinance credit rate is 72% p.a.
	May	Refinance credit rate is 59% p.a.
	July	Refinance credit rate is 50% p.a.
	August	Refinance credit rate is 44% p.a.
	September	Refinance credit rate is 40% p.a.
1992	July	Refinance credit rate is 38% p.a.
1993	March	Refinance credit rate is 35% p.a.

Foreign exchange and exchange rate policy

1989		Preliminary devaluations, official NBP rate approaches free market rate.
1990	1 January	Devaluation of Zloty to 9500 zl/USD, unification of the foreign currency market, introduction of partial current account convertibility, reaction of interbank deposit market.
1991	May	Zloty devalued by 15%, exchange rate pegged to basket of 5 currencies.
1992	February	Zloty devalued by 12% versus market basket, crawling peg introduced; Zloty devalued maximum of 9 Zlotys per day (5 days per week).
1993		Crawling devaluation, 11 Zlotys per day, then 12 Zlotys then 15 Zlotys per day maximum. Interbank foreign exchange market with spot and forward transactions.

Table 3.6   Monetary policy calendar for Poland 1989—1993
(continued)

Date	Policy change

Reserve requirements

1989	March	Introduction of reserve requirements: 15% on sight deposits and current accounts, 10% on savings deposits, 5% on term deposits.
1990	March	Reserve requirements set at 9% on all three types of accounts.
	April	15% on all three types of accounts.
	July	Change in calculation of obligatory reserves; up to 50% of vault cash may be included.
	August	Reserve requirements differentiated and changed to 27% on sight deposits and current accounts, 17% on savings deposits, 7% on term deposits.
	October	30% on sight deposits and current accounts, 20% on saving deposits, 8% on term deposits.
	December	30% on sight deposits and current accounts, 30% on saving deposits, 10% on term deposits.
1991	September	30% on sight deposits and current accounts, 25% on saving deposits, 10% on term deposits.
1992	April	25% on sight deposits and current accounts, 25% on savings deposits, 10% on term deposits. Interest payments on excess reserves over 10% of required reserves.

Other policies

1989		Replacement of the credit plan with credit ceilings in general and for individual banks.
1990	July	Auction sales of NBP bills. Introduction of Lombard credits.
1991	May	Introduction of auction credits (and repurchase agreements).
		Introduction of auctions of Treasury Bills.
1992	April	Introduction of interbank market for CDs and commercial paper.
1993	March	Open market operations to stabilize interest rates.

Source: Marta Golajewska and Pawel Wyczański, National Bank of Poland

Table 3.7   Outstanding debts of the banking sector by risk in Hungary

Rating	31 December 1992		31 March 1993	
	HUF bn	%	HUF bn	%
Standard	1451.0	89.0	1491.3	88.5
Sub-average	39.2	2.4	38.4	2.3
Doubtful	61.6	3.8	67.5	4.0
Bad	79.0	4.8	88.4	5.2
Total Debt (included in rating)	1630.8	100.0	1685.6	100.0

Source: NBH (1993), p. 11.

Discussion of Part One

Douglas Kruse

In my remarks, I want to focus on two major points common to both chapters: first, the need for 'the continued enhancement of commercial bank management skills', as Kemme puts it, and second, the bad loans problem facing banks throughout the region. To quote Kemme, 'The most important issue with respect to the transition of industry ... is how to resolve the issue of non-performing loans to state-owned enterprises'. These two subjects are closely linked: the bad loans problem is among the major challenges confronting bank management, and developing the skills within banks (and their regulators) to manage bad loans is one of the most important facets of the bad loans problem.

First, however, a couple of technical comments. Montias suggests that US banking law, in particular the Glass-Steagall Act, restricts the ability of commercial banks to take equity in exchange for debt in the context of restructuring a non-performing loan. While US banking laws and regulations generally prohibit banks from owning equity in non-financial enterprises, there is a specific exemption that permits banks to hold such equity if they receive it in full or partial settlement of previously made loans, the so-called debt previously contracted (DPC) exception. Also, it is less than certain that the departments responsible for working out trouble credits ('DTKs') will 'become the nuclei of the investment departments of commercial banks'. The experience of Western banks suggests that the skills required in these two areas are different and not readily transferable.

In his remarks on the instruments available to central banks for implementing monetary policy, Kemme calls for 'a new set of market-oriented instruments' and appears to prefer these to more traditional methods, such as 'direct quotas and ceilings on bank credits', as a 'means of providing liquidity to the economy'. This section would be strengthened by putting it in the broader context of monetary policy development in Western economies. Direct controls on credit creation, through credit ceilings, rediscount quotas, and other instruments, were major tools of monetary policy in Western Europe in the postwar period and remained in use throughout the 1970s and in some cases considerably later. Also, it is not certain that 'we will see an increase in investment banking relative to commercial banking' in Eastern Europe during the 'remainder of this century'. There is already considerable investment banking activity throughout the region. Stock exchanges have been established, and privatization programmes have generated much investment banking business. It remains to be seen, however, whether there is sufficient indigenous savings and capital to support a growing investment banking sector. The experience of Western Europe may be instructive in this regard. An equally plausible scenario for Eastern Europe is one where banks, as lenders and possibly investors, are the principal suppliers of corporate financing.

Let me turn now to the topic I would like to discuss, developing the skills to manage the bad loan problem. Both chapters make a useful contribution by focusing on the issue of system change, looking beyond such superficial changes as the creation of instruments and institutions to study the 'customary ways of doing things, the formal and informal rules and procedures that may be said to constitute an economy's system'. This provides an illuminating perspective through which to examine how banks in Eastern Europe are managing their non-performing assets. While many have established work-out departments, often at the suggestion of the World Bank or another external agency, most bankers from East and West question whether these departments do in fact function as work-out departments, actively managing the bank's non-performing assets so as to realize the maximum value. Similarly, several countries have adopted loan consolidation programmes and established specialized agencies to take over the management of bad loans. Once again, there is the question of whether this is only a change of form, in which responsibility is shifted from one institution to another, or a more fundamental shift in the way bad loans are handled.

Managing individual problem loans

In discussing the bad loans problem, it is useful to recognize that it is not one but three interrelated problems. Distinguishing between these intertwined but conceptually distinct problems, each at a different level of the banking system, is helpful in highlighting the different tools and types of solutions appropriate for each. The first, most basic of the three problems is how to manage the problem loans of a bank. The focus here is at the level of individual loans in a bank's portfolio. Detailed analysis is required on a loan-by-loan basis to determine the cause of the borrower's inability to service its debt. If the problem is financial in nature, such as excessive leverage, then it is amenable to the classic work-out techniques, such as debt restructuring. If not — if the company's difficulties are operational — it must be recognized that the problem cannot be solved by financial means and therefore that it is beyond the ability of the banking system to fix it. Using such financial expedients as capitalizing interest, extending maturities, or granting additional credit may keep the firm afloat temporarily, but can only mask, not cure, the underlying weaknesses. This is not to say that the only alternative is to liquidate the firm. On the contrary, a host of tools can potentially be used to salvage some or all of it, such as restructuring, closing divisions, selling the salvageable units as independent entities, or cutting wages and reducing the labour force. But these are operating rather than financial issues, and bankers generally play only a secondary role.

Let me briefly raise a few of the issues confronting Eastern European banks and regulators in addressing the bad loans problem at the level of individual credits. First, the number of problem loans at a given bank can be large. Analysing them properly, let alone devising and implementing appropriate strategies, may overtax the bank's capacity in terms of human resources. Training qualified staff is a major challenge, especially as work-outs is an area where they lack prior experience. This applies equally to such vital internal tasks as evaluating the loan portfolio and creating appropriate reserves and to working externally with the borrower and other creditors to restructure a loan. Availability and reliability of information make these tasks even more difficult.

Second, what policies should banks and regulators adopt towards debt/equity swaps? As I have suggested earlier, this is different from the broader question of the role banks should play in underwriting and brokering securities, the familiar debate over a universal banking system vs. separation between banking and securities. In the context of bad loans, what matters is the conditions under which banks can hold equity acquired in exchange for debt. Because the approach that is chosen has repercussions on the safety and soundness of banks as well as on the locus and concentration of economic power, deciding on limitations on amounts of equity, the periods it may be held, and/or capital requirements imposed on what is a relatively illiquid asset of questionable credit quality, is a complex and delicate task.

Third, should problem loans be handled by the bank(s) that made the loan or by some other entity? Let me stress that this is not a question of who should bear the financial burden of credit losses, but of where the job can best be done. The case for transferring responsibility for managing non-performing assets outside the banking system rests, therefore, on demonstrating that the requisite expertise is located primarily outside banks, for example in investment management companies. It is far from certain that this is so in Eastern Europe; or indeed even in Western Europe or the United States, where the asset management industry is relatively more developed. On the contrary, most problem loans are managed by work-out units within banks, where the requisite expertise is generally found, in developed as well as transition economies. In addition, experience suggests that managing bad loans inside a bank is cost-efficient, takes advantage of the bank's existing knowledge of the borrower, internalizes the experience with problem loans and thereby strengthens the credit function, and builds expertise in identifying and resolving credit problems, which are an unavoidable part of the banking business. In the context of Eastern Europe, these arguments apply with particular force. Financial and human resources are scarce. Banks and bankers need to refine their understanding of, and their willingness to accept, risk as well as their ability to make trade-offs between risk and reward. And they need to develop skills in monitoring and evaluating the quality of the credit portfolio.

Let me digress very briefly to mention two other interesting issues. First, in the particular circumstances of Eastern Europe, would it be more efficient to assign responsibility for managing problem loans where more than one bank is involved to only one bank, perhaps the one with the largest exposure? Although this could raise nettlesome allocation questions, it might help to reduce the demands on the staff of individual banks. Second, to what extent should banks be involved in restructuring debtors whose problems are operational rather than financial? As this question is broadly analogous to the one we have just been discussing, I would suggest that the same analytical approach is appropriate, with the decisive factor being where the necessary expertise is located. It bears reiterating that the requisite skills are not those of a credit-trained commercial banker. If banks are the institutions best suited to this task, it is because of the skills found or believed to be found in their work-out departments, units already stretched with their existing workload. If one is to assign them additional duties, one must address the risks of overloading the system. At a minimum, banks will need additional skilled staff, already a scarce resource, and training on a substantial scale if they are to have a reasonable chance of shouldering this burden successfully.

Managing banks with bad loan problems

The second bad loan problem is managing 'troubled' banks, i.e. banks whose level of problem loans is so high that the bank itself has insufficient capital, after reserving for loan losses, to support its business. This is the aggregate at the bank level of the problems at the loan level we have just discussed. One part of the problem is managing an institution, a large part of whose resources and attention are devoted to work-outs. This entails managing the handling of troubled credits, but equally important it requires developing and implementing a strategy to return the bank to profitability. Let me also mention the 'good bank' 'bad bank' approach often raised in this context. To the extent that it illuminates the need to promote the development of the efficient parts of a bank as well as the treatment of its inefficient parts, this may be a useful concept. I would caution, however, that creating a separate legal entity to manage some or all of the problem credits is merely a legal technique employed in situations where a new corporate entity was necessary, usually because of the way in which a particular country's regulatory authorities operate. It is not clear that such a legal framework confers any practical advantages in managing the bank or its non-performing assets, or that it is appropriate in Eastern Europe.

Let me raise a provocative question. How urgently does this problem need to be addressed? In other words, should infusing additional capital into banks, through recapitalization or other schemes, be a priority? It may be necessary for privatization, but does it have to be done now? And is it necessary to 'recapitalize' all the state-owned banks when at most two or three will be privatized in the next 12 months? Is recapitalization essential to keep a bank from closing down? Experience suggests that it may not be in the case of state-owned banks. Is recapitalization a necessary, let alone sufficient, condition for a bank to improve its performance; for a (state-owned) bank to manage its problem loans; or to break the link between public money and bank losses?[1] The answers to these questions are of vital importance not only to the banking system but to the economy as well. For the banking system, misdiagnosing the ailment may lead to focusing on the wrong problems. For the economy, it may take scarce resources away from areas where they are badly needed. Assessing the interrelationships between bank capitalization and the functioning of the banking system and establishing the appropriate priorities is thus one of the major challenges facing bankers and finance officials in Eastern Europe.

If we turn to the question of how to address the 'troubled bank' problem, an instructive approach is to look at the bank as a company in financial difficulty and to use the same methods that banks apply to 'troubled' borrowers. If the bank's difficulties are financial in nature, the result perhaps of an unbalanced capital structure or inherited bad loans, and the bank is otherwise a viable economic entity, then financial measures may resolve the problem. Such techniques fall broadly into two categories, which are not mutually exclusive: the bank can 'earn' its way out of the problem by generating and retaining sufficient income, or it can raise capital from outside sources through a recapitalization by the owner(s), through the sale of equity to third parties, or through the sale of assets (such as bad loans) at above-market prices.[2] Many such approaches have been tried in Eastern Europe, with varying success. In the interests of time, let me offer just one comment. The experience in Western countries with guarantee schemes and creative accounting, such as net worth certificates in the United States, has not been positive.

It may be worth stating explicitly that if a bank's problems are operational rather than financial, such as a bad loan problem caused by loans the bank has made rather than inherited, financial measures will not be successful. This does not mean that the bank should or will fail. The techniques discussed earlier in the context of borrowers with operational problems, for instance, may be appropriate. Judging by Western experience, it is likely that some or all of a troubled bank will be bought by or merged with another institution. But an important part of this reforming process is the bank's releasing resources it had used. At the macroeconomic level, this allows resources to be used more productively and thereby potentially increases output, and at the micro-economic level, it strengthens the incentives linking the bank's interests with those of its owners (if it is privately owned), managers, and executives. In this latter respect, it may help reduce the moral hazard problem to which both authors refer, and it may promote system change by potentially disrupting Montias's 'lines of hierarchic subordination'.

Situations in which this problem is widespread, creating a so-called 'systemic' problem, may be seen as special cases of the troubled bank problem. The issue occurs on a broader scale, and it may suggest a role for the government as well as the owners, if these are different. But the same analytical approach and techniques can be applied. Extensive experience in a large number of Western countries has shown that to resolve a crisis in the banking sector one has to address the problems at the level of individual banks, where injecting capital and/or changing the way the bank operates is usually required.

The bad loan problem of the enterprise sector

The third and final bad loan problem is the challenge of designing the economic structure of the enterprise sector. Here, the bad loan problem facing Eastern Europe assumes a dimension not generally found in Western experience. This is due to the scale of the problem, the lack of institutionalized procedures for dealing with restructuring and bankruptcy, the scarcity of experienced managers, and dislocations occasioned by the transition from a planned to a market economy. There are two main sets of critical questions. First, what is the bank's role in the restructuring process: is it only a creditor or an instrument of its owner (especially the state) or the government with a broader responsibility for promoting the necessary changes? We have discussed earlier the implications for the bank of taking on a broader role; here the focus is on the consequences for the corporate sector. Second, what should the banks' role be in owning non-financial business? If they are allowed to acquire equity through debt/equity swaps, should that equity be 'upstreamed' to the bank's owner (especially if the state), perhaps as part of a capital infusion? If the bank itself holds equity, should it be limited to a maximum share of each firm? These questions go to the heart of the structure of industrial ownership, and it is important to recognize that while the answers have great impact on the banking system, they transcend it and need to be addressed in a broader context.

While this is of necessity a rapid overview, it indicates the magnitude of the challenge facing banks and governments, bankers and financial officials, in managing the bad loans problem in Eastern Europe. Their task is intensified because the need to acquire experience must be balanced against the costs of deferring decisions; investing in training to build essential expertise must be balanced against the scarcity of and demand for skilled human resources; and the banking system's need for additional capital must be balanced against the claims of other parts of the economy. Successfully meeting this challenge will require rigorous discipline in allocating and managing resources and single-mindedness in concentrating on the truly essential tasks.

Notes

1. Lack of capital may constrain privately-owned banks in managing their bad loans because, for instance, they cannot afford a write-off. Does this apply equally to state-owned banks in Eastern Europe?
2. Restructuring the bank's liabilities is a theoretical alternative, but in practice it is rarely viewed as an option because the liabilities are predominantly deposits. Writing down deposits, converting them into equity, or similar measures are generally ruled out because they would damage confidence in a bank. It is interesting to note, however, that if the bank is allowed to fail, depositors may share its losses, depending on the regulatory and deposit insurance system.

PART TWO

The Banking System:
The Foundation for Emerging Financial Markets

4 Central Bank Independence in the Transitional Economies: a Preliminary Investigation of Hungary, Poland, the Czech and Slovak Republics

Pierre L. Siklos

1 Introduction[1]

The notion that central banking authorities should have independent control over monetary policy gained credence during the 1980s, following the severe stagflation faced by industrialized countries during the 1970s and early 1980s. Many came to believe that the primary task of the central bank was to ensure some kind of price stability.[2]

The collapse of central planning toward the end of the 1980s in Central Europe, in particular in Czechoslovakia, Hungary and Poland, meant first the end of the monobank concept of the banking system and the introduction of a two-tier banking system with a central bank and an independent commercial banking sector. Kemme (1992), Calvo and Kumar (1993), and Borensztein and Masson (1993) review the reforms undertaken in this sphere in the so-called transitional economies.

Arguably, the evolution of any transition will be dependent on the model for the central bank chosen by the former centrally-planned economies (hereafter CPEs). Hence, this paper provides an assessment of the legal and economic independence of the newly-reformed central banks as well as some tentative estimates of central bank reaction functions to economic and political fundamentals.

The chapter is organized as follows. The next section provides a brief overview of existing concepts of central bank independence. I then construct estimates of an index of central bank independence for the Czech and Slovak Republics as well as for Hungary and Poland, based on the new legislation governing their central banks. I also compare these indexes with the current inflation performance in the same countries as well as in relation to existing indexes based on the legislation under the central planning regime. A separate section presents econometric estimates of selected central bank reaction functions for the same three countries. A concluding section summarizes and suggests the lessons learned so far.

2   The meaning of central bank independence

While relatively few central banks are mandated to achieve price stability alone, the notion that independent action by central banks in the area of monetary policy can be evaluated via inflation performance has received considerable attention lately. Beginning with the work of Parkin and Bade (1978), with more recent contributions by, among others, Burdekin and Willett (1991), Grilli *et al.* (1991), Cukierman (1992), Alesina and Summers (1993), Banaian *et al.* (1993), qualitative comparisons of central bank legislation and inflation performance suggest that more independent central banks deliver less inflation.[3] Except for Cukierman (1992) pp. 427—430, however, these studies tend to assume rather than demonstrate empirically the idea that more central bank independence *causes* lower inflation. Yet, the causal relationship between central bank independence and inflation can easily be reversed. Germany is the archetypal case in this regard because its inflation record has long been associated with a historical aversion to inflation which has, in turn, reinforced central bank independence rather than having been caused by it.[4]

As another illustration of this point consider Figures 4.1 and 4.2. Figure 4.1 shows the annual rate of inflation in the G-7 countries. The first vertical bar represents the approximate date of the collapse of Bretton Woods in the early 1970s. The second vertical bar marks the beginning of the European Monetary System (EMS) in 1979. Figure 4.2, by contrast, plots the annual rate of inflation for progressively smaller samples, also for the G-7 countries. The first observation gives the average rate of inflation for the period 1960—1990 based on quarterly data. Every observation thereafter gives the average rate of inflation for samples which omit one year at a time from the beginning of the sample. Thus, the second observation is for the sample 1961—1990, and so on, until the last observation represents the average inflation rate in 1990 only. Notice that average inflation rates diverge considerably even under the Bretton Woods system but divergence is even more apparent following the collapse of the adjustable peg exchange rate system. Convergence in inflation is more apparent during the last few observations which essentially represent the decade of the 1980s.[5]

Yet, even by the most detailed accounts of central bank independence based on an analysis of the legal provisions governing their behaviour (Cukierman, 1992, Chapter 19, Appendix A) only Canada and Italy (see Rymes, 1993, for Canada and Cottarelli, 1993, for Italy) experienced any major changes in central bank legislation since the 1960s among the G-7 countries. Less fundamental changes took place in France and the UK. Notice, for example, that the UK inflation rate is consistently higher than France's and that the gap between their inflation rates widened during the 1980s despite the fact that neither central bank is formally independent of the government. Similarly, Italy's inflation rate has been substantially higher than Canada's even though, at least until 1987 in the case of Italy, both central banks have been considered formally dependent.[6] The European exchange rate target zone mechanism may have played a relatively more dominant role in explaining the relative inflation performance of these two countries than central bank behaviour alone. Japan, too, offers a lesson in contrasts between inflation performance and central bank legislation. While the Bank of Japan is not considered to be formally independent of the government and the legislation governing its behaviour has hardly changed over the last 30 years, inflation in Japan has varied considerably since 1960. A low inflation country until the early 1970s, Japan posted the highest inflation rate among the G-7 in the aftermath of the two OPEC oil price shocks. But by the mid-1980s Japan's inflation rate was one of the lowest among the G-7. Thus, Japan has proved to be difficult to classify for some authors who associate the degree of legal independence with inflation performance.[7] Instead, what Figure 4.1 suggests is that one important determinant of central bank independence is the exchange rate regime, about which more is said below.

The most ambitious attempt at providing a numerical measure of legal or statutory independence is in Cukierman (1992, Chapter 19). He constructs an index of central bank independence for 68 countries by deriving numerical values for more than 17 different characteristics of central banking legislation such as term of office, conflict resolution, legislated goals of the central bank, to name but a few of the aspects of the legislation considered. This approach is useful because it allows for a comparison between legislated goals and actual economic performance. At the same time, however, focusing too narrowly on the legislation can lead to a confusion between what a central bank actually does as opposed to what it is legislated to do (see also Mayer, 1976, and Cargill, 1989, in this connection). Famous examples come from the Japanese and US experiences noted previously. In the US case, the Federal Reserve is guaranteed independence but has often been seen as acting to improve re-election prospects of the President (Woolley, 1988).[8]

A separate strand of the literature estimates, via econometric techniques, central bank reaction functions. This approach seeks to determine how instruments of monetary policy (I) react to aggregate economic information (Z; presumably available with a lag) as well as political factors (P). The equation

$$I_t = B(L)Z_{t-1} + C(L)P_t \qquad (1)$$

where B(L) and C(L) are distributed lags, describes the formulation of a typical reaction function. Political factors are ordinarily represented by dummy variables. These are active around election dates or when there are changes in the ideological make-up of government. Johnson and Siklos (1993) provide a brief survey of the literature on central bank reaction functions, while Alesina (1988), Nordhaus (1989), and Cukierman (1992, Chapter 17) review the literature on political and partisan effects on aggregate economic activity. The exact specification of the dummy variables is a function of how economic agents form expectations. However, as these types of political influences are not yet feasibly measured for the transitional economies I shall instead examine the estimates of reaction functions in light of the role played by economic fundamentals and by introducing a measure of the influence of political events on central bank behaviour.

3   Legal and economic independence in three former CPEs

3.1   Credible central bank reforms?

Several authors (e.g., Jindra, 1992; Boguszewski *et al.*, 1992; Rudka, 1992; Balassa, 1992) have emphasized the fact that the new central bank laws in the former CPEs of Hungary, Poland, and the former Czechoslovakia were modelled after the statutes of the Bundesbank. Presumably, the belief is that the transitional economies can, at least eventually, inherit the enviable inflation record of Germany. Yet, there exists a myth about the Bundesbank's whole legal autonomy which is, in fact, quite limited. In the first place, there is no legal prescription to maintain price stability unlike the legislation in Austria, the Netherlands or New Zealand. Indeed, the legislation governing the Bundesbank stipulates that it is ultimately required to support the economic policy of the federal government (Article 12, see Aufricht, 1967, p. 255).[9] Nor is the Bundesbank absolutely mandated to act independently of the government.[10] Thus, unless the former CPEs can import the German 'cultural' aversion to inflation, the design of the existing legislation is flawed. Even if one does not believe that Germans are predisposed to desire low inflation the Bundesbank is a creature of the federal system in which representatives of each Land or regional state generate *de facto* independence for the central bank (Lohmann, 1993).[11] Since neither Hungary, Poland, the Czech or Slovak Republics are federal states in the German sense it becomes more likely that the design of central bank laws in the former CPEs may have relied too heavily on an inappropriate model. Indeed, one could argue that the legislation in the transitional economies should be much clearer about the responsibilities of the central bank than in industrialized countries in view of the concerns expressed by international organizations, such as the

IMF, about inflation following the adoption of market economics over the central planning model. An exception to this interpretation may be the Czech Republic which has adopted a price stability objective, but whether this goal is a credible one is open to question, as we shall see, not least because none of the financial systems in the transitional economies is mature.

3.2 Measurement

Independence is defined in terms of a central bank's ability to use instruments of monetary policy to accomplish primarily an inflation objective. Clearly, central banks may also be concerned with the possible existence of a short-run trade-off between inflation and output or unemployment. This would lead to a broader definition of legal independence. By examining the legislation governing central banks we can provide a sense of notional independence conferred on a central bank by legislators, that is, the degree of independence legislators intended to give the central bank. One difficulty with this approach is that central banking legislation changes very infrequently. Thus, it is possible that subsequent governments or legislators may interpret the meaning of the legislation differently over time even if the central bank laws remain unchanged. Once again this raises the point made earlier about the subtlety of the notion of central bank independence. For example, when the US Congress mandated, under the Humphrey-Hawkins Act of 1978, that the Fed produce target growth rates for monetary aggregates this was viewed as an attempt to influence the Fed's independence even though the Federal Reserve Act was not modified. A second example is the so-called Coyne-Rasminsky directive which occurred in Canada in the early 1960s when a disagreement over monetary policy led to the resignation of the Governor of the Bank of Canada, James Coyne. Louis Rasminsky, Coyne's successor, issued a directive to the effect that, in the event of a disagreement between the Governor and the Government about monetary policy, the Minister of Finance would be required to issue a directive indicating what policy the Bank should follow. If the Governor disagreed with the directive, resignation would follow. Although a version of the directive was later enshrined in the Bank of Canada Act it has since been seen as an instrument of more, not less, independence, which was the original intention (Rymes, 1993).

Table 4.1 largely follows the indexing system created by Cukierman. The Table codifies key elements in the central banking legislation in the four countries considered in this study. The index values range from zero to one, with zero meaning least independence and one signifying maximum central bank independence. However, as there are special considerations for the transitional economies, a number of new variables are introduced into the construction of an index of legal and economic central bank independence. Table 4.2 gives the index values assigned as well as a brief definition describing how the values were assigned.

The characteristics of central banking legislation should be broadly interpreted as follows. The longer the term of office of the head of the central bank, the less likely it is that it will overlap with the electoral cycle, thus reducing the possibility that a government can always appoint the central banker of its choosing. This is interpreted as enhancing central bank independence. Similar observations apply to the other categories under the group heading termed *CEO*. The next set of variables, under the heading *Policy Formulation*, measures the responsibility for monetary policy actions. Thus, for example, if the legislation assigns complete control over monetary policy to the central bank, this is taken as a sign that politicians intended to confer independence on the central bank. An important consideration in this respect is whether clear provisions exist for conflict resolution. As noted earlier, the absence of such provisions proved to be critical in Canada's case. Thus, statutes which clearly outline how conflicts between the government and the CEO of the central bank are resolved are assumed to enhance independence.

A third variable, called *CB Objectives*, determines whether the central bank is supposed to satisfy a single and clear objective or a multiplicity of possibly incompatible objectives. For example, specification of the single objective of price stability is an indication that the central bank be permitted to pursue such a goal. By contrast, if the legislation specifies several vague objectives these can be opened to government influence thereby eroding central bank independence.

A fourth variable, under the heading *Limitations on Lending* represents a group of variables which evaluate the extent to which the government can freely borrow from the central bank. Clearly, the fewer the limitations on lending to governments, the less room exists for independent central bank action.[12]

As useful as these indicators of central bank independence are, they fail to capture some potential constraints on central bank behaviour which are peculiar, but not exclusive, to economies in the transition to market. One such characteristic is the choice of exchange rate regimes. Table 4.1 suggests that central bank independence is at a minimum under a rigidly fixed exchange rate regime.[13] The reason, of course, is that a rigidly fixed exchange rate implies that inflation would, in equilibrium, be the same as in, say, Germany, the largest trading partner of the three countries studied here. While this is a desirable condition, it nevertheless eliminates any scope for independent monetary policy and, consequently, for the establishment of a credible record on inflation based on central bank action.

The greatest scope for central bank action would occur under a pure float which would then permit the monetary authorities to independently influence domestic inflation. The acquisition of credibility by central banks can be important since it is certainly the case, based on the historical record, that governments do change the exchange rate regime over time. Thus, a peg of any kind does not permit the central bank to develop or to demonstrate the credibility of its actions. While the choice of the exchange rate regime would be important in assessing the degree of independence enjoyed by any central bank, this is especially important for the transitional economies since, rather unusually,[14] the central bank laws in *all* the countries considered here have explicit provisions dealing with the fixing of exchange rates. For example, in the case of Hungary, Section 13 of the Act on the National Bank of Hungary 1991 states:

(1)   NBH (National Bank of Hungary) quotes and publishes the exchange rates serving to convert foreign currencies into Forint and the Forint into foreign currencies.
(2)   The order of fixing and/or influencing the exchange rates is determined by the Government in agreement with NBH.[15]

Another characteristic of the Central European economies in transition is the role played by enterprise arrears credit and bad loans, a legacy of the financial structure under central planning and an outcome of the drive to introduce market mechanisms.[16] However, the degree to which the newly-reorganized central banks in these countries are affected by this legacy depends in part on the reforms undertaken in the banking sector. If, for example, banks are required to meet Bank for International Settlements (BIS) standards (see Siklos, 1993, Chapter 10, for the details), this is likely to mean considerable risk of insolvency for the banking system as a whole if the central bank is required to bail out failing institutions either directly or indirectly via the government's budget. Thus, at the outset of the transition, banks which inherit loans with a low probability of repayment, as in Hungary, or who shun commercial lending, thereby exacerbating the financial difficulties experienced especially by the large enterprises, raise the likelihood that liquidity shortages will have to be underwritten by the central bank. This condition is exacerbated by the low capitalization of such banks. It is these conditions rather than the BIS standards themselves which can create difficulties for the banks and, by implication, affect the central banks. This problem is also likely to be aggravated by the ability of banks to borrow regularly from the central bank under unspecified extraordinary conditions since this is interpreted as a looser requirement than the expectation that the central bank act as a lender of last resort. Again, provisions for such loans exist in the legislation in some of the countries examined in this paper and they clearly impinge on central bank independence.[17] However, the impact of such provisions may be somewhat mitigated by the formation of consolidation banks[18] which manage existing bank loans separately or foreign loan forgiveness which can increase the ability of the central bank to operate autonomously.

An additional determinant of central bank independence is the maturity of the financial system, that is, the degree to which the financial system is developed. Four characteristics of the maturity of the financial system are considered: whether there are limitations on the operations of foreign banks concerned, that is, whether they can operate legally on an equal footing with domestic banks; whether the financial system is viewed as being competitive; whether an active stock market exists which can generate a significant amount of liquidity; and the variety of financial instruments that the public can hold. More mature financial systems (i.e., ones where the public's share of wealth in financial assets is large) imply that the public has a greater stake in price stability which enhances the role of the central bank in meeting such an objective and thereby improves the likelihood of its independence. Put differently, as the fraction of wealth in financial assets rises, the public is likely to become more sensitive to the importance of policies which have an impact on the real interest rate. A central bank which is independent is more likely to attempt to maintain a real interest rate than one which would prevent nominal interest rates from rising when inflationary expectations rise.

A particular concern in several of the former CPEs is the high level of foreign debts accumulated under the previous economic regime. A high proportion of foreign debt to GDP increases the costs of the transition. If these costs are perceived to be too high, political pressure on the central bank to inflate its way out of the constraints imposed by such debts may grow over time, thereby reducing its independence. Alternatively, because high foreign debt, in effect, represents a type of externally imposed constraint, this is interpreted as having a negative influence on central bank independence.[19]

An additional risk facing the former CPEs stems from the absence of deposit insurance. Although Hungary has proposed and implemented a modest plan for deposit insurance in 1993, the shaky nature of the financial sector in the countries examined here potentially creates another source of risk — that central banks will be called upon to bail out the commercial banking sector (also see Calvo and Kumar, 1993, and Borensztein and Masson, 1993, in this connection). This potentially affects the autonomy of the central bank and it represents a characteristic that could be incorporated into an index of central bank independence.[20]

While the newly-reformed central banks discussed here have instituted appointment procedures to avoid the overlap of the term of heads of central banks with those of their political masters, the same is not necessarily true of the Board or Council of these central banks where actual monetary policy decisions are made. As a result, if the Board or Council of the central bank is largely government appointed for terms shorter than the electoral cycle, this reduces the ability of the central bank to act independently.

A final ingredient in the independence equation concerns a problem peculiar to the former CPEs, namely the monetary overhang question. This refers to the large quantities of notes in circulation, as a share of GDP, apparently created by the double coincidence of shortage of desirable goods and services available to consumers as well as the failure of the banking system to provide sufficiently attractive or varied savings vehicles yielding realistic returns. Although there is disagreement about both the size and importance of the monetary overhang, its existence threatens inflation and, therefore, central bank independence in the transition to market. Unless confiscatory measures are put into place, there is little a central bank can do to stop the consequences of the release of the overhang.[21] Of course, the monetary overhang question is allied with the concept of the financial system's maturity since the prospective overhang could, in principle, be channelled into newly-created financial instruments instead of being reflected in an increase in aggregate expenditures.

Table 4.2 gives the values assigned to each variable listed in Table 4.1 as well as providing a variety of aggregate index measures of central bank independence. The first aggregate index considers only those variables which also appear in Cukierman's index. The next line gives the aggregate index value as computed by Cukierman (1992, Table 19.3) for Hungary and Poland (Cukierman did not construct an index for Czechoslovakia). Other indexes were constructed for the newly-introduced variables, as well as indexes for the transitional variables alone and all of the variables listed in Table 4.1. To construct the indexes the mean of the codes assigned within each of the five categories was constructed. Next, each of these mean values was again averaged to produce a mean of means which represents the value of the indexes reported in Table 4.2. It was thought preferable to use an unweighted scheme but to present several index calculations since it is unclear, *a priori*, how one would assign appropriate weights.

On the basis of all the indexes shown, it appears that the Czech National Bank is the most statutorily independent while the Slovak National Bank is the least independent. The National Bank of Poland, by almost any measure, now rates as slightly more independent than the National Bank of Hungary, although this result is sensitive to the variables included in the index. Both the National Bank of Hungary and National Bank of Poland appear to be more independent than under central planning. The rise in the index relative to Cukierman's previous estimate is large in both cases, especially in Poland's case, suggesting considerably more legal independence than under central planning.[22] The results are fairly insensitive to the selection of variables included in the index calculations. If we rely on the variables said to be most closely associated with inflation performance, namely the *Policy only* variable, then the central banks of Hungary and Poland are equally independent. Otherwise, the rankings are the same as the more highly aggregated indexes. Indexes which exclude the monetary overhang (*overh*) and the choice of exchange rate regime (*forex*) also do not change the conclusions much, except that the National Bank of Poland appears to be more legally independent than the National Bank of Hungary when *overh* is excluded but is seen as slightly less independent when both *overh* and *forex* are excluded from calculations. Nevertheless, the differences between the two indexes are not very large. Only when *overh* and *forex* are excluded is the Slovak National Bank shown to be more independent than either the National Banks of Hungary or Poland when the transitional variables alone are considered.

It is also interesting to note that the central banks of Hungary, Poland, and the Czech Republic all have index values for the broadest index measure above the median of the index values for the 68 countries previously tabulated by Cukierman (1992, Table 19.3). This was not the case for either Hungary or Poland prior to the transition to market. Indeed, the Czech National Bank would now rank as statutorily independent as the US Federal Reserve if Cukierman's index alone is considered while Poland's central bank would rank as more independent than the Bank of Canada, according to the same index. Finally, Table 4.2 suggests that the index of central bank independence is inversely related to inflation,[23] as predicted by theory, but *only* when the new variables introduced in this study are alone considered. Otherwise, the correspondence between inflation and central bank independence is weak.[24]

4   Estimation of central bank reaction functions

Given the availability of data it may be rather precarious to consider econometric estimates of central bank reaction functions, in part because one could argue that it may take some time before the newly-reformed central banks can reduce or stabilize inflation. Nevertheless, because legal measures of independence are fraught with difficulties, as explained above, it would seem useful to consider how inflation and economic growth are assumed to be, at least partially, the consequence of central bank actions as well as how central bank behaviour may have been influenced by political and policy variables since the reform process was introduced in 1987 in Hungary, in 1990 in Poland and 1991 in Czechoslovakia.[25] To accomplish this objective I consider two sets of econometric tests.

4.1 Panel data set

In one exercise I consider Czechoslovakia, Hungary, and Poland together, for a sample of monthly data which, except for Czechoslovakia, begins in 1987 and ends in 1992 (details are provided in the notes to the Tables). Because there are too few elections in the available sample considered to test either electoral or partisan influences on selected macroeconomic aggregates, a political events measure with potential consequences for central bank behaviour is considered.[26] Following the literature on political business cycles the political events variable is a dummy variable active whenever an economic or political event is believed to be likely to influence central bank behaviour or performance. Based on the chronology of events in Siklos and Ábel (1993), Table 4.1,[27] two political events dummies were constructed. Economic events which directly influence the countries considered, such as, for example, the suspension of IMF credit, results in an active dummy(=1) for the month in which the event takes place. Political events, such as an election or a change in government, earn a greater weight (dummy is active in the month of the event with a value of 2).

Alternatively, it could be argued that the series of economic and political shocks affecting these countries produce cumulative type pressure on the respective central banks. If this is the case then the value of the political events dummy is a function of whether economic and political events occur in consecutive months or not. For example, if an economic event occurs in February 1990, and then again in April of the same year, the dummy is active in February and April only. If, however, economic and political shocks occur in February through April the value of the political stability dummy is cumulated until such shocks disappear and the political stability dummy eventually becomes inactive the month following the latest economic shock.

Following, for example, Alesina and Roubini (1992), I then ran the following panel regressions of time series cross-section data on inflation and output growth. The general form of the single equation specification is:

$$x_t = \alpha_0 + \alpha_1 x_{t-1} + \ldots + \alpha_n x_{t-n} + \alpha_{n+1} x_{t-1}^f + \ldots + \alpha_{n+k} x_{t-k}^f + \alpha_{n+k+1} POLEV_t + e_t \quad (2)$$

where x represents either pooled inflation (INF or π) or output growth proxied here by industrial production (PROD or y) for the three countries considered and x^f represents foreign inflation or output growth. Standard specification searching is used to select the 'best' lag length in (2) subject to data limitations. POLEV represents the dummy variable for political events defined two different ways, as explained previously. Because the economies considered are all small and open, foreign shocks are controlled for by the addition of the German inflation rate or the growth in US industrial production which serves as a proxy for world output conditions, as determined by the relevant dependent variable.[28] Tables 4.3 and 4.4 present the regression results based on specification (2). Inflation is proxied by the annualized monthly per cent change in the Consumer Price Index and output growth is proxied by the annualized monthly per cent change in the index of industrial production. Both series were obtained from the International Monetary Fund's *International Financial Statistics* CD-ROM with some observations from country sources (see Siklos and Ábel, 1993). The coefficients in column (2) of Tables 4.3 and 4.4 are for the political events dummy active in the months in which some political or economic event is active while column (4) is for the political events dummy in which economic or political events have a cumulative impact on either inflation or output growth. According to the results in Table 4.3 political events have no statistically significant impact on inflation in either Hungary or Poland. When output growth is considered in Table 4.4, political events have a statistically negative influence on output growth when economic and political shocks are permitted to have only a transitory impact on industrial production. This means that these political events have had a negative impact on output growth in the countries considered. Note also that Hungary and Poland had statistically significantly higher inflation rates while Czechoslovakia's inflation rate is explained, in part, by German inflation. This represents some evidence that the Czechoslovak pegged exchange rate had the desired effect on its inflation rate.

4.2 Individual country results

Data limitations prevent the estimation of a reaction function for Czechoslovakia alone. Consequently, Tables 4.5 and 4.6 show separate estimates for Hungary and Poland only. In generating these estimates I have assumed that a vector autoregression (VAR) consisting in one case of an interest rate,[29] the inflation rate (defined as before) and output growth characterizes the central bank's model of the economy. In a separate VAR, money growth (measured by the narrow aggregate M1, the monetary base being unavailable in the monthly frequency) replaces the interest rate. The interest rate and money growth variables are assumed to proxy the central bank's instrument of monetary policy over which it exerts control.[30] The VARs were estimated recursively to ensure that forecasts of the variables are based only on information that would be available to policy makers. Johnson and Siklos (1993) explain in greater detail the advantages of this procedure for estimating central bank reaction functions.

If the central bank targets interest rates or money growth rates independently of political influences then it should react only to unanticipated movements in inflation and/or output growth. Given that central bank reaction is measured via either a change in the interest rate or via money growth this leads to the following two reaction functions.[31] In the case where monetary policy actions are measured via the interest rate we have

$$\Delta R_t = \alpha(L)[\pi_{t-1} - \hat{\pi}_{t-1}] + \beta(L)[y_{t-1} - \hat{y}_{t-1}] + \delta(L)POLEV_t + \zeta(L)\Delta R_t^W + u_t \quad (3)$$

When the stance of monetary policy is measured by money growth the reaction function is written

$$\dot{M}_t = \alpha^*(L)[\pi_{t-1} - \hat{\pi}_{t-1}] + \beta^*(L)[y_{t-1} - \hat{y}_{t-1}] + \delta^*(L)POLEV_t + \zeta^*(L)\dot{M}_t^W + u_t^* \quad (4)$$

where inflation (π) and output (y) growth forecasts are generated by the VARs [R,π,y] or [$\dot{M}$,π,y]. Four lags were used to estimate the VAR and generate forecasts for Hungarian data, two lags in the case of Polish data, owing to the smaller sample for the latter country. No restrictions, other than the ordering of the variables in the models as shown, were imposed. Equations (3) and (4) specify that interest rate changes (or money growth) react positively (negatively) to greater than expected inflation, and positively (negatively) to higher than forecast output growth. If the central bank is dependent, however, it will respond by reducing interest rates (increasing money growth) when the frequency of political events falls (i.e., political instability rises). Finally, as with the panel data, a small open economy is likely to be influenced by conditions in the rest of world. These are here proxied by German interest rate changes or money growth.[32]

Reaction functions for Hungary are presented in Table 4.5 while those for Poland appear in Table 4.6. For Hungary, interest rate changes are unrelated to unanticipated errors in either inflation or output, nor does the chosen Hungarian interest rate react to German interest rate changes. Political events do have a positive impact on interest rates when these types of shocks are allowed to accumulate over time but not when they are transitory. That is, political events appear to have permitted the central banks to raise interest rates and demonstrate their independence from government influence.[33] Turning to the reaction functions specified with the money growth policy variable, an unanticipated rise in inflation leads to a fall in money growth (the sum of the lagged terms is statistically significant in all cases) but there is no cumulative impact (statistically speaking) from lagged unanticipated output to current money growth. Moreover, political events have no statistically significant impact on money growth. The results based on both reaction functions suggest an independent National Bank of Hungary although this conclusion is somewhat stronger when money growth proxies monetary policy actions.

The results for Poland (Table 4.6) suggest that while the Polish National Bank does not respond either to unanticipated inflation or output growth there is a little bit of evidence that money growth is reduced in the face of rising political instability when the latter is permitted to have a cumulative impact on monetary policy variables. Though the evidence is weaker than for Hungary there is no econometric evidence that the Polish National Bank is dependent.

5   Conclusions

An analysis of the legislation of the reformed central banks in the former CPEs of Hungary, Poland, the Czech and Slovak Republics suggests, not surprisingly, that they are now clearly less subject to government influence than under central planning. A similar regime change is evident from the available econometric evidence. Nevertheless, to suggest that these central banks are independent because they are modelled after the German Bundesbank ignores the fact that the German central bank is not legislated to guarantee price stability which, if for historical reasons only, is a natural goal for the central banks of former CPEs to set. The Bundesbank has de facto behaved as if it were mandated to guarantee price stability because of its disastrous experience with hyperinflation during the 1920s as well as the federal structure of the German state. Czechoslovakia, Poland and Hungary have each experienced hyperinflation this century, twice in the case of Hungary, so perhaps it is sufficient to follow the German model. Yet, there is little evidence that low inflation is seen by the public as a desirable goal in itself, except perhaps in the Czech Republic, which is puzzling. As discussed in the paper, the existing legislation in the countries considered in this study is not sufficiently clear about central bank goals and responsibilities to behave *as if* they were the Bundesbank. Nevertheless, the little econometric evidence that is available does point to the conclusion that the Hungarian and Polish central banks appear to act fairly independently of political influences while the exchange rate policy of the Czech Republic appears to be delivering the desired disinflation. More generally, one has to ask whether price stability or low inflation is a desirable goal in itself. After all, price distortions are still significant as these economies drive toward market-determined prices. Moreover, the financial systems in the transitional economies are rather immature in the sense that relatively few financial instruments are available and liquidity is in short supply. It is particularly important then to be wary of associating measures of statutory independence with the ability of the transitional economies to deliver low or stable inflation.

It will be interesting to consider how well the estimated reaction functions will perform in the future. Given a sufficiently long time horizon, the political events variable could be augmented with electoral variables. It will take a considerable amount of time, however, before distinct partisan influences are detected. Also, a longer sample will enable researchers to delineate the transitional effects from the permanent effects of central bank reforms on inflation in the countries studied here. After all, it is too early to conclusively evaluate the independence of central banks in the transitional economies faced with a multitude of internal and external economic constraints simultaneously.

Notes

1. I am grateful to István Ábel and Tomás Baliño for supplying copies of the relevant legislation for the countries examined in this study. I also wish to acknowledge the financial support of the Social Sciences and Humanities Research Council of Canada under grant 410—93—1409. I am grateful to King Banaian, Richard Burdekin, Peter Dittus, Edi Hochreiter, Jerczy Konieczny, Werner Riecke, Aurel Schubert, István P. Székely and Tom Willett for comments on an earlier draft and to the International Monetary Fund for its hospitality while I was a Visiting Scholar in October 1993.
2. While references to price stability exist in the legislation of a few central banks (e.g., Austria; see Aufricht, 1967, p. 4, Art. 2(3) and Hochreiter, 1990) it is rare that a precise definition is given to the concept of price stability. An exception is the Reserve Bank of New Zealand Act of 1989 which stipulates the path inflation must take to achieve a target range of 0—2 per cent inflation in the Consumer Price Index by December 1993 (see Dawe, 1992, and Reserve Bank of New Zealand, 1991). The Bank of Canada also has an inflation target to meet but it is part of the Federal Government's 1991 Budget rather than forming an integral part of the legislation governing the Bank's activities.
3. Alesina and Summers (1993), however, find that central bank independence does not appear to be associated with real macroeconomic performance.
4. Below, I consider an alternative explanation of the Bundesbank's independence relevant to the transitional economies.
5. Siklos and Wohar (1993) consider a formal test of whether inflation rates have converged among industrialized countries, and find evidence favourable to this hypothesis.
6. In the sense that qualitative studies of central bank independence have tended to classify the Bank of Canada, for example, as dependent.
7. For additional details on this point, see Johnson and Siklos (1993).
8. Fratianni *et al.* (1993) propose a model which suggests that Japan is the 'odd man out' because the qualitative approach to measuring central bank independence ignores the role of political stability. Walsh (1992) posits a model which leads to the interpretation that the relatively superior Japanese inflation performance stems from the fact that the income of its Governor is more closely tied to government action than is the Fed Chairman's income in the US.

9.   Article 3, however, does state that the Bundesbank '... shall regulate the note and coin circulation and the supply of credit to the economy with the aim of safeguarding the currency...' (Aufricht, 1967, p. 252).

10.   Decisions by the Central Bank Council can be deferred for not more than two weeks (Article 13, see Aufricht, 1967, p. 256). This has generally been interpreted as an independence enhancing device.

11.   The Central Bank Council determines the direction of monetary policy. It consists of the President and Vice-President of the Bundesbank, up to eight members of a Directorate, and the Presidents of the Land Central Banks.

12.   If, as seems clear, Hungary, Poland and the Czech Republic wish to join the European Community then the Maastricht Treaty will resolve the problem of lending since this is explicitly forbidden under the provisions for the establishment of the European Central Bank.

13.   Estonia, for example, has established a currency board arrangement which fixes the value of the Kroon to the DM although some fluctuations are permitted. See Hanke *et al.* (1993) Chapter 4. In this case some might argue that lack of independence is a desirable characteristic. What is being discussed is the nominal exchange rate as an anchor. This does not prevent the real exchange rate from being a target of policy makers with consequences for inflation. See Calvo *et al.* (1993) for a description of relevant models. Siklos and Ábel (1993) describe the current real exchange rate policy in Hungary, Poland, and the Czech and Slovak Republics as resulting in a real appreciation of their respective currencies.

14.   Relative to central banking legislation in Western industrialized countries. See Aufricht (1967).

15.   The Czech National Bank Act (Article 35) stipulates that the Bank 'shall proclaim the exchange rate of the Czech currency *vis-à-vis* foreign currencies'. This does not preclude the government ultimately determining the exchange rate but officials of the Czech National Bank do not see it this way, according to Miroslav Hrnčíř of the Institute of Economics of the Czech National Bank.

16.   For the relevant details, see Siklos and Ábel (1993) and references therein.

17.   For example, the legislation governing the Czech National Bank has no specific provisions dealing with the problems arising out of inter-enterprise arrears. The Act on the National Bank of Hungary (para 17) has explicit provisions regarding credits to financial institutions in emergency situations. However, the modalities of interest and repayment are not clearly spelled out. Maturity, collateral and related conditions are specific in the case of the National Bank of Slovakia (see the Law about the National Bank of Slovakia, part 6, para 22 to 25). Provisions for credits to banks and other institutions also exist in the case of the National Bank of Poland.

18.   Unless such an approach exacerbates difficulties in working out bad loans.

19.   To the extent that a high level of foreign debt — which tends to be denominated in foreign currencies — requires an inflow of funds to service it may impose discipline on the authorities to ensure low inflation which is assisted by having an independent central bank. The foreign debt situation can also conflict with (real) exchange rate targeting when, say, an appreciation reduces the competitiveness of domestic producers. The resulting deterioration of the current account, especially on the still large former state enterprises with poor balance sheets, might result in pressure on the monetary authorities to extend credit thereby exacerbating inflation in the future.

20.   While deposit insurance did not exist in most industrialized countries until after World War II, except in the US, these financial systems were also not jeopardized to the same extent by the prospect of large-scale failures or bad loans. Previously, in centrally-planned economies, the state could underwrite deposits. The point being made here is that, until formal deposit insurance schemes are implemented, the impression is left that the central bank may be called upon to underwrite losses of the commercial banking sector. Note that this provision is not entirely independent, for example, of the item dealing with competition in the banking system.

21.   One of these could be the impact of price liberalization on real balances. See Siklos and Ábel (1993). While the overhang problem may be one which impacts the transitional economies only temporarily, central bank behaviour may have important consequences for the credibility of its actions, at least viewed from the public's perspective and for this reason is included as a separate determinant of legal and economic independence.

22.   Though one cannot express the 'significance' of the change in statistical terms. One should also ask to what extent it makes sense to regard the operations of 'central banks' in CPEs as resembling anything like the ones in conventional central banks. After all, under the monobank system, National Banks were simply passive suppliers of the domestic currency and did not engage in the kind of domestic or foreign currency operations performed by central banks in most other countries. It is thus odd that Cukierman would include these countries or that the value of the independence index would be a number greater than zero.

23.   One difficulty here is that I am unable to provide separate data for inflation in the Slovak Republic although casual evidence suggests it is considerably higher than in the Czech Republic.

24.   With only 13 observations it proved not to be possible to conduct a proper pooled cross-section time series test of the statistical link between the rate of depreciation in the real value of money (defined as in Cukierman, 1992, p.418) and the major groupings of codes in Table 4.2. Regressions (not reported) suggest that the greater the independence of monetary policy of the central bank, the more specific the central bank objectives, and the less binding the transitional constraints on central bank action, the smaller the depreciation in the real value of money. However, because the regressions could not be run with all the variables jointly these results should be viewed with some caution.

25.   In what follows, Czechoslovakia as a whole is examined up to its break-up into the Czech and Slovak Republics at the end of 1992. Separate Czech or Slovak data were unavailable.

26.   In earlier drafts, I had called this variable a political stability variable but as the political science literature equates political stability with coups d'états, revolutions and similar events, I preferred to call the relevant variable by the political events name.

27.   The list of events is contained in a separate appendix available in a working paper version of this study.

28.   US industrial production was more readily available and is perhaps more representative of international conditions than German industrial production data which excludes the former East Germany and may not, therefore, be entirely representative of the economic conditions in Germany overall.

29.   For Hungary, the enterprise loan rate was used; for Poland, the working capital loan rate; for Germany, the three month Treasury bill rate.

30.   Here I follow the methodology of Johnson and Siklos (1993) except for the use of a monetary aggregate in the VAR. Johnson and Siklos (1993) describe the reservations they have about monetary aggregates in reaction functions as well as outlining the arguments for resorting to an interest rate measure even in a world of capital controls. In the context of the former CPEs, however, the major drawback of the interest rate measure of monetary policy actions is that it is not yet clear to what extent movements in it are influenced by the market for debt which is still very much in its infancy in these countries. Moreover, since the currencies considered here are not really convertible on the capital account, the interest rate need not be the chosen instrument of the central bank.

31.   See, for example, *National Bank of Hungary: Annual Report 1992*, Chapter 3, for a description of interest rate and credit policies of the NBH. The exchange rate could be an additional policy variable but, as made clear earlier, it is essentially under government control rather than at the discretion of the government. This appears to be also true in the other countries considered in this study.

32.   A specification more representative of the existing literature on reaction functions, as in Abrams *et al.* (1980) or Woolley (1988), where the monetary policy variable reacts simply to lagged changes in the right hand side variables in (3) or (4) was also considered with no effect on the conclusions reported below.

33.   The events considered are typically ones which increase the pressure on governments to inflate or are the result of events which have led to the resignation of governments which attempted to implement or continue to implement inflation stabilization policies. To the extent that pressure on governments to inflate or to go against policies imposed externally, such as those of the IMF, which would translate into pressure on central banks to lower interest rates (or increase money growth) while higher interest rates reflect more independence.

References

Abrams, R.K., Froyen, R. and Waud, R. (1980), 'Monetary policy reaction functions, consistent expectations and the Burns era', *Journal of Money, Credit and Banking* 12, 30—42.

Alesina, A. (1988), 'Macroeconomics and politics', in Fischer, S. (ed.), *NBER Macroeconomics Annual*, Cambridge, The MIT Press.

Alesina, A. and Roubini, N. (1992), 'Political cycles in OECD economies', *Review of Economic Studies* 59, 663—688.

Alesina, A. and Summers, L.H. (1993), 'Central bank independence and macroeconomic performance', *Journal of Money, Credit and Banking* 25, 151—162.

Aufricht, H. (1967), *Central Banking Legislation, Volume II: Europe*, Washington, D.C., International Monetary Fund.

Balassa, Á. (1992), 'The transformation and development of the Hungarian banking system', in Kemme, D.M. and Rudka, A. (eds), *Monetary and Banking Reform in the Postcommunist Economies*, New York, Institute for EastWest Studies.

Banaian, K., Burdekin, R.C.K. and Willett, T.D. (1993), 'On the political economy of central bank independence', in Hoover, K.D. and Sheffrin, S.M. (eds), *Monetarism and the Methodology of Economics: Essays in Honour of Thomas Mayer*, London, Edward Elgar, (forthcoming).

Boguszewski, P., Czulno, W., and Prokop, W. (1992), 'Monetary and credit policy of the National Bank of Poland', in Kemme, D.M. and Rudka, A. (eds), *Monetary and Banking Reform in the Postcommunist Economies*, New York, Institute for EastWest Studies.

Borensztein, E., and Masson, P.R. (1993), 'Financial sector reform and exchange arrangements in Eastern Europe. Part II', Occasional Paper No. 102, International Monetary Fund, Washington, D.C.

Burdekin, R.C.K. and Willett, T.D. (1991), 'Central bank reform: the Federal Reserve in international perspective', *Public Budgeting and Financial Management* 3, 619—650.

Calvo, G.A. and Kumar, M.S. (1993), 'Financial sector reforms and exchange arrangements in Eastern Europe. Part I', Occasional Paper No. 102, International Monetary Fund, Washington, D.C.

Calvo, G.A., Reinhart, C.M. and Végh, C.A. (1993), 'Targeting the real exchange rate: theory and evidence', (mimeo), International Monetary Fund, Washington, D.C.

Cargill, T.F. (1989), 'Central bank independence and regulatory responsibilities: the Bank of Japan and the Federal Reserve', Solomon Brothers Center for the Study of Financial Institutions Monograph Series in Finance and Economics No. 1989—2.

Cottarelli, C. (1993), 'Divorce: the theory and practice of limiting central bank credit to the government', Working Paper, International Monetary Fund, Washington, D.C.

Cukierman, A. (1992), *Central Bank Strategy, Credibility and Independence*, Cambridge, The MIT Press.

Dawe, S. (1992), 'Reserve Bank of New Zealand Act, 1989', in *Monetary Policy and the New Zealand Financial System*, Third Edition, Wellington, Reserve Bank of New Zealand.

Fratianni, M., von Hagen, J., and Waller, C. (1993), 'Central banking as a political principal-agent problem', Discussion Paper No. 752, Centre for Economic Policy Research, London.

Grilli, V., Masciandro, D., and Tabellini, G. (1991), 'Political and monetary institutions and public financial policies in the industrial countries', *Economic Policy* 13, 342—392.

Hanke, S., Jonung, L., and Schuler, K. (1993), *Russian Currency and Finance: A Currency Board Approach to Reform*, London, Routledge.

Hochreiter, E. (1990), 'The Austrian National Bank Act: what does it say about monetary policy?' *Konjunkturpolitik* 36(4), 246—256.

Jindra, V. (1992), 'Problems in Czechoslovak banking reform', in Kemme, D.M. and Rudka, A. (eds), *Monetary and Banking Reform in the Postcommunist Economies*, New York, Institute for EastWest Studies.

Johnson, D.R. and Siklos, P.L. (1993), 'Empirical evidence on the independence of central banks', (mimeo), Wilfrid Laurier University.

Kemme, D.M. (1992), 'The reform of the system of money, banking and credit in Central Europe', (mimeo), The Wichita State University.

Lohmann, S. (1993), 'Designing a central bank in a federal system: the Deutsche Bundesbank, 1957—1992', in Siklos, P.L. (ed.), *Varieties of Monetary Reforms: Lessons and Experiences on the Road to Monetary Union*, Dordrecht, Kluwer Academic Publishers, (forthcoming).

Mayer, T. (1976), 'Structure and operations of the Federal Reserve System' in *Compendium of Papers Prepared for the Financial Institutions and Nation's Economy Study*, Committee on Banking, Currency and Housing, 94th Congress, Second Sess., General Printing Office, Washington, D.C.

Nordhaus, W. (1989), 'Alternative approaches to the political business cycle', *Brookings Papers on Economic Activity* 2, 1—68.

Parkin, M. and Bade, R. (1978), 'Central bank laws and monetary policies: a preliminary investigation', in Porter, M.G.(ed.), *The Australian Monetary System in the 1970s*, Monash University, Clayton.

Reserve Bank of New Zealand (1991), *Monetary Policy Statement*.

Rudka, A. (1992), 'Reform of the banking system in Poland', in Kemme, D.M. and Rudka, A. (eds), *Monetary and Banking Reform in the Postcommunist Economies*, New York, Institute for EastWest Studies.

Rymes, T.K. (1993), 'On the Coyne-Rasminsky directive and responsibility for monetary policy', in Siklos, P.L. (ed.), *Varieties of Monetary Reforms: Lessons and Experiences on the Road to Monetary Union*, Dordrecht, Kluwer Academic Publishers, (forthcoming).

Siklos, P.L. (1993), *Money, Banking and Financial Institutions: Canada in the Global Environment*, Toronto, McGraw-Hill Ryerson.

Siklos, P.L. and Ábel, I. (1993), 'Fiscal and monetary policy in the transition: searching for the credit crunch', in Sweeny, R.J., Wihlborg, C., and Willet, T.D. (eds), *Establishing Monetary Stability in Emerging Market Economies*, Boulder, CO, The Westview Press.

Siklos, P.L. and Wohar, M.E. (1993), 'Convergence in interest rates and inflation rates across countries and over time', (mimeo), Wilfrid Laurier University.

Walsh, C. (1992), 'Incentive contracts for central bankers and the inflationary bias of discretionary monetary Policy', (mimeo), University of California, Santa Cruz.

Woolley, J.T. (1988), 'Partisan manipulation of the economy: another look at monetary policy with moving regressions', *Journal of Politics* 50, 335—360.

Table 4.1   Index of central bank independence: definitions

Variable definition	Symbol	Hungary	Poland	Czech R.	Slovak R.
1. CEO					
Term of office-head	**too**	6	6	6	6
Who appoints CEO	**app**	PM	PM	Pres.	Pres.
Dismissal of CEO	**diss**	non-pol	Par.recall	Pres.recall	Pres.recall
2. Policy					
Who formulates it?	**monpol**	with gvt	with gvt	Bank alone	with gvt
Conflict resolution	**conf**	NO	NO	NO	NO
CB active in gvt budget?	**adv**	YES	YES	YES	NO
3. CB objective					
Single, multiple?	**obj**	multiple	multiple	price stability	stability of currency
4. Lending limitations					
Advances	**lla**	3% of planned revs.	2% of budgeted exp.	5% of previous year's revs.	5% of State Budget revs.
Maturity of loans	**lmat**	None	YES	YES	YES
Interest rate restrictions	**lint**	YES	YES	YES	YES
5. Transitional variables					
Exchange rate regime	**forex**	adj. peg	adj. peg	adj. peg	adj. peg
Enterprise arrears	**enter**				
BIS standards?		YES	NO	NO	NO
Consolidation Bank?		YES	YES	YES	NO
Foreign loans forgiven?		NO	YES	NO	NO
Access to CB funds?		YES	YES	YES	NO
Maturity of the financial system	**mat**				
Limits on foreign banks?		NO	YES	YES	YES
Competition in banking?		NO	NO	NO	NO
Active stock market?		YES	NO	YES	NO
Variety of fin. instr.?		YES	NO	YES	NO
Foreign debt load?	**debt**	high	high	low	low
Deposit insurance?	**depins**	NO[a]	NO	NO	NO
CB Board structure	**board**				
Who appoints?		PM	PM	Pres.	Pres.
Term		3 years	6 years	6 years	6 or 4 years
Gvt representative adv+vote					
adv.		YES	YES	YES	YES
attend only					
Monetary overhang?	**overh**	NO	YES	YES	YES

Notes:

For items 1 to 4, see Cukierman (1992), Chapter 19. For description of items under 5, see Section 3.2.

a) A deposit insurance scheme was proposed and passed in 1993 but, as it is not yet clear what the impact of the scheme will be, it was deemed preferable to list Hungary as having no deposit insurance scheme for the period considered.

Sources of Data: State Banking Supervision, *New Banking Act in Hungary II*, Budapest, 1 December 1991; Ministry of Finance, *Act on the National Bank of Hungary*, Budapest, 1991; Changes to the Bank Law and Act of the National Bank of Poland, 28 December 1989; Act of 31 January 1989, *The Banking Law* (Poland); *Foreign Exchange Law* of 1 January 1990 (Poland); Act of the Czech National Council No. 61, 1993, *On the Czech National Bank*; The Law of the National Council of the Slovak Republic, 18 November 1992 about *The National Bank of Slovakia*.

Table 4.2   Indexes of central bank independence

Group/Variables	Numerical coding			
	Hungary	Poland	Czech R.	Slovak R.
1. CEO				
too	.75	.75	.75	.75
app	0	.5	0	0
diss	.67	.33	.33	.33
2. Policy				
monpol	.67	.67	1	.67
conf	.20	.20	.40	0
adv	.50	.50	.50	0
3. Objectives				
obj	.4	.4	.8	.4
4. Limitations on lending				
lla	.67	.67	.67	.67
lmat	0	.67	.67	.33
lint	0	0	0	0
5. Transitional variables				
forex	.5	.5	.5	0
enter	.25	.5	.5	.5
mat	.75	0	.5	0
debt	0	0	1	1
depins	0	0	0	0
board	0	.375	.375	.125
gvt	.5	.5	.5	0
overh	.25	.11	.14	.14
Aggregate indexes				
items 1 to 4	.39	.46	.56	.33
Cukierman	.24	.10	NA	NA
policy only	.46	.46	.63	.22
item 5	.28[a]	.25	.44	.22
items 1 to 5	.34[a]	.36	.50	.31
Above less:				
overh	.21	.27	.48	.23
overh&forex	.25	.23	.48	.27
inflation rate	18.8[b]	103.1[c]	16.4[d]	16.4

Note: The Notes to this table are on the next page.

Notes to Table 4.2:

For description of variables see Table 4.1 and Section 3.2.
Coding for items 1 to 4 is from Cukierman (1992), Chapter 19.
For items under 5, coding is as follows:

Variable	Codes[e]
forex	fixed=0, adj. peg=.5, float=1
enter	BIS?: YES=1, NO=0
	Cons. Bank?: YES=1, NO=0
	Loans forg.?: YES=1, NO=0
	CB borrowing?: YES=1, NO=0
mat	Foreign banks?: YES=1, NO=0
	Competition?: YES=1, NO=0
	Active stock market?: YES=1, NO=0
	Variety of fin. instr?: YES=1, NO=0
debt	low=1, high=0
depins	yes=1, no=0
board	follows *app* and *too* in Cukierman
overh	=1/{m2/GDP} ratio
gvt	advise+vote=0
	advise=.5
	attend only=1

a) If *depins* is coded as .5 then Hungary's index becomes .34 for item 5 and .37 for items 1 through 5.
b) Mean of monthly inflation in consumer prices, 1987.01—1992.12.
c) Same as (b), except sample is 1989.01—1992.10.
d) Same as (b), except sample is 1991.02—1992.11, and data are for Czechoslovakia as a whole.
e) The higher the value for the index the more independent the central bank.

Table 4.3   Pooled time series data regressions

Dependent variable: Inflation (INF)[a]

Independent variables	(2) coefficient	(3) t-stat.	(4) coefficient	(5) t-stat.
INF(-1)	0.32	3.90*	0.33	4.02*
INF(-2)	0.12	1.34	0.12	1.42
INF(-3)	0.22	2.67*	0.22	2.71*
German INF(-2)	-4.93	-2.28*	-5.10	-2.31*
Dummies				
Czechoslovakia	21.03	1.30	20.12	1.21
Hungary	20.25	2.02*	18.44	1.87*
Poland	52.48	3.28*	44.48	3.26*
POLEV[b]	-1.79	-0.84	0.98	0.10
R^2 adj.	0.42		0.41	
S.E.	68.47		68.65	
Observations	147		147	
Dummies=0[c]	1.52 (0.22)		1.32 (0.25)	

Notes:
  a) Annualized monthly inflation in the Consumer Price Index (International Monetary Fund, *International Financial Statistics* (line 64), calculated as 1200*(log P_t- log P_{t-1}).
  b) In column(2), estimates are based on [0,1] political stability dummy. In column (4) estimates are based on cumulative political dummy. An appendix (not shown) provides a plot of the two dummies considered.
  c) Test of the null hypothesis that all dummies are jointly equal to zero. Significance level in parenthesis.

  *   Statistically significant at the 5% level.

Table 4.4 Pooled time series data regressions

Dependent variable:	Rate of growth in industrial production (PROD)[a]			
Independent variables	(2) coefficient	(3) t-stat.	(4) coefficient	(5) t-stat.
PROD(-1)	-0.43	-5.52*	-0.49	-5.97*
PROD(-2)	-	-	-0.18	-2.21*
US PROD(-2)	2.41	2.13*	1.40	1.25
Dummies				
Czechoslovakia	-47.53	-1.84#	-23.71	-0.89
Hungary	-16.16	-1.48	-10.21	-0.96
Poland	-10.36	-0.72	3.57	0.28
POLEV	-0.18	-0.28	-35.85	-2.90*
R² adj.	0.18		0.25	
S.E.	85.22		81.61	
Observations	137		137	
Dummies=0[b]	3.52 (0.06)		0.86 (0.35)	

Notes: See Notes to Table 4.3 for pertinent details.
a) Industrial production is an index (1985=100) from International Monetary Fund, *International Financial Statistics* (line 94).
b) Dummies=0 tests the joint significance of the dummy variables. The test is distributed as an F.
For sample information, see the following tables. For Czechoslovakia, the sample is 1991.02—1992.12.

*   Statistically significant at the 5% level.
\#   Statistically significant at the 10% level.

Table 4.5   Reaction functions for Hungary

(Sample: 1988.12—1992.12)

Independent variables	Dependent variables					
	ΔR	ΔR	ΔR	M	M	M
Constant	.09	-.13	-.01	14.75	16.43	14.83
	(.47)	(.69)	(.08)	(4.56*)	(4.73*)	(4.15*)
$\pi_{t-1} - \hat{\pi}_{t-1}$	.0004	.008	.002	-.13	-.21	-.13
	(.073)	(1.13)	(.26)	(1.19)	(1.67#)	(1.16)
$\pi_{t-2} - \hat{\pi}_{t-2}$	-.006	-.004	-.01	-.02	-.041	-.02
	(.76)	(.516)	(.79)	(.23)	(.43)	(.23)
$\pi_{t-3} - \hat{\pi}_{t-3}$	-.010	-.003	-.01	-.16	-.23	-.16
	(1.33)	(.459)	(1.30)	(1.55)	(1.98#)	(1.53)
$y_{t-1} - \hat{y}_{t-1}$	-.003	-.003	-.003	.12	.12	.12
	(.64)	(.74)	(.68)	(2.80*)	(2.88*)	(2.76*)
$y_{t-2} - \hat{y}_{t-2}$	-.004	-.005	-.004	.002	.005	.002
	(1.17)	(1.287)	(1.22)	(.039)	(.11)	(.041)
$y_{t-3} - \hat{y}_{t-3}$	.003	.004	.004	-.08	-.09	-.08
	(.537)	(.581)	(.613)	(1.97*)	(2.06*)	(1.92#)
ΔR^{Ger}	.37	.41	.42	-	-	-
	(.69)	(.88)	(.77)			
M^{Ger}	-	-	-	.25	.29	.25
				(2.10*)	(1.30)	(2.08*)
POLEV	-	.19	.39	-	-1.95	-.21
		(1.84#)	(1.15)		(1.27)	(.04)
R^2	.16	.22	.18	.34	.37	.34
S.E.	1.35	1.31	1.35	18.80	18.65	19.04
Observations	49	49	49	47	47	47

Notes to Tables 4.5 and 4.6:

Inflation and output are as defined in Tables 4.3 and 4.4. R^{Ger} is the German treasury bill rate. R is the enterprise discount rate for Hungary and the working capital loan rate for Poland. M is M1 for both countries. For M^{Ger} a special problem arises because of the effect of German unification in 1990. Since the International Financial Statistics publication makes no adjustment for this shock there is a huge jump in German M1 between 1990.12 and 1991.01 (DM 90.5 bn out of an M1 value of DM 453.1 bn in 1990.12). To adjust the figures for the growth rate in M1 between 1990.12 and 1991.12, an estimate from the *Monthly Report of the Bundesbank*, vol. 44 (September 1992), Table 2, p.4*, was used to project data from 1990.12 to 1991.12. This resulted in a downward adjustment factor of 0.8308843 from the IFS figures for 1991 and 1992. Growth rates in M1 were thus preserved despite the unification effect. In the first two columns of results, owing to heteroskedasticity in the residuals, White's heteroskedasticity adjusted standard errors were computed.

*   Statistically significant at the 5% level.
#   Statistically significant at the 10% level.

Table 4.6 Reaction functions for Poland

(Sample: 1989.08—1991.12)

Independent variables	ΔR	ΔR	ΔR	M	M	M
			Dependent variables			
Constant	2.50 (.23)	2.44 (.15)	-3.13 (.24)	135.03 (4.42*)	199.72 (6.68*)	-149.83 (4.34*)
$\pi_{t-1} - \hat{\pi}_{t-1}$	-.03 (.32)	-.03 (.31)	-.05 (.45)	.07 (.30)	.001 (.04)	.08 (.36)
$\pi_{t-2} - \hat{\pi}_{t-2}$	.02 (.18)	.02 (.18)	.02 (.13)	-.15 (.66)	-.18 (1.04)	-.12 (.56)
$\pi_{t-3} - \hat{\pi}_{t-3}$	.13 (1.20)	.13 (1.17)	.14 (1.26)	.23 (1.01)	.04 (.23)	.20 (.87)
$y_{t-1} - \hat{y}_{t-1}$	-.07 (.42)	-.07 (.41)	-.06 (.36)	.22 (.59)	-.10 (.32)	.21 (.55)
$y_{t-2} - \hat{y}_{t-2}$	-.12 (.69)	-.12 (.68)	-.13 (.73)	-.23 (.56)	-.19 (.58)	-.18 (.44)
$y_{t-3} - \hat{y}_{t-3}$	-.07 (.43)	-.07 (.43)	-.06 (.41)	.10 (.26)	-.21 (.63)	.06 (.14)
POLEV	-	.01 (.01)	10.78 (.74)	-	-19.17 (3.69*)	-36.04 (.94)
ΔR^{Ger}	-25.60 (.51)	-25.62 (.50)	-28.67 (.57)	-	-	-
M^{Ger}	-	-	-	-1.49 (1.48)	-.88 (1.09)	-1.08 (.98)
R^2	.12	.12	.13	.16	.50	.19
S.E.	65.91	66.93	66.37	131.13	103.71	131.51
Observations	41	41	41	29	29	29

Note: See Notes to Table 4.5.

Annual Rate of Inflation In Consumer Prices

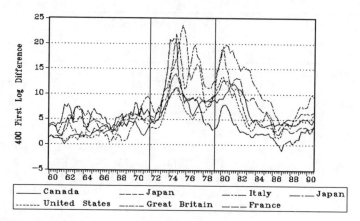

Figure 4.1 Annual rates of inflation in the G-7

Annual Inflation Rates in Consumer Prices

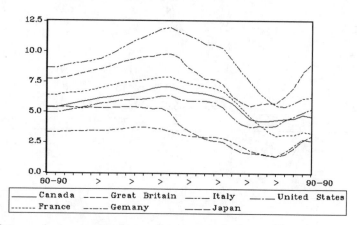

Note: Average annual rates for progressively smaller samples.
         For more details, see Section 2.

Figure 4.2 Average annual inflation rates in the G-7

Discussion
Peter Dittus[1]

Pierre Siklos has made a first attempt to understand better the issues of central bank independence in Central Europe. Only through such research will our knowledge improve, and he is therefore to be commended for having attempted such a difficult task. The chapter has been advertised modestly as a preliminary investigation but nonetheless provides much food for thought. As it presents a step in the exploratory journey of a rather new strand of economic research which has excited both economists and lawmakers in recent years, it is useful to stand back and reflect on the state of our knowledge in this area. This will be the first part of my comments. The second part will examine more closely the evidence Siklos has presented in his chapter.

Why should we be interested in whether central banks are independent or not? Presumably the answer is that we believe central banks to be better at achieving low inflation when they are independent than when they are directly controlled by their governments. Through the ages governments have imposed taxation without representation by debasing the currency. Democratic governments, in addition, are tempted to improve re-election prospects through inflationary policies. The result of this policy game between the government and the public can be a nasty Nash equilibrium: little real gain but definitely much higher inflation. The agreement to make the central bank independent may be interpreted as a way to credibly commit government to a lower rate of inflation.

In parenthesis I may add that another — and more sceptical — interpretation is also possible. By making the central bank independent, the government may be able to shift the blame of unpopular policies on the independent central bank, while still retaining effective control in critical periods through various means (Kane, 1980).

Surely the proof of the pudding must be in the eating. Research in the last few years (e.g. Alesina, 1989 and Grilli *et al.*, 1991) has appeared to support the notion that over longer periods of time independent central banks have achieved lower rates of inflation than more dependent ones. Is this finding robust? So far it appears not. For example, if the sample is extended beyond the narrow circle of OECD countries, the correlation between central bank independence and inflation performance is weakened to the point of disappearing (Cukierman, 1992). This may be partly because most work to date has examined simple correlations that do not control for other relevant factors in explaining inflation performance.

It is also partly due to the fact that central bank independence is difficult to measure. Two methods are found in the literature. The first one constructs indices of economic and political independence based mainly on central bank laws. Whether what is measured really proxies for independence is an open question. For one, the correlation between different types of such indices is not very high (De Haan and Sturm, 1992). More importantly perhaps, the comparison between such indices and questionnaire results of informed market participants suggests rather large discrepancies between legal provisions and actual practice, in particular in developing countries (Cukierman, 1992). This must nourish doubt on the validity of inferences based on any one of these indices.

A second approach analyses how the central bank reacts to economic and political developments. Significant political variables are interpreted to indicate a low degree of de facto independence. The findings of the reaction function approach appear not robust either. For example, Khoury (1990) analysed 42 estimated reaction functions for the Federal Reserve Board, concluding that results are extremely sensitive to the time period chosen and the conditioning variables included.

What can we learn from this brief overview of the contours of a rapidly expanding literature? Three points stand out. First, we have as yet no satisfactory way of measuring independence. In particular, in many countries the discrepancies between the law and actual practice seem large. This casts doubt on our ability to draw valid conclusions from research based on such measures.

Second, the belief that more independence buys lower inflation is — for the time being — a plausible and promising working hypothesis. But it needs to be explored in more detail. Perhaps both independence and low inflation can be explained by third factors. The fashionable citation of German inflation aversion as the result of hyperinflation, however, seems too simplistic. After all, other countries have experienced similar traumatic hyperinflation without drawing, apparently, the same conclusions.

Third, even if we think that there is a relationship between independence and inflation performance, we should bear in mind that the unexplained fraction of cross-country variation in inflation is substantial. There are many more elements to understanding inflation in a particular country than knowing the degree of independence of its central bank.

Let me now turn to the analysis of Siklos' chapter. It consists of two parts. He first constructs an index of central bank independence following Cukierman (1992). He then estimates reaction functions. I will discuss these two in turn.

To the usual components of Cukierman's index of independence Siklos has added factors that are intended to capture 'true' independence in economies in transition. As standard indices are poor proxies for independence in the case of non-OECD economies, this decision can only be applauded. According to the author, the Czech National Bank ranks as the most independent one in Central Europe, while the Slovak National

Bank is characterized as the least independent. This classification appears to confirm the opinion of a number of observers, but is it correct? While any classification involves some judgmental decision, my impression is that the indices in the paper can and should be improved. Let me explain how by taking the example of the Slovak National Bank.

First, some interpretations of the National Bank Act are debatable. For example, the maturity of central bank loans to the government is said — in Table 4.2 — to be limited to a maximum of more than one year. The Law states, however, in Section 25:2 that the National Bank may 'offer the Slovak Republic short-term credit through the purchase of Government treasury bills maturing within three months from the date of purchase for the purpose of covering fluctuations in the State budget in a current year'. This is very similar to the formulation in the Czech law and thus would seem to merit the same coding.

Second, there are problems with some of the transitional variables introduced by Siklos. For example, the exchange rate regime in all four countries can be characterized as an adjustable peg. The author argues that this circumscribes central bank freedom. It then proceeds to give only the Slovak Republic the lowest possible mark for independence without justifying why it does so.

Moreover, there is an important difference between an exchange rate regime which is imposed on a central bank and one it chooses itself. Would we say that the Austrian National Bank has little independence in exchange rate matters because it has decided that a fixed peg to the DM is its preferred policy? In Hungary and Poland exchange rate policy is the joint responsibility of the government. But most freedom appears to be given to the Slovak National Bank which has the right to 'establish' the exchange rate, similar to provisions in the Czech Central Bank Law. Thus, it would appear, based on the legal texts, that the Slovak National Bank merits the highest ranking for independence in this case, not the lowest one.

The relevance of some of the variables seems doubtful, too. Does it really matter for central bank independence now whether two years ago there was a monetary overhang?

The overall point I want to make is clear: more work is needed to make these indices of central bank independence reliable and therefore useful. More analysis is also required to make the central bank reaction function approach convincing. Siklos estimates a VAR system in three variables that is taken to constitute the central bank's model of the economy. He then analyses how the central bank reacts to unexpected developments in these variables and whether political variables help explain changes in the interest rate or of the rate of monetary expansion. I cannot comment on the political variable which was not available to me. Therefore let me focus on the model of the economy on which the results are conditioned.

Vector-autoregressive models have been used with success to describe the development of OECD economies. We know, however, that autoregressive systems are bad at tracking systems undergoing rapid structural change. But this is precisely the case in the economies in Eastern Europe. A VAR model of the economy is therefore unlikely to explain much. Out of curiosity I have estimated some VAR systems with the same variables Siklos is using for Hungary. Indeed, they explain very little except for the lagged dependent variable in some equations. More importantly perhaps, they track poorly. Surely central banks in Eastern Europe have more information on the economy than the little which is embedded in a few and poor autoregressive equations. Let me explain what I mean by a little example.

A simple model might try to explain inflation by changes in the lagged money stock. In the case of Hungary, such a model with four lags, all significant, explains just a quarter of the variation of inflation. But we, and also central banks, know better. Administrative price adjustments in Hungary as in other Eastern European countries are usually concentrated in January. This information should not be thrown away. If we include a dummy variable for January in the equation, two-thirds of the variation of inflation can be explained. Other factors known to central banks beyond the simple VAR include the timing of the elimination of consumer subsidies; the introduction of value-added taxes; the decline of CMEA trade and the concomitant decline in industrial production; and many more.

The point I wish to make is that a VAR is not an appropriate model for economies in transition. Technical analysis which builds on such a shaky foundation cannot be convincing. The reaction functions Siklos has shown us may therefore be best understood as a progress report on a difficult piece of applied economic research.

To sum up, Pierre Siklos has ventured into uncharted waters by examining central bank independence in Central Europe. Research on central bank independence in general and its influence on the performance of economies in particular is still in its infancy. Therefore we cannot know whether useful policy conclusions may emerge in due course. This should not prevent us from branching out. Only through such pioneering work will our knowledge ultimately increase. But, as I have attempted to show, many obstacles are in the way, and more work is needed to convince us that they have been truly overcome.

Note

1.   The views expressed are those of the author and do not necessarily reflect those of the Bank for International Settlements.

References

Alesina, A. (1989), 'Politics and business cycles in industrial democracies', *Economic Policy* 8, 58—98.

Cukierman, A. (1992), *Central Bank Strategy, Credibility, and Independence: Theory and Evidence*, Cambridge MA., The MIT Press.

De Haan, J. and Sturm, J.E. (1992), 'The case for central bank independence', *Banca Nazionale del Lavoro Quarterly Review* 182, 305—327.

Grilli, V., Masciandro, D., and Tabellini, G. (1991), 'Political and monetary institutions and public finance policies in the industrial countries', *Economic Policy* 13, 342—392.

Kane, E.J. (1980), 'Politics and Fed policymaking', *Journal of Monetary Economics* 6, 199—211.

Khoury, S.S. (1990), 'The Federal Reserve reaction function: a specification search', in Mayer, T. (ed.), *The Political Economy of American Monetary Policy*, Cambridge, Cambridge University Press.

Discussion
Aurel Schubert[1]

Pierre Siklos has written an interesting and useful paper with not very surprising results. Central bank independence already seems to be important for the inflation and output performance of Central and Eastern European countries. But I have some doubts as to whether we are really in a position yet to prove this fact empirically for the countries in transition.

This is a very timely topic to be studied. Not only because of all the interest of researchers — the book by Cukierman (1992) being the most visible sign of this interest — but also because it is a very relevant issue for practitioners. France, Spain, the UK and also the US are some of the countries where the political debate around central bank independence has gained momentum lately. The statutes of the planned European Central Bank (ECB) are the most prominent expression of the newly-found relevance of and interest in this topic.

The topic of central bank independence has received considerable interest reaching far beyond the economics or political science profession by the discussions surrounding the Treaty on European Union, the so-called Maastricht Treaty (Commission of the European Communities, 1992). In that treaty it is laid down that not only the planned ECB but also all national central banks of the member countries will have to be granted independence before entry into stage three of Economic and Monetary Union. Independence is defined in the statute of the ECB as 'neither the ECB, nor a national central bank, nor any member of their decision-making bodies shall seek or take instructions from Community institutions or bodies, from any government of a Member State or from any other body. The Community institutions and bodies and the governments of the Member States' it continues 'undertake to respect this principle and not to seek to influence the members of the decision-making bodies of the ECB or of the national central banks in the performance of their tasks.'

All of us who followed the discussion in the Community more closely remember very vividly what pains this paragraph caused and continues to cause some of the member countries and their politicians. Even in the market economies of Western Europe the concept of an independent central bank is not yet fully accepted or acceptable. In words maybe, but definitely not yet in deeds.

But this paragraph only covers part of the independence. Other important elements are in the objectives ('... the primary objective of the ECB shall be to maintain price stability ...'), in the employment conditions of the directors ('their term of office shall be eight years and shall not be renewable'), in the financial aspects of the statutes (own budget for the ECB), or in the prohibition of government financing via the central banks.

But are central banks ever really independent? I would argue that their independence is always a conditional one. Central banks are part and parcel of the overall economy and as such have to take into account the general economic situation of the respective country. The situation in the Central and Eastern European countries is presently characterized by systemic transformation, which restricts the possibilities of central banks. They have less freedom than under more normal economic conditions, less freedom than their sister institutions in the West. Therefore they also have to be judged differently.

Independence is not a one-dimensional thing, it is not a simple yes-or-no issue. Siklos is correct in pointing out how many aspects there are, and he also shows how difficult it is to measure all these aspects. He has to be commended for attempting to extend Cukierman's extensive indexation exercise by one more country and several new dimensions. As Cukierman (1992, p. 349) points out correctly, the basic objective difficulty in characterizing and measuring central bank independence is that it is determined by a multitude of legal, institutional, cultural and personal factors, many of which are difficult to quantify and some of which are unobservable to the general public.

To answer his questions, Siklos examines the empirical evidence. I was tempted to say that he examines the historical record but in view of the extremely short time span there is not much history to be examined — yet.

The empirical side of Siklos' chapter consists of two distinct parts. The first of these is the attempt to run panel regressions of time series cross-section data on inflation and output growth using lagged values of these variables, as well as foreign inflation or output growth and a dummy for political stability as explanatory variables. The second empirical part tries to estimate reaction functions of the central banks of Hungary and Poland. Data limitations prevent him from estimating a reaction function for Czechoslovakia alone. He does not find evidence that either the Hungarian or the Polish National Bank behaved in an obviously dependent manner.

In my view, the results of Siklos' study are very preliminary. Considering the short time span since the new central banking laws were adopted in the countries concerned this might not be surprising. With data covering not more than two to four years, detecting the influences of central bank dependence or independence on inflation or output performance appears close to impossible, especially in the economic and political environment in which these central banks have to act, namely systemic transformation.

Siklos speaks of the need for the former centrally planned economies to import the German 'cultural' aversion to inflation. I think this is a crucial point about successful anti-inflationary central banking, although I would argue that this aversion to inflation is not limited to Germany. The legal framework might be important but the 'cultural' framework seems even more relevant. Unless the public and the most influential political groups have an aversion to inflation, even a legally very independent central bank will not be able to perform well. On the other hand, even without many legal safeguards against political influences a central bank can behave in a very stability-oriented way, if the public wants it to. Therefore it is crucial to create that kind of environment in the CEE countries. Incidentally, the same necessity exists in several Western European countries, should the European Economic and Monetary Union become a stability union.

Increased financial sophistication might be one important way of creating more anti-inflation feelings in the CEE countries. People only care about inflation if they have something to lose. During 40 years of communism there was nothing to lose, but as they start to acquire financial assets their concern for a stable store of value will increase very rapidly.

Austria is in the very fortunate position of having a wide-ranging consensus for the need to follow stability-oriented policies. The institutionalized involvement of the most relevant groups of society in monetary policy making is one important element of that strategy. This might be something for countries in Central and Eastern Europe to copy, more so than the German model which is based on a federal political structure. In addition, the Austrian National Bank Act states that the Austrian National Bank (ANB) 'shall ensure with all the means at its disposal that the value of the Austrian currency is maintained with regard both to its domestic purchasing power and to its relationship with stable foreign currencies' (Article 2:3). But the Act also states that 'in determining the general lines of monetary and credit policy by the Austrian National Bank ... due regard shall be paid to the economic policy of the Federal Government' (Article 4). At the same time it prohibits the Federal Republic from adopting 'measures which are liable to hinder the Bank in the performance of the functions entrusted to it' (Article 41:2). Independence, yes; but not without limits and, at the same time, combined with an obligation for the government not to restrict the freedom of the Bank. In addition, the Act (Article 41:1) forbids government financing by the ANB (except on a very limited short-term basis).

Inflation is likely to remain one of the most pressing problems of Eastern European economies as the liberalization of prices needs to be continued and the present large-scale distortions in relative prices have to be further corrected (Duchatczek and Schubert, 1992, p. 22). In addition, fiscal problems will test the central banks' true independence, as David Kemme pointed out in his remarks at the conference. In Central and Eastern Europe the public has to regain confidence in the respective currencies; money must become a store of value again. To achieve this restoration of confidence and trust a good track record of the institutions issuing money is required, which means that inflation rates have to come down rapidly into the single digit range. Independence might be an important element in this process.

I see the importance of the work Siklos is doing in the fact that it gives prominence to an issue that requires great attention in the CEE countries during their transformation toward market economies. The politically responsible institutions and persons should constantly be reminded of the necessity to give their monetary authorities the freedom and means to pursue stability-oriented policies. The policy makers should feel constantly observed, not only by their electorate but also by economists, foreign economists in this case.

Let me make two small technical remarks. First, because the economies considered are small and open, Siklos controls for foreign shocks by adding among others the growth in US industrial production as a proxy for world output conditions. For the CEE countries and their trade orientation I consider German output to be more relevant than US output.

Second, the equations use monthly output growth (production index) in the CEE countries, both as dependent and independent variables. I have great doubts about the reliability of the output measurements in CEE in general, and monthly data in particular. Can one really have such confidence in the data to use it on a monthly basis? Is the strongly growing private sector really accounted for in an appropriate way?

In conclusion, I remain a little bit sceptical about whether we can really read from the data all we want to read, or find all we want to detect. I completely agree with Siklos' conclusion that it seems too early to conclusively evaluate the independence of central banks in the transition economies, faced with a multitude of internal and external economic constraints simultaneously. This should not keep us from attempting to evaluate it, although we should always remain conscious of the limitations.

In any case, it is a very interesting research topic and it should be further investigated. As more data points are accumulated, more analysis and better supported conclusions will be possible. This might be a very fashionable topic at the moment, but I am convinced it will also endure, at least for those genuinely interested in understanding the behaviour of central banks or the art of central banking. Pierre Siklos is on the right track and I encourage him to follow this path. Perhaps he should be a little more patient.

Note

1. The views expressed are those of the author and not necessarily those of the Oesterreichische Nationalbank.

References

Commission of the European Communities (1992), *Treaty on European Union*, Brussels.

Cukierman, A. (1992), *Central Bank Strategy, Credibility, and Independence: Theory and Evidence*, Cambridge MA., The MIT Press.

Duchatczek, W. and Schubert, A. (1992), 'Monetary policy issues in selected East European countries', SUERF Papers on Monetary Policy and Financial Systems No. 11, Tilburg.

5 Financial Sector Reform in the Economies in Transition: On the Way To Privatizing Commercial Banks

István Ábel and John P. Bonin

1 Introduction:[1] Why is the transition stalled?

The transition to a market economy in Central Eastern Europe (CEE) involves replacing one set of institutions and 'economic culture' with another. The CEE countries are experiencing simultaneously the two worst fears of capitalism, namely deep recession and significant inflation. In each country, the liberalization of prices and external trade resulted in a significant decline in the real economy. The fiscal deficit has been increasing as the recession erodes the tax base and transfer payments increase dramatically. The composition of government support changed as direct subsidies to companies and households were eliminated but the financial needs of the social side of the budget grew. Fiscal financing soaked up increased household savings that would have been available for financing business investment. Without sufficient financing, the real sector continues to stagnate or decline.

Nurturing growth in the real sector depends crucially on replacing institutions and developing the proper economic culture in the financial sector. Financial markets are at the core of any well-functioning capitalist economy but they have failed to develop sufficiently in the CEE countries. The relatively high level of savings in financial instruments observed in all CEE countries during the first few years of the transition has not been intermediated effectively to business investment. Rather it has disappeared into a 'black hole' to finance increasing fiscal deficits as businesses found it difficult to compete with the state for loanable funds.[2]

The retarded development of financial institutions and market culture can be attributed to the differences between the operation of the old system and the requirements of emerging financial markets. In the traditional central planning system, financial institutions and instruments were used mainly to record transactions and monitor compliance with plan directives. Investment decisions were taken directly by the state, formalized in development plans, and financed by issuing state directives to the commercial department of the national bank. The financial authorities had little or no independent decision-making authority as the bank acted as the financing wing of the state. A national savings bank served as the collection agency for household savings deposits. Thus, investment decisions were driven by the directives of central planning while intermediation between savings and investment occurred within the state sector.

In contrast, financial institutions have a crucial role to play in resource allocation in the market economy. Commercial banks settle payments between companies and individuals, provide liquidity for financing business activity (e.g., trade credit and working capital) and intermediate savings and investment by developing a longer term relationship with their business clients (e.g., line of credit, renewable short-term credit). The financial instruments used to provide liquidity and to perform intermediation are short- and long-term debt respectively (in the case of universal banks, equity shares are also part of the intermediation process). Hence, an essential ingredient of a successful transition is the creation and nurturing of commercial banks that will act like their market-economy counterparts.

As a necessary condition for facilitating the transition to a market economy, the state has withdrawn from the direct allocation of resources. In a typical CEE, a two-tier banking system has been created with the central bank separated from its commercial division. Public commercial banks were formed by dividing up the existing assets and some of the liabilities of the commercial division of the central bank. However, foreign loans were not transferred from the monobank; rather a new liability, a refinance loan, was created making the balance sheets of the newly-born commercial banks different from their Western counterparts. A public foreign trade bank, established in the planning period to deal in foreign currency and finance the external transactions designated in the plan, continues to operate now as a fully licensed commercial bank. The national savings bank, which is usually the largest bank in terms of assets and the principal collector of household deposits, operates with an extensive branch network. The central bank has become responsible for monetary management and exchange rate policy.

Although this separation is necessary for the establishment of a financial sector supportive of the market economy, it is not sufficient. In the process, the CEE states deserted their financial sectors leaving them unfairly burdened with the legacies of the past. The state bequeathed to the newly-formed commercial banks highly concentrated (non-diversified) loan portfolios of dubious quality. These distorted portfolios were inherited from a discredited (or soon to be discredited) political regime without the necessary financial compensation (e.g., loan-loss reserves). Hence, the large public commercial banks which were designed to be the pillars of the financial system in the transition were created as undercapitalized, financially distressed, weak institutions without solid financial foundations.

In each country, the bad[3] debt of the banks increased with the domestic recession and the disruption of trade patterns following the dissolution of the CMEA. As many companies were unable to reorient their products immediately and effectively to Western markets, bank loan portfolios deteriorated further. The transition requires the adoption of new market-type legislation including regulations for prudent management of banks to address issues of governance. Yet banks are also being held financially accountable for the decisions of the past. Inherited debt, either loans that were bad when the bank was established or loans that became non-performing due to the macroeconomic shocks, renders the newly-created commercial banks technically insolvent by international accounting standards (IAS). The extent to which the current bank management should be held responsible for this situation is difficult to assess.

Why should such weak financial institutions be preserved? As in the market economy, CEE commercial banks play a central role in the payments settlement system. The state savings bank is the primary depository of the financial savings of the populace and, as such, it plays an important role in intermediation. Either directly through central bank refinancing or indirectly in interbank markets, commercial banks acquire loanable funds to distribute to their clients. Commercial banks, by virtue of their lending activity with business clients, also become the depository of much of the financial information on companies. Although commercial banks may be financially weak, they do play a crucial role in settling payments and they do possess information, the essential commodity for well-functioning financial markets. Whether the current management is well-equipped and properly motivated to process and use this information is a separate question.

In deserting the financial sector, the state placed the burden of supporting ailing companies on the commercial banks. When the state eliminated direct fiscal subsidies to state-owned enterprises (SOEs), the banks had little choice but to protect their clients. Hence, non-performing loans were rolled over, interest arrears accumulated, and fresh credit was even extended to some of the better-connected but ailing clients. Good companies, those that serviced their debt, paid for these subsidies in the form of the high cost of services and high borrowing rates. What had been transparent fiscal support of nonprofitable SOEs was transformed into non-transparent support intermediated by the commercial banks.

The high borrowing rates coupled with low deposit rates generated large spreads. That newly-emerging banks which were not burdened by bad loans did not exploit this opportunity by offering loans on better terms than those offered by the large state-owned banks indicates a market imperfection. Minimum capital requirements for new banks found in the banking acts coupled with impacted financial information may offer some explanation for the current non-contestability of this market.[4] Consequently, the current large spreads maintained by the cartel of large state-owned banks provide the potential for severe disintermediation as good clients avoid, whenever possible, the domestic banking system and search out cheaper sources of credit. Commercial banks left with poorer credit risks seek better assets for their portfolios. Presently, CEE banks are turning to government securities for a better risk-return package and for the liquidity needed in their portfolios to accumulate the loan-loss reserves required by regulation. Hence, the increased household savings in financial instruments that accompanied the beginning of the transition are being squandered away in financing an increasing fiscal deficit. In essence, fiscal crowding out has effectively blocked the intermediation between savings and business investment.

The failure of credit markets in the CEE countries is the primary reason for the stalled transition. To jump-start (and then nurture) real growth, savings must be channelled to the business sector. Commercial banks can play a major role in this process but not if they are saddled with the excessive bad debt found currently in CEE banks. The state should accept responsibility for the burden that it imposed on the commercial banks at their conception. However, state intervention should be enabling and stop short of direct intervention in the allocation of resources. Market institutions and economic culture must be created to ensure that credit decisions are taken by competent financial managers operating independently of the government.

In what follows, we develop the conceptual basis for appropriate government policy to remedy the credit market failure. Then we focus on the Hungarian experience with an initially misguided attempt at resolving the bad-debt problem. Since Hungary is at the forefront of financial sector reform, the lessons learned from a careful analysis of Hungarian policy are relevant to many of the other countries in the region. Finally, we discuss how sound government policy can provide the preconditions necessary for bank privatization. This last step, privatization, is crucial if commercial banks in CEE countries are to act like their market counterparts and support the development of the business sector in a prudent way.

2   Breaking credit market gridlock

The purpose of government intervention should be to break the credit market gridlock by inducing commercial banks to allocate fresh capital to the business sector in a prudent way. With this objective in mind, it is crucial that financial sector reform be distinguished from industrial (and social) policy. Both companies and banks are suffering from financial distress but the two problems, although conceptually interrelated, must be separated in order to design proper policies. When the two issues are considered together, one policy tries (and fails) to achieve two objectives.

As an illustration of this problem, consider the following scenario. Large ailing loss-making SOEs desperately need financial support to prevent further reductions in output and employment. Without new capital, these enterprises cannot be restructured successfully and rendered capable of competing in emerging markets. Yet commercial banks are required by their supervisory agencies to accumulate provisions against all outstanding bad debt. The prospect of adding more qualified debt to the portfolio is not appealing to the prudent manager. Hence, the connection between financial distress of banks and companies and the tendency for governments to confuse several aspects of the problem.

To clarify the objectives of any proposal for financial sector reform, we divide the resolution of financial distress in the CEE countries into three aspects. The recapitalization (and, if necessary, restructuring) of public commercial banks is the crucial first step in breaking the credit market gridlock. A second and logically related issue is the consolidation and working out of the existing bad debt on the banks' balance sheets. For the purpose of policy design, these two interrelated components should also be separated. The third component of resolving financial distress is enterprise reform which must ultimately take one of three forms, restructuring and subsequent privatization, liquidation, or continuation as a public company. Although the commercial banks will have a critical role to play in this issue, they must first be financially sound. When properly endowed, banks can be privatized to establish the economic culture necessary to promote further the market economy.

Inherited bad loans and a further deterioration in the portfolio due to macroeconomic conditions have left commercial banks in the CEE countries severely undercapitalized. Due to the provisioning requirements in the new banking regulations, a significant portion of bank earnings is used to accumulate loan-loss reserves. Commercial banks are also incurring abnormally high costs as they develop rapidly both their payments settlements capacity and a more extensive branch network. Hence, the capital base is further strained. Therefore, banks require an injection of fresh capital from the state that conceived and deserted them leaving them in their present weak condition.

Any government programme that increases the capital of the commercial banks is fraught with tensions. First and foremost, the securities used to recapitalize the banks must consist of good assets which yield a market rate of return (Begg and Portes, 1992). Otherwise the programme will consist simply of replacing bad loans with tainted government securities. However, government securities yielding a market rate of return and issued in sufficient amounts to replace a significant portion of the qualified part of the banks' portfolios would add substantially to the fiscal deficit. The first tension is between the need to recapitalize the banks with good government securities and the cost to the fiscal budget of financing such securities (calculated as the market interest on the stock of bad debt).

Second, if the securities used in recapitalizing the banks are both highly liquid and yield a market rate of return, inflation management will become more difficult as banks would essentially be receiving cash. Monetary policy would have to walk a tightrope between too much base money that would rekindle inflationary fires and an overly tight credit policy that would retard the increase in lending to companies which is precisely what recapitalization is meant to accomplish. In a system in which the foundations for market-based monetary policy (e.g., open market operations) are rudimentary at best, such fine-tuning would be extremely difficult. Hence, government securities that can be used in transactions with the central bank but are not highly marketable may be the appropriate financial instrument for recapitalization.

Any recapitalization programme should be based on three sound principles. First, the establishment of proper governance to preclude a recurrence of the bad loan situation is crucial. If a programme does not reward prudent management when it has already occurred, it sends an inappropriate signal to managers. Hence, the temptation to level the playing field and recapitalize all banks to some target capital adequacy ratio (CAR) would run counter to the encouragement of proper governance.

Second, that CEE economies are in serious financial distress must be recognized. Fifty years of bad (by economic criteria) management is being dealt with in a very short period of time. Hence, international standards and prescriptions should be applied cautiously and judiciously. It is inappropriate to try to raise financial indicators immediately to levels considered healthy in normal conditions. Hence, CARs considered to be minimally acceptable by international standards may have to be phased-in over some period of the transition.

Third, and related to the first principle, the issue of using public money to bail out present bank management and current shareholders may be unpopular (and unfair). To the extent that the bad debt is truly inherited, management cannot be held accountable for it; to the extent that it results from poor governance, it must not be forgiven. Management and the current shareholders (usually state-owned agencies and organizations) should share in the cost of recapitalization. The actual proportions can vary from country to country depending on the specifics of the situation and the characteristics of existing shareholders (public companies vs. pension funds). To the extent that all existing shareholders are public institutions, the issue may look like an accounting exercise. However, the incidence of recapitalization may not be purely distributional; rather the cost born by certain groups (e.g., municipalities or pension funds) may affect their activities.

Recapitalization of the banks is often linked to removing the bad loans and arranging for their work-out. However, these two aspects of the problem should be separated at the initial stage of policy design. Loan consolidation and work-out has a dual purpose, to identify and package effectively the bad debt and to manage the resulting portfolio to maximize the present discounted value of the eventual return. The basic principle for efficient work-out is to match expertise in managing the portfolio with the necessary financial information. Many recapitalization proposals involve replacing the bad debt on the banks' balance sheets with government securities. What to do with the bad debt?

After removing the bad debt from the balance sheets of the commercial banks, the government should consolidate the loans of any individual debtor into a single package. It may also be useful to group together the loans of several companies to make the resulting package more attractive in size and diversity. A market-based approach would then involve the sale of these loan packages at auctions, thus transferring the rights to work out the bad debt to the purchasing agent. This scheme is attractive because market-type auctions lead to the commodity being sold to the buyer who values it most highly. Thus the bad debt would be worked out by the agent who can benefit most from such a procedure. If bidding is competitive enough, the agent will be the one most adept at work-out and the government will earn maximal return on bad debt from its 'sale' at auction. In CEE countries, a secondary market for bad debt is likely to be extremely thin. The agents with the best financial information on the debtors are the commercial banks themselves. Will these few large public institutions generate competitive bidding in an auction for *their own* bad debt? If the answer is negative, the market-based option will not exhibit the desired efficiency properties due to impacted information.[5]

An alternative centralized, state-directed approach consists of placing the bad debt in a 'sink' or 'hospital' bank. Again the issue is an informational one. How is the sink bank (or any government agency) going to extract the information that the commercial banks have on their clients? Without this information, the work-out procedure will not satisfy the objective of maximal returns to the government.[6]

Can an intermediate strategy that both uses the information where it resides and encourages the participation of agents with the necessary expertise be designed so as to maximize the return on bad debt to the government? An incentive contract could be designed with a lead bank (presumably the commercial bank with the most information on the loans involved) to induce it to seek the maximal eventual value (in discounted terms) of the package. The contract would encourage the involvement of a partner with particular expertise in loan work-out (e.g., a foreign financial company). Although state-directed, this proposal uses the information that resides in the commercial banks to work out the loan. Given that loan work-out takes time, having the informed commercial bank involved as a monitor of managerial activity during the work-out period should help to prevent asset erosion. Since asset erosion reduces the recoverable value of the loan, state-directed, commercial-bank-based work-out may lead to higher eventual returns to the government (Bonin and Mitchell, 1993).

Although related to bad debt work-out, policies for enterprise restructuring should be designed separately with commercial banks playing a major *informational* role. The three possible outcomes for an enterprise are privatization, eventual (or immediate) liquidation, and continuation as a public company. Privatization requires preparation and restructuring. Moreover, the decision of whether to privatize or liquidate a particular company depends on the future profitability of the company. Hence, the financial information that the commercial banks have on their clients is a crucial input into this decision.

Furthermore, transparency is a crucial principle for industrial policy. If the government wishes to support certain companies and sectors for reasons of national security or critical importance (e.g., public transport), the funding should come from the fiscal budget. If the goal of employment maintenance argues for a gradual restructuring of companies (in particular in certain regions of the country due to the relative immobility of the regional labour force), sunset procedures should be adopted and funded directly from the fiscal budget. In short, industrial policy must be recognized explicitly by direct fiscal financing whether it be a transitory part of the safety net or a decision to support a public company. The burden of providing nontransparent support for government programmes must be removed from the commercial banks.

In virtually all cases, the process of resolving the fate of a large SOE will take time and resources. During this interim period before privatization or liquidation occurs, the management of the company must be monitored to preclude asset stripping for personal gain. The commercial bank having the most experience with the company is in the best position to assume this trustee responsibility. However, the costs of industrial policy must not be born by the banking sector. Rather, the temporary subsidies required in the sunset plan should appear in the fiscal budget. If the enterprise is scheduled for privatization, the privatization agency should bear the costs of restructuring with the intention of recouping its expenses from privatization revenues. With the cost of enterprise sector reform made transparent, rational choices can be made by costing out the alternatives.

Whether commercial banks should hold equity positions to carry out their monitoring role is arguable. To the extent that banks take ownership of collateral against bad debt, they have already taken an equity position with their client. Some suggestions for dealing with the weak portfolio problem of the banks involve swapping bad debt for equity in the company so long as commercial banks are licensed as universal banks. However, replacing bad debt with bad equity does not help the bank's financial position but actually *increases* its risk exposure. The bank's cash flow is available to subsidize directly the losses of the companies it owns. A partnership between the state and the commercial banks in which the state holds the majority equity position in large companies and the banks use debt as a monitor of managerial behaviour is preferable to debt/equity swaps.

If commercial banks were to exchange debt for equity, the debt-equity ratios of companies would decline towards zero. In such a situation, managers have little incentive to improve short-term performance. Debt is an effective inducement to encourage cash flow in the short term when the overall business environment is weak (Stiglitz, 1992). In this situation, especially if management thinks that little or nothing is at stake over the longer term because the enterprise will be liquidated, short-term monitoring is crucial. Consequently, during the transitional phase, debt-equity ratios should be neither infinite nor zero.

In summary, commercial banks are the main depositories of crucial financial information and the appropriate agents to monitor proper company governance during the transition. They serve as effective payments settlements agents, act as lenders of short-term credit to satisfy the liquidity needs of companies, and establish longer term relationships with their clients. To ensure that commercial banks act prudently, a sound supervisory and regulatory system must be put in place. Well-trained personnel at both the banks and the supervisory agency is a necessary prerequisite. Technical improvements are also necessary to ensure timely payments clearing. In essence, resources must be allocated to infrastructure development in the financial sector. The state must accept financial responsibility for creating a sound financial system with strong commercial banks as its pillars.

3 Hungary's financial shock: from bad loans to tainted bonds

Denton (1993) attributes to the World Bank the statement that the banking system in Hungary is unable to finance the transformation to a market economy. The core of the problem is the financial situation of three large public commercial banks, in descending order of asset size, Hungarian Credit Bank (HCB), Commercial and Credit Bank (CCB), and Budapest Bank (BB). These three banks were created by dividing up the commercial credit division of the Central Bank in 1987. A fourth public commercial bank and financially sounder than the other three, the Foreign Trade Bank (FTB), was established in 1950 for handling foreign trade related banking and given a full commercial licence in 1978. By far the largest Hungarian bank, the National Savings Bank (NSB) accounts for about 40 per cent of all deposits and is also on shaky financial grounds. An interbank market exists on which the savings deposits of households held mainly at the NSB are transferred to commercial banks. The basic problem is the lack of efficient bank intermediation. The main stumbling block is the serious financial shock that the commercial banks were asked to absorb in 1992.

Credit market failure in Hungary is attested to by the virtually zero growth in the stock of bank credit issued to the business sector in 1992.[7] The banks' reluctance to finance new business investment is attributable partially to two legislative acts. The New Banking Act, effective on 1 December 1991, introduced three categories for rating the loan portfolios of the banks, mandated the accumulation of provisions (loan-loss reserves) against the qualified loans in the portfolio, and specified a schedule for meeting capital adequacy targets. The New Bankruptcy Law, effective 1 January 1992, began to have significant impact in April 1992 when a company with *any* outstanding debt more than 90 days overdue was required to initiate bankruptcy proceedings or the responsible parties would be subject to criminal prosecution. Each law addressed an important economic problem, i.e, ensuring the prudent operation of the banking system in the face of substantial qualified debt and counteracting creditor passivity in the face of a growing amount of involuntary and doubtful inter-enterprise debt, respectively. However, these two laws combined to deliver a serious financial shock to the Hungarian credit market by imposing an immediate flow solution on two stock problems.

According to the Banking Act, banks must classify assets in their portfolios as '*bad*'[8] if the borrower is in default for more than one year or the claims are held against a company that has filed for bankruptcy. Provisions equal to 100 per cent of the 'bad' debts must be accumulated over a three-year period. The banking act legislates two other categories of qualified loans — *substandard* and *doubtful* — with provisions equal to 20 per cent of the former and 50 per cent of the latter to be accumulated over the same time period. By the end of 1992, the aggregate stock of qualified loans stood at HUF 262 bn[9] which amounted to 17.2 per cent of the total loan portfolio and about 10 per cent of GDP. Full statutory provisions for the banking system increased from HUF 83 bn to HUF 222.5 bn from 1991 to 1992, an increment that exceeds 1992 profits *before* tax and provisions by almost 300 per cent. Total equity and provisions of the banking system amounted to HUF 267.9 bn at the end of December 1992. Hence, the solvency problem.

Of the total statutory provisions in 1992, HUF 118 bn is deferrable according to Hungarian accounting procedures (HAP). IAS treats deferred provisions differently. For loans classified as qualified by the end of 1992, banks are required to hold one-third of the prescribed provisions leaving two-thirds of this amount as a deferred liability. Although these deferred provisions are not subtracted from bank capital by HAP, IAS requires such deductions.

The trigger mechanism applied in April 1992[10] by the bankruptcy legislation led more than 10 000 companies to begin restructuring or liquidation procedures in 1992, an almost ten-fold increase over the number filing in 1991.[11] Since banking legislation requires that these companies' loans be classified as 'bad', the bankruptcy act was a significant contributor to the rise in the provision liability of the banking system in 1992. As a result, three of the four Hungarian commercial banks (the exception being FTB) were insolvent by IAS in 1992.[12] However, all four banks maintained reasonably high cash flow although the market began to change toward the end of the year.

High spreads and an inefficient payments system drove good commercial customers away from the domestic banks to seek credit and services elsewhere.[13] Some companies used internal funds whereas others sought financing on international markets. Some companies floated their own issues of commercial paper to circumvent the credit gridlock. The banks found themselves caught in a squeeze having to generate sufficient income to accumulate rapidly the required loan-loss reserves but finding no small-risk creditworthy commercial clients. Having no better alternative, banks turned toward government securities which provided both a reasonable risk-return package and the necessary liquidity (Treasury Bills) to support the increased provisioning. Thus, the budget deficit was financed by household savings and the productive sector was crowded out of the credit market as bank intermediation between individual savers and business investors ceased.[14]

After several revisions, the Ministry of Finance (MOF) and the Hungarian Investment and Development Ltd. (HID) announced in March 1993 the terms of a loan consolidation programme (LCP) applying retroactively to 1992 balance sheets with the intention of alleviating the bad-debt burden on commercial banks. All commercial bank debt classified as 'bad' by 1 October 1992 was eligible for participation. The arrangement allowed the banks to swap loans so classified for a special state financial instrument. Debt that was guaranteed by the government and certain types of 'bad' loans (e.g., debt held from a company that is being bailed out by either the State Property Agency or the State Assets Holding Company) was eligible to be swapped at 100 per cent of face value. Other 'old' debt, i.e., loans that were classified as 'bad' as of December 1991, would be swapped at 50 per cent of face value. Loans that were classified as 'bad' in 1992 from January to October, were exchanged at 80 per cent of face value. Once removed from the balance sheets of the commercial banks, the 'bad' loans were to be placed with HID to arrange the contractual terms for their work-out.

To replace the principle of the eligible 'bad' debt on the commercial banks' balance sheets, the government issued consolidation bonds (CBs) with a maturity of 20 years bearing interest equal to the average yield of 90-day Treasury bills (series A bonds). The capitalized accumulated interest arrears was treated differently in that it was eligible for compensation with series B bonds which paid only 50 per cent of the interest earned by series A bonds. Furthermore, the MOF retained the option to levy a stabilization tax on the participating banks at a rate not to exceed 50 per cent of the interest income generated by the LCP. Fourteen banks and 69 savings cooperatives contributed HUF 104.9 bn worth of 'bad' loans totalling over 4000 accounts to the programme in exchange for HUF 80.3 bn in *face value* of CBs.

With respect to recapitalization, the 1992 LCP was not successful. Since the stabilization tax was a deferred liability for the banks, IAS required a computation of the net present value (NPV) of the CBs adjusted for the tax. The series B bonds were also discounted because they did not yield market interest rates. Taking these factors into account, one estimate reduced the value of the CBs from HUF 80.3 bn to a NPV of HUF 32.5 bn. According to this calculation, less than one-third of the face value of the 'bad' debt was replaced. In essence, 'bad' loans were exchanged for tainted bonds and the banks were not recapitalized sufficiently. In response to this problem, the Hungarian government embarked on a new programme of bank recapitalization, dubbed the 1993 phase of loan consolidation. In June 1993, series B bonds were changed into series A bonds and the stabilization tax was rescinded. Thus, the full face value of the CBs used in the 1992 LCP was restored. In December 1993, the government announced a recapitalization programme for the nine largest state-owned banks in which USD 2 bn of new funds would be provided through a two-phase bond issuing, although further details are not available at this time of writing.

Although a large number of 'bad' loans were consolidated by the 1992 LCP, no procedures were designed to work out the accounts. In particular, no mechanism with appropriate incentives was established to use the banks' information on its clients in the work-out procedure. Furthermore, much of the old inherited 'bad' debt was removed from consideration by the banks because of its 50 per cent replacement coefficient. Banks acted strategically to reduce the tax liabilities that would result from excess provisioning once the 'bad' debt was removed. Furthermore, no consideration was given to inducing proper bank governance to ensure that the 'bad' loans problem would not recur. Since the commercial banks have a crucial input, information, that is needed to restructure companies and jump-start the floundering real productive sector, they cannot be left out of financing the transition. Hence, the importance of promoting proper bank governance. Hungary is taking the first necessary step in this process by endowing the state-owned commercial banks so that they will be ripe for privatization in the near future.

4 Bank privatization

Privatization is a crucial component of promoting proper governance of commercial banks. If recapitalization of the banks simply provides rent to the current management and shareholders, the public money will have been squandered. Banks must be induced to make new loans on an economically rational basis, to manage prudently their portfolios, and to preserve and increase their equity. Although privatization is a necessary condition for promoting these objectives, it is not sufficient. Bank behaviour is influenced strongly by the regulatory environment, the market structure, and other inherited conditions.[15]

By definition, privatization is the shift of any activity from the public to the private sector. In the case of CEE commercial banks, the first stage of privatization involves a transfer of only some portion of ownership from the government to private hands. The state's share and influence will be diluted but complete state divestiture will not occur immediately.[16] Nonetheless, privatization is expected to concur substantial benefits on the commercial banks including an injection of fresh capital, the upgrading of technical and management skills, and access to lower cost funding partly through economies of scale. In essence, all CEE governments are searching for international financial institutions as strategic partners for their commercial banks in order to promote these ends.

Such a privatization strategy contains at least four paradoxes. Before any CEE bank is attractive enough to a foreign institution, it must be solvent. Domestic banks are attractive because of their branch system and local knowledge but strategic partners are very cautious about buying into a bad debt problem. Hence some combination of recapitalization and government guarantees on old debt will be necessary preconditions to entice a strategic foreign partner. Nonetheless, part of the bank's recapitalization is expected to come from an injection of fresh capital from the foreign partner. Hence, the crucial issue of determining the maximum allowable share of a CEE bank that can be held by a foreign investor arises.

In most countries, foreign ownership of banks cannot exceed 50 per cent. In Hungary, the Banking Act requires government approval for a foreign investor to hold more than a 10 per cent share. Nonetheless, Bokros (1993) argues that the institutional situation in Hungary and the recapitalization needs of some of the large banks make it necessary for the strategic foreign partner to take over more than 50 per cent of the shares. However, he does suggest techniques by which the government can maintain its national interest in the event of a majority takeover by a foreign institution (e.g., the government can retain a golden share). The first paradox is between the desire to share the costs of recapitalization with the foreign partner and the share of ownership implied by such cost sharing.

Prior to allowing a strategic foreign partner to obtain controlling interest in a CEE bank (or a significant core of its equity) consideration must be given to the regulatory environment and the domestic market structure in commercial banking. In the CEE countries, commercial banking is dominated by a few large public banks. The financial market in the CEE countries is not a fully contestable one. Yet competition in banking and financial liberalization are the perfect ingredients to foster a banking crisis.[17] Hence, a regulatory environment sufficient to prevent the newly-privatized banks from exploiting monopolistic positions is a necessary precondition for privatization. If supervisory gaps exist because the regulatory mechanism is too primitive or because different regulatory bodies coexist[18], privatized banks will not behave properly. Allowing a foreign financial institution to earn unregulated monopoly rents does not constitute successful bank privatization.

The second important paradox is the tension between the regulatory environment and the attractiveness of the CEE bank to a foreign partner. If expected profit is not sufficiently high, the CEE bank will not entice its strategic foreign partner. Therefore, the regulatory authorities must allow some transitory monopoly rents to be earned after privatization takes place. Thus banking regulation must suppress competition to some extent so that the privatization deal is sufficiently attractive to the foreign bank.[19] However, sufficient contestability of financial markets must be fostered to provide the appropriate discipline in the longer run. Regulation must be fine-tuned to balance these conflicting objectives.

Information is a crucial ingredient to any privatization transaction. The potential foreign partner must have sufficient information about the client base of the bank to decide whether or not to bid and undergo the cost of due diligence. As in privatization of companies, the potential exists for the prospective partner to use the information provided to set up a greenfield venture and eschew the privatization process. This temptation is especially acute in the financial sector where joint ventures and foreign subsidiary banks are not saddled with the legacy of bad debt and long-term relationships with doubtful clients. The newcomers can 'cherry pick' from amongst the clients and leave the 'pits' for the CEE bank. Hence, the third paradox. Although information must be provided to attract the foreign partner, the potential exists for that information to be used privately and for the CEE bank to be left at the altar.

Finally, the foreign partner is expected to bring updated management skills and techniques in exchange for significant executive control over the CEE bank. Yet the process of privatization requires the participation of the *current* management of the CEE bank. It is with them that the knowledge and needed information resides. Why should they cooperate in a process that will lead to a significant decrease in their own stature? Perhaps they would even act as opportunists and misrepresent information for their own gain. One obvious way to elicit proper information is to assure present management that their position will be secure after privatization. However, this may be at odds with modernizing the management team and even with proper governance. The fourth paradox is the tension between enlisting the cooperation of current management without foregoing necessary improvements in management that are expected to accrue from privatization.[20]

Given the paradoxes identified in privatizing the large CEE banks, the virtually empty scorecard is not too much of a surprise.[21] However, the crucial problem is to ensure that the recapitalization which must occur before privatization is not squandered away due to mismanagement. Hence, Levine and Scott (1992) recommend tying recapitalization to bank privatization. Unfortunately, this would mean that the recapitalization of large banks would be delayed significantly. While such a strategy may be pursuable in the enterprise sector, it would have obvious deleterious effects in a financial sector that lacks both competition and a sufficiently well-developed and sophisticated regulatory mechanism.

Privatization of the large state-owned commercial banks is the natural consequence of any policy designed to break the credit market gridlock. Foreign banks have entered the market but they are not expanding into the riskier segments. Waiting for new domestic entrants to contest various portions of the market is too slow a process. Capital markets are underdeveloped so that few other financial instruments are currently available. Even if the large commercial banks should ideally be downsized, this restructuring must *follow* improvements in the real sector. Potential new entrants await better investment opportunities; these in turn can be provided only if the financing necessary for successful enterprise restructuring and for nurturing the newly-emerging private sector is provided. But it is only the large commercial banks that are currently positioned to accept this challenge. However, they require financial support and the proper governance to carry out this task efficiently. Bank recapitalization aimed at attracting a foreign partner to share the costs and also the benefits of this venture as soon as possible is required.

5   Conclusion: Can the transition be jump-started?

Replacing one set of institutions with another and developing the economic culture necessary for the market economy to function effectively has been a frustrating experience for the CEE countries. The current roadblock is the gridlock in financial markets. The credit crunch perpetrated by asking weak banks to bear the burden of past mistakes weighs heavily on the real economy. With little or no financing from the commercial banks, the business sector is not primed for a recovery. The state must concentrate on improving the health of the banks to encourage them to perform the intermediation role for which they were established. However, the state can do so only at significant cost.

Presently, the CEE commercial banks are accumulating government securities to improve the quality of their ailing portfolios. The banking system is financing the large fiscal deficits in the CEE countries by intermediating the increased flow of household savings. The state must halt this fiscal crowding out of business investment and nudge the commercial banks to lend to the real sector. Since any government policy must be carried out at arms length, the only possible solution is to recapitalize the banks and, thus, add to the fiscal deficit. Furthermore, the government must separate financial sector reform from industrial policy and make transparent its support of ailing enterprises. Again the budget will bear the brunt of such action.

Can this vicious cycle be broken by bank privatization? Will a foreign financial institution come to the rescue with fresh capital, management expertise, technical assistance, and its own broad-based network for raising funds? The likelihood seems remote in the near term. First the banks must be recapitalized to some extent and arrangements must be made to work out the bad loans. Then a regulatory environment sophisticated enough to ensure that the newly-privatized banks behave prudently must be established. Lastly, the real sector must become a reasonably attractive place for banks to do business. As a result, enterprises must also be restructured and privatized with the cost born in a transparent way by the fiscal budget. Unfortunately, the transition cannot be jump-started unless the state both commits additional resources to the financial sector and removes the burden of financing its industrial policy from the backs of its commercial banks.

Notes

1.   We acknowledge gratefully the support provided by the *National Council For Soviet and East European Research* (grant number 807—07) and *MTA OTKA Research Fund* (grant number 681).

2. The Czech Republic (formerly Czechoslovakia) is an exception to this statement.
3. Here and throughout the first two parts of this chapter, the term 'bad' is used in a generic sense to refer to all qualified debt. When the example of Hungary is considered in part three, the term 'bad' (i.e., in quotes) will be used in the specific sense defined in the Hungarian Banking Act.
4. Székely (1993) argues the necessity of a credible threat of contestability in each segment of the financial market to achieve market competition.
5. Even in US financial markets, the auction of bad debt from the bankrupt savings and loans was initially very difficult. When the government provided some financial assistance, the bad debt sold quickly but only at deep discounts.
6. In the former Czechoslovakia, this method was applied to a particular type of bad loans when the Consolidation Bank was established as a sink bank. Progress to date has not been encouraging.
7. According to the National Bank of Hungary, total credit to the entrepreneurial sector on 1 January 1992 was HUF 766.8 bn and it stood at HUF 774.2 bn on 31 December 1992. (NBH Monthly Report, 1/1993, p.42)
8. In this section, we restrict the term 'bad' to refer to loans so classified in Hungary.
9. This amount and the amounts to follow immediately are not adjusted for the government's loan consolidation programme which was instituted in 1993 but applied retroactively to 1992 balance sheets.
10. The trigger was subsequently suspended after September 1993 and more flexible rules were introduced to achieve and enforce agreement among creditors.
11. The National Bank reports that, in 1992, 4231 companies filed for bankruptcy and roughly 10 000 liquidation applications were received. Of these latter, about half were cancelled. (NBH Monthly Report 1/1993, p.23)
12. Before recapitalization, these three commercial banks had estimated CARs of 2.2, -7.9, and -8.5 per cent.
13. By the second half of 1992, the difference between lending and deposit rates with less than one year maturity was around 12 per cent. (NBH Monthly Report 1/1993, p.7)
14. The net household savings rate remained high at 11.6 per cent of disposable income in 1992 while the fiscal deficit as a ratio of estimated GDP was 7 per cent. (NBH Monthly Report 1/1993, pp.6—7)
15. Perotti (1992) demonstrates that value-maximizing banks burdened by inherited bad debts have an incentive to redirect funds from more profitable new loans toward their clients who are currently not servicing existing debt. Hence, the inherited bad debt problem must be resolved prior to privatization.
16. In Hungary, the Banking Act requires the state to hold no more than 25 per cent of the assets and one vote in the four large commercial banks by 1997.
17. See Stiglitz (1992) for a clear presentation of the theoretical reasons and Hinestrosa (1992) for a discussion of this problem in the context of bank privatization in Mexico.
18. In Hungary, the responsibility for banking supervision is shared between the Hungarian National Bank and the State Banking Supervision.
19. Because of the concentrated market structure, Székely (1993) points out that privatization of the large commercial banks is not sufficient for the true competition that is desirable in CEE financial markets. Rather he argues that regulation should not prohibit the entry of new financial institutions that will themselves promote contestable markets.

20. In the Mexican experience, a combination of incentives for current management and the takeover of bank operations by the Committee for Privatization from the beginning of the process was employed to solve this problem (Hinestrosa, 1992).
21. The first successful case of privatizing a state-owned commercial bank that had been created from a national bank is Wielkopolski Bank Kredytowy S.A. in Poland. A second such Polish bank, Bank Śląski S.A. w Katowicach, is in the process of being privatized. In both cases, no foreign commercial bank was found to become a strategic partner. Rather the European Bank for Reconstruction and Development (EBRD) provided the injection of new capital.

References

Begg, D. and Portes, R. (1992), 'Enterprise debt and economic transformation: financial restructuring in Central and Eastern Europe', Discussion Paper Series No. 695, Centre for Economic Policy Research, London.

Bokros, L. (1993), 'The role of commercial banks in privatization', Working Papers No. 6, Budapest Bank.

Bonin, J.P. and Mitchell, J. (1993), 'Creating efficient banks during the transition: do bad loans lead to bad policy?', paper presented at the American Economic Association Meetings in Anaheim CA, January.

Denton, N. (1993), 'The hole at Hungary's banking heart', *Financial Times*, 20 May.

Hinestrosa, P. (1992), 'Privatizing banks, the Mexican experience', paper presented at conference on banking reform and regulation in Eastern Europe, EBRD, October.

Levine, R. and Scott, D. (1992), 'Old debts and new beginnings: a policy choice in transitional socialist economies', Policy Research Working Paper Series No. 876, The World Bank, Washington, D.C.

Perotti, E.C. (1992), 'Bank lending in transition economies', (mimeo), Boston University.

Stiglitz, J.E. (1992), 'The design of financial systems for the newly emerging democracies of Eastern Europe', in Clague, C. and Rausser, G. (eds), *The Emergence of Market Economies in Eastern Europe*, Cambridge MA., Blackwell.

Székely, I.P. (1993), 'Economic transformation and the reform of the financial system in Central and Eastern Europe', Discussion Paper Series No. 816, Centre for Economic Policy Research, London.

Discussion
Richard A. Golden

This discussion analyses the authors' viewpoint from the position of a practitioner of privatization, who sees first hand the impact made on both the Hungarian corporate sector and the financial system by the stalled reform of the financial sector. The topic holds considerable interest, since I started my banking career at Continental Illinois, one of the early benefactors of an FDIC rescue operation, and also managed a joint venture that had one of the Hungarian commercial banks as a shareholder.

Since I agree with the authors' conclusion that reform has to be carried out by the state and not by the commercial banking system, I hope to address: (1) some of their basic assumptions of the role played by these banks to date; (2) the banks' culpability for the current situation; and (3) to what extent these institutions can act in future reform and in the financial system. In particular, I want to attempt to address the human and institutional aspects involved in the problem, and the incentive structure in existence at the banks, and how these factors serve as additional, deeply ingrained obstacles to reform.

I wish to point out that most of the research for this discussion consists of conversations with State Property Agency staff and financial advisors involved in either Hungarian bank privatization or in the recent bank rescue operations held in the United States, and includes only a limited amount of reading material.

To a certain extent the authors appear to contend that the state used the break up of the monobank system and spin-off of the three big commercial banks to abrogate its responsibilities to clean up the debt overhang in the state enterprise system. To use their words, 'In deserting the financial sector, the state placed the burden of supporting ailing companies on the commercial banks'.

In their view, the commercial banks were mostly passive agents in a government attempt to initiate financial and industrial reform by establishing a nascent commercial banking system. They portray the banks as having been largely helpless, with the conclusion that the continued deterioration in the commercial banks' condition occurred through no fault of the bank managers.

In the authors' opinion, the state then continued to make matters worse by recapitalizing the banks with low-yielding securities and failing to impose an appropriate corporate governance system. The authors also contend that the commercial banks are most suited to be involved in the clean-up of bad debts due to their superior level of information on these companies, with the missing element being partners with technical expertise, who would have to be subcontracted.

Lastly, the authors assume that these banks deserve to be coddled as regards the imposition of capital adequacy ratios and competition from foreign competition, which in my opinion remains an open question.

The authors' contention that the beginning of the transition was 'squandered away in financing an increasing fiscal deficit' and that effective intermediation of saving and investment was blocked by a credit market failure is undoubtedly correct.

There are three key points I want to address in this regard: (1) the commercial banks' culpability for their own crises; (2) whether they are capable in terms of human and institutional capital to eventually become an effective financial intermediary; and (3) what alternatives the state has.

My research and conversations indicate that several factors endemic to the system led the commercial bank managers to effectively participate in the steady expansion and worsening of their credit portfolios after the spin-off in 1987. According to several informed sources, two-thirds of the bad debts on their books stem from after 1987.

Although the authors are correct in contending that no effective controls were put in place, the fact is that the institutions allowed a system of incentives to prevail which led to the worsening of their credit portfolios. In many instances, individual performance incentives were solely based on loan growth and related revenues, hardly constraining the appetite for credit of individual managers. Also, cross-share holdings between commercial banks and the state enterprise sector, which still stand at 19 per cent, may have lessened the banks' ability to decline several requests for rollovers or extensions of credit.

A more difficult motivation to evaluate and eventually change, is the personal incentives that accrued to individual bank managers from helping out their fellow managers in state enterprise, who most likely were key members of their social peer group. Since these people were probably convinced that their respective institutions would be bailed out by the state in any case, they had absolutely no incentive to halt the habit of helping out other members of their social elite.

Lastly, not to mention the often-cited absence of corporate governance, these banks had no existing corporate credit culture to determine what was a good or bad loan. This inability to properly assess the quality of their loan portfolio was frequently compounded by an absence of the necessary internal management or reporting systems which could provide a consolidated overview of the loans outstanding throughout their network to their large clients.

According to the latest information from CSFB, the result of the banking crisis is that by the end of 1992 nearly 26 per cent of all loans in the banking sector were non-performing. If the government were to take this as a one-time hit it would more than double the 1993 budget deficit.

Ultimately, it would appear that the banks are largely responsible for exacerbating their own crisis. Not having closely studied recent bank developments, I am not aware if the necessary internal changes have now taken place to change management incentives, and create an internal culture with an appreciation of proper credit analysis.

Commercial banks do have the best source of information about these creditors and their files are invaluable in recovering the bad loans, so they do need to play a role. However, a means has to be found to break the institutional attitude and personal incentives that continue to build up bad loans.

Not being a trained management consultant, I do not know how to accomplish this. I can only refer to the example of Continental Illinois, where the clean-up was handled by in-house staff, on loan to the FDIC, whose management reported to the FDIC. The loans handled by this 'bad bank' had been sold to the FDIC at 66 per cent of their face value. Incentives of the in-house team were based on the percentage recovered relative to the purchase price paid. Ultimately, the FDIC's loss was limited to approximately 10 to 19 per cent the amount it paid for the loans.

Important elements in the Continental Illinois bail-out were: (1) the severing, albeit only temporarily, of the team assigned to the work-out from Continental's management structure; (2) the severing of the incentive scheme of the individuals involved; and (3) the fact that the bank no longer owned the loans, which meant that it was neutral about the work-out result.

Aside from the question of whether the Hungarian commercial banks can build up a strong base of credit analysis, let me briefly look at their ability to handle other roles. In regard to setting up an efficient money transfer system, internal bickering has continued to delay the establishment of a fires system despite the availability of World Bank funding.

As to alternatives to the state rescuing the banks, I cannot evaluate whether the state can afford to allow any bank to fail. However, I have never understood why this sector needed to be protected from foreign competition, as the authors seem to contend. In my opinion, they will only change their behaviour once serious competition arises.

The failure to resolve these problems will benefit one interested party: the investment banking community. In its efforts to provide the private corporate sector with the necessary capital, this community will continue to find instruments which lead to the disintermediation of the state-owned commercial banks.

Discussion
Paweł Wyczański

I would like to start with some rather technical remarks which are of minor importance, but which make a small contribution and help make the chapter more reliable. These deal with the following issues. The characteristics of the command economy were in reality different from the theoretical models of the planned economy, presented very briefly in the chapter, as a reference point to the new economic environment. The main phenomenon was the interplay between the enterprise sector and central planning, in which the central decision-making body was in many cases forced to follow a pattern which was in the interest of the enterprises themselves, and to allocate scarce resources to inefficient projects and in some instances to projects that were not even feasible from a micro-economic point of view.

Shortly after the emergence of new commercial banks the burden of bad loans and bad borrowers was almost unimaginable. In Poland this was mainly the result of hyperinflation in 1989, and then the stabilization programme and the transformation undertaken in 1990. A large number of state-owned enterprises failed to adjust to the new economic environment. All this was coupled with the loss of external as well as internal markets.

A question of much greater importance is that of information. We should analyse this further to find out the potential problems. The authors are right that the information rests in the banks' possession, but is highly dispersed and in many cases not analysed, and what is worse still, not utilized in full. There is a lack of a proper interbank information system. Though the Polish Bankers Association gathers information on default borrowers, not all the banks are willing to participate in that programme and to update the information, or they are not prepared to use it efficiently.

The auction sale of loans is highly unlikely or even impossible, given the results of published offerings of various banks. The authors are right that only banks might have sufficient information and ability to manage the acquired loans, but the major goal for the sellers should be to get rid of bad loans, not to accumulate (acquired from others) new doubtful assets.

The question of debt into equity swaps must be seen as extremely troublesome. Experience shows that those transactions can be a trap for the bank involved, as the bank becomes the slave of the company in which the bank holds the equity stake. The bank is then being forced to extend new loans or to reschedule outstanding ones to avoid a total compromise. The case of involuntary debt into equity swaps forms a part of the restructuring package, but should be put last in the list of likely solutions.

The most difficult question is perhaps the issue of privatization of banks or the establishment of new banks with foreign participation — which might be preferable, but in the latter alternative, in the Polish situation the newcomer is perceived by the public as being in a privileged position. (Foreign banks operating in Poland are granted three years tax release and they do not pay a tax on wage increases.) A foreign bank, with a good reputation, enters the new market with no burden of default borrowers. The bank may be very competitive and attract first-class corporate customers. It may, however, lead to a worsening of the position for domestic, but not yet privatized banks, left with a bad loans burden or with second-class customers. The proposal to recapitalize banks before privatization has some political implications, which makes it not directly feasible in our situation. One cannot imagine foreign banks operating in Eastern and Central European countries directly involved in solving the problem of bad loans. They are more likely to be concentrated in the most profitable market segments. These banks may be helpful in creating a competitive environment for domestic banks, easing and speeding up the process of consolidation of the banking industry.

Taking charge of the restructuring of insolvent enterprises would be an obvious task for the fiscal budget makers, but political implications make it much easier to transfer this responsibility to the banks. The banks are then to blame for making wrong decisions if they are not successful.

One of the 'big nine' banks was successfully privatized in 1993 and shares are now traded at a price three to seven times higher than the issue price. A second bank will be sold in the coming weeks, the first tranche to large institutional investors, the second to smaller and the rest to the general public.

As experience shows, the sale of Wielkopolski Bank Kredytowy (WBK) to institutional investors caused rather mixed results, as the shares are highly diluted and there is no active investor except the EBRD. The EBRD obtained two seats on the bank's supervisory board. It is too early to come to any definite conclusions on the results of privatization of the WBK. The new strategy is under discussion as well as internal organization and staffing questions.

In other cases of privatization we could see no major differences. Export Development Bank, sold at a public offering in 1992, has not greatly changed its strategy and has no major shareholders. The foreign shareholder, notably Girocredit Bank from Austria, is actively offering assistance in training and providing new products and skills.

So far, the major benefit for privatized banks is freedom from bureaucratic control, and a competitive advantage due to tax treatment, as there are no penalty taxes on wage increases.

6 Bankruptcy and Banking Reform in the Transition Economies of Central and Eastern Europe

Kálmán Mizsei

1 Introduction[1]

The problem discussed in this study is the proper policy approach to handling enterprise insolvency in the period of economic transition from centrally-controlled to market economies. The issue is twofold. On the one hand, since these economies have lived for many decades without any bankruptcy, the infrastructure (legal, human, institutional and administrative) was not present when the transition started. On the other hand, the systemic transition has, out of necessity, incorporated major macroeconomic adjustments, causing a huge liquidity squeeze in the enterprise sector. In addition, the disintegration of CMEA-trade also contributed to the severe financial conditions. So, even if the procedure had been set up by the time of the big changes, the wave of insolvencies would have forced the countries to take some policy measures.

The chapter relies primarily on the experiences of the 'fast-track' reformers, i.e. Poland, Hungary and, to a lesser extent, the Czech Republic, since insolvency regulation becomes an urgent policy issue when the monetary and fiscal system stops automatically guaranteeing enterprise liquidity. My own policy activities have also led me to Russia; I am also using that experience here although institutionally Russia is obviously not yet in the same category.

The general purpose of the economic reform, to use Kornai's suitable terminology, is to 'harden the budget constraint' of businesses. In this context the issue of dealing with enterprise and bank insolvency is a critical one. The policy goal should be to arrive in the long term at a situation where timely payment of dues is treated seriously on both enterprise and bank levels. What this study can do is to assess the early experiences of the 'fast-track' East Central European countries in dealing with enterprise insolvency and the impact government approaches have had on the banking sector. Also, one can speculate on the impact of initial experiences on the long-term hardening of the budget constraint.

The remaining part of the chapter is organized as follows. Section 2 deals with the macroeconomic environment of the bankruptcy regulation. Section 3 turns to the experiences of Hungary with its pioneering bankruptcy regulation in 1992 and its impact on the banking sector. Finally, Section 4 looks at the experiences of Poland and the Czech Republic to try to gauge whether a softer initial approach helps these countries in consolidating their market reforms faster.

2 Macroeconomic conditions

As said before, transition had to be accompanied by major macroeconomic adjustments. All the Eastern European countries started the transition with macroeconomic imbalances although their intensity differed largely by country.[2] Therefore, adjustment was needed in each post-communist country, although to a different degree. Where it did not occur, there were far-reaching consequences for the whole transition. As known, macroeconomic adjustment has been the most successful in the 'fast-track' countries, the least successful in the CIS-countries, while the Balkans and the Baltic countries are in between.[3]

Russia is the only country in the transforming region where recent acute imbalances (near hyperinflation and continuing major shortages) and extremely soft budget constraints are accompanied by arguably meaningful micro-economic reforms, notably rapid privatization. Elsewhere, acute imbalances go hand in hand with mediocre performance in the micro-economy; likewise, energetic macroeconomic adjustments in the Czech Republic, Hungary and Poland are accompanied by very rapid micro-economic reforms.

One important, yet not often emphasized determinant of the macroeconomic conditions of enterprise insolvency in the transition period is wage policy. In this respect (former) Czechoslovakia pursued the toughest course in the region and, consequently, the liquidity crisis in the enterprise sector, although present, was the mildest here in the 1990—1992 period (Mizsei and Rostowski, 1993). Some analysts criticize this policy, claiming that it postponed structural change in the Czechoslovak industry. However, more important is that in the very critical initial period of transition, the burden on the enterprise and banking sectors was somewhat mitigated by repressed wages. In other words, the Czechs gained some degree of institutional stability by introducing tough policies on wages in the critical time of reorganizing almost everything. Also, in the early period of the transition, policy makers could afford two major operations to improve the liquidity positions of the enterprise and banking sectors by increasing the national debt. Poland and Hungary had to be less generous with such operations, as their national debt had already reached dangerous levels before the 1990s. Obviously, this did not mean that these two countries could not pursue a policy of debt conciliation or state financial support to the banking and enterprise sectors, but the room for manoeuvre was much more limited than in the Czech case. Moreover, Polish and Hungarian economic policy makers could afford less mistakes than the Czechs (or even the Slovaks for that matter).

Unfortunately, at least in the Hungarian case this danger did not prevent the authorities from making major policy mistakes. One can legitimately say that the authorities did not understand the consequences of the liquidity squeeze in 1990—1992. Only this can explain the sequence of policy steps during this period.[4] In 1990 and 1991 there were two simultaneous concerns of economic policy. On the one hand, price liberalization and the elimination of price and production subsidies put strong upward pressure on consumer price inflation; on the other, monetary austerity and the disintegration of CMEA trade, while moderating the inflationary pressures, had a huge effect on industries exporting to the region. Needless to say, in the short term the two concerns were pushing economic policies in opposite directions and the long-term implications were not clearly realized.

An important fact of Hungarian political economy is that in that period, similarly to communist times, these two considerations appeared as a battle between different government departments. I think it was unnecessary because the political situation was favourable for creating an operative government. Besides agriculture (where the Small-holders' Party had particular interests), the senior coalition party did not have to face any real political constraint in shaping its economic policies. And yet, due to a lack of experience and, to some extent, competence and to the fact that the conservative forces concentrated much more on abstract national grievances than on problems of economic transition, the unity of economic policy was not established. One group in the government followed the conservative IMF policies in good faith (believing that it was plainly the only policy option), while another one opposed it with rather obsolete pro-growth arguments. There was no intellectual centre in the government during this period that could have worked out feasible alternatives to the option of doing nothing for enterprises undergoing enormously rapid changes, including the collapse of the Eastern markets and the sudden jump in energy and other basic input prices. In 1990 enterprises were quasi-subsidized by having received the price of their Soviet exports from the Hungarian authorities, in spite of the fact that already at that time the Russians had not paid their dues. This solution in 1990 was again more a result of a lack of coordination than of any conscious policy to maintain liquidity.

In 1991 automatic payment for Eastern European exports by the Hungarian state was terminated; enterprises were pushed one step closer to the harsh realities of the market. In this year (and in 1990) enterprises were able to dynamically reorient their trade towards the Western markets. However, it is still not clear how much of the reorientation was attributable to the presence of competitive goods, better marketing, etc., and how much to a strictly temporary mobilization of reserves, i.e. the non-profitable, low-priced export of whatever was available to sell. Due to the rapid changes in the environment (such as programmes for privatization), enterprise managers' time-horizons became shorter. This was probably one of the main reasons for the policy of 'exporting at any price in order to survive for a little longer' followed by a large number of enterprises. Enterprise profitability, already in bad shape after several years of austerity, quite obviously plummeted in this period. Inter-enterprise payment arrears were probably at their peak. And yet, there was no institutional mechanism or policy programme to break the chain of liquidity gaps in the period of export reorientation and price/trade liberalizations.

The Ministry of Finance fiercely opposed any enterprise bail-outs in 1991, arguing that the government would soften the budget constraint by offering bridging finance for the enterprises. Moreover, (consumer goods) inflation was at its peak and inflationary fears were, probably justifiably, high. It is also a defendable argument that the knowledge and financial know-how was simply not there to choose the right subjects and tools to help restructure enterprises; the troubled large Soviet export industries could clearly not be chosen and nobody had an idea of who to support as the future 'winners'.

Yet, retrospectively it might be useful to draw two lessons from the inaction of the Hungarian government.[5] One lesson is that the lack of enterprise bail-outs in 1991 probably cost more in terms of later loan consolidation, that is, the situation became worse by doing nothing. This does not, of course, mean that in *every* case inaction is worse than action; quite the contrary, in many situations the opposite is true. But in this particular case, some bail-out of enterprises could have prevented the more expensive actions banks had to take later. The other lesson is that the situation would have been significantly better if some large industrial enterprises had been put on sale in 1989 or 1990 when the interest in 'buying Hungarian' was immense. Obviously, there is a limit to what the government apparatus can do in a given time (and voucher sale and other quasi-privatization methods could not have saved the short-term troubles either), but in those two years there was a real chance to sell such large enterprises as Ikarus, Rába, etc., along with some major commercial banks.[6] However, there was a fear of 'selling the family silver' (when it was not silver but quite used aluminium) cheap to foreigners. Retrospectively, one can say that the Hungarian economy would be significantly better off had some of the large firms been privatized early on.

One has to remember, in order to maintain perspective, that none of the post-communist reformers reacted to the collapse of the CMEA any better than Hungary in 1991; arguably the contrary was the case in Czechoslovakia where the illusion about clearing mechanisms in their Soviet trade prevailed much longer than in Hungary. Nor did Polish economic policy makers react in time to this challenge.

The accumulating inter-enterprise indebtedness pressed the Hungarian government in 1991 to implement quite radical bankruptcy legislation to achieve a turn-about in the payment discipline of firms. The lack of proper policy coordination in the government, mentioned earlier, led to several unexpected phenomena in the economy. In 1992 the combined effect of three new regulations created a real shock in the Hungarian economy: the bankruptcy law, as well as the consequences of the accounting and banking laws, forced economic agents to reveal the true values of their financial assets and to face the consequences. It was a real 'shock therapy' the extent of which, as many argue, exceeded the micro-economic effects of the Polish stabilization programme in 1990. While this probably goes too far, it is true that the conservative Hungarian government showed a radicalism unprecedented in Eastern Europe in this regard.

With respect to the financial sector, the Hungarian government and the public lived under an illusion until this operation and even afterwards for some time. The big state banks showed large windfall profits in the early years of transition precisely because they were not yet forced to confront the true quality of their asset portfolios. The Ministry of Finance was happy because this was one of the important sources of revenue for the embattled state budget and in the press there were constant attacks on the overspending of the 'rich' banks while the nation was suffering. The overspending was true in the sense that, should the banks have lived according to their real financial situation, they could not have afforded the pace of expansion of their operations, the salaries they paid their employees and other benefits they handed out to their managers. In 1992 it came as a shock for the uninformed public (including, unfortunately, major parts of government) that the banks' profits had dried up altogether and their bail-outs became a major policy issue, unless one wanted to take the risk of allowing the large state-owned banks to go bankrupt.

How little the government sensed these problems is illustrated by an episode in early 1992 when the Minister of Finance wanted to force the banks to pay back the money they had received from the tax authority due to overpayment of profit tax during 1991. In early 1992 the Minister of Finance still believed that banks were in good shape and were only hiding their wealth from the fiscal authorities. In fact at that point, being faced with the new rules and provisions against doubtful assets, the government started many of its frequent programmes aimed at the long-term reform of banks. In many instances this has also involved large scale and costly state assistance.[7]

3 The impact of bankruptcy legislation on the economy and the banking system in Hungary

Vaclav Klaus, Prime Minister of the Czech Republic, often says publicly that there is no such thing in the course of reforms as sequencing different steps. While I appreciate the political function of such a statement, many people have taken it seriously as an analytical one. Yet, if we analyse the three countries' reform steps, very significant differences can be recognized regarding the timing of introducing bankruptcy legislation.

In what follows, I would like to investigate the following questions related to the sequencing of reform steps.

— Should the introduction of bankruptcy proceedings be postponed during reforms or should the government go ahead with it aggressively? Should it be preceded by the bulk of firm and bank privatization?
— Should transition-related rules be introduced at first or can one immediately establish 'normal' rules, characteristic of well-established market economies?
— Should the rules encourage financial restructuring of companies in trouble?
— Should the government force by regulation the initiation of bankruptcies or should it leave this to the agents of the economy?

In trying to answer these questions, I will rely primarily on the Hungarian experience. As mentioned earlier, Hungary adopted the toughest bankruptcy rules (together with accompanying banking and accounting legislation) in the whole region at the beginning of 1992. This goes against the popular perception of Hungary's transition being soft, or too gradualist as compared with the so-called shock therapy of Poland or the boldness of the Czech approach. The Hungarian bankruptcy legislation did two things which made it so radical. On the one hand it instituted the 'automatic trigger', i.e., enterprises which could not meet their payments to any of their creditors had to file for financial restructuring or for liquidation. This is a crucial point, because the Polish example tells us that in the absence of such measures the introduction of bankruptcy as a real option is very delayed.[8] The other thing was that the Hungarian law made it very difficult to reach an agreement between debtor and creditors by requiring unanimous consent of the creditors to the restructuring of the company's debt.[9]

From such tough bankruptcy legislation the policy makers expected radically increased financial discipline in the economy. They probably did achieve this (see Chapter 13), at least in the short run. Payment arrears decreased in real terms at that time. Of course, one has to ask whether this was the only way to achieve that. I think the answer is that some radical insolvency rules were badly needed to give credibility to the economic policy; in Poland the initial phase of the Balcerowicz programme had this credibility and it certainly resulted in shrinking payment arrears (in real terms, naturally). But even there this initial credibility bonus needed reinforcement; ultimately regulation of financial default and execution of the rules carried the weight of disciplining the companies. In Hungary there was no macroeconomic shock so the micro-economic reforms had to demonstrate credibility from the very outset. Also, the Hungarian business infrastructure was more mature to face such a shock than the Polish economic environment in 1992. And yet, as I will argue below, the harshness of the automatic trigger was probably too severe and caused too many enterprise failures for the system to handle. The domino effect of this harsh regulation was also an issue of clear concern.

One of the effects of the bankruptcy legislation was a huge wave of bankruptcy filings from April 1992 (the starting date for the real application of the law, see Table 6.1). The system (i.e., courts, judges, trustees, banks, etc.) was unable to meet the time requirements of the law; even now only about one-third of the announced liquidation cases (and one-tenth of the filed cases) have been finalized and an even smaller share of cases has led to real liquidation. Thus, the short-term increase in the credibility of the system is likely to erode over time. Also, other dysfunctions of the legal system, related to bankruptcy, such as slow and difficult execution of claims, have raised questions about the overall credibility of law enforcement in the economy.

A lack of policy coordination was also very visible in this issue; in spite of the courts' (most notably the largest Budapest commercial court) repeated appeal to invest in the technology and staffing of the court, the Ministry of Finance refused to do so. The size of the requested investment was incomparably lower than the losses caused by the delays and ineptness in the courts' processing of bankruptcy cases. This would have been a public investment with an unusually high rate of return. On the other hand, the weakness of the infrastructure strengthens Schaffer's argument (presented below in the Discussion[10]) that the reason for the low level of bankruptcy filings in post-communist economies is not necessarily caused by 'creditor passivity' (Mitchell, 1992) but in many cases partly by the creditors' rational calculation that the liquidation values of firms will be lower than what can be recovered without bankruptcy (Fan and Schaffer, 1993).

The broad picture is that in spite of the far too severe regulations of reorganization, at least half of the finalized cases actually ended successfully with agreement. Part of the explanation for this is, though, that the creditors were in a forced situation precisely because the expected liquidation values of firms were very low due to the poor legal and capital market infrastructure.

However, a large number of the agreements were too optimistic, and ended in liquidation after a few months. The good part of the bad news is that these applications were spread over a period of time and therefore were not too extreme a burden on the courts' and banks' capacities, current accounts, etc. However, this slowness highlights the problem of long liquidation procedures required. The commonsense argument is that liquidations always take a long time, even in countries with a well-established economic and legal infrastructure. However, I strongly feel that this is yet another field where the Eastern European countries unfortunately cannot afford the slowness of well-established market economies.[11] There are ways to accelerate the process, such as establishing aggressive success fees and connecting them not only to the sales price but also to the speed of the process.

From the very beginning the new bankruptcy rules were criticized on the grounds of being too harsh, too strict on the reorganization side and creating too many cases for the legal infrastructure. It was also felt that it followed German bankruptcy philosophy too much, while at least in the present phase of development, the US concept might be more applicable, even if it is very questionable in the American setting. A recent meeting of international experts with Ministry of Finance officials concluded that the requirement of unanimous consent was certainly counterproductive; and the processing of liquidations should be given even more aggressive incentives.[12] On the other hand, I would not have eliminated the automatic trigger; it would have been enough to establish minimum debt levels (in absolute terms and/or in relation to the debtor's capital base). Changes came very late, in the summer of 1993[13] and only did good in the elimination of unanimous consent. However, application for reorganization became unnecessarily complicated[14] and no additional incentives have been introduced in order to accelerate liquidations which lag behind tremendously, causing many delays and in fact abuses, too. Moreover, the complete elimination (rather than mitigating) of the automatic trigger probably gave wrong signals to businesses concerning the government's commitment to maintain financial discipline in the economy.

As said above, the shock effect of the set of new rules, especially the bankruptcy law, revealed in early 1992 the quality of the Hungarian banks' assets portfolios. The question is, then, whether a different sequencing and/or less tough measures would have made the banks' books brighter in the long run; and furthermore, whether the way the Hungarian government handled its large banks' problems was right, or whether it had any alternatives? First, one has to underline again the impact of macropolicies on the liquidity of enterprises and, consequently, on the banks' financial position. Here, I would differentiate between three groups of issues. First, one should look at the problem of labour relations within the policy mix used to fight inflation. Second, one should also take into account the different trade-offs between present and future inflation. And third, it is very important to keep in mind the importance of government expectations (especially in practising its supervisory role) towards the large banks.

As far as the first issue is concerned, let me point out that Hungarian economic policy makers did not recognize the central role of wages in inflationary processes. The voice of those who tried to impose more discipline on wages (such as those in the top management of the National Bank) was very weak. The government wanted to compensate for its lack of popularity by avoiding confrontation with the trade unions at the triangular negotiations about yearly wage increases. This is not to suggest that government policy was irresponsible towards wages; it just did not recognize the critical relevance of wages for short-term inflation, and more importantly in the present argument, for securing enough enterprise liquidity to survive the few critical years of trade reorientation.

The Czech example again shows that even more prudent wage policies would have been beneficial for the balance of payments, short-term inflation and the enterprises liquidity position. So it is an oversimplification to argue that Hungary just endured this hardship earlier.[15]

In the second category of macro issues, I would mention exchange rate policy and the government's general attitude towards banks and the enterprise sector. The government hesitated too long to give up the rigidity of its policy of real appreciations in 1992 and 1993. The rationale for the policy was that, on the one hand, institutional innovation improved the relative efficiency of the Hungarian economy and it made room for real appreciation. On the other hand, many economists have also argued that solving the liquidity problem through devaluations relieved enterprises of the burden of adjustment. While these arguments may be valid in the long term, I believe that policy makers need to recognize when it is best to temporarily abandon the principle of appreciating the domestic currency, because the (short-term) costs of maintaining it (either on the balance of payment side or on the enterprise insolvency side) are greater than the benefits to be gained from it (in the long run). The Hungarian National Bank's policies seemed to change in the right direction at the end of 1991, but then again devaluation lagged behind inflation. Moreover, the reaction to trade balance deterioration in 1992 was too late and too hesitant.

The changes in the government's attitude towards the banking sector were again very slow. Already in 1991 it was clear that the asset portfolio was in a bad shape and deteriorating. The Ministry of Finance still lived under the naive illusion that it was enough to squeeze the banks to make them continue delivering fat tax payments. The Ministry's attitude towards the enterprise sector was similar. While the conventional argument about industrial policy does not have much relevance for East Central Europe, I think it is valid to question whether the government should have done more to help the enterprises' trade reorientation with additional financing of credible programmes right after the CMEA crisis.[16] The exchange rate policy and bridging loans are examples of inflationary finances where, I believe, the short- and long-term inflationary impacts might well have clashed.

This leads to the third point to mention here, which is the unexplored opportunities (or duties) of banking supervision in a situation where the hard budget constraint is not fully achieved on an institutional level. In this kind of situation, the supervisory body has to force the banks to maintain prudent policies. In other words, the main role of banking supervision at this time should be to substitute for the lack of management control by the banks' owners. However, not only banking skills but also the government's ability to control the banks' activities were absent. Also, the supervisors of the banks have to be made personally responsible for imprudent banking practices, i.e. for failing to maintain the financial stability of the bank. In reality, the supervisory organization was not up to its job and coordination (again) between the Ministry of Finance and the State Banking Supervision was poor in the critical period of 1991—1993.

Was the government's management of the emergency situation, which followed the micro-economic shock in 1992, correct? In mid-1992 it was clear to people dealing with economic policy that something had to be done with the banks' balance sheets. I would step back and emphasize again that the crisis of 1992 could have been much smaller were some of the large banks already privatized in a credible way, i.e. to minimize the need for future state bail-out. The chance was present in 1989—1990 to privatize some of the large banks (even one bank would have been much better than none); and later, the chance was there to privatize at least the Foreign Trade Bank. Recapitalization of some of the others with the help of the EBRD and possibly IFC could also have helped if the government had been prepared to take this step. In fact in 1991 and 1992 and even in 1993 the government was very slow and overcautious in trying to develop a philosophy of bank privatization.

Despite the fact that there was no outright bank privatization (some privatization occurred mainly in the form of foreign investment, and in this respect the government's policy is to be admired), the loan consolidation action in 1992 could still have been much better. In fact, I believe this was the worst economic policy action of the Antall government. The government could not create a meaningful strategy during 1992 and at the end of that year it allowed itself to be blackmailed by the top managers of the large banks on the grounds of the urgency of cleaning the balance sheets if they wanted to privatize the banks in the foreseeable future.

The initial fallacy of this idea is that it was quite clear that the two largest banks could not be privatized without a more fundamental improvement in their balance sheets than the action allowed. The second problem was that the conditions for swapping debt for government bonds were made at very unfavourable terms for the banks. Although the immediate threat of negative capital adequacy was eliminated, the new assets would generate such a low rate of return that it might well depress the prices of the banks in case of privatization. Thirdly, as a consequence of this action, recovery of the poor quality assets was more doubtful than before since these were taken over by an organization (Hungarian Investment and Development Corporation) which had no practice in such an activity nor possessed a similar depth of information as the previous owners of the assets. Fourth, it was impossible to match the maturity structures of assets and liabilities, which made the bank quite vulnerable to future inflation. Fifth, and most importantly, the action did not reflect in any way the efforts of the bank managers themselves. Policy makers did nothing to eliminate the potentially huge moral hazard involved in relieving the bank managers of the responsibility for lending decisions, nor did it bring bank privatization any closer[17] (see Chapter 5).

The situation was somewhat similar at the 1993 recapitalization of the banks: its hasty preparation was not justified by any urgency related to privatization. Without that perspective, recapitalization will again ease the pressure on the banks themselves. Selectivity, focusing on those banks which can be privatized relatively quickly, is badly needed. Instead, the government has prepared a recapitalization package which does not solve anything, does not bring bank privatization closer and increases the moral hazard. By adopting the principle that each large state-owned bank would be recapitalized to the extent that their net risk-adjusted capital position would be zero, it sent a wrong message to the banking community: performance does not matter, on the contrary, it worsens one's chance to obtain state subsidy.

Another part of the 1993 recapitalization episode is that the Ministry of Finance is going to take over a 'golden share' of ownership from the State Holding Company and the recapitalization contract gives extensive rights to the Ministry to execute control over the banks. However, the Ministry does not possess the skills to control the functioning of the banks and by duplicating other organizations' overseeing functions clear responsibilities will be impossible to establish. In any case, politicization of state control over banks has intensified tremendously on the eve of the 1994 election. Therefore, one of the most immediate tasks of the new government after the election will be to reshape the country's banking policies and to establish order in the recent confusing situation.

To sum up, one's intuitive reading of the Hungarian lesson is this: the policies towards the enterprise sector as well as the bankruptcy regulation could have been somewhat softer (perhaps by helping out the enterprises selectively in 1991 and by adopting somewhat more lenient bankruptcy regulations in 1992) and macro policy makers could have taken better advantage of their opportunities during the transition years; furthermore, the government missed several good opportunities to privatize parts of the financial sector. In this respect a case-by-case approach to bank privatization still seems to be the most feasible one, now of course in somewhat worse conditions than if the process had started earlier.

I do not expect the bankruptcy regulation to have such an impact on the economy in the future as it did during 1992 and 1993. In this respect improvement of the courts' absorption capacity as well as developing more aggressive regulations to shorten liquidation proceedings is not yet complete. However, in the meantime, the macroeconomic situation has worsened markedly in many respects: the current account is in a deep deficit, national debt has increased significantly and inflation seems to be resurgent to some extent. Economic decline has stopped but growth perspectives at this point seem to be worse than in the Czech Republic and Poland. If the economic policy, including policies towards troubled enterprises and the banking sector, had been more consistent in the last three years, macroeconomic fundamentals would be more solid and the chances for sustained growth would be better now.

4   Have the Czechs and Poles fared better?

The question is whether Polish and Czech policies concerning troubled enterprises and bad loans in the financial sector offer better (combined) solutions than the Hungarian ones, and whether these policies can explain differentials in recent growth performance.

None of the three countries was able to take the necessary measures in time when the liquidity problem of the enterprise sector (due to the collapse of regional trade) appeared. Each of them was cutting enterprise subsidies (except agricultural ones) to minimal levels. Although in the former Czechoslovakia the level of subsidization was somewhat higher than in the other two countries, it did not serve any restructuring goal since it targeted structurally weak companies, for instance, in the steel industry. Similarly, none of the three countries pursued any industrial (in the sense of sectoral) policy ('picking the winners'). Regarding these issues, one cannot detect any significant difference between the three countries in the initial period. This is about to change in Poland and Hungary as more enterprise bail-outs happen in a case-by-case manner. In Hungary, 13 large enterprises were chosen in 1993 for financial restructuring, financed or guaranteed by the state. One can only say that in 1991 this action would have helped much more as its chain-effect would have been stronger than now. On the other hand, the election campaign has softened the government not only towards the banks but also towards the enterprise sector; a large-scale enterprise bail-out scheme is being hastily prepared.

Bankruptcy regulations were either not in place (Czechoslovakia) or not applied (Poland) until quite recently. Hungary is the first country in the region with a working bankruptcy regulation. Is this good or bad? The argument against it is that a regulation which sends one-third of the enterprises bankrupt is simply not feasible. The counter-argument is that in Poland and especially in Czechoslovakia no noticeable restructuring on the basis of insolvency occurred in the first four years of transition.

In Hungary the bankruptcy law forced the banks and companies to concentrate on solving the financial problems of their troubled partners. Creative solutions emerged which also fostered ownership changes through explicit or implicit debt-equity swaps. This kind of learning process is probably still in the future for Poland and the Czech Republic. In this respect, whether good or bad, we see a marked difference between Hungary and the rest of the region.

Does this have any consequence on the development of the banking sector and more broadly of the economy? We need to refer to the question of whether Hungarian insolvency regulations (and the banking law and new accounting rules) have simply brought the structural problems to the surface or whether they have deepened them through too much shock therapy and through generating chain reactions of insolvency among enterprises. In trying to answer these questions, of course, we face the additional problem of variables such as the impact of macropolicies on growth performance.

I think that by the time the Hungarian legislators adopted the bankruptcy law the country was already institutionally prepared to discipline the enterprise sector; and structurally the economy badly needed it. This does not automatically mean that in the other two countries the situation was the same; in fact, I believe that the Czech policy makers had good reason to choose to postpone the introduction of the law primarily because they started building a market economy much later and there is a limit to the changes an economy can absorb. On the other hand, it is also true that the Czechs, by adopting voucher-privatization as one of the key legitimizing factors of the government, created a vested interest in the stability of the enterprise sector which made them overcautious in their policy towards insolvent enterprises (Brom and Orenstein, 1993).

The bankruptcy law led to a deterioration of the quality of the assets of Hungarian banks, making it more difficult to privatize them. However, delaying the introduction of this law would have caused a loss in terms of credibility of market reforms.[18] It is too early to know if postponing the hardship has compromised the Polish and Czech reforms.

These two countries have taken roads which differ as much from each other as from the way Hungary handles its bad debt and enterprise insolvency problems. In Poland nothing really happened in this respect until early 1993.[19] In fact, after the heroically fast design and implementation of the Balcerowicz plan in 1989 and 1990, not many policy decisions related to micro-economic reform were made. The bulk of private sector growth occurred outside privatization; privatization itself was successful where it was decentralized, such as 'liquidation type privatization', a misleading name for MBO- or LBO-type mechanisms. So between 1990 and 1992 very little occurred, for various reasons, in terms of our interest.[20] However, at the end of 1992 the Polish parliament adopted a complex set of actions (called 'banking conciliation' in World Bank language) aimed at comprehensively handling technically insolvent yet potentially promising enterprises and accumulated bad debts in the banking sector. There are no clear data available to show the scale of bad banking assets; the Polish Ministry of Finance officials believe that recent economic growth has sufficiently eased the situation; also, they believe that the recapitalization of the banks in the beginning of 1993 was based on rather conservative estimates, i.e. the banks are slightly overcapitalized.

There are contradicting interpretations of the related issue of inter-enterprise arrears. As Schaffer points out in his discussion below, the scale of the problem is no larger in terms of relative size of overdue receivables than in established market economies. Other reports estimate the scale and dynamics of the problem (and of enterprise indebtedness generally towards the enterprise sector, banks, the tax authority and the social security fund) much more pessimistically. Unfortunately, the data of Fan and Schaffer (1993) mostly apply only until 1991. Nevertheless, their argument is convincing enough that one should not overreact on this issue.[21]

By omitting a description of the general legal framework of enterprise insolvency in Poland, it is important to concentrate here on the 'banking conciliation' framework which is so far the only complex policy action in Eastern Europe which aims to tackle the bad debt problem and enterprise insolvency in a comprehensive way. It grants the lead-banks of indebted firms the right to conduct financial restructuring of the firm, should the firm initiate it. In the first step the Ministry of Finance has recapitalized the state banks so that their risk-weighted capital adequacy reaches 12 per cent, that is, theoretically they became significantly overcapitalized. After that, for a limited period of time (until the end of March 1994), the banks can accomplish the restructuring of those state enterprises which have applied. For an agreement to be valid, the enterprises have to get the consent of 50 per cent plus one of the creditors and 50 per cent plus one of credits involved. Firms above a minimum level of indebtedness can apply. The Ministry of Finance supports the agreements by contributing a similar proportion of its overdue receivables to the other creditors. The banking conciliation law specifically permits debt-for-equity schemes as part of the agreements. Also, after the expiration of the March 1994 deadline, the lead-bank has to sell its overdue claims on the market (the affected banks have started to create the market infrastructure for those transactions) or to announce bankruptcy of the debtor (Groszek, 1993).

The promising thing about the Polish approach is that it considers all aspects of the problem. Purely for the benefit of other countries it is worth asking ourselves whether, as in Hungary, it would have been better to carry out the 'debtor consolidation' earlier, after the collapse of the CMEA. The answer is probably yes, but at that time the strategy was not ready in the Ministry of Finance. The political process (voting the banking conciliation law) took a long time in the confused politics of Poland, too.

Also, one can legitimately ask whether the Polish programme brings us any closer to bank privatization. It might, in the sense of making the banks more attractive because of a stronger capital base behind the asset portfolio; however, the World Bank scheme itself does not require subsequent bank privatization. Moreover, recent political changes might mean that bank privatization will be further delayed. Nor are the banks forced to be active on enterprise debt restructuring, although better capitalization makes actions here somewhat easier. The Ministry of Finance can (and does) exert a strong informal influence to get the banks more involved in the project. At the end of August 1993, 214 initiated cases were registered at the ten largest banks.[22] However, by the time of writing this paper, only a few sporadic cases have actually been finalized.

Again, the new government might, as many are afraid,[23] exert political pressure on creditors to be lenient towards the restructuring plans of debtor enterprises. This could cause a dangerous precedent and might result in an avalanche of restructuring applications that would be difficult to resist. The next logical long-term question is whether the banks will need frequent and regular financial assistance from the government since there is no pressure on them to improve their efficiency. To sum up, the Polish programme is a uniquely intelligent one in the recent history of Eastern European government loan consolidation programmes. However, the danger is still there that this will not be the last one as one cannot be sure that the recent government will pursue the same economic philosophy as its post-communist predecessors.

In both countries (Poland and the Czech Republic) privatization of the banks can help in inching towards less dependence of the banking industry on government support. The question here is whether the way the two countries have started privatizing their banks (by dispersing stock ownership) will lead to efficient management control in the foreseeable future. One gets the impression that in both places the policy makers might have to face another round of requests to help out their banks; in the Czech case probably, in Poland perhaps including the privatized banks as well.

The usual criticism of the Czech government's approach is that it has postponed micro-economic restructuring; I think this criticism would be less vocal if Czech 'success propaganda' were not so loud. But in itself, I think, the reform sequencing in this country has been reasonable. Also, the Czech Republic has an enviable inherited macroeconomic situation: low debt, low current deficit and healthy external balance. The only worry might be the structure of privatization. What seems to emerge is a situation where investment funds owned by the major commercial banks own a too high share of the economy. This, accompanied by the dispersed ownership of the banks themselves (and the 'real' introduction of bankruptcy proceedings from October 1993) raises some questions. Will not this cross-ownership (undoubtedly the strongest in regional comparison) lead to irresponsible lending practices which might threaten the health of the financial sector? What will prevent inexperienced banks (with presumably no effective management control) from lending extensively to firms which they also own in order to avoid enterprise failure?

It appears that clear answers to these questions are not yet formulated. The Czech economy has sufficient reserves to subsidize the financial sector further, if necessary; but if one wants to limit the additional financial burden on the state in years to come, more professional investors are needed to run the economy. As a recent article in *The Economist* suggests, after two loan consolidation/bank recapitalization actions in the Czech Republic, the government is preparing a third one since the bad loan problem has recurred very fast; this trend of too many bail-out operations is threatening (*The Economist*, 1993).

5   Summary

Systemic treatment of financially-troubled enterprises is one of the crucial issues of reforming previously planned economies. This is an issue where one can not rely entirely on established Western wisdom as philosophies of Western countries also differ from each other. What seems to emerge from the experiences of the 'fast-track' reform countries is this.

Whatever the ultimate goal of insolvency regulation should be,[24] it is certain that some kind of interim regulation is necessary because credible market reforms everywhere have to incorporate macroeconomic shocks, which lead to so many liquidity troubles that cannot be managed only by establishing long-term bankruptcy regulations. The task of the economic policy is to balance the extremely important general policy goal of establishing credible property rights, and the more immediate task of keeping hardship within politically manageable limits. The Hungarian bankruptcy regulation of 1992 was excessively severe, but it would be a mistake to make regulations that are not strong enough. Probably the right mixture for the transition economies is to create a creditor-friendly legislation which, however, is not made too extreme by such measures as excessive use of the automatic trigger. However, CIS countries in particular might need special government guidance over the initial phase of the process, since the legal and institutional infrastructure is far less developed there than in East Central Europe.

It would be overambitious to draw far-reaching lessons about loan consolidation issues on the basis of the episodes mentioned in this text. Certainly the tough Hungarian bankruptcy rules not only revealed the poor quality of the asset portfolios of the large commercial banks, but probably caused this to deteriorate further. This made it even more urgent for the Hungarian government to concentrate on the complex issues of banking reform. One should, unfortunately, conclude that this has been one of the weakest points of the Hungarian government's economic policy in the years of economic transition so far. The main reason for this failure is that the government had no clear goal for banking sector reform. Also, its treatment of the financial sector has been heavily overpoliticized.

So far, the performance of the other 'fast-track' reform countries has not been dramatically better in these fields either, although the jury is still out concerning the question of proper bankruptcy philosophy in the transition period. Banking reform will be a long process in each East Central European country, let alone the slower reformers.

Notes

1. I would like to express my gratitude to the discussants of the earlier version of this paper, especially to Christian Kirchner and Mark Schaffer. I have also benefitted from the comments of my colleague, Lado Gurgenidze. Obviously, all the remaining mistakes and shortcomings are my own responsibility.
2. It is a misunderstanding to believe that Czechoslovakia or Hungary did not have those imbalances at all. Czechoslovakia had them mainly in the form of acute shortages. Hungary also experienced some shortages, price regulation and, in particular, had accumulated a large amount of foreign debts.
3. This categorization is obviously rough; Estonia, for instance, might belong to the first category, Bulgaria's and Romania's performances are not nearly identical, etc.

4. This goes back even further and only for the sake of brevity I do not discuss earlier mistaken policy perceptions.

5. Let me again emphasize that nobody, including the author, had clear and right answers to the problem in time; events developed too quickly and our knowledge was limited.

6. A recent survey of the *Financial Times* mentions two examples: that of the chemical concern TVK which was approached by Eastman Kodak and the pharmaceutical company Richter Gedeon where Takeda of Japan would have been a buyer, both in 1990. The latter case illustrates particularly well that the collapse of CMEA caused a sharp depreciation in the values of Hungarian (generally Eastern European) companies. In the case of pharmaceuticals, Russia was the largest market; its collapse made the companies in that industry much less attractive. (See N. Denton, 'Utilities take up the torch', *Financial Times*, 17 November 1993, p.31.)

7. Again I want to emphasize that this paper does not discuss the regulation of banking failure. Especially, I avoid discussing the possibility of the bankruptcy of a large state-owned bank in an environment of highly concentrated financial markets. However, this does not mean that this issue is irrelevant in the present context. On the contrary, it deserves considerable attention — especially in countries where financial markets are less concentrated, like in Poland, Russia, or until very recently, in Bulgaria.

8. Again, this is not a normative but an analytical statement; at this point I would not dare to evaluate which policy is better.

9. This paper cannot provide a full description of the philosophy of the Hungarian bankruptcy law. A detailed analysis is given in Mizsei (1993).

10. The comments in the discussion of this chapter were made on a previous version of this paper presented at the international conference mentioned in the Introduction (Chapter 1).

11. Other examples, where Eastern Europeans are forced to be quicker than more fortunate states, are the introduction of VAT and the privatization of state-owned enterprises.

12. Even though the success fee is generally built into the system, it is worth noting that in environments of strong law enforcement and civil service traditions the costs of building in success fees can easily exceed the benefits. Such an example is probably Britain. In Hungary and, as a matter of fact, elsewhere in Eastern Europe the benefits, at least for the time being, strongly exceed the possible costs.

13. Yet another illustration of a lack of coordination and prioritization in Hungarian economic policy.

14. Even for accepting the application the agreement of two-thirds of the creditors is required.

15. In the whole range of issues of labour relations, I only considered the yearly wage bargain since it has the most immediate relevance to the issue we are discussing. But several other excessive burdens on the business sector could also be named; these have a lesser or more indirect impact on the enterprise balances.

16. Even though it is clear that the government is by and large unable to check the feasibility of restructuring programmes on the company level.

17. The government could have launched the privatization of the Budapest Bank by a more comprehensive assistance programme on account of the recent relatively better performance of that bank's management as well as quite lively international interest in investing in that bank. Helping out the two other large banks did not

bring their privatization any closer but it helped to lower their morale in trying to improve their own efficiency.

18. Nonetheless, as pointed out earlier, the actual law caused a short-term loss of GDP in Hungary which would have been more moderate with milder laws and more government investment in the courts. When the most obvious shortcomings of the law came to the surface the legislators should have reacted quickly; instead they waited about a year to adopt the necessary changes.

19. Actually the pre-war Polish legal situation was reinstated in 1989; however 'nothing happened' in the sense that the reinforcement of the legal regulation was not followed by a significant amount of bankruptcy filings. See Mizsei (1993) for more details about development of institutionalizing bankruptcy in Poland.

20. This in itself is not a normative statement; there are also arguments for doing nothing in terms of bailing out enterprises and banks. While I do not go that far, I would not swing the other way either by presuming that major government actions are always needed in case of large bad debt problems; this is the bias of World Bank analysts who are institutionally interested in large-scale actions.

21. Obviously, the nature of the problem is different with the bad banking assets; their accumulation to a level which threatens the stability of the financial system would be a situation where the government could not be neutral.

22. See Oddluzanie dla najlepszych, *Nowa Europa*, 23 November 1993.

23. See, for instance, Balicka (1993)

24. The author's views on what the ultimate shape of bankruptcy regulation should be are discussed in more detail in Mizsei (1993).

References

Balicka, M. (1993), 'Amnestia dla molochow', (in Polish), *Wprost*, 3 December.

Brom, K. and Orenstein, M. (1993), 'Restructuring and corporate governance in the Czech Republic', (mimeo).

The Economist (1993), 'A second spring', 13 November.

Fan, Q. and Schaffer, M.E. (1993), 'Government financial transfers and enterprise adjustments in Russia, with comparisons to Central and Eastern Europe', Working Paper No. 394, Centre for Economic Performance, London and The World Bank, Washington, D.C.

Groszek, M. (1993), 'Ogolna charakterystyka problemu "zlych" dlugow', (in Polish), (mimeo).

KOPINT (1993), 'Konjunktúrajelentés', (in Hungarian), No. 2, June 1993.

Mitchell, J. (1992), 'Creditor passivity and bankruptcy: implications for economic reform', (mimeo).

Mizsei, K.(1993), *Bankruptcy and the Post-Communist Economies of East Central Europe*, New York, Institute for EastWest Studies.

Mizsei, K. and Rostowski, J. (1993), 'Fiscal crisis during economic transition in East Central Europe: an overview', (mimeo).

Table 6.1   *Financial reorganizations and liquidations in Hungary since the introduction of new bankruptcy regulations*

	Financial restructuring			Liquidation			
	1992	1993 Q1	Total	1992	1993 Q1	Total	%
Filed	4231	372	4603	10062	2180	12242	100
Administrative end	1254	162	1416	4963	1026	5989	49
Announced	2500	295	2795	2227	591	2818	23
Finalized	1099	349	1404	562*	431	993	8
of which							
reorganization agreement	682	140	882				
liquidation initiated	417	165	582				

Source: KOPINT (1993), p. 160.
Note: * Four counties' data are missing, therefore incomplete.

Discussion
Christian Kirchner

Kálmán Mizsei's chapter is informative and analytical; it provides an excellent insight into the problems of institutional reform of Central and Eastern European countries. The chapter centres on one specific aspect of institutional reform: the relationship between the functioning of bankruptcy law on the one side and that of the banking system on the other side. It draws attention to the fact that bankruptcy procedures have a direct impact on the banking system. It stresses the point that reforms in bankruptcy law have to be accompanied by simultaneous reforms of the banking system, a fact which has been realized in these countries very late.

In order to comment on Mizsei's chapter it is necessary to clarify the functions of bankruptcy law in transition economies and to analyse the specific function of the banking system in the reform process. I must add that the discussion of Mizsei's chapter is a special pleasure for me because both of us have cooperated in some projects concerning the reform of bankruptcy law in Central and Eastern European countries. That does not mean, however, that I agree with everything which has been said in the chapter.

In order to clarify the functions of bankruptcy law in transition economies *vis-à-vis* its function in established market economies, one has to start with its functions in developed market economies. Here, bankruptcy law serves two particular purposes:

— selecting those business enterprises which should no longer participate in the market process;
— serving as a threat to existing business enterprises in order to force them to fulfil their obligations and to try to reorganize the enterprise in the event of pending illiquidity or overindebtedness (a disciplining function).

The first issue is connected with the functioning of markets and the reallocation of resources, insofar as the exit of bankrupt enterprises lowers market entry barriers for potential market entrants and sets free such resources which may be strategic for market entrance (for example, real estate).

The second function is necessary in order to curb the owners of business enterprises who otherwise would be inclined to lay the burden of reorganization on the shoulders of creditors without paying their own share. Furthermore, it leads to negotiated, rather than publicly enforced solutions.

There is a controversial discussion between experts of bankruptcy law about whether or not bankruptcy law should be used as an instrument for the reorganization of failing business enterprises. Under the influence of the American approach to bankruptcy (which is not very successful in practice) there is a strong — and growing — group of experts who stress that bankruptcy procedures must be arranged in a manner such that reorganization is not only a potential goal but also the rule rather than the exception. This position seems to be very attractive in transition economies because one may hope to use bankruptcy law for the restructuring process of the economy.

If one transfers the overall concept of bankruptcy law to transition economies one realizes that to leave the whole selection process for restructuring the economy to bankruptcy law may be very dangerous. This is because the failing of a business enterprise may indeed be caused by mismanagement and/or misallocation of economic resources, but on the other hand there are also several external factors, such as the breakdown of the CMEA-trade system (as mentioned by Mizsei) and the fact that these enterprises were formed in a non-market environment.

As far as the disciplining function of bankruptcy law is concerned there are hardly any differences between developed market economies and transition economies.

In the question of bankruptcy law as an instrument for reorganizing business enterprises, one has to be very careful even if one accepts this function. Introducing reorganization procedures as part of bankruptcy procedures may eventually lead to a weakening of the disciplining effect of bankruptcy law and may promote strategic behaviour on the part of managers of failing businesses. If they can expect to gain an advantage by putting pressure on creditors or just by delaying the whole procedure, they are disinclined to seek a settlement with the creditors (and owners) prior to the opening of bankruptcy proceedings. The second problem is rooted in the scarcity of resources which need to be employed if reorganization is part of bankruptcy procedures. In order to employ bankruptcy law for reorganization purposes in transition economies, it is necessary to have well-trained judges and lawyers.

The links between the banking system and bankruptcy law in developed market economies are characterized by *ex ante* safeguards to be employed by creditors, i.e. using collateral. On the grounds of the civil law procedures loans can be secured in different ways so that normally banks are affected by their debtors' failure only insofar as they have not been able to secure their loans. Furthermore, banks are normally forced by law to write off doubtful loans in a piecemeal manner, so that bankruptcies in normal cases (there are exceptions) do not totally disrupt their balance sheets. Under these circumstances, banks are mostly interested in bankruptcy law as a means of protecting their particular type of credit securitization against any threat of bankruptcy law.

In transition economies the situation of banks is totally different. Most loans are those from business transactions under the old economic and legal regime. This means that the creditworthiness of the debtor was not a major determinant. Securitization of loans was not possible since collateral was not available. If, with the introduction of bankruptcy law, the threat arises that a debtor may go bankrupt the bank is — according to the new legal provisions of accounting law — obliged to write off part of these debts, or perhaps to write them off totally. Thus the introduction of bankruptcy law has a direct impact on the banks' balance sheets (this has been accurately analysed in Mizsei's chapter). If banks are later privatized they may hope to be bailed out by the state, so the pressure put on debtors by banks may be mitigated substantially. Even under existing bankruptcy laws banks may not be interested in the disciplining effect of bankruptcy; on the contrary, if bankruptcy law introduces a so-called automatic trigger banks may prefer — in collusion with their debtors — to prevent this automatism.

Applying these deliberations to Mizsei's chapter the first impression — that he has provided a very informative and analytical insight into the link between the banking system and restructuring the economies of reform countries by means of bankruptcy law — is confirmed. But some critical remarks seem to be necessary. I have chosen six issues to highlight sensitive political decisions of legislation.

— The author stresses the importance of wage policy and dumped exports. This is a good point. But whether or not business enterprises can take this road depends on the disciplining effect of bankruptcy law. In the case of dumped exports which only bring short-term relief to an enterprise but which may lead to an excess of liabilities over assets (overindebtedness), bankruptcy law acts as a threat if overindebtedness is a criterion to start bankruptcy proceedings.

— When the author criticizes the harshness of Hungarian bankruptcy law and points to the automatic trigger, he should have included an analysis of how banks and their debtors are able to circumvent these legal provisions. When he criticizes the principle of unanimity which the former Hungarian bankruptcy law provided for reorganization decisions, he is totally right. I have stressed this problem several times in discussions with officials of the Hungarian Ministry of Finance.

— When Mizsei criticizes the lengthy bankruptcy proceedings in Central and Eastern European countries and the scarcity of human and technical resources, I am fully in accordance with him. In the Warsaw conference of spring 1993 both of us brought forward some proposals to mitigate these problems.

— When Mizsei draws links between bankruptcy law, the banking system and bank supervision, he makes a very fine point. Failures in bank supervision have led to many inefficiencies in handling the problems of defaulting debtors by banks. On the other hand, it should be mentioned in this context — which is done in the chapter under another aspect — that reforms of accounting law have forced banks to make their bad portfolios transparent; these accounting rules are in some way an alternative instrument *vis-à-vis* bank supervision. Whereas such an instrument is not very costly, bank supervision needs very valuable human resources.

— The author mentions the issue of bank recapitalization and discusses the positive response to the new Polish legislation. I am fully in accordance with him on this issue. But in order to avoid problems of moral hazard it might be prudent to distinguish between those bad credits handed out under the old economic and legal regime and those of the transition period when banks were able to take into account the creditworthiness of their customers.

— My last comment refers to Mizsei's critique of the banks' role in the Czech Republic and the problem of cross-ownership. Here he touches on one of the sensitive issues of the universal banking system. The implicit assumption of his arguments, that banks are more lenient towards their debtors under this system, is not supported by evidence in countries where banks are allowed to hold equity of business enterprises. I see a real danger in the potential advantages of banks to better secure their loans compared to those of other creditors. The legal instruments to deal with these dangers are to be found in developed market economies in bankruptcy law provisions and corporation law.

To sum up, the most important issue is the following: analysing the links between bankruptcy and the functioning of the banking system may lead to the promulgation of proper legal provisions to cope with these problems only if one accurately takes into account the feedback processes between the various legal fields at stake, namely bankruptcy law, accounting law, banking law, securitization of loans and corporation law.

Discussion

Mark E. Schaffer[1]

What is the purpose of the mechanism of bankruptcy, in general and in a transition country in particular? Mizsei's chapter, and Kirchner's comments above, suggest two possible answers. First, bankruptcy law can facilitate the restructuring or liquidation of troubled firms and the settlement of competing claims of creditors. Second, bankruptcy can impose 'financial discipline' on firms. In my comments on Mizsei's chapter I want to argue that in fact bankruptcy is mostly about the former role, and is not central in the second. Specifically, I want to suggest that a substantial degree of financial discipline can, and in the leading transition countries typically does, exist even in the absence of widespread bankruptcies. But before I do this a few remarks about the first role of bankruptcy are in order.

There are in general two possible outcomes to bankruptcy proceedings, depending on whether the firm that entered bankruptcy exits as a going concern or not. Under a properly functioning bankruptcy regime, the first outcome means an insolvent but viable firm can resume normal operations following a settlement of the competing claims of the firm's creditors, possibly after the firm adopts a restructuring plan. In the second outcome, the liquidation value of the firm is greater than its value as a going concern, and bankruptcy allows for the orderly dissolution of the firm and the disposal of its assets in favour of the creditors, followed (hopefully) by the redeployment of the assets via the market.

Why is this process so slow and bankruptcies so few in transition economies? Here I am mostly in agreement with the views expressed in Mizsei's chapter. There are few bankruptcy courts in transition economies, and little experience with bankruptcy law. Court proceedings are slow, costly, and the outcomes are uncertain. Mizsei notes that bankruptcy laws may be structured so that creditors find it difficult to come to an agreement; these difficulties may in turn be a deterrent to creditors to file. I may add that highly indebted firms may have a very low liquidation value, making it uneconomic for a creditor to try to recover his debt. Furthermore, if the indebted firm is state-owned, the best creditor strategy may be 'wait-and-see', since the government may end up injecting cash into the (potentially) bankrupt firm (say as part of privatization).

This brings me to the second oft-mentioned role for bankruptcy in transition countries, namely 'imposing financial discipline on firms'. In my view, the absence of financial discipline is not a reason for the rarity of bankruptcies in these countries. Indeed, I want to argue that one may have a reasonable degree of 'financial discipline' and yet have a 'weak' bankruptcy law and few or no bankruptcies. I will do this by looking at an example, namely 'inter-enterprise debt' and 'payment discipline'. It is often suggested that the large volumes of inter-enterprise debt in transition countries indicates a lack of financial discipline among (state-owned) firms; or, to use Kornai's terminology, that firms continue to have 'soft budget constraints'. But in my view this problem is at the very least greatly exaggerated for the leading transition countries: the available evidence suggests levels of inter-enterprise credit and payment discipline are actually quite reasonable.

To simplify the question a bit: how does a supplier in these countries react when a customer fails to pay for goods received? My reading of the enterprise-level evidence from these countries is that the usual outcome is that eventually the supplier figures out that the customer is not paying his bills and refuses to ship any more goods until the past debt is paid, or only if the customer will pay in advance, etc. Firms also learn to apply the lessons from these experiences to dealings with other firms, and for example start to ask for partial payment in advance. In this way firms learn to impose 'payment discipline' on each other.

The available aggregate data support this view (for more details, see Fan and Schaffer, 1993).

—   A convenient way of measuring the stock of inter-enterprise debt is to convert it into average payment times. I have calculated average payment times for the Hungarian and Polish enterprise sectors in the transition period. The figures are not very large — about 1.5 to 2 months in both cases.

—   Average payment times in both Hungary and Poland have apparently increased only slightly in the transition period: perhaps by one or two weeks between the end of 1989 and the end of 1991. Average payment times have subsequently levelled off and started falling in Poland (data are not available for Hungary). So non-payment does not seem to be a very large or widespread phenomenon.

—   These average payment times appear rather low by Western European standards, where the average payment period is in excess of two months (it is three months or more in France and Italy). Furthermore, it is standard business practice in Western Europe for firms to pay late. A survey of UK firms, for example, found that on average firms were paid one month late (that is, one month beyond the due date).

The key point here is that reasonable levels of 'payment discipline' emerged despite the apparent ineffectiveness of bankruptcy law, low numbers of bankruptcies, etc. More generally, in Fan and Schaffer (1993) we argue that in general the financial environment of firms in the leading transition countries is moderately 'hard'. Not only do firms learn to impose payment discipline on each other, but banks (eventually) learn not to extend new credits to firms that fail to service old ones. The main source of 'softness' in the financial environment of enterprises is the government (via subsidies and tax arrears), and here the scale of the problem, while serious, is limited. Troubled firms in these countries have typically downsized dramatically despite the absence of the practical threat of bankruptcy, for the simple reason that the limits on their budget constraints imposed by customers, suppliers, banks and government gave them no choice. These firms may at some point enter formal bankruptcy proceedings, but even if they do so with a substantial delay this does not mean that these firms have 'soft budget constraints'. As I noted earlier, if the liquidation value of these firms is low enough, it may simply be uneconomic for creditors to pursue the formal bankruptcy route. I will not go into the details of the empirical evidence here, except to suggest that if financial discipline were absent and budget constraints were soft, it would be difficult to explain why state-owned industrial firms in these countries would have shed so much labour (around 30 per cent for industry as a whole in the former Czechoslovakia, Hungary and Poland).

That is not to say that bankruptcy law has no role in the emergence of financial discipline: a firm is more likely to pay its bills if it is easy for the unpaid supplier to pursue its claims against the firm through the courts. But we should not necessarily be worried about financial discipline simply because we do not observe many bankruptcies. Indeed, the recent Hungarian experience with its reform of the bankruptcy law provides a warning of what can go wrong if policy makers try to artificially impose the bankruptcy penalty. I am more critical of the novel '90 day trigger for self-bankruptcy' clause in the Hungarian bankruptcy law than is Mizsei; in my view it was simply a costly mistake and made things worse rather than better, and the fact that this clause was recently removed suggests that Hungarian policy makers share this view.

Note

1.   I am grateful to the Austrian National Bank, Creditanstalt and the Centre for Economic Performance for support in making my participation in the conference possible. The Centre for Economic Performance is funded by the Economic and Social Research Council. Some of the comments made here (on an earlier, conference paper version of Chapter 14) were taken into account by Mizsei in producing his contribution to this volume.

References

Fan, Q. and Schaffer, M.E. (1993), 'Government financial transfers and enterprise adjustments in Russia, with comparisons to Central and Eastern Europe', Working Paper No. 394, Centre for Economic Performance, London, and The World Bank, Washington, D.C.

PART THREE

Financial Liberalization:
Lessons from Experience

7 Financial Liberalization in Central and Eastern Europe and its Impact on the Exchange Rate

György Sándor

1 Introduction[1]

By the end of 1993 Central and Eastern European countries (CEECs) had made significant progress in transforming their economies. An important element of the transition process was the reform of the financial system and the concomitant liberalization of financial transactions. Though the present state of financial liberalization differs across CEECs, a number of lessons can be drawn from the different experiences.

This chapter concentrates on the four leading reforming economies, the Czech Republic, Hungary, Poland and Slovakia. These countries have gone the furthest down the deregulation road. Therefore, their experiences are the most informative for studying the process of financial deregulation in CEECs. Nonetheless, most observations, in particular the conclusions, are relevant for other transition economies, as well.

The remaining part of the chapter is organized as follows. Section 2 summarizes domestic and foreign deregulation steps taken until now by CEECs. It also compares the experiences of CEECs to those of developed market economies. Section 3 investigates the conditions for and consequences of financial liberalization. Section 4 discusses the problem of setting the proper level of exchange rate that can be supported during economic transformation and the nature and extent of changes in the exchange rate that can be expected in the immediate future. This section also identifies the difficulties in measuring and comparing consumer prices across countries. Finally, Section 5 summarizes the conclusions.

2 The present state of financial liberalization in CEECs

Financial liberalization consists of the liberalization of domestic financial activities and foreign exchange transactions. The present extent of liberalization is very different in the domestic and foreign exchange activities in CEECs. While restrictions on domestic financial activities have been substantially removed, a large number of foreign exchange restrictions are still in force on capital account transactions, and both resident households' and non-residents' current account transactions.

2.1 Domestic liberalization

When investigating financial liberalization in CEECs, comparisons are frequently made with the experiences of those developed and developing countries that have recently undergone this process. However, the fact that domestic liberalization has been carried out relatively quickly and almost completely in CEECs has not been fully appreciated. Credit rationing systems were scrapped and interest rates were freed. The Czech Republic, Hungary, Poland and Slovakia are the most advanced in this regard.

One of the major reasons that made quick deregulation possible was probably the strong political commitment of the new administrations to a decisive dismantling of central planning. The system of central planning was the most rigid and restrictive in the financial sector. Consequently, the disadvantages of this system were the most visible there. This was true to such an extent that there was no political force in any of the CEECs under investigation that would have objected to domestic financial liberalization.

An additional important factor for the swift, smooth domestic deregulation was that policy makers recognized that, in an only partially deregulated environment, economic agents would be able to circumvent rules that were not abolished, a lesson policy makers in developed economies had had to learn previously (see Chapter 9 below).

Interest rate deregulation

Interest rates were widely deregulated at the early stages of liberalization, and by now there remains no restrictions on them. Interest rate liberalization was gradual and in some cases governments had to act to mitigate the adverse effects of their earlier decisions. Short-term deposit rates were deregulated first; long-term deposits last. Due to their political sensitiveness, mortgage rates were kept low for as long as possible. However, this asymmetry in policy caused serious trouble for savings banks because it became almost impossible for them to cover the costs of their funds from their incomes on mortgage loans. Savings banks are key institutions in CEEC banking systems and unfortunately this uneven policy had a long-term effect on their financial health.

In spite of the advanced level of liberalization, central banks still have considerable influence on interest rates, not only through their regulatory power, but also because they are the largest agents in a number of markets.

Central banks still set preferential interest rates for special segments of refinancing (see Estrin *et al.* 1992, pp. 793—794). Moreover, financial markets are rather underdeveloped and thin in CEEC countries. Therefore, central bank influence is overwhelming in these markets; interest rates offered or requested by central banks significantly influence the average interest rates (see, e.g., Kurcz, 1992, p. 41).

However, the Hungarian experience with the supportive discount rate for bills of exchange that was applied by the central bank to support the use of bills in payments shows the limits of central bank influence on monetary policy targets. Despite the lowered rediscount rate, commercial banks kept their discount rates on bills high by widening their margins.

Deregulated but fragmented financial markets

Due to the lack of certain wholesale markets and financial instruments, financial markets in CEECs are fragmented (see Király, 1992) and consequently provide very limited degrees of liquidity for financial investors. On the other hand, this gives central banks a larger than desirable degree of influence over these markets. Moreover, it makes monetary policies more vulnerable because in formulating policies, policy makers cannot rely on market signals (feedback) carried by rates determined in distortion-free or less distorted markets.

Another implication of the segmentation and underdevelopment of financial markets, especially foreign exchange markets, is the possibility for governments or central banks to run separate, independent interest rate and exchange rate policies. The development in the forms and sizes of the foreign exchange markets would require capital account liberalization. As we shall discuss later, this would in turn link domestic and foreign financial markets more closely, limiting the room for manoeuvering that governments can have in influencing domestic markets.

2.2 Foreign exchange regulations

The leading reforming countries (Czech Republic, Hungary, Poland and Slovakia) achieved relatively high levels of convertibility at an early stage of economic transformation (see Poret, 1992 and Oblath and Marer, 1992). Nonetheless, the convertibility of domestic currencies is limited to certain types of agents and transactions:

— *Foreign trade*: Trade is liberalized for resident businesses. Exporters must hand over their export earnings to the commercial banks but importers have free access to foreign currencies at the official rate.

— *Other current transactions*: Resident businesses have free access to the official foreign exchange market to obtain foreign currency for their service (transport, insurance, etc.) payments. Non-residents working for foreign-owned companies can exchange some of their earnings into foreign currencies. In Poland, resident households also have free access to foreign currencies at the official exchange rate for tourism. In the Czech Republic, Hungary and Slovakia there are yearly limits on the amount of foreign currency available to residents for travel.[2]

— *Foreign currency accounts*: Resident households are permitted to keep foreign currency denominated accounts in domestic banks, but they are not allowed to keep accounts abroad. Foreign businesses and households in these four countries are allowed to keep foreign currency accounts. Deposits and interest are freely withdrawable.

— *Direct investment*: Foreigners are allowed to invest without prior authorization, though some restrictions apply to certain industries. Profit, principal and capital gain can be repatriated without restriction. Outward direct investments are subject to restrictions but in the Czech Republic, Hungary and Slovakia permission is liberally given.

— *Portfolio investment*: Both portfolio investments abroad by domestic investors and portfolio investments by foreign investors are restricted in these countries.

— *Credits*: Foreign trade credits are subject to prior government authorization in all four countries. However, authorized banks and resident businesses in Hungary are allowed to issue corporate bonds abroad. Hungarian banks that have general authorization to carry out foreign exchange operations can borrow from abroad without prior permission for each individual transaction.

2.3   Similarities and differences to developed economies

As, for example, the discussions in Chapters 8 and 9 below indicate, CEEC experiences with financial deregulation show some similarities to those of developed economies. However, there are a number of important differences, mainly on the micro-economic level. Regulated services in developed economies were carried out by a number of well-established private banks seeking profit maximization. Moreover, there was a viable non-banking sector that was worthwhile financing, unlike in Central and Eastern Europe where the non-banking sector was inefficient and became bankrupt after losing government support and its eastern markets.[3] On the other hand, emerging private ventures in CEECs lack proper track records, making it very difficult for them to obtain bank finance.

Another important difference is that in developed market economies deregulation measures were forced by newly-emerging products and practices reflecting the needs of non-bank businesses, as well as by the ability of the banking sector to improve its competitiveness at home and abroad.[4] In the CEECs under investigation, deregulation was initiated by politically-motivated governments. Besides governments, only a small segment of the private sector and the most competitive state enterprises were ready to use and benefit from the more advanced financial services. The other banks and non-bank businesses were satisfied with the safety provided by the old system.

However, it was a false sense of security since the conditions for fierce competition from foreign banks and other financial instruments were already present, though muted by the long and severe recession. Another reason for the banks' reluctance was that they were overburdened with bad loans in their portfolios, partly inherited from central planning, partly accumulated after the decline in production and foreign trade. Unless these loans are dealt with, banks will remain seriously handicapped in competing with other financial institutions or foreign banks.[5]

In developed market economies, deregulation took place in an environment where most banking institutions already existed or were newly created by private banks and businesses. In the CEECs under investigation, however, almost all the necessary agents and institutions were absent at the beginning of the process. The only existing institution was the dominant monobank. Consequently, markets were highly distorted (monopolized).

Furthermore, the monopolistic structure was kept alive by government protection. A monopoly can be vulnerable even if its monopolistic position results from competition: after a while it will lack experience with competition. Therefore any major structural changes can easily wipe out such a firm from the market. The exposure to competition is even more deadly for banking monopolies in CEECs, since their monopoly was created by government restrictions in the first place. Naturally, this makes governments more reluctant to open up their banking system to foreign competition.

As of now, there is no sign of fierce competition among banks for market shares in CEECs. State-owned banks created from the monobank are busy transforming themselves from government agencies into real banks.[6] This exercise is exhaustive in itself. Moreover, any major restructuring is further hindered by the lack of capital, making these banks unfit to compete.

Financial liberalization is frequently accompanied by a relatively fast build-up of bad loans. To this extent, recent developments in CEECs are similar to those in developed market economies undergoing financial liberalization. The underlying processes are, however, markedly different in nature. While in the West competition for a market share and excess funds available fuelled lax credit practices, in CEECs the process was driven by inherited bad debts and the vested interest accompanying them, as well as by the lack of experience and sophistication in credit evaluation. Put differently, the major problem for CEECs at present is not credit expansion, as it was in most deregulating Western economies, but credit crunch.

As a result of deregulation in CEECs, real interest rates turned positive, lifting households' saving. On the other hand, this had an adverse effect on the corporate sector which was not ready to adjust from low (negative real) interest rates to market-determined ones. Moreover, the imperfect banking sector and distorted (or non-existent) financial markets were not very efficient in bringing down interest rates when demand for loanable funds declined. Besides the inefficiency of these markets, there were two additional reasons for the high loan rates. Due to the newly-introduced banking legislation, banks had to build up loan loss provisions, resulting in wide margins. On the other hand, high (and increasing) government deficits were consuming large parts of household savings, i.e., funds that otherwise would have been available for business finance.

2.4 Further expected developments of financial markets not resulting from liberalization

There are certain developments in the financial system that take time. Even after liberalization, one cannot expect agents' behaviour to change overnight. Similarly, after the legal establishment of institutions, it takes time for them to become fully functional.

A possible list of such existing (or planned), but not yet fully functioning institutions is as follows:

— Sizeable, liquid stock exchange.
— Sizeable, liquid money market, i.e., short-term credit market.
— Further steps towards (full) convertibility, i.e., lifting restrictions on keeping accounts abroad denominated in currencies of CEECs, and on transfers abroad. This would mean external convertibility for current transactions.
— Futures and options markets (for foreign exchange).
— Long-term credit market (bond market) that can convey the inflation expectations of the market. The necessary instruments are government bonds, but with a long enough maturity and wide enough market to make the market efficient and liquid. Furthermore, there is a need for a corporate bonds market making funds available for special investment needs when credit institutions are not appropriate creditors.
— Mortgage market.

3 Conditions and consequences of further foreign exchange liberalization

Historically, capital account convertibility is simply a consequence of foreign trade. Its original function was to make foreign trade financing cheaper. The experience of the early liberalizers shows that it removes the possible financial obstacles to economic growth. In the case of excess domestic demand for investment finance, it can provide the necessary additional supply. In the opposite case, when there is an excess supply of loanable funds in the domestic market, it can channel these funds abroad where they can be invested more efficiently. In general, capital account convertibility improves the efficiency of worldwide resource allocation. For CEECs, it could supply the additional funds needed to finance the transition. However, there are certain conditions and short-term adverse effects as well as political considerations that should be taken into account.

3.1 Price liberalization before convertibility

While there has always been a market for consumer goods, capital markets did not exist even in the most advanced centrally-planned economies. Levcik (1991) points out that de-etatization and de-monopolization can be seen as preconditions for avoiding dysfunctional or perverse supply responses on goods markets. The same is true for financial markets. However, there are a number of reasons why one cannot expect the same results from deregulation of financial markets. First of all, a major part of financial firms, in particular banks, will remain state-owned for a longer period, thus maintaining the highly monopolistic nature of the financial markets. The fact that the government remains the biggest borrower is an additional hindrance to the development of financial markets.

For the new economic environment the financial sector must provide new products, that is, financial innovation must enter Eastern European financial markets. Financial innovation, however, cannot be expected from markets where competition is hindered by highly concentrated ownership and other factors discussed below.

There is an additional reason on the demand side that slows down financial sector development. Customers, both corporate and household, lack the experience to evaluate risks and returns on financial transactions. Therefore, expectations are uncertain and volatile. Moreover, financial markets are dominated by the overwhelming influence of government, resulting in distorted and volatile prices.

3.2   Banks' portfolios

Banking systems in CEECs are burdened with a large amount of bad debt inherited from the old systems or accumulated during the subsequent deep and lengthy recession. As Chapter 13 points out, due to the vested interest in those companies that are currently indebted to the banks and the special ownership structures (some of these companies are minority shareholders of the banks), the banks cannot terminate loans to these virtually bankrupt companies. Therefore, they have to roll over these low-quality credits with relatively low rates. At the same time, new debtors are squeezed out of the credit market or have to pay extremely high interest rates to pay for the banks' losses on the above-mentioned loans. In trying to avoid paying for others' losses, good debtors turn to other markets for finance, leaving the banking system with the worst clients. This tendency is shown by the fact that companies with foreign — mainly multinational — owners were the first in the region to issue corporate bonds and commercial papers.

3.3   Stabilization

Although the connection between the sequencing of financial liberalization and stabilization is widely discussed, the literature usually concentrates on the role that financial liberalization can play in stabilization. However, there can be a reverse connection where stabilization can help to underpin the institutions of the financial system.

As pointed out above, the lingering inflation and recession-induced government budget deficit hinders the development of financial markets by absorbing large proportions of household savings, and thus diverting the banks' funds from other investment possibilities. This leaves the creditworthy borrowers with foreign borrowing as the only liquid source of funds. This tendency makes governments more cautious because of the already high level of foreign indebtedness characterizing most countries in the region. This explains why foreign exchange deregulation lags behind domestic liberalization. The large stock of household savings denominated in foreign currencies and kept in domestic bank accounts further increases government caution in attempting foreign exchange deregulation. These savings are a major part of the foreign exchange reserves that currently give these countries freedom in foreign trade liberalization and in maintaining their debtor positions.

There is another connection between the delay of capital account liberalization and the budget deficit. It is widely believed that high government budget deficits are responsible for the high real interest rates observed in CEECs. Budget deficits typically amount to 5 to 8 per cent of the GDP in these countries (with the exception only of the Czech Republic).

The role of the government deficit becomes more important during economic transformation. The transition process requires a massive amount of new investments to restructure large segments of the economy. The question is where to obtain the necessary finance. Although domestic saving has increased significantly, the government deficit absorbs much of this. Foreign finance, which is an alternative source, can have two forms: foreign debts and direct investments. Any increase in foreign debt is limited by the already high level of foreign indebtedness. Though foreign direct investment contributed significantly to the transition process, it cannot be expected to finance the whole process by itself.

3.4 Market structures and micro-economic changes

In CEECs, a specific precondition for convertibility is the responsiveness of demand and supply to price changes. For capital account transactions, price elasticity would be enhanced by wholesale markets that connect all possible market agents, bringing demand and supply together. However, the development of these markets lags behind other markets. Besides, as pointed out above, the government is still the overwhelmingly biggest agent in these markets. Governments own the biggest shares of equities and central banks handle the majority of foreign exchange transactions. As central banks will continue to manage foreign debts, the latter will not change for a long time. However, this should not deter the introduction of capital account convertibility. Market distortions should be addressed: government influence on banks must be limited to prudential regulation and supervision providing more security for the banking system, and government deficit should be decreased to a sustainable level. Due to the uncertainty surrounding the impact of deregulation steps, prudential regulation and banking supervision must be extremely cautious and flexible in following developments in financial markets.

Székely (1993) points out the importance of mortgage markets. The importance of the housing market makes it vital for CEECs to overcome the inherited difficulties in this regard. The way the mortgage market was regulated excluded other participants from retail banking. Usually, only one institution was entitled to provide subsidized mortgages that were financed by artificially low (stipulated) deposit rates on household deposits. To keep household funds available, other competitors were excluded by regulation. This monopoly was removed by liberalizing mortgage interest rates and deposit rates for household accounts. However, the monopolistic position of savings banks persisted because they were the only ones having a wide enough branch network to reach a large number of retail customers.

3.5 International financial environment

Since the international environment changed dramatically in the 1980s, liberalization cannot be carried out gradually over a long period. While early liberalizers in the 1960s and 1970s, such as Japan and Denmark, accomplished full financial liberalization in one and a half decades, in the 1980s it took Austria only about ten years. For others that joined even later, the transition period shortened significantly. Norway, Finland and Sweden had to carry out full liberalization in less than five years. Spain and Portugal, countries that kept capital control untouched until 1990, liberalized in under two years. Turkey did it in one stroke in 1989 (see Poret, 1992). This indicates that international financial markets led by early liberalizers have reached a size and level of flexibility and efficiency that makes any gradualist approach carry a great risk of evasion.

3.6 Capital account convertibility and the freedom of government

Capital controls have a crucial impact on the economic system of a country. With quantitative capital control, interest rates are determined domestically while, with free capital movements, domestic interest rates of a small country are determined by world interest rates (see Bacchetta, 1992).

Governments have greater freedom in influencing exchange rates when capital account transactions are limited in size (see Streissler, 1991). Since capital account convertibility presumably increases the size of these transactions, it limits governments' freedom in setting or influencing the exchange rate.

That is, capital account convertibility links the exchange rate policy of a country with its interest rate policy. Since these four CEECs are committed to fixed or crawling pegged exchange rate regimes, after this link is established the only way to influence exchange rates would be to use interest rates. However, it is politically difficult for governments to give up a major tool to boost the economy and decrease the cost of financing the budget.

The reason for maintaining these exchange rate regimes is that, being open economies relying heavily on foreign trade, it is advantageous to maintain relatively stable exchange rates *vis-à-vis* the currencies of major trading partners. This also plays a role in the anti-inflationary commitments. Floating exchange rate regimes increase the risks of import-led inflation through devaluation.

However, the recent experience of the French Franc shows the great dangers a country with capital account convertibility has to face. Although the French Franc appeared undervalued *vis-à-vis* the DM judged on the basis of usual indicators, France's macroeconomic conditions, its position in the business cycle and desperate need to lower interest rates raised the expectation of devaluation. However, without capital account convertibility, market agents with such expectations would not have had the necessary tools to attack the Franc and bet on their expectations.

3.7   Impact on economic growth and asset prices

Deregulation in Scandinavia, the UK and US provides clear evidence that, without a cautious approach by governments and central banks, financial deregulation may first cause unsustainedly high rates of economic growth and, later on, recession. This cycle may well be accompanied by parallel price movements and an undesired volatility in the liquidity of the banking system which is neutralized by asset price changes (see Fromlet, 1993). In Finland, for example as pointed out in Chapter 9, the earlier liberalization of capital exports could have helped to offset the influence of capital imports on asset prices and interest rates.

However, this does not seem to be a real danger for financial deregulation in CEECs. Though some countries have already liberalized certain parts of their capital imports, this has not led to a decline in interest rates and a concomitant increase in (real) assets' prices. Although foreign investors had opportunities for portfolio investment in CEECs, the underdevelopment of financial markets and consequent lack of a wide range of (derivative) financial instruments kept the risk attached to this type of investment high. Consequently, portfolio investment in the region has remained insignificant.

3.8   New markets and instruments as tools of sharing increased risks

The financial system has several vital roles in an economy. First, to channel savings to investments. Second, to convey market signals to economic agents, without which economic decisions can be distorted. More recently, the literature brought attention to a further role of the financial sector (see, e.g., Saint-Paul, 1992). Financial intermediation can decrease the risk attached to a greater division of labour, allowing firms to engage in more division of labour. This enables them to achieve higher productivity; and the same holds for foreign financial intermediation.

There are extensive studies available on the impact of foreign exchange futures markets on the behaviour of multinational firms. The results reported by Broll and Zlicha (1992) show that in the presence of efficient futures markets, exporting firms will choose their levels of output as if they were in a position of certainty.

In CEECs banks typically provide only short-term loans. Consequently, the proportion of short-term loans is increasing (at least in Hungary). One reason behind this is certainly the high risk of default on bank loans. However, the uncertainty surrounding future inflation and interest rates is also an important factor in this development. Banks and companies cannot protect themselves against interest rate risks due to the lack of the necessary instruments and markets.

There are some other conclusions to draw from the development of leasing markets in Eastern Europe. Domestic leasing markets are handicapped by the high level of domestic interest rates. This makes it easier for cross-border leasing companies to compete with domestic firms. However, a general problem that cross-border transactions have to face is the absence of credit information.

3.9   Liberalization and regulation

As deregulation proceeds, banking legislation and supervision need to be strengthened. Even countries with a long history of good banking supervision have to face new challenges as the BCCI story showed. Frauds in Poland and bank failures in Hungary surrounded by a suspicion of illegal actions show that CEECs have to pay extra attention to these problems. The lack of experience of regulators combined with the inherited legal structures and arrangements can cause unexpected delays in financial sector development.

4   Convertibility: but at what level of exchange rate?

CEEC governments would like to use the fixed exchange rate as a kind of nominal anchor for their economic policy. At the same time, they want to use the exchange rate as a policy tool to boost exports and curb imports. These two aims together point to an undervalued exchange rate. This is in line with the high indebtedness of these economies and the consequent need for foreign exchange to service foreign debts. However, it contradicts the financial needs of the transition that require net inflows that usually push up the exchange rate. An additional problem governments have to face is that, due to the distorted nature of goods and financial markets, it is very difficult to identify what is an undervalued exchange rate and what is not.

Vaclav Klaus, the then finance minister of Czechoslovakia, stated that the introduction of internal convertibility of the Koruna was based on a realistic exchange rate (see Klaus, 1991). However, this exchange rate still shows a deep undervaluation if compared to the purchasing power parity (PPP) of the Koruna. On the other hand, Klaus was right as the then established rate turned out to be defendable against market forces and expectations. This shows that there are legitimate reasons for a deviation from PPP rate.

4.1 Exchange rate and economic policy

Economic restructuring requires massive new investments, increasing the demand for loanable funds. With restrictions on capital account transactions in place, this increased demand leads to an increase in real interest rates for a relatively long period. On the other hand, the high marginal gains from the transition itself can support the higher rates. With capital account convertibility and highly flexible capital markets, however, rates higher than international ones cannot be sustained for longer periods, unless some government restrictions on certain elements (exchange, interest rate or banking regulation) are preserved.

The argument for the existence of high interest rates comes from studies of Japan, postwar Europe or, more recently, Korea. Meanwhile, international capital markets have become global and do not have this kind of disparities. The late-comers (such as Thailand and Malaysia) could not repeat the examples set by their earlier predecessors of government-led development. Worldwide financial markets, however, make high domestic interest rates unnecessary since additional external funds are available and thus there is no need to give extra incentives to domestic savers. Similarly, in the new, global financial environment it would be impossible for governments to maintain undervalued exchange rates for a longer period.

Some historical arguments can be raised for the use of PPP. After big exchange rate disturbances like world wars and following hyperinflationary periods, when exchange rates had to be set, PPP was always used as an anchor (Dornbusch, 1992, pp. 270—271). One can argue that transition economies are in a similar position to that after a war or hyperinflation.

The Hungarian Blue Ribbon Commission argues that, during the transition period, producers in the tradeable sector need some cost advantage (meaning undervaluation to PPP rate) in competing in the developed world (Oblath and Marer, 1992, p. 60). The argument is not developed further; however, it is obvious that the transitional cost advantage is needed to buy time during which those producers can improve their efficiency and competitiveness. This gradual improvement in efficiency makes it possible for the cost advantage (undervaluation) to diminish gradually, leading to a gradual movement of the exchange rate towards PPP.

The recent success of CEECs in attracting outward processing clearly shows that the lack of efficiency of manufacturing exporters of the region stems mainly from their weak management, high finance costs and lack of access to the competitive markets of suppliers. Though at present exchange rates CEEC wage producers pay around five to ten per cent of those prevailing in Western European countries, after the spectacular performance of 1991 and 1992, many countries in the region face difficulties in maintaining their competitiveness abroad and at home. This indicates that the present exchange rates provide very little room for any significant appreciation. Nonetheless, sizeable real appreciation has already taken place in the Czech Republic, Hungary and Poland, partly explaining the export difficulties these countries now experience.

4.2   The concept of PPP and the problem of measurement

The current method of measuring PPP gives the wrong impression that PPP is a useless concept. This is because PPP overestimates the value of the currency of an underdeveloped country and especially that of a formerly centrally-planned economy (CPE). This failure is due to the fact that the usual techniques used to calculate PPP are unable to properly account for the differences in the quality of goods and attached services (retail trade, warranty, etc.) across countries.

Technically, the PPP rate compares the stated prices of goods and services in different countries. The question is whether the stated prices or their averages represent the purchasing power of the currencies or not. In CPEs, this assumption does not hold. Shortages reduce consumers' ability to exchange money for goods. This decline in the level of 'moneyness' represents a deterioration in the purchasing power of the currency.

When prices are liberalized and become market clearing ones, associated with the removal of price subsidies, there are two parallel movements in the purchasing power of a currency. On the one hand, prices increase to compensate producers for the lost state subsidies. This increase is made possible by the elimination of the price regulation allowing prices to reach higher, market clearing levels. This represents a measurable decline in the purchasing power of the currency. On the other hand, the availability of goods improves rapidly. The Polish experience with price liberalization represents this impact very clearly: after decades of persistent shortages, shop shelves were filled with goods immediately after price liberalization. This change represents an improvement in the purchasing power of the currency. Unfortunately, this improvement can hardly be measured. Though surveys can estimate the amount of time saved by not having to search and queue for goods, this can only reflect part of the increase in the degree of 'moneyness' of the currency.

The underlying theory for many practical comparisons or studies of exchange rates relates to PPP theory, which has also been described as the 'inflation theory of exchange rates' (see Dornbusch, 1992). This theory implies that the exchange rates of currencies are related to the prices of the goods that can be purchased for them, i.e., to their PPP. The weak version of PPP theory is represented by

$$e = \theta P / P^*$$

where *theta* is a constant representing the given obstacles to trade (and exchange). An increase in the home price level relative to that abroad implies an equiproportionate depreciation of the home currency.

The assumption that *theta* is constant may be reasonable for developed economies where structural changes are slower and occur in a more synchronized way in the countries compared. However, for CEECs in transition to market economies where 'artificial' obstacles to trade and exchange are being torn down, it does not hold. This would mean that the more *theta* is changing the less devaluation is needed for balancing the domestic price changes.

Exchange restrictions and lack of developed money, capital and foreign exchange markets can be seen as obstacles to trade since they represent costs or opportunity costs as compared to other more developed regions of the world. Even if exporters to Hungary ask the usual price and payment conditions, it might be (and in fact it was) very expensive for Hungarian importers to get the foreign exchange needed for the imports ready in time. The same is true for exports. Western companies normally pay after a few months' delay. For Western producers with access to relatively inexpensive, short-term export credit facilities, this delay causes no serious problem. However, for Hungarian exporters without access to such finance, this results in a significant increase in costs, leading to a level of foreign trade below the optimal one.

The PPP theory is based on the assumption of a uniform price for each traded good across countries. If practical evidence shows that PPP theory does not hold, either there are factors that deviate exchange rates from PPP, or the 'one-price' assumption does not hold. In the latter case there should be a specific reason, such as trade (and other) restrictions that prevent prices from levelling out.

Due to exchange restrictions and the lack of a liquid foreign exchange market, the actual return of an investment in, for example, Hungarian Forint was always smaller than direct estimations indicated, based on interest rates and expected exchange rate changes. In calculating expected yields, one had to take into account the additional costs of currency exchange (black market) and different type of risks (high and volatile inflation, interest rate not reflecting the market-set equilibrium level).

4.3 Inflation

Although inflation occurs as prices change, at the same time the purchasing power of the currency increases as the monetization of the economy proceeds and more goods are sold for money instead of being centrally distributed. Moreover, (money) prices of goods reflect to an increasing extent the total costs of acquisition of a product. In the past, besides the official prices of goods, additional efforts and sometimes payments had to be made in order to acquire goods. Therefore, by simply taking average price changes, one does not take into account this change. Put differently, in spite of nominal price changes the amount of traded goods (that are standing against money in circulation) has increased dramatically, resulting in an increase in the purchasing power of the currency.

The monetization of an economy takes more time than expected. It has an impact on inflation and money demand. Even after an all-out price liberalization, there are several hidden price subsidies such as benefits in kind (free electricity, fares, natural gas or clothes) for employees of state (natural) monopolies and enterprises with still soft budget constraints. The elimination of these factors causes an equivalent price increase and an increase in money demand. Thus, if money supply did not keep pace with these, it would cause a deflationary, recessionary pressure on the economy: other prices would have to decrease. Consequently, money supply increases that accommodate these price increases do not represent inflation proper, since prices of other goods and services are left almost unaffected. The only impact on other prices comes from the substitution effect.

Similarly, any elimination of price subsidies, even if compensated in wages, does not necessarily represent an inflationary pressure. The increase in the money supply is matched by the increase in the value of goods. If pressures from wage increases can be tamed by tight monetary policy and improving efficiency, monetary equilibrium can be maintained.

5   Concluding remarks

Financial liberalization in CEECs has two phases. The first phase that has been accomplished by a number of countries involves domestic liberalization and the deregulation of current account transactions. The second phase consists mainly of the deregulation of capital account transactions. Although most countries are committed to the eventual liberalization of capital account transactions, none of the CEECs has made significant steps towards this end until now.

Governments in CEECs have several reasons for opting for a more gradual approach in this respect. First, the results of domestic liberalization are still controversial. Governments and central banks dominate the newly-created markets. Therefore, these markets, though they exist, are not functioning efficiently. Banks, which are the major agents, are burdened with bad loans, while other participants are not yet ready to explore the advantages of new instruments. The dominant role of central banks in the new financial markets has an adverse effect on the policies pursued by central banks. It makes it impossible for these markets to convey the appropriate signals to economic policy makers.

Second, governments are overburdened with foreign and domestic debts. This makes them overcautious about the undesired consequences of capital account liberalization. Third, governments are reluctant to give up their option to use both exchange rates and interest rates in influencing economic growth and the costs of financing public debt.

CEECs have no choice other than to continue the reforms leading to capital account convertibility. To accomplish economic transformation, they need the foreign capital that otherwise would not be available. Moreover, new global financial markets do not make it possible for countries to stop short of capital account transaction. Flexible products would provide ways to circumvent remaining restrictions.

Current account liberalization coincided with sizeable devaluation in all CEECs. The present levels of exchange rates seem to reflect the competitiveness of these economies, since they lead to sustainable balances of payment. There are arguments suggesting that, in the medium term, as the transition proceeds, real appreciation can be expected. This, however, depends upon whether structural changes will result in tangible improvements in efficiency and international competitiveness.

The standard methods for measuring changes in real exchange rates, or their relations to PPP rates, may very well be misleading due to difficulties in both cross-country and intertemporal price comparisons for CEECs.

Notes

1. I am grateful to István P. Székely for his comments and suggestions. Any opinions expressed are those of the author and not those of the Hungarian National Bank.
2. At the end of 1992, the limits were USD 250 in Czechoslovakia and USD 350 in Hungary, while in Poland, legally USD 2000 (per person per year) could be used for any other current transaction.
3. In this respect, the Finnish experience is rather similar. In Finland, manufacturing industries that relied mostly on Soviet markets got into a similar situation.
4. Chapters 8 and 9 provide excellent examples to support this point.
5. For a detailed discussion of this issue, see Chapter 5.
6. This is not meant to be a criticism, only an observation.

178   György Sándor

References

Bacchetta, P. (1992), 'Liberalization of capital movements and of the domestic financial system', *Economica* 59.

Broll, U. and Zlicha, I. (1992), 'Exchange rate uncertainty, futures markets and the multinational firm', *European Economic Review* 36.

Dornbusch, R. (1992), 'Purchasing Power Parity', in Dornbusch R. (ed.), *Exchange Rates and Inflation,* Cambridge, MA., London, MIT Press.

Estrin, S., Hare, P. and Surányi, M. (1992), 'Banking in transition: development and current problems in Hungary', *Soviet Studies* 44(5), 785—808.

Fromlet, H. (1993), 'Lesson for survival', *The Banker,* February.

Király, J. (1992), 'Pénzpiaci szegmensek — szegmentált irányítás', (in Hungarian), *Közgazdasági Szemle* 39(7—8).

Klaus, V. (1991), 'Price liberalization and currency convertibility: twenty days after', in Williamson, J. (ed.), *Currency Convertibility in Eastern Europe,* Washington, D.C., Institute for International Economics.

Kurcz, A. (1992), 'A tartalékráta fokozatosan csökken', (in Hungarian), (An interview with Sándor Czirják, Vice President of the NBH), *Figyelő,* 10 December.

Levcik, F. (1991), 'The place of convertibility in the transformation process', in Williamson, J. (ed.), *Currency Convertibility in Eastern Europe,* Washington, D.C., Institute for International Economics.

Oblath, G. and Marer, P. (1992), 'Forint convertibility', Policy Study No. 1, the Joint Hungarian International Blue Ribbon Commission, Hudson Institute.

Poret, P. (1992), 'Liberalizing exchange controls, a challenge for Central and Eastern Europe', *the OECD Observer* No. 178, October/November.

Saint-Paul, G. (1992), 'Technological choice, financial markets and economic developments', *European Economic Review* 36, 763—781.

Streissler, E.W. (1991), 'Árfolyamrandszerek, valutaunió és konvertibilitás — Magyarország lehetőségei', (in Hungarian), *Közgazdasági Szemle* 38(7—8).

Székely, I.P. (1993), 'Economic transformation and the reform of the financial system in Central and Eastern Europe', Discussion Paper Series No. 816, Centre for Economic Policy Research, London.

8 The Austrian Experience With Financial Liberalization

Heinz Glück

1 Introduction[1]

In 1931, in the wake of the Credit-Anstalt crisis, exchange controls were introduced in Austria. After World War II, very restrictive exchange controls had to be observed for some years in order to cover at least the basic import needs of the population and for the reconstruction of the country. Although some careful steps towards a more generous practice of authorizing foreign exchange transactions were soon undertaken, it took until 1962 to declare IMF Article VIII convertibility.

The 1970s brought the evolution of the hard currency policy, as it was termed later, and the struggle to make the close link between the Austrian Schilling (ATS) and the German Mark (DM) credible to exchange markets. In the 1980s, with the increasingly successful accomplishment of this task, it became possible to approach capital account convertibility. In doing so, Austria followed OECD guidelines and EC directives. Although Austria was not (and is not yet) a member of the EC, the Oesterreichische Nationalbank (OeNB) followed the community's liberalization programme closely as it fitted into the logic of the long-term evolution of its monetary and exchange rate policy. On the other hand, the banking sector had to be re-regulated to some extent after having experienced a very liberal period since the late 1970s.

By 4 November 1991, the OeNB abandoned the remaining few restrictions on capital transactions between Austria and the rest of the world. From that day on, the Austrian financial markets were fully liberalized after a period of 60 years of exchange controls.

In this chapter we will follow the evolution of Austrian currency from the disastrous economic situation after World War II to full convertibility, and the experience gained from this process; the development of the hard currency option; and, more recently, the approach towards joining the European Community, and the implications for financial deregulation.

Section 2 gives a short historical outline of this evolution, the accompanying gradual abolition of exchange controls, and the regulatory

179

reforms in Austria. Section 3 then turns to the experiences which were gained in the course of those years, and especially in the two years since the complete liberalization of financial transactions, and to possible lessons for the evolving financial markets in Eastern Europe. Section 4, finally, draws some conclusions.

2   A short history of Austria's exchange rate and monetary policy with special emphasis on financial liberalization[2]

2.1   Starting from zero

In April 1945, at the end of World War II, Austria disposed of virtually no foreign exchange reserves, and there was no other choice than to introduce strict capital controls. Consequently, the Foreign Exchange Law of 1946 forbade any exchange transaction unless it was explicitly allowed. For three years, exchange allocations were only available for the most essential goods and could only be obtained from the OeNB which was responsible for the execution of this law.

The exchange rate of the ATS to the US dollar (USD) was set at 10 ATS per USD by the Allied Military Government. In 1949, a two-tier exchange rate was introduced and later extended by a third tier, the tiers ranging then from 14.40 ATS per USD (the basic rate) in the case of goods, to 26 ATS (the premium rate) in the case of capital transactions, services and tourism. Forty per cent of export receipts had to be surrendered to the OeNB at the basic rate, whereas the remaining 60 per cent could be used for imports within 60 days or had to be sold to the OeNB at the premium rate.

The Foreign Exchange Law of 1946 was very strict, but it was also very flexible as it authorized the OeNB to liberalize certain kinds of transactions by simple notification if it appeared appropriate and possible. Of course, these notifications could also be withdrawn if liberalization conditions changed.

This opportunity to notify was first used in 1949, when it became the starting point for some first, very careful signs of liberalization of foreign exchange transactions, relating to a very few general authorizations for the import of specified goods. By the end of 1950, the basic exchange rate was dropped and the mixed rate of 21.36 ATS per USD was used for all imports and exports of goods while the premium rate continued to be used for services and capital transactions.

Again, three years later in 1953, the exchange rates were unified into one rate of 26 ATS per USD which was quite close to the black market rate of those days. At about the same time, in 1954, the first timid steps towards decentralization of foreign exchange transactions were taken by allowing banks to get involved. Further, the number of general authorizations was gradually increased. By this time, about 35 per cent of merchandise imports were generally liberalized.

In 1948 Austria became a member of the Organisation for European Economic Co-operation (OEEC), the International Monetary Fund (IWF), and the World Bank, thus participating in the Bretton Woods System. In 1950, it was a founding member of the European Payments Union (EPU) whose goal was the provision of facilities for multilateral settlement between its members. This purpose was achieved in late 1958 and the Austrian Schilling was declared externally convertible together with the other currencies of the EPU.

The following year, 1959, marked the beginning of an increasingly generous practice of exchange controls. The payments for all imports — merchandise as well as services — from countries that settled their transactions with Austria in freely convertible currencies were generally authorized. Also some first measures towards liberalization of capital transactions, for example, for the purchase of real estate and domestic securities by non-residents, were taken.

Finally, in August 1962, Austria achieved the so-called IMF convertibility according to Article VIII of the IMF Charter. Section 2 of this article states that 'no member shall, without the approval of the Fund, impose any restrictions on the making of payments and transfers for current international transactions'. However, a distinction was still made between current account convertibility and capital account convertibility, allowing members to restrict convertibility for capital transactions.

2.2 Reorientation

When the Bretton Woods System came to an end and the United States closed the gold window in August 1971, Austria had to reconsider the anchor for its exchange rate and monetary policy. The option of a free float was rejected because of the supposed uncertainties connected with it. It was widely believed that these uncertainties would permanently lower economic activity and make it more volatile. As a result, Austria was one of the first countries to monitor an effective exchange rate and to use it as an 'indicator' for policy which comprised in a weighted basket the currencies of nine important trading partners.[3]

The adoption of such a basket as an indicator for policy was based on Austria's National Bank Act which defines price stability as the primary task and responsibility of the Austrian National Bank. Article 3 of Paragraph 2 explicitly says that the Bank '... has to ensure with all the means at its disposal that the value of the Austrian currency is maintained with regard both to its domestic purchasing power and to its relationship with stable foreign currencies'.

Following the breakdown of the Bretton Woods Agreement this task was interpreted as requiring that the value of the ATS be stabilized relative to currencies with comparatively stable domestic prices, that is, currencies whose external value had been rising relative to other countries with higher inflation rates. This was expected to keep the rise of Austrian import prices relatively low.

In 1973, Austria unilaterally declared its adherence to the European snake. However, the observed depreciation of snake currencies against the DM implied, given attempts to stabilize the indicator, a concomitant weakening of the ATS against the DM, as long as the snake's fluctuation limits (plus or minus 2.25 per cent) were adhered to. This problem was resolved first by doubling the band acceptable to Austria and then by dropping the snake orientation altogether and pegging the ATS exclusively to the DM, letting exchange rates to other currencies float freely. Policy makers were convinced that an alternative exchange rate policy that focused on competitiveness or employment would not succeed because wage earners would react to devaluation-induced price increases and a 'vicious circle' would result.

Thus, three considerations were decisive for the development of the hard currency policy. First, price stability could be imported via the pass-through from the prices of imported goods to consumer prices or to the prices of production inputs. In some periods even real appreciations were accepted despite adverse effects on the current account. Second, appreciations caused a profit squeeze in the exposed sector that led to rationalization, innovation, rising productivity, and improved structure. This also prevented excessive wage increases. Third, by these mechanisms — a lower inflation rate as a precondition for income policy and a profit squeeze in the exposed sector limiting the possibilities for wage increases — some 'virtuous circle' effects were brought into play, validating the appreciated exchange rate in the longer run.

This reorientation brought the liberalization process to a transitory halt. The turbulence in the foreign exchange markets and rising domestic inflation led to the reintroduction of some restrictive measures. The authorization for non-residents to buy domestic securities, introduced in 1959, was suspended, as well as the right of residents to borrow abroad. ATS deposits by non-residents were only allowed to be augmented in relation to current transactions between Austria and the rest of the world. These restrictions were in force until the end of 1975.

2.3 Stabilization of expectations and the struggle for credibility

Issues of credibility and reputation and their benefits have been central to the transformation of exchange rate and monetary policy in Austria over the past 20 years.[4] In carrying out the hard currency policy it was soon recognized that by increasing liberalization and rising capital mobility the variability of exchange rates would grow and that this effect would influence the public's expectations about future exchange rates. Once a devaluation was effected — and reputation lost — these expectations would change. More volatile capital flows and movements in the interest rate differential could result. Policy makers came to the conclusion that an important role of the central bank was to stabilize the market participants' expectations by reducing, as much as possible, the uncertainties about the future exchange rate.

In the short term, this is done by limiting exchange rate fluctuations to an absolute minimum through the permanent presence of the OeNB in the foreign exchange market and by the adjustment of interest rates. Austrian exchange market intervention goes beyond the scope of conventional intervention. For example, it encompasses measures to coordinate the timing of the federal government's capital imports with intervention policy.

In the long run, however, stabilization of exchange rate expectations can only be achieved if underlying macroeconomic aggregates, or economic fundamentals, are also stabilized. Thus, economic policy had to be coordinated with the anchor country if the feasibility of the hard currency option was to become and remain credible. In this respect, successful policy coordination was a precondition for credibility and ongoing liberalization.

In the beginning, the hard currency policy was not widely perceived to be feasible.[5] The measures taken in 1974 (revaluation of the ATS after a steep increase of inflation in the wake of the first oil-price shock) were followed by a massive deterioration of the current account deficit which reached 4.4 per cent of GDP in 1977. The strategy became increasingly criticized and confidence that it could be maintained was low. Industry opposed this policy and favoured a real exchange rate rule instead of pegging to the DM.

In this period, however, the central bank did not leave any doubt that it would maintain its exchange rate objectives, and if necessary, intervene and adjust the interest rate differential to whatever level required. Key policy makers had come to the conclusion that it was the economy which had to adjust to the exchange rate and not the other way round. A deviation from the course would leave central bank, budget, and unions worse off.

Later, in October 1978, in order to placate critics of the policy, a realignment in the snake was handled in such a way that the ATS lost about 1 per cent against the DM. Obviously, this change was inconsistent, so that credibility and reputation were damaged.

In 1979, however, when oil prices rose quickly in the wake of the Iranian revolution, the idea of appreciating the nominal exchange rate to keep inflationary pressures low was again discussed. In September of that year the ATS was revalued against the DM by 1.5 per cent, followed by gradual appreciations until in late 1981 it amounted finally to 4.5 per cent. Since then, the ATS/DM relation has remained nearly constant.

Subsequently, credibility and also reputation were rebuilt. Official and press statements increasingly supported this option and the public attached increasingly high probability to the consistent pursuit of the announced policy. Thus, Austria was enabled to borrow an anti-inflationary reputation from the Bundesbank by credibly fixing the exchange rate to the DM. Maintaining credibility and reputation became a precondition for further liberalization in the following years.

2.4 Monetary policy

The development of the hard currency policy required alterations of monetary policy. Generally speaking, the room for manoeuvre for monetary policy was reduced and subordinated under the exchange rate target.

From the breakdown of Bretton Woods until 1979, monetary policy tried to keep nominal long-term interest rates stable while pursuing the exchange rate objective for the indicator. The domestic interest rate level, it was believed, should be protected as far as possible from exogenous influences in order to stabilize it as a cost factor. No balance of payments problems were expected to result because of the still prevailing foreign exchange restrictions, market segmentation and investors' preferences.

This interest rate component of policy was maintained until 1979, when it could no longer be defended against a sharp rise in international interest rates. After one-third of Austria's international reserves was lost, interest rate policy was redesigned from its domestic orientation towards an instrument supporting the exchange rate target. This change also reflected the view that the weakening of financial market segmentation due to liberalization and globalization of world capital markets meant that domestic interest rates would have to become more closely linked to international interest rates. In Austria's case, given the exchange rate regime, this link was with Germany, so the differential between Austrian and German rates became a target for the exchange rate policy. The short-term interest rate especially is to be considered as an intermediate target controlled by means of direct interest rate policy, such as key interest rates and open market interest rates, or liquidity policy measures like the use of the domestic or foreign source components of money supply creation.

2.5 Temporary deliberalization and further steps

As a consequence of the above-mentioned deterioration of the current account and the reduction of foreign exchange reserves in the mid-1970s, a ceiling on the growth of consumer credits had to be imposed in 1977 which remained in force for some years. For the same reason, the authorizations for capital exports had to be handled in a more restrictive manner. In particular, the growth in the volume of foreign exchange loans to non-residents was restricted. However, in July 1981 further liberalization steps could be taken, relating to the purchase of domestic securities, domestic real estate, and shares in domestic companies.

2.6 A new Banking Act

In 1979 a new Banking Act was passed which was intended to provide the legal basis for a more competitive era in this sector. The previous act which was in force since 1939 had been very restrictive with regard to the establishment of new branches, the scope of activities allowed for the banks, and the interest rates on deposits. In the context of this chapter, the main goal of the new act was the principle of non-intervention in the free disposition of the banking sector; only general rules to guarantee the realization of economic and monetary policy goals in the interest of stability and a distortion-free economic development should be imposed. Thus, since 1979 all banks were allowed to operate as universal banks; domestic banks could establish branches freely and interest controls were removed (with some exceptions).

However, it turned out that the freedoms granted by this act produced undesired results. Thus, relatively soon after the act came into force a discussion on its amendment started, since balance sheet growth regularly exceeded growth in capital resources. This was prompted by the desire to ensure public trust in the banks, to reduce competition via balance sheet growth and excessive expansion of the number of branches, to strengthen profitability and to reduce costs. The rising risk exposure of banks as well as shrinking margins of the Austrian banks led to a fundamental reorientation of the banking law as authorities obviously were not willing to accept the potential damage — also for the credibility of the exchange rate policy — of a larger bank going bankrupt. In the light of increasing international integration and competition the risk-bearing capacity of the system needed to be improved.

For this purpose, a regulatory system had to be created which would oblige and enable the supervisory authority to intervene promptly in case of difficulties. The Amendment of 1986 introduced capital adequacy requirements and established two classes of liquidity to be observed by the banks and examined by the Ministry of Finance in its capacity as supervisor. The most important innovations in the amendment were:

— the obligation to hold liable capital in certain relations to assets;
— upper limits on large credits, large investments, and foreign exchange exposure;
— new liquidity rules;
— enlarged reporting requirements to OeNB and Ministry of Finance;
— the obligation to establish internal control systems.

2.7   The last steps

From the mid-1980s the remaining restrictions on capital flows were reduced stepwise. This happened almost simultaneously with the liberalization of capital markets in the EC. There, instead of ideas dating back to Keynes which emphasize the threat of speculation and the possible appearance of bubbles or chaotic price developments in the financial markets which might impede investments and foreign trade, neoclassic arguments had gained ground, stressing the efficiency of deregulated financial markets. Although there may be some doubts about the assumptions which underlie this theory (atomistic markets, rational expectations, symmetric information), it became dominant in the EC[6], striving for 'the four freedoms' and was also regarded as relevant in Austria.

On 1 November 1986, a large number of liberalization measures were put into effect in Austria. Among others:

— the limit on domestic notes and coins which residents were allowed to take with them for travelling purposes was raised from 15,000 to 50,000 ATS per head and trip;
— the limit on foreign exchange which residents were allowed to buy for travel purposes from authorized banks was also raised to 50,000 ATS per trip. In cases of need for larger amounts the additional sum had to be authorized by the OeNB;
— the use of credit cards was allowed for the purchase of goods to be imported for personal use;
— the permission for the purchase of securities quoted on foreign official securities markets was extended to cover all securities quoted on a recognized securities exchange.

The emphasis of the next step which was set on 1 February 1989, was on long-term capital movements. Thus, the number of reservations *vis-à-vis* the

OECD Code for Liberalization of Capital Movements was reduced from 12 to four. Also from this date, almost all transactions conducted by banks for their own account were liberalized.

From 1 January 1990, the exchange control philosophy of the postwar period was changed completely. From this point in time, everything was allowed that was not explicitly forbidden. All transactions were permitted if they were done through Austrian banks. Only the holding of accounts abroad and related transactions, the issuing of securities by domestic borrowers abroad and by non-residents in Austria, and loans raised by domestic non-banks from non-residents were still subject to individual authorization. Foreign securities could only be purchased via Austrian banks and had to be deposited there.

On 4 November 1991, the OeNB took the final step in abolishing exchange controls. All impediments to the free movement of capital, as far as they were under the influence of the OeNB, were abandoned. The Foreign Exchange Law of 1946 remained in force but the OeNB granted a general licence to carry out all transactions covered by the regulations of the Law.

This general licence, however, was issued on condition that broadened reporting requirements were observed. Obviously, the withdrawal from exchange controls also reduced the OeNB's access to data on capital transactions. But there was still the necessity to compile a reliable balance of payments and to report these data to international organizations (e.g., the IMF). For this purpose, reporting requirements had to be extended: banks, businesses, and private households became obliged to report their capital transactions to the OeNB, as soon as they surpassed certain thresholds. In order to fulfil this task, the OeNB implemented a new data collection and presentation scheme at the same time as full liberalization came into force.

With these steps now performed, Austria belongs in the group of the most liberal countries concerning capital movements. There remain only two reservations under the OECD Capital Movements Code, reflecting restrictions concerning inward direct investment and real estate purchase by non-residents, a topic to be discussed also in the EC negotiations.

3   Experiences and possible lessons

What are the experiences to be gained from almost 50 years of development of the Austrian Schilling from the end of World War II to full convertibility, and especially from the two years since all foreign exchange transactions were liberalized? After some general considerations, the following sections deal with the consequences for the conduct of monetary policy, for the banking sector, and for the capital market.

3.1   Some general remarks

It seems important to emphasize that the relatively frictionless Austrian way towards convertibility and liberalization was a slow and careful one. While the authorities scrupulously calculated possible risks, banks, enterprises, and finally the general public were gradually given the opportunity to become accustomed to new freedoms and the dangers involved in them. Over the full period, the very strict Foreign Exchange Law was in force, but the authorities generally followed an increasingly generous practice of authorizing capital transactions. Within this framework, the economic agents could develop their activities, but the threat that the authorities might in case of need change their liberal attitude always remained. So it was rational for the public not to overextend the given room for manoeuvre.

Further, no contradictions and inconsistencies arose between the liberalization process and monetary and exchange rate policy. Thus, '... Austria managed to avoid any forced retreats that would have devastated the credibility of the process' (Schubert, 1992, p. 9).

Since practically any foreign exchange transaction was de facto allowed for Austrian residents since January 1990 — or, as an EFTA-study puts it: the improved capital allocation had already taken place[7] — no capital movements larger than normal were expected after 4 November 1991.

In fact, no capital outflow such as might have been feared was observed immediately after this day; on the contrary, there was an inflow of ATS 1.5 bn on the first day and even more on the second day immediately after full liberalization. Throughout November 1991, the reserves remained virtually unchanged. The development of the capital account over the last few years (see Table 8.1) shows a marked intensification of capital movements after 1991 (EFTA, 1989, p. 50) with a relatively high net inflow in 1992; the first half of 1993 reveals a tendency towards equilibrium under persistently high transactions volumes.

Thus, the process of liberalization seems to have been completed successfully. On 15 September 1993, Austria's foreign reserves amounted to ATS 139 bn, about 28 per cent higher than on 31 October 1991. The number of accounts of Austrians held abroad — one of the last items to be liberalized — remained relatively modest; the desire to hold such accounts does not seem to have been very strong. There are, of course, some problems left which will be taken up in the next sections.

The Austrian case seems to be an example of a successful gradual approach to the liberalization of financial markets. Generally speaking, financial deregulation means new market conditions with sometimes unpredictable consequences, and market participants need time to adapt to deregulation. It is, of course, frequently questioned whether such an approach is still viable in the 1990s with worldwide highly mobile capital and considerable sophistication to circumvent any kind of restriction. This points to the difficult question of sequencing which, however, cannot be dealt with here in detail. Generally, a useful approach might be to start liberalizing payments for foreign trade sufficiently to avoid impeding external trade. In the long term, it would be advisable to keep an especially careful eye on the banks; the private sector will need to be taken care of only when there is a savings volume of some weight. The further course of events will depend on the speed of the development of financial markets themselves.

3.2 Monetary policy with completely liberalized capital transactions

It is a commonplace that the increasing integration of financial markets has made them more efficient, but also more volatile. Through the liberalization process described above the Austrian Schilling also has become exposed to this environment.

The most obvious consequence for the conduct of monetary policy is that the principle of stabilizing expectations by credible control over the fundamental data has gained considerable additional weight, i.e., the need for even more discipline in macroeconomic policy has become evident. Interest rate policy plays an increasing role as a means to support the exchange rate target. The need for the flexibility of instruments has increased, and also the task of prudential supervision has become more important.

In interest rate policy the room for autonomous action is even more restricted. Thus, market mechanisms have to be increasingly relied upon to level out disturbances. If there were, for instance, undesired short-term capital movements caused by interest rate differentials — which might easily happen between ATS and DM assets because of the almost non-existing exchange rate risk — the OeNB would not run counter to interest rate reactions. On the other hand, the OeNB is still in a position to influence the structure of money supply with regard to its domestic and foreign sources. This is done, among other ways, by the above-mentioned coordination of volume and timing of capital transactions related to the federal budget.

In a situation of reserve losses it is therefore appropriate for the central bank to strengthen the foreign component of money supply by tolerating the changes of domestic interest rates and not sterilizing these effects via the domestic component. This should induce capital transactions compensating for the initial ones.

These considerations, of course, apply to so-called normal business. In the case of speculation and exogenous shocks to the financial markets the problem is more difficult, but stable expectations and convergence of fundamentals should prevent such a case.

There have been important innovations relating to the flexibility of instruments. In 1985, short-term open market operations in the form of pensions were introduced in order to fine-tune the money market. This instrument permits very rapid influence on liquidity and interest rates. Further, the use of swap transactions has been intensified since the end of 1986. Then in 1987, futures transactions in DM were offered to the banks. Since 1988, a special open market window has been installed.

Recently, a minor problem came up in that after liberalization foreign exchange deposits are not subject to reserve requirements. These deposits showed substantial growth (from ATS 20.0 bn at the end of 1988 to ATS 126.4 bn in July 1993) as banks discovered them as a way to circumvent minimum reserves. An attempt will be made to solve this problem via a gentlemen's agreement between OeNB and commercial banks.

A related problem can be seen in the increasing cross-border deposits after liberalization. Deposits of this kind make monetary aggregates less precise. In the Austrian case, however, monetary aggregates do not play an essential role for monetary policy, and reports from banks indicate that the extent to which ATS accounts are held abroad is not very large. In countries with other types of monetary policies this problem might, of course, be more severe.

To sum up, destabilizing effects from liberalized financial transactions can be avoided, or at least reduced, if:

— a credible and long-term oriented intermediate goal of monetary policy exists;
— this policy is credibly coordinated internationally;
— sudden changes of policy which may not be consistent with expectations are avoided;
— domestic financial markets exhibit international standards concerning quality and efficiency (Pech, 1993, p. 7f).

3.3   The banking sector

In contrast to the liberalization of financial transactions, a further need for some regulative measures in the banking sector was felt, as liberalization and integration increased the pressure for structural adjustment. This structure is still characterized by a large number of small banks, a smaller number of medium to large banks by Austrian standards, and the absence of banks of international scale. There is still overbanking, though in 1993 a slight shrinking of the number of branches will be observed, mainly caused by the closing-down of branches through the merged institutes

Länderbank and Zentralsparkasse. Further, there is still the fact that a strict distinction and division between the various sectors is maintained making cooperation between them difficult, though almost all of them are offering universal banking services. Three of these sectors, the savings banks, the rural credit cooperatives (Raiffeisen), and the industrial credit cooperatives (Volksbanken) are constructed as multi-tier systems existing together and each of them often maintaining branches in small villages.

Although banks generally fulfil liable capital ratios stricter than the Basle prescriptions and are sound from this point of view, it will be necessary to create larger and (which is not necessarily the same) more efficient unities to cope better with international competition in a world of free capital movements. The important point is to ensure that such mergers really result in rationalization and cost-reducing organizational changes.

Some smaller and one big merger have already taken place, the latter, as mentioned, bringing together Österreichische Länderbank and Zentral-sparkasse und Kommerzialbank Wien as Bank Austria. This fuelled another change when Girozentrale, the wholesale bank of the savings banks, bought Österreichisches Credit-Institut from Bank Austria to form GiroCredit. Further talks are taking place concerning the reorganization and rationalization of the savings bank sector; the idea is to create a strong ownership structure in the form of a holding to perform this task.

To make banks more robust and to pave their way into the EC, a completely new Banking Act has been designed which is to be put into effect in 1994. In general its character will be of a re-regulating kind and will, among others functions:

— incorporate into Austrian law the EC capital ratio requirements, putting into effect the Basle minimum ratios of 4 per cent core capital and 4 per cent supplementary capital;
— endorse the relevant EC legislation such as the Banking Law Coordination Directives, the Share Capital and Reserves and the Solvency Directive as well as the Balance Sheet Directive;
— establish the 'single passport' principle not only when Austria joins the EC, but more immediately under the planned European Economic Area (EEA);
— incorporate the EC Money Laundering Directive;
— improve the norms for supervision;
— provide more security by further developing internal control.

3.4 The capital market

A well-functioning capital market is essential for the smooth working of exchange rate policy even under conditions of liberalized financial transactions. The advantages of fully liberalized capital movements can only be exploited and potential negative effects on exchange rate and monetary policy avoided if domestic capital markets match international standards.

In Austria, there seems to be considerable room for further development in this respect. Though the volume of the Austrian capital markets has been increasing quickly and many innovations have been undertaken over the last few years, the bond market remains relatively small compared to the size of the credit market but is still considerably larger than the equity market.

In 1979, a Capital Market Committee was established in accordance with the Securities Act (Wertpapier-Emissionsgesetz) of the same year which was to promote the development of the market by carefully introducing international standards, practices and innovative instruments. Later, in 1989, a new auction system for the issuance of government bonds and a market maker system were introduced in order to increase trading volumes and reduce transactions costs. As of November 1991, as mentioned, any restrictions or authorization requirements were removed for foreign issuers, though authorization practice had already been very liberal since 1989.

Until the end of 1991, the issuance of bonds required the recommendation of the Capital Market Committee. These requirements were abolished when the new Capital Market Act (Kapitalmarktgesetz) came into force at the beginning of 1992. Extensive disclosure requirements replaced the former procedure for publicly offered issues; a prospectus with detailed information must be published before the beginning of the subscription, after being verified by a bank or an auditor.

Despite these achievements, some structural weaknesses remain. Especially as far as long-term papers are concerned, a persistent disequilibrium is observed. While domestic investors increasingly use foreign investment opportunities, foreign interest in domestic papers is restricted simply by the fact that the supply of Austrian papers is relatively small. This disequilibrium leads to capital outflow, reduces potential income for the banks, and produces an upward pressure on interest rates. Furthermore, negative consequences for the real side of the economy are implied insofar as the high volume of savings in Austria cannot be mobilized efficiently for cheap and long-term financing of the Austrian economy.

There are different reasons for this situation: one is that the small- and medium-sized structure of the Austrian economy may not be favourable for capital market financing. Another reason is the relatively high portion of subsidized credits which leads to a preference for this kind of financing instead of using the capital market.

More work is still needed to bring the Vienna Stock Exchange up to date. Recently, stricter regulations against insider trading have come into force. Improved transparency with respect to information and fair conditions for all participants are essential preconditions for a lasting acceptance of primary and secondary markets by the public. Currently, a group of high-level financial specialists is looking for further ways to improve the performance of the Vienna stock market. But banks and other participants will need to adapt more rapidly to a different and less protected environment.

4   Conclusions

The Austrian approach to full convertibility and liberalization was a slow and cautious one; it developed credibility of exchange rate and monetary policy on the one hand and liberalization on the other hand in a narrow and interdependent way. Steps were only taken if it seemed that banks and the public were able to use new freedoms in a responsible and sensible manner and, even more important, if it seemed that these freedoms also corresponded to the fundamental situation of the real economy.

Thus, disturbing effects on credibility could be avoided which might have appeared if liberalization measures had had to be withdrawn. On the other hand, however, authorities did not hesitate to re-regulate the banking sector when it turned out that the freedom given to it was not used in a constructive manner.

From this experience of a successful gradual approach it may not be surprising that most Austrian economists remain sceptical about the 'shock treatments' of Central and Eastern European economies on their way towards financial reform. It is believed that the convertibility of a currency as well as the liberalization of a financial sector must correspond to the competitiveness of the productive sector and the soundness of fundamental data. In achieving this, the factor of time must not be neglected.

Notes

1.   The views expressed in this chapter are those of the author and not necessarily of his affiliated institution.
2.   This section draws on Schubert (1992) and Glück *et al.* (1992).
3.   These were the German Mark, Swiss Franc, Dutch Guilder, Belgian Franc, Swedish, Norwegian and Danish Krona, Lira and Pound Sterling.
4.   The role of credibility and reputation was first modelled by Kydland and Prescott (1977) and further developed by Barro and Gordon (1983). The distinguishing feature of this work is that government is not exogenous in the analysis. Policy is made endogenous by specifying a government objective function and assuming that the government maximizes its objective function under the constraints imposed by private equilibrium behaviour (Persson, 1988).
5.   See Hochreiter and Winckler (1991) for details.

6.   According to Directive 88/361 of 24 June 1988, member countries of the EC are obliged to liberalize all short-term and long-term capital transactions: credits, money market operations, the right to hold deposits in other member countries, export and import of assets of any kind, etc.
7.   This intensification, however, may not necessarily be a direct consequence of liberalization.

References

Barro, R. and Gordon, D. (1983), 'Rules, discretion and reputation in a model of monetary policy', *Journal of Monetary Policy* 12, 101—121.

EFTA (1989), 'Working group on liberalization of capital movements: consequences and problems of liberalizing capital movements in the EFTA countries', Doc EFTA/EC 7/89, Geneva.

Glück, H., Proske, D., and Tatom, J.(1992), 'Monetary and exchange rate policy in Austria: an early example of policy coordination', in Motamen-Scobie, H. and Starck, C.C. (eds), *Economic Policy Co-ordination in an Integrating Europe*, Helsinki, Bank of Finland.

Hochreiter, E. and Winckler, G. (1991), 'Signaling a hard currency strategy: the case of Austria', Working Paper No. 10, Auslands-analyse-Abteilung der OeNB, Vienna.

Kydland, F. and Prescott, E. (1977), 'Rules rather than discretion: the inconsistency of optimal plans', *Journal of Political Economy* 85, 473—492.

Pech, H. (1993), 'Globale Kapitalströme und ihre Implikationen für die Funktionsweise des internationalen Währungssystems aus österreichischer Sicht', (in German), (mimeo), Economics Department, OeNB, Vienna.

Persson, T. (1988), 'Credibility of macroeconomic policy. An introduction and a broad survey', *European Economic Review* 32, 519—532.

Schubert, A. (1992), 'The history of currency convertiblity in Austria', paper presented at the Akademieaustausch and NÖG-Treffen Öster-reich-Ungarn 'Währungsfragen der internationalen Wirtschaftsinteg-ration', 2—4 November 1992, Vienna and Budapest.

Table 8.1   Capital movements in Austria before and after liberalization

ATS bn

	1989	1990	1991	1992*	1993* 1st half
Short-term capital					
change in liabilities	17.2	14.4	11.3	70.2	33.2
change in claims	-6.7	-5.4	13.5	-53.9	-60.3
net	10.5	8.9	24.8	16.3	-27.1
Long-term capital					
change in liabilities	55.7	46.7	49.6	76.7	51.3
change in claims	-49.6	-56.9	-74.0	-71.1	-23.1
net	6.1	-10.2	-24.4	5.6	28.2
Total capital account	16.6	-1.3	0.4	22.0	1.1

Note: * preliminary data

9 The Finnish Experience with Financial Market Liberalization: Some Lessons for Economies in Transition

Jouko Rautava

1 Introduction[1]

The Finnish economy is essentially based on private enterprise, with over 80 per cent of manufacturing output produced by private companies, and it is highly dependent on foreign trade. Compared with many other industrial countries, Finnish financial markets have traditionally been narrow and dominated by banks.

After World War II, economic policy in Finland focused on economic development through promoting rapid growth of output. The main instrument to this end was monetary policy, relying on low interest rates to stimulate investments. This policy was supported by high savings by the public sector and by a rather extensive financial market regulation system.

During the 1980s, the Finnish financial markets underwent a transformation from a rather strictly regulated system to an unregulated regime. Thus, Finland followed the general process of deregulation in Europe, although with a lag and at a slower pace than elsewhere. Because of the similar characteristics of their economies, Norway's and particularly Sweden's experiences of financial market deregulation are broadly similar to those of Finland.

In Finland, deregulation of financial markets was a result of both deregulation measures taken by the authorities and the expansion of unregulated markets outside the authorities' control. In part, the authorities sought to give new momentum to the deregulation process by relaxing current rules, in part they merely legalized activities that had already become commonplace. However, owing to the underdeveloped state of domestic financial markets and fears of the possibly disruptive effects of liberalization, the authorities tried to pursue a strategy of gradual deregulation.

In the transition economies, the same questions related to the speed and sequencing, and more generally, to a strategy of deregulation are under discussion. In this chapter, we give an overview of the Finnish experience of deregulation and try to highlight some points which we believe are also relevant for the economies in transition.

The chapter is organized as follows. First, we give a short description of the regulatory system that existed in Finland from World War II until the end of the 1970s and the reasoning underlying it. We then look at how deregulation was implemented in the 1980s. Next we discuss the major problems related to financial market deregulation as well as some of the advantages that attach to it. In the concluding section, we raise three issues related to the deregulation process which we believe are of special interest in the transition economies. These are: (1) the speed and sequencing of deregulation; (2) the role of foreign competition in the domestic financial markets; and (3) the need for a general commitment to deregulation.

2 A short history of Finnish financial market developments

Thanks to favourable foreign trade developments after Finland had to abandon the gold standard at the end of 1931, there was no need to maintain exchange control or regulation of imports until problems emerged again in the latter half of 1939. Thus, Finland was, in addition to Belgium and Luxembourg, the only European country to return to completely free foreign exchange markets after a short period of exchange control.[2] In the domestic sector of the financial markets the only element of regulation before 1939 was an agreement between the banks not to compete for deposits with interest rates.[3] Thus, at the end of the 1930s the financial markets in Finland were almost totally deregulated but, due to other regulations and market structures, the significance of financial deregulation in the 1930s apparently differs from that today.

However, with the onset of World War II, the situation changed dramatically and it marked a clear turning point in the history of Finnish — as indeed of other countries' — financial markets.

2.1 The regulation period until the end of the 1970s

One of the principal reasons for restoring regulation in the Finnish financial markets after 1939 was to meet the special needs of the wartime economy. During the war, exchange control was extensive and covered all foreign payments. In the domestic money market, a system of tax-exempt deposits and regulation of lending rates were introduced alongside the existing interbank deposit rate agreement.

After World War II conditions in Finland favoured the continuation of financial market regulation. The Great Depression in the 1930s, the wartime experiences of government intervention, the ideas raised by the Keynesian revolution as well as the increasing power of the Soviet Union and the birth of the new socialist states in Europe all had a strong influence on the political climate in Finland.

A dominant feature of Finnish economic policy in the postwar decades was the emphasis on growth-oriented structural (industrial) policies. This was in line with the general atmosphere favouring government intervention and regulation, and had an immediate impact on monetary policy and the financial markets. It was believed that the rapid growth of the economy was best achieved by keeping interest rates sufficiently low to boost investment. Low interest rates were also seen as essential for securing the operation of firms, for keeping rents and prices low and for alleviating the government's debt burden. Incidentally, this notion of the cost-push effect of interest rates on inflation dominated the Finnish discussion on interest rate policy until the beginning of the 1980s.[4]

Since it was not possible to use interest rate policy to balance demand for and supply of financing, a credit rationing system was needed to clear the financial markets.[5] Already in the latter part of the 1940s, quotas for the banks' central bank borrowing were introduced and this system was made more effective by applying penalty interest rates to borrowing in excess of quotas. It is also worth mentioning that, starting in the mid-1950s, there was an extensive indexation system for deposits and government debt in Finland. Owning to high inflation and low nominal interest rates at that time, it was judged that indexation was needed to protect savings.

Exchange control and the licensing of imports were also guided by structural policy considerations in the postwar decades. The central bank gave preference to borrowing for long-term investments supporting the balance of payments and economic growth and it took a favourable attitude towards foreign direct investments.[6] Thus, the main elements of the postwar Finnish financial market regulation were already in place in the early 1950s.

Although the main characteristics of the financial markets and the instruments used in them remained essentially the same, some changes already occurred before the period of more intensive deregulation started at the beginning of the 1980s. In the latter part of the 1950s, exchange controls were lifted on the major part of trade-related current payments along with the general changeover to more liberal foreign trade and payments practices in Western Europe. The Markka was made externally convertible at the end of 1958 and investments by foreigners in Finnish securities were allowed in the late 1950s. Later on, the further liberalization was implemented in keeping with the free trade agreements that Finland concluded in the 1960s and 1970s with EFTA, the EEC and, on a bilateral basis, with most of the CMEA countries. In addition to lifting customs duties, the maximum period for financing export receivables was extended to 12 months and the authorization procedure for direct investments abroad was alleviated in the late 1970s. In contrast, the regulations concerning import financing and capital imports were tightened in the 1970s.

In the domestic money market, the indexation system was abolished in the late 1960s as part of a comprehensive economic stabilization package and the call money market was set up by the Bank of Finland in 1975. The call money market provided the commercial banks with a flexible channel for levelling fluctuations in their liquidity. The new system gradually replaced the old system based on quotas for central bank borrowing and penalty interest rates on borrowing in excess of quotas. Moreover, the call money rate became the first market-based interest rate in the Finnish financial markets in the postwar period, thus enabling the authorities to obtain important information on the state of the markets.

In the latter part of the 1970s, both domestic and foreign factors created mounting pressures for change in the Finnish financial markets. However, owing to the underdeveloped state of domestic financial markets and the existing tax system, the most striking elements of which were the tax exemption of deposits and bonds and the tax deductibility of interest costs, the regulation system remained more or less intact throughout the 1970s.

2.2 The deregulation period of the 1980s

The transformation which the Finnish financial markets underwent in the 1980s was a result of both the growth and development of the unregulated market segment and of the deregulation measures taken by the authorities.[7]

In the late 1970s and early 1980s, rapid inflation, together with favourable income developments and the increased cost and yield awareness of many economic agents, increased pressures for the introduction of higher-yielding financial instruments. These pressures were intensified by the world-wide internationalization of financial markets and deregulation of capital movements and by the internationalization of the Finnish banks through the setting up of subsidiaries abroad. Also, changes in sectoral financial balances[8] and financial market innovations and advances in information technology added to pressures for more liberal financial markets. As a result of these developments, short-term lending between firms at unregulated interest rates increased rapidly. Lending between firms was channelled both through the banks — although outside their balance sheets as trust department loans and deposits — and directly between firms. The expansion of unregulated financial markets was further stimulated by the introduction and growth of factoring, leasing and hire purchase services by bank-owned finance companies and by corporate bonds and debentures.

The growth of unregulated markets was also spurred on by the liberalization measures taken by the authorities (Figure 9.1), although these measures only reflected or responded to developments that had already occurred in the financial markets. The deregulation measures by the authorities were partly a response to the fact that economic agents could circumvent rules with increasing ease, which was thought to lead to distortions in the markets. The general atmosphere was also more favourable to market-oriented reforms than before. This was evident, for example, in changes in terminology: after the initial years of the 1980s unregulated finance began to be referred to as 'market money' instead of 'grey money'. The debate on deregulation related merely to the speed and sequencing of deregulation. Maintenance of an extensive regulation system was not seen as a viable option. Despite some debate on the principles and sequencing of liberalization, actual deregulation decisions were usually based more on practical considerations than intellectual debates.[9]

In 1980, the Bank of Finland withdrew from the forward markets and, at the same time, banks were granted permission to use foreign credits and deposits to cover their forward purchases and sales. These measures proved to be very important for the growth of the unregulated market in the 1980s, since the forward exchange market provided a flexible channel for short-term capital movements and formed a true link between unregulated Finnish and international interest rates. Foreign influence and competition were also increased by allowing foreign banks to operate in Finland and in 1984 they were granted access to the call money market on the same terms and conditions as Finnish banks.

In 1983, Bank of Finland started the step-by-step dismantling of average lending rate controls and this process was completed in 1986, when banks were allowed to freely determine the level of interest rates on new loans. In 1986 and 1987, a set of major liberalization measures was effected. At the beginning of 1986, the Bank of Finland introduced a spread between borrowing and deposit rates in the call money market to encourage banks to settle differences in their liquidity in the interbank market rather than at the central bank. The growth of the money market was further stimulated by exempting certificates of deposits (CDs) from the cash reserve requirements and by agreeing on a code of conduct to be applied in the money market. As a result of these measures the market for CDs, commercial paper, local authority paper and Treasury bills started to expand rapidly. At the same time, the focus of monetary policy shifted to money market operations, as was demonstrated by the central bank's decision to discontinue its practice of periodically issuing guidelines on credit policy to the banks.

Deregulation of domestic money market was followed by liberalization of capital movements. The restrictions on borrowing and investing abroad were progressively removed from the mid-1980s. These measures led to the more widespread use of financing and transactions denominated in foreign currencies and, consequently, increased interest rate and exchange rate risks. The need to manage these risks, again, acted as a spur to the development of markets for derivatives.

Trade and payments with the former Soviet Union were the last foreign trade operations to remain regulated. Because of bilateral trade and clearing agreements, these operations were strictly regulated by means of licensing and exchange control. However, the changes in the former Soviet Union that started in 1985 led to pressures for conducting trade more on the basis of freely convertible currencies. Finally, at the end of 1990 it was agreed to terminate the remaining bilateral trade and clearing agreements.[10]

The deregulation of the Finnish financial markets continued until the beginning of 1991, when almost all remaining exchange controls were lifted.

3   The effects of liberalization

Until the mid-1980s, the Finnish financial markets were characterized by the dominance of banks, by an administratively regulated interest rate system with credit rationing and by fairly effective exchange control. The liberalization of the domestic money market and exchange control in the latter part of 1980s strongly affected the structure of the Finnish financial markets, monetary and fiscal policy and the behaviour of economic agents.

However, before we look at some obvious results of deregulation, some reservations must be made. First, no comprehensive study has been made on financial market liberalization in Finland and therefore we have to focus on some of the most obvious consequences of deregulation.[11] Second, as already mentioned, many deregulation measures only legitimized practices already applied by economic agents. Thus, a widely shared view is that there was no viable alternative to deregulation. Third, the Finnish economy in the late 1980s and early 1990s was influenced not only by financial market liberalization, but also by exceptional international events and domestic policy measures other than deregulation.[12] Therefore it is difficult to distinguish the effects of deregulation from other factors. Fourth, one cannot pass over the peculiarities of the Finnish tax system, which greatly accentuated the problems related to financial market deregulation. The change in the tax system started step-by-step only at the end of the deregulation process.

3.1 The credit boom

In Finland, the major problem related to deregulation was a sharp increase in bank lending and subsequent overindebtedness. With hindsight, it is clear that all agents, including households, firms, banks, the authorities and politicians, were at fault in not taking adequate account of the changing financial environment. Consequently, they continued to operate on the basis of partly outdated principles.

Before the mid-1980s, the tax deductibility of interest costs, together with relatively high inflation, effectively decreased the cost of borrowing. Lending, on the other hand, was restricted by credit rationing, by strict bank-customer relationships and by the need for prior savings. Access to credit became an important criterion for investments, which most probably affected the borrowing behaviour of economic agents. This is one reason why the common understanding in Finland is that the investment ratio has been high but the profitability of the investments low.

After decades of pent-up demand for credit, deregulation combined with exceptionally favourable income expectations led to a demand boom, which was financed by the banks. The credit boom was reinforced by a very sharp increase in asset prices, particularly real estate and housing prices.[13] Moreover, people had no experience of falling prices for real estate and housing after World War II. Thus, in 1987 households and businesses started to borrow as never before (Figure 9.2).

In the peak year of 1988 bank lending rose by 30 per cent, household debt grew from 60 per cent of disposable income at the beginning of 1987 to 80 per cent in 1988 and the household savings ratio became negative.

One extraordinary feature of the Finnish credit boom in the late 1980s was the explosion of foreign currency borrowing. Following assurances by the Bank of Finland and the government, companies and banks thought that the Markka would not to be devalued. This belief was not diminished by the fact that Markka interest rates were much higher than other interest rates, indicating that the markets did not exclude the possibility of a future devaluation. Nor did the revaluation of the Markka in 1989 make borrowers worry about the external value of the Markka. When expectations of continuing growth and a fixed Markka proved to be wrong at the beginning of the 1990s, economic agents were severely hit by unemployment and by increased debt service payments. As a consequence of this, they were forced to cut spending, thereby aggravating the recession.

The tendency of deregulation to give rise to larger surges of borrowing in a boom and correspondingly greater retrenchment in recession has also been shared with other countries. The danger of imprudent lending and borrowing without adequate risk assessment has also been revealed, for example, in the UK and the US. However, although many countries already liberalized their financial markets in the late 1970s and early 1980s, the disadvantages of deregulation only became evident in the late 1980s, at the same time as in Finland. Thus, Finland was unable to benefit from their experiences.[14]

3.2 Problems in the banking sector

For the banks, competition for market shares was the dominant objective, and this led to a lowering in banks' credit standards in the late 1980s. Insufficient attention was given to the value of collateral, credit risk was not correctly priced and interest risks attracted too little attention. Although banks balanced their foreign lending and borrowing, they did not pay adequate attention to the risks associated with devaluation and subsequent credit losses.[15]

Before deregulation started, the dominance of the banks in the Finnish financial markets was supported by the tax exemption of deposits, which decreased the funding costs of the banks. Because of interest rate regulation, it was impossible to compete for these deposits by the means of price competition. Thus, to attract these savings the banks built up very extensive branch networks and invested heavily in banking technologies.

Increased price competition in financial markets since deregulation has reduced the role of tax-exempt deposits. At the same time, it has become evident that the banks' service networks, even if technically very efficient, are too heavy and costly in the new environment. Hence, between 1989 and 1992 the number of employees in the banking sector was cut by some 20 per cent and a change of similar magnitude occurred in the number of branches.[16]

Deregulation has not, however, diminished the central role of the banks in the Finnish financial markets. The role of the banks was even reinforced as the release of the households' pent-up demand for credit led to a sharp increase in bank lending. Moreover, the increase in foreign financing intermediated by banks has further consolidated the role of banks. Thus, the bulk of financial intermediation still takes place through deposit banks.

3.3 Policy problems connected with deregulation

Today, with the passing of time, it is clear that fiscal and monetary policies were not geared to restrain the expansionary effects of financial deregulation. The mild counter-cyclical fiscal stance was more a result of incorrect forecasts, which underestimated the strength of the boom and budget revenues. Partly due to the same assessment errors concerning the state of economy, the monetary authorities did not take timely action to restrain credit expansion. However, the lack of restrictive measures was partly associated with the overriding target of a fixed exchange rate. In practice, the only option available to the monetary authorities, in addition to issuing strong formal statements, would have been a revaluation of the Markka in order to induce devaluation expectations, which would have curbed foreign borrowing and pushed domestic interest rates higher. This action was finally taken in 1989. But today there is general agreement that the decision to revalue the Markka was taken too late.

In addition to these policy mistakes, which were connected with the misjudgment of the prevailing state of the economy and future prospects, there are at least two additional aspects open to criticism. First, existing banking legislation and supervision were not adapted to the new financial environment. Finland did not have any general legislation governing financial institutions and different acts governed the various types of deposit banks. The laws in force dated back to 1970 and it was only in the early 1990s that the legislation governing financial markets underwent a fundamental reform. Today it is also clear that during the deregulation process the regulatory authorities did not pay enough attention to their own monitoring and supervision practices. Thus, banking regulation focused for too long on judicial compliance rather than risk evaluation.[17]

Second, Finnish tax legislation was not adjusted in time to meet the needs of deregulated financial markets. The fact that interest expenses could be deducted from taxable income at a high marginal rate constituted a tax distortion, the impact of which was greatly increased with deregulation. Hence, although real lending rates have been positive since the beginning of the 1980s, real after-tax lending rates were still negative at the height of the boom in 1987—1989 (Figure 9.3).

The other feature of the tax system that should have been removed along with financial regulation was tax-exempt accounts. Tax-exempt accounts constituted a subsidy to banks and boosted their capacity to lend. Furthermore, the act on tax exemption precluded interest rate competition and delayed the necessary adjustment of banking capacity. Finally, excess borrowing was also stimulated by the fact that equity capital was taxed more than debt.

With hindsight, we can also say that it was a mistake not to introduce market-based long-term reference interest rates at an earlier date and to request the banks to use these rates as reference rates in their lending. What happened in Finland was that, until the end of 1987, the central bank required interest rates on housing loans, in particular, to be tied to the central bank's base rate, and long-term reference rates were introduced only at the beginning of 1988. As a consequence, a large part of new lending was tied to an administrative interest rate which was for political reasons very difficult to change.[18] In addition, one can argue that capital exports could have been liberalized earlier to offset the effects of capital imports on domestic interest rates. However, here too the authorities' discretionary power was limited by political realities.[19] Moreover, the liberalization of deposit rates could have preceded that of lending rates — as in Norway and Sweden — so as to create pressures for higher interest rates and to make banks aware of the real market price of their own funding.

3.4 Advantages of deregulation

Owing to the general nature of the favourable results of deregulation, it is more difficult to identify them than the readily discernible adverse effects. In general, the favourable effects of deregulation are related to enhanced competition in the financial markets and to more effective use of financial resources. There are, however, some more concrete results worth mentioning.

Maybe the biggest advantage of deregulation is related to improved availability of finance. Given the fact that credit rationing and interest rate regulation have been abolished, credit decisions are based more on price and risk considerations. Hence, it is easier for new and growing businesses to obtain finance whereas inefficient old firms can no longer earn excess profits based on subsidized credits. Free access to and market pricing of credit have also very likely changed the investment behaviour of firms. Now it is no longer rational to invest whenever you get a loan and hence the use of financial resources has became more efficient.[20]

Despite the continuing dominant role of deposit banks, deregulation has improved the availability of finance from sources other than the banks. In particular, direct borrowing by firms from both domestic and foreign markets has increased, and thus the capital market has started to develop.

Moreover, rent-seeking and speculation based on the existence of unregulated and regulated markets is no longer possible. This has also contributed to increased efficiency of financing, since now there are fewer distortions and problems associated with them. Also, resources needed to administer the regulatory system can now be diverted to more productive use. Finally, savers have benefitted greatly from deregulation as a result of price competition for savings. Positive real deposit rates have increased the attractiveness of saving and the household saving ratio has risen sharply after the initial collapse related to the release of pent-up demand, tax distortions and a bubble in housing prices.[21]

4   Some possible lessons for the economies in transition

In Finland, financial market regulation continued for longer than in many other European countries and the deregulation which began at the beginning of the 1980s was not completed until 1991. Thus, the Finnish experience may reveal some interesting points that are also relevant for the economies in transition. In this summary, we focus on the following three topics: (1) speed and sequencing of deregulation; (2) the role of foreign competition in the domestic financial markets; and (3) the need for a general commitment to deregulation.

Financial market liberalization in Finland was a gradual process and domestic financial markets and foreign exchange markets were deregulated more or less at the same time. Moreover, deregulatory measures were often planned to support monetary policy considered appropriate at that time. The authorities also tried to take into consideration the possible influence of deregulation measures on agents' risk behaviour, market stability and interest rate volatility.[22] On the other hand, the Finnish experience also demonstrates that financial market liberalization is a process which — once started — is very difficult to stop and there are even limits to the authorities' ability to manage it. Even partial liberalization makes it easy to circumvent the existing rules and increases pressures to continue liberalization in order to avoid market distortions.

The question of sequencing between domestic and foreign deregulation clearly illustrates the more general problems related to sequencing. Arguments have been put forward both for deregulation of domestic financial transactions before foreign transactions and vice versa. However, for any such argument to hold one has to believe that the two types of regulation can be separated. In practice, this is doubtful once companies learn how to lend lawfully acquired domestic and foreign funds directly to each other.[23] Hence, after the initial steps of deregulation, the process develops a momentum of its own. This is not to say that the authorities responsible for deregulation have no influence on the process, but the limits to continuing regulation or to sequencing the process should be recognized.

It seems that gradual deregulation during the boom alleviated some problems related to foreign indebtedness and investments in real estate, because agents did not have time to make all possible mistakes before economic recession put a limit on borrowing. However, despite major efforts by the authorities to determine the sequencing of liberalization, it is not at all clear whether the strategy based on gradualism and sequencing in general was successful.

There are at least two policy measures directly related to sequencing which could have been taken earlier than they actually were. These options were (1) the abolition of tax exemption on savings and tax deduction of interest costs in the early stage of liberalization and (2) earlier adjustment of banking legislation and supervision practices. The general lesson related to these options is that preserving old structures and practices in some sectors while deregulating others tends to raise severe problems. In liberalized financial markets, the tax system should not be allowed to disturb basic market relations and incentives to borrow or lend in the same manner as it is possible in regulated markets. Banking legislation and supervision must also be adapted so that the risks of the new environment can be identified. In deregulated financial markets, it is no longer sufficient to keep to legal aspects of banking activities; rather, focus must also be placed on risk evaluation.

Moreover, the strategy of gradual deregulation in Finland was based on the idea that agents need time to adjust to the new environment. Unfortunately, it seems that they did not make use of the opportunity provided to them. In particular, banks did not take advantage of the transition period to adjust their structure and operations, though they knew that conditions would change in the near future. Instead of running down excess capacity, banks exploited all the possibilities of the old and new systems to obtain very short-run benefits, and, for example, the number of bank employees even increased until 1989. Thus, the transition period was not used to adjust to the new environment; rather the subsequent adjustment problems were even enhanced by intensified use of market distortions related to the concomitant existence of regulated and unregulated markets. Some outsiders also take the view that the pace of deregulation in Finland was not unduly fast and could have been even faster.[24]

The role of foreign competition in financing has attracted interest both in Finland and in the economies in transition. The usual argument is that the opening up of domestic markets — although in principle a reasonable measure — poses a serious threat especially to domestic banks. However, the Finnish experience of financial market liberalization does not bear this out. On the contrary, the foreign banks have not been able to shake the position of Finnish banks. Moreover, despite a small market share of foreign banks, there is at least one concrete example of the positive impact of increased competition by foreign banks. In 1984, the central bank was able to use foreign banks to break the domestic banks' agreement to control money market interest rates.[25] In addition, it seems that there is no evidence that the decision to delay deregulation of capital exports was beneficial. On the contrary, earlier liberalization of capital exports could have helped to offset the influence of capital imports on asset prices and interest rates.

In general, it seems that the caveats related to the opening up of financial markets for foreign competition are exaggerated. At least in the case of Finland, we can say rather that if we want more competition in domestic financial markets it is necessary to open them up for foreign competition. However, opening up is not a sufficient measure to get foreign banks to invest in domestic markets; other conditions must also be favourable.

Finally, the importance of a general commitment to deregulation can hardly be overstated. In the case of Finland, the lack of such commitment is well illustrated by the difficulties experienced in coordinating the reform of tax legislation with other deregulation measures. Also, the fact that the effects of financial market liberalization on monetary and fiscal policies were not understood more widely in the economy reflects the lack of general commitment to deregulation.

However, to convince all parties that deep-going changes are needed in the financial markets as well as to inform the public of the prerequisites for and consequences of deregulation is not an easy task. In Finland, there were strong 'vested interests' related to the old system and hence it was difficult to show that deregulation was unavoidable and that prolonging regulation would be harmful to the economy as whole. In retrospect, one can say that deregulation in Finland was too much a central bank-led process without enough commitment and support on the part of politicians. As a consequence, it is frequently argued that all economic problems stem from financial market liberalization, which makes it difficult even to discuss relevant topics and corrective policy measures.[26]

How could we then strengthen the general commitment to deregulation and improve information on it? One obvious answer is to be found from the experiences of developing countries and the economies in transition: with the help of a deregulation programme. Financial market deregulation is a social operation of such magnitude that it would be beneficial to have a definite programme for it. To be useful, the programme should be supported at least by the government and the authorities responsible for deregulation. A credible programme makes it easier to manage problems connected with policy coordination. It also makes it easier to inform and convince the public of the coming changes. In general, a credible programme helps to reduce uncertainty about the pace of transition to unregulated markets.

5   Conclusions

The Finnish experience in financial market deregulation reveals once again that, despite many country-specific factors, there are several common problems related to any economic transition: transition periods tend to increase market distortions from which the agents try to benefit as long as possible; if there are uncertainties about the coming changes, agents seem not to use the transition period to adjust to the new environment; after the initial steps of transition, the authorities capability to manage the process is limited; and the lack of a general commitment to transition tends to intensify all problems related to it.

Unfortunately, it seems that in domestic policy making it is difficult to differentiate between general and domestic features of any problems. Moreover, there seems to be a tendency in domestic policy making to belittle the common problems and experiences of other countries and to highlight domestic factors and the special short-term needs of certain groups at the expense of the benefits to society as whole.

Notes

1. The opinions expressed in this chapter are those of the author and do not necessarily represent official Bank of Finland views.
2. See Lehto-Sinisalo (1992) for a detailed description of the history of exchange control in Finland.
3. The agreement was reached at the instigation of the Bank of Finland and its initial purpose was to lower lending rates. Around this time, many countries introduced similar arrangements to protect the profitability of banks and the stability of the financial system as a whole (e.g. regulation Q in the US); See Tarkka (1988) p. 34.
4. See Tarkka (1988) for a more detailed discussion.
5. However, from time to time there was disagreement concerning monetary policy. According to Tarkka (1988) p.3, conflicts frequently arose between the central bank and politicians when the bank tried to implement a more market-oriented interest rate policy.
6. Lehto-Sinisalo (1992) p. 5.
7. A detailed description of the structure of and developments in the Finnish financial markets is given in 'Financial Markets in Finland', Bank of Finland Bulletin Special Issues (1986 and 1991).
8. In the latter part of the 1970s, the sizeable surplus in central and local government finances disappeared but, on the other hand, private sector savings increased.
9. See Nyberg (1992) pp. 3—4 on the debate concerning the speed of foreign exchange deregulation and its impact on decision making. For an example of theoretical argumentation before more intensive liberalization started, see Swoboda (1986) pp. 24—31.
10. Although the changeover to convertible-currency trade with the former Soviet Union created many adjustment problems in Finland, the major reason for the collapse of that trade in 1991 was the domestic problems in the former Soviet republics. See Hukkinen and Rautava (1992) for more on trade between Finland and the former Soviet Union.
11. Reference is nevertheless made particularly to the works of Bordes (1993), Currie (1993) and Söderström (1993). In these three independent reports, commissioned by the Bank of Finland, deregulation is seen as one of the major factors affecting the Finnish economy in the late 1980s. Other major sources for this paper are Nyberg (1992) and Nyberg and Vihriälä (1993).

12. The most important factors, in addition to financial market liberalization, influencing the Finnish economy in the late 1980s and early 1990s were: (1) a sharp increase in the terms of trade in the latter part of the 1980s and a subsequent decrease after 1989; (2) the collapse of the Soviet Union and subsequent problems in trade with the former Soviet republics; and (3) the tax reform which started in the late 1980s.

13. In addition to the incentive to borrow, rising asset prices boosted banks' ability to lend after the Banking Supervision Office allowed banks to increase their equity capital through value adjustments. Unfortunately, this new capital did not prove to be as permanent as expected. See Brunila and Takala (1993) p. 10.

14. See Currie (1993) p. 116.

15. See Nyberg and Vihriälä (1993) p. 13 and Currie (1993) p. 119.

16. For a broader discussion of the problems of the Finnish banking sector, see Nyberg and Vihriälä (1993).

17. The list of deficiencies in banking legislation and supervision included: (1) banks' operating prerequisites were not linked to the size of a bank's capital base and the nature of the business; (2) no risk weighing system was introduced to calculate capital adequacy and deposit banks were subject to different capital adequacy requirements; (3) banking supervision was delegated to several authorities. See Bordes (1993) p. 23.

18. This point has been made by the former governor of the Bank of Finland; see Kullberg (1991).

19. See Åkerholm (1990).

20. Many of these points are made, e.g., by Abrams (1989).

21. Incidentally, there is one more point to make here. The Finnish authorities no longer need to try to convince their foreign colleagues why Finland should have more regulation than other OECD countries.

22. See Nyberg (1992) pp. 4—7 on linking foreign exchange deregulation to monetary policy.

23. See Nyberg (1992) p. 10 and Swoboda (1986) pp. 24—27 for arguments on the sequencing of external and internal deregulation.

24. See Abrams (1989) p. 17 and Bordes (1993) p. 22.

25. See Tarkka (1988) p. 232.

26. See Åkerholm (1990) for a more detailed discussion on arguments put forward concerning deregulation at the end of the 1980s.

References

Abrams, R. (1989), 'The financial market liberalization in Finland', (in Finnish), *Kansallis-Osake-Pankki Economic Review* 1, 6—19.

Åkerholm, J. (1990), 'Is financial market liberalization a cause of our problems?', (in Finnish), *The Finnish Economic Journal* 1, 95—101.

Bank of Finland (1986), 'Financial markets in Finland', *The Bank of Finland Bulletin* Special Issue.

Bank of Finland (1991), 'Financial markets in Finland', *Bank of Finland Bulletin* Special Issue.

Bordes, C. (1993), 'The Finnish economy: the boom, the debt, the crisis and the prospects', in 'Three assessments of Finland's economic crisis and economic policy', Series C:9, Bank of Finland, Helsinki.

Brunila, A. and Takala, K. (1993), 'Private indebtedness and the banking crisis in Finland', Discussion Papers No. 9, Bank of Finland, Helsinki.

Currie, D. (1993), 'The Finnish economic crisis: analysis and prescription', in 'Three assessments of Finland's economic crisis and economic policy', Series C:9, Bank of Finland, Helsinki.

Hukkinen, J. and Rautava, J. (1992), 'Russia's economic reform and trade between Finland and Russia', *Bank of Finland Bulletin* 4.

Kullberg, R. (1991), 'Deregulation of financial markets', (in Finnish), press release of a speech given at the Ekonomiska Samfundet.

Lehto-Sinisalo, P. (1992), 'The history of exchange control in Finland', Discussion Papers No. 3, Bank of Finland, Helsinki.

Nyberg, P. (1992), 'Foreign exchange deregulation in Finland: principles, practice and consequences', Financial Markets Department Working Papers No. 3, Bank of Finland, Helsinki.

Nyberg, P. and Vihriälä, V. (1993), 'The Finnish banking crisis and its handling', Discussion Papers No. 8, Bank of Finland, Helsinki.

Söderström, H.T. (1993), 'Finland's economic crisis: causes, present nature, and policy options', in 'Three assessments of Finland's economic crisis and economic policy', Series C:9, Bank of Finland, Helsinki.

Swoboda, A.K. (1986), 'Ongoing changes in Finnish financial markets and their implications for central bank policy', Series A:62, Bank of Finland, Helsinki.

Tarkka, J. (1988), 'The era of money: the decades of financial market regulation in Finland', (in Finnish), in 'Money, inflation and economic policy', Department of Economics, University of Helsinki.

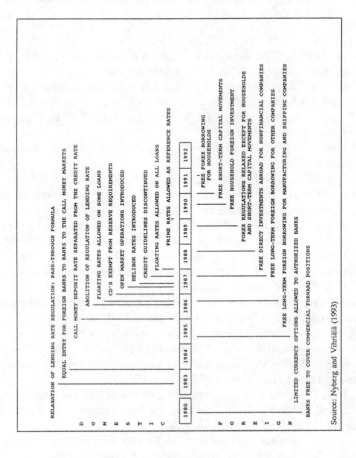

Figure 9.1 Financial market liberalization in Finland

Source: Nyberg and Vihriälä (1993)

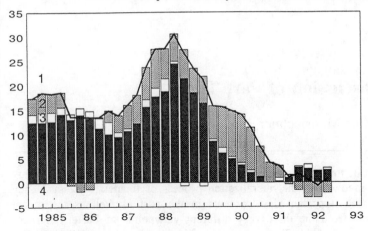

1 Total lending
2 Contribution of foreign currency loans
3 Contribution of bonds
4 Contribution of markka loans

Source: Bank of Finland

Figure 9.2 Bank lending to the corporate and household sectors; per cent change

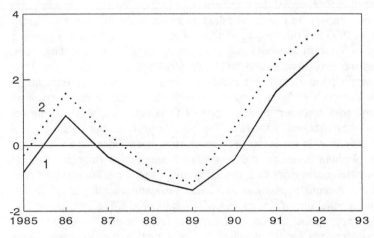

1 Outstanding loans
2 New loans

Source: Bank of Finland

Figure 9.3 Real after-tax lending rates

Discussion of Part Three

Peter Mooslechner

In general, the three chapters give us a very stimulating picture of many aspects involved in the liberalization process of financial systems. They analyse the important developments in the past as well as the recent challenges from the three very different viewpoints of Eastern Europe, Austria and Finland. The main topic of interest in this respect is not the specific history of financial liberalization in these countries but the preliminary conclusions that can be drawn from a comparison between the different starting conditions and experiences of financial liberalization for the Eastern European countries in transition.

It will therefore be helpful to point out some basic and essential features of the liberalization process. They are centred around the problems of the degree, speed, sequencing and preconditions of financial market liberalization for successfully transforming a former command economy into a market economy. In this respect the turbulence in the European Monetary System in 1993 and the severe problems of the banking system in a growing number of Western countries may lead one to the general expectation that there are no easy answers and no simple solutions.

One main point is that, for much too long, financial developments in Eastern Europe have been discussed mainly with regard to their impact on Western banks' exposure to this region. This perspective, although not yet obsolete, has changed to focus on the need to promote the transition to a market economy, in particular to establish an efficient financial and banking system. Without doubt the development of competitive financial markets and financial institutions is a crucial prerequisite for a successful transformation. Adequate payment facilities, sufficient mobilizing of funds, efficient channelling of domestic savings into productive investment and raising an appropriate amount of risk capital are — to mention only four — important features for the development of a market type economy. This argument holds even if in the transition process the situation has to be complemented by an additional inflow of foreign savings, in particular at an early stage of development.

Contrary to this need, the repressed financial systems of Eastern Europe were characterized by distorted interest rates, 'privileged' financial circuits and administratively determined credit flows. An overhang of bad loans to loss-making enterprises, lack of capital, non-competitive behaviour and inadequate regulatory systems are the most visible consequences. To avoid financial fragility and macroeconomic instability, it is necessary to address these key structural problems along with the question of the liberalization of the financial sector.

Certainly a viable banking reform strategy must be among the first priorities, but this strategy must be in line with the needs of transformation in the real sector of the economy. It has to deal with the financial restructuring of enterprises, an early privatization of banks themselves and a stable legal environment as basic conditions.

The experiences of Austria, Finland and some other countries (Fischer and Reisen, 1993, Mathieson and Rojas-Suarez, 1993, Galy *et al.*, 1993) indicate that successfully liberalizing financial markets is a very time-consuming process of trial and error, consisting of many small steps. For example, we had to learn that even under the most developed economic conditions, it is very difficult to establish a safe, stable and sound banking system that is at the same time economically efficient. And as recent banking history in Scandinavia or the US has shown, there is always a substantial risk of financial fragility that may be harmful for the real side of the economy.

Pure economic theory leads to fairly clear-cut conclusions about the advantages of a fully liberalized financial environment. But one has to learn from history that these comparative static results, derived under conditions of perfect markets and rational economic agents, are not automatically applicable to any stage of economic development or any market structure in the real world.

One of the most important elements in this respect is the meaning of the term 'efficiency'. As Tobin (1984) has stressed the term, efficiency is used with very different meanings in economics. The arguments in favour of financial liberalization are based on the concepts of information-arbitrage efficiency, fundamental-valuation efficiency and full-insurance efficiency in an Arrow-Debreu type of world of competitive markets. But even the US financial markets, the most developed financial structures in the world, are falling short in fulfilling these assumptions. Speculation on the speculations of other speculators dominate the pricing of assets, moral hazard is a real problem and oligopolistic rivalry rather than perfect competition is typical for financial market structures as well.

On the other hand, the importance of the functional efficiency of a financial system, of promoting real economic activity and growth, is widely neglected. This underlines the general dilemma, as Keynes saw even in his day, that the possible advantages of financial liberalization come at the cost of functional inefficiency and real distortions. Certainly many regulations of financial markets have been counterproductive. But the process of financial liberalization — in particular under Eastern European circumstances — should not be a routine application of free market philosophy. It has to be a pragmatic approach to dealing with what a financial system can be expected to contribute to growth at an early stage of development, and an assessment of the social costs of liberalization.

It should be remembered that the Western European market economies were allowed to realize their successful economic development after World War II under a regime of heavily regulated financial markets on the domestic side and also, in particular, in international capital transactions and exchange rate management. After World War II there was a consensus in international economic policy that at the beginning priorities had to be set for liberalizing real trade and real economic integration. This consensus determined economic policy, although Keynes' proposals didn't carry much weight in the formulation of the rules of the Bretton Woods system.

Today, the starting position for the Eastern European countries seems rather different and much more difficult. Under the severe pressure of financial market credibility they are urged by their creditors to establish domestic and international financial liberalization as soon as possible but, on the other hand, they suffer from substantial restrictions in real trade and from entry barriers in their supply of goods to Western markets. The Finnish example may tell us that even for a very developed economy it is extremely difficult to achieve and preserve an optimal degree of financial liberalization. And, of course, it would be very harmful to the process of establishing a market economy if it is disturbed by speculative bubbles and continuing financial instability.

The most important lesson from comparing the preconditions and experiences of financial liberalization in different countries should be that Western countries themselves realize from their own history that transformation, development and the process of establishing sufficient market structures and institutions require a long time. It is not as clear as sometimes proposed in the literature that forced financial liberalization is an appropriate instrument for transformation and economic development, in particular in situations at a very early stage of development when great institutional adaption is necessary.

References

Fischer, B. and Reisen, H. (1993), 'Liberalizing capital flows in developing countries: pitfalls, prerequisites and perspectives', OECD Development Centre, Paris.

Galy, M., Pastor, G., and Pujol, Th. (1993), 'Spain: converging with the European Community', Occasional Paper 101, International Monetary Fund, Washington, D.C.

Mathieson, D. and Rojas-Suarez, L. (1993), 'Liberalization of the capital account — experiences and issues', Occasional Paper 103, International Monetary Fund, Washington, D.C.

Tobin, J. (1984), 'On the efficiency of the financial system', *Lloyds Bank Review* No. 153, 1—15.

PART FOUR

Reforming Financial Markets:
Case Studies in Central and Eastern Europe

10 Reform of the Banking Sector in the Czech Republic

Miroslav Hrnčíř

1 Introduction[1]

The key importance of workable factor markets for the entire transition and for its ultimate success has been underlined by a number of observers since its early stages (Hinds, 1990). While these markets were effectively lacking under the former centrally-planned economy framework, they form the core of any market economy. The stage of their development in the given country thus marks the progress this particular country made in transition: the more flexible and rational the allocation of resources mediated via factor markets is, the closer the transition economy is to a market-type system.

This conclusion applies in particular to financial markets and to financial intermediation. Though the establishment of a modern capitalist economy cannot be judged only by the existence of a stock exchange (as some in transition economies appeared to believe), any sustainable recovery of transition economies is conditioned by the mobilization of savings and by their efficient allocation and reallocation to prospective users.

Compared to the initial conditions, substantial progress has been accomplished within a relatively short period of transition years and, at least the former three (currently four) Visegrád countries, Poland, Hungary and ex-Czechoslovakia, can claim to have their financial and banking systems already closer to a market framework.

Nevertheless, as was also pointed out by Dittus (1994) and Ábel and Bonin in Chapter 5, the degree of functional efficiency and competitiveness of financial markets and financial intermediation evidently lagged behind demand and expectations even in the more advanced transition economies.

It is the links and interactions between the state of financial markets and real economy developments, and not so much the financial markets per se, that are a matter of concern for both 'insiders' and foreign observers and institutions. The drop in economic activity in all transition economies has been greater and more protracted than expected. The signs of economic recovery, though differentiated across individual countries, started to assert themselves slowly and remained mostly uncertain in 1992 and 1993.

Identifying the causal factors, the existing underdevelopment, weaknesses and constraints of factor markets came to the fore. Given the continued low functional efficiency of financial markets and misallocation of savings, the prospects for sustainable recovery and growth of transition economies remains rather gloomy.

The interaction runs, however, the other way round also, from the state of the real economy to the degree of stability and soundness of the financial and banking systems. A tough lesson about this link was learned in the recession of the early 1990s in the developed world. The well-established financial and banking systems of a number of developed market economies fell into crisis (e.g., in the Nordic countries, Nyberg and Vihriälä, 1993).

Though more severe than previous ones, this recession was still not so deep as the economic downturn in Central and Eastern Europe (CEE) economies. The recession in the West had a predominantly cyclical character compared to the mostly structural causes of the downturn in CEE countries. It is no surprise, therefore, that signs of the banks' fragility and of a potential financial crisis have been gaining in intensity and urgency in CEE economies, including the more advanced ones.[2]

In these circumstances, both external and domestic observers seemed to agree that financial markets and financial intermediation were the spheres where a further radical advance was most urgently needed in all transition economies. The 'second' financial and banking reform was on the agenda. Views, however, diverged as to what should be done and how the existing constraints should be handled.

This discussion concentrated in particular on banks and their functional efficiency and stability. This reflects the fairly general consensus that banks are and should be the core of financial systems during transition, and especially in its early stages (see, e.g., Lampe, 1992). The relevant issue is therefore not whether banks have a key role, but what types of banks there should be and what changes in their environment and incentives are required to secure a more satisfactory standard of financial intermediation for transition economies.

Should the old-established banks continue to play their dominant role, providing restructuring, privatization and changed incentives (Dittus, 1994); or should the newly-emerging banks (Phelps *et al.*, 1993) or banking institutions from the West (Schmieding and Buch, 1992) be increasingly responsible for these changes?

A related strategic issue is what type of banking system is best for transition economies. While banks of a universal type, implying integration of commercial and investment banking, are increasingly given preference in the literature (Saunders and Walter, 1991), the significant risk implied in their adoption by transition economies is linked to the potential re-emergence of their traditional behaviour patterns (Hare, 1992).

Are these issues similar in all transition economies and, consequently, could there be a common solution? Such an assumption seemed to prevail in the literature on transition, addressing the financial markets' development in general terms, without reflecting specific features of individual transition economies. However, these economies appear to be increasingly differentiated. Therefore, to avoid biased conclusions, their common and specific features should be evaluated in a more balanced way, if relevant policy assessments are to be worked out.

Certainly, it can be claimed that most outcomes are similar; surprisingly enough even the fall in economic activity was almost the same among Visegrád countries, despite their different transition strategies. It is also true that they still have to cope with the common constraints inherited from the past and, no doubt, the goals of the second financial and banking reform will also be roughly parallel in all transition economies.

At the same time, the transition economies of CEE became much more differentiated compared with the conditions of the first financial reform when two-tier banking systems were introduced. This reflects developments in the economic, institutional as well as policy spheres, including finance and banking. In this respect, the policies addressing bad, non-performing loans, undercapitalization of banks and inter-enterprise arrears, to name just the main structural constraints, diverged widely in the instruments used and in their timing even across the relatively homogeneous group of Visegrád countries.

The type, intensity and time horizon of financial and banking reform in each country can be viewed as an outcome of the three interrelated dimensions: heritage of the past; present state and existing properties of financial markets and banks; policy goals and preferences.

The reform options available for individual countries, their viability as well as their costs and benefits depend on these characteristics. The more differentiated they prove to be, the more the discussion of the financial markets and of second banking reform should allow for the specific features of a particular country. Generalizations based on the experience of a representative country, be it Poland or Hungary as the most discussed cases, should therefore not be carried too far without qualifications.

2   The quest for functional efficiency and stability of the banking system

The properties which should be secured in any financial and banking system can be grouped into two dimensions: functional efficiency[3] and safety and stability. As discussed by Saunders and Walter (1991), financial systems in Western market economies, however varied they may be, aim to provide static (allocational) and dynamic efficiency (in financial innovations and in accelerated rates of capital formation) with simultaneous safe and sound financial intermediation.

The goals of efficiency and stability are interrelated. Though complementary in the long run, the policies for their achievement in reality can be conflicting. The waves of regulation and deregulation in the banking and financial fields experienced in the world economy since the 1920s and 1930s should be interpreted just as efforts to establish and re-establish a proper balance between the stability and efficiency objectives, given the conditions and preferences of the particular development stage.

With the start of transition and the initiation of institutional changes in both financial and real spheres, another issue arose for the emerging market economies (EMEs): what should be the proper balance between the goals of functional efficiency on one side and the stability and safety of the banking system on the other, and how to accomplish the adjustment in the follow-up stages?

The main driving force for the enhancement of functional efficiency is definitely competition; not so much in the Marshallian, but rather in the Schumpeterian sense, i.e., what matters are the incentive aspects of workable, contestable competition. If competition is weak and too constrained, functional efficiency is not likely to advance. But if it is too tough, it may become destructive in its pressure on profit margins and capital, with the resulting chain of bank crises and/or bail-outs, in each case undermining the stability of the entire banking system and public confidence.

Assessments of financial markets in EMEs more or less unanimously highlighted the absence of effective competitive pressure (see e.g., OECD, 1991; Schmieding and Buch, 1992; Corbett and Mayer, 1991). The evidence for this conclusion was provided, among others, by the existence of banks' high nominal profits (sometimes even super-normal in the early stage of transition, however artificial they could be in reality). As the main source of these profits was the spread between the banks' borrowing and lending interest rates, the argument was that these spreads could be maintained significantly higher than the customary 1—2 per cent on competitive financial markets of developed economies just because of the low competitive pressure.

High profit margins coexisted with a persistently low standard of banking services, only gradual extension of the range of products offered to clients, overstaffing and high operating costs of the profitable banks. Low competitive pressure was thus associated with persistently low functional efficiency. The existing soft, non-demanding environment could hardly generate incentives for quick adjustment and for a spectacular increase in banks' efficiency.

At the same time, the banking sector seemed to be stable in the initial stage of transition, despite technical insolvency of most existing banks according to international standards and despite the dramatic fall in economic activity in all transition economies. The conditions for such stability were implied in the continued state umbrella over the banking institutions, in low competitive pressure in the real economy, and in almost no occurrence of bankruptcies, keeping the entire business sector afloat.

To conclude, the financial and banking systems which came into existence after the first wave of reforms were associated with low competitive pressure and low functional efficiency, and their stability was secured mostly from outside, exogenously. The established balance was thus of a 'bad equilibrium' type. The challenge of the transition was to accomplish the shift from bad to good equilibrium.

Though differentiated across individual countries, the policies and developments initiated in the first transition stage started to work towards increased efficiency in both real and financial spheres. The state authorities were more and more relieved of their previous ownership functions, privatization programmes were initiated, competitive pressure gradually became stronger and bankruptcies increased.

As a consequence of the changes, the inherent fragility of the former seeming stability of the banking system was revealed. Policies aimed at increased efficiency inevitably eroded the status quo. To cope with the changed conditions, the banks were induced to increase their allocations for reserves and for loan-loss provisions. This should explain why despite tougher competition, interest spreads continued to increase rather than decrease in transition economies and, at the same time, banks' profits margins showed a decreasing tendency — according to the IAS they fell mostly into the red (for ex-Czechoslovakia and the Czech Republic see Table 10.1, for the data on Hungary see Chapter 12).

In this context, the alarming weakness of a number of Hungarian banks revealed in the above cited report by the international monetary institutions (see endnote 2) did not necessarily imply that their standard was worse than elsewhere. Rather, their constraints and fragility apparently came more rapidly to light due to the more demanding environment which had recently been imposed in Hungary compared to other EMEs. This refers in particular to the provisions of the new bankruptcy and banking legislation which came into force at the beginning of 1992 (see Chapter 5).

It follows that the characteristics of a banking system which appeared satisfactory in the given conditions of a particular country and/or transition stage may prove entirely deficient in others. While the records of individual countries in promoting competitiveness, functional efficiency and stability of their banking systems differed widely, the rationale of the second banking reform applied without doubt to all EMEs.

3   Legacy of the past: an unsolved issue

As Ábel and Bonin point out in Chapter 5, the current roadblock for transition is the financial markets. However, one should ask the following question. To what extent are the existing constraints, deficiencies and risks implied in the financial sector of all EMEs inevitable by-products of the given development stage or, conversely, attributable to the policies followed? The diverging stances and even disagreements both inside transition countries and among outside observers relate in particular to the policies which addressed (or did not address) their heritage (Begg and Portes, 1992; Herr *et al.*, 1991; Klaus, 1992; Schmieding and Buch, 1992).

Institutional and ownership changes progressed everywhere more slowly than expected. When trying to identify the reasons, the explanation could be rather simple: initial over-optimistic expectations not properly taking into account the inherently long-term character of institutional and behavioral changes, unlike macroeconomic stabilization and liberalization.

However, there are grounds for arguing that the one-sided preoccupation with macroeconomic policies and goals in the first transition stage, coupled with the failure to address the legacy of the past effectively and early on, delayed the progress of financial markets in transition economies, at the same time hindering output and restructuring (Nuti and Portes, 1993).

The properties of financial and banking systems in EMEs can be viewed as an outcome of the three main causal factors: legacy of the past; developments in the course of transition; the type of banking system adopted.

3.1   Options in coping with the legacy of the past: stock versus flow approach

The occurrence of bad loans, debt contract failures, bankruptcies and banking crises is certainly not confined to EMEs. However, unlike in the developed world, in the reforming countries of CEE debt contract failures became a widespread, mass phenomenon. The main causal factor must be seen in the specific feature of EMEs: a legacy of the past.

This legacy imposed a number of constraints on the development of financial intermediation, including a lack of expertise and qualified personnel. However, the most important structural ones proved to be undercapitalization of banks and bad, non-performing loans in their portfolios coupled with inter-enterprise arrears.

There are two main reasons why debt contract failures and bad loans became persistent features of EMEs and thus acquired a structural character.

The first one is the inertia of the traditional behaviour pattern of economic agents. In the established regime of a standard market economy any enterprise is encouraged (and induced) to make all efforts to comply with the 'rules of the game'; being required, among other things, to honour debt contracts at their maturity. However, parallel micro-economic and institutional prerequisites which could provide both the incentives to adhere to contract conditions and the means to enforce them were initially lacking in the EMEs.

In the given environment, neither banks nor suppliers were ready to initiate procedures, including bankruptcy, against their defaulting clients. Commercial banks appeared to be dependent on the survival of their major clients and their apparent passivity in enforcing credit contracts (Begg and Portes, 1992) was conditioned by their own fragile situation, given their sub-standard capital/assets ratios, along with non-existent or rather limited loan-loss provisions.

The unsolved inherited problems interacted with the parallel consequences of transition itself. These resulted in particular from the impact of a deep recession, from both exogenous and endogenous shocks and discontinuities as well as from by-products of the ongoing restructuring. The consequences of old and new bad loans and debt contract failures mutually reinforced themselves. This was the second major reason why bad loans and debt contract failures in EMEs acquired a persistent, structural character. As a result, the disease proved to be a long-term and contagious one.

In principle, in coping with the legacy of a centrally-planned economy two alternative strategies could be adopted. First, to draw a clear dividing line with the past at an early stage of transition, i.e. to eliminate monetary overhang and clean the balance sheets of banks and firms when they were still only parts of the all-comprising state sector. Second, to postpone the principal solution to the privatization phase and to the follow-up restructuring of privatized enterprises.

The former approach addresses the inherited stock first, aiming to avoid its distorting impact on the emerging flows. The latter one, on the other hand, leaves the accumulated stock untouched, relying on partial corrections via flows and struggling along until privatization takes place.

The companies' performance in the past, their balance sheets, profits and liabilities had hardly any correlation with their current standing in the changed conditions and even less with their potential. The merit of eliminating inherited financial liabilities at the very start of transition was therefore seen as a levelling of the ground, with the assumption that once not locked-in, both banks and enterprises could proceed in accordance with rational criteria and incentives, addressing the present problems instead of being absorbed and constrained by the distorted past.

This was also the rationale behind the former approach. Its conclusions underlined the importance of the cleaning of banks' balance sheets and re-capitalization (Brainard, 1991). The sooner these are accomplished, the better are the prospects for economic recovery.

The crucial constraint of this approach was the dominance of state ownership in both banking and non-banking institutions at the start of transition. It made any write-off and recapitalization subject to the risk of an unchanged behaviour pattern and of early re-emergence of former ills. At the same time, it also implied the moral hazard problem when it became clear that the bail-out was strictly not a once and for all measure.

Within the framework of this approach a number of options have been suggested, including currency reform, general or partial debt cancellation, and debt socialization via some form of debt swaps (bad debt for good debt, debt for equity, debt for bonds, and debt for savings). Though intensively discussed in literature, neither the option of currency reform nor the general cancellation of old debts or their transformation via some form of debt swaps have been adopted in any transition economy.

The comparative advantage of the latter approach was the link between privatization and implementation of recapitalization and financial restructuring. Privatization, though not a panacea solving alone the issue of corporate governance, provides for a clear identification and enforcement of property rights and for changed incentives in both banks and enterprises. In the course of time, more and more observers highlighted this link as a necessary prerequisite for success (see, e.g., Begg and Portes, 1992).

The drawback of this approach was the implied time span of policy vacuum in dealing with the debts and bad loans accumulated in the past. As their impact on flows was not alleviated, the volume of bad loans was likely to increase and the occurrence of debt contract failures become further disseminated. The resulting risk was increased destabilization of payments flows and worsened payments discipline in the interim period. The longer such a period, the higher the costs incurred.

3.2   Stock versus flows policies in ex-Czechoslovakia and in the Czech Republic: a pragmatic compromise

The Czechoslovak authorities initially did not foresee any interference with the inherited stock of enterprise liabilities, at least not until the first wave of voucher privatization was over.

This stance was based on the assumption that swift mass privatization could and would be accomplished, in particular through voucher schemes. At the same time, potential interim measures such as efforts to change management incentives, commercialization of state firms and their transformation into legally separate entities were not considered capable of hardening the state firms' budget constraint and, accordingly, the government did not intend to resort to them to any considerable extent.

However, the prolonged privatization horizon compared to initial expectations, as well as emerging constraints in the flow of funds and increasing disarray in financial intermediation prompted the authorities to implement a number of interim pragmatic measures. The initial policy stance notwithstanding, ex-Czechoslovakia took the lead among transition economies in correcting the legacy of the past. The steps effected included the following in particular.

The establishment of Consolidation Bank

Consolidation Bank, a form of recovery agency, was founded by the Treasury and the Central Bank in March 1991 with the assignment to manage the state's long-term assets. Its immediate role was, however, to take over perpetual credits for inventories from the commercial banks.

These special credits (extended without any fixed maturity and at an artificially low interest rate fixed at 6 per cent) supplanted firms' funds confiscated by the government's budgetary authorities in the early 1970s. As its first big transaction, Consolidation Bank took over a substantial part of these credits, amounting to CSK 110 bn, i.e. almost one-fifth of the total bank credits then extended to enterprises and households.

The transfer was relatively easy to effect as it concerned only two banks, Commercial Bank, Prague and General Credit Bank, Bratislava; moreover, the perpetual credits for inventories as a special class could be easily sorted out. Though the move helped to clean the balance sheets of these banks, the respective credits were sorted out because of their special type. However, they could not be labelled 'bad loans' as a whole. This is also suggested by the fact that a substantial share has already been recovered by Consolidation Bank.

Only later did Consolidation Bank extend its activities to normal non-standard (classified) loans. Unlike the above identified mass shift, commercial banks had to negotiate their transfer from the balance sheets on a case-by-case basis and arrive at an agreement on the discount in the deal, incurring thus some nominal losses. To support these activities, Consolidation Bank was recapitalized by the National Property Fund, drawing on the proceeds from privatization.

In accordance with the legislation on privatization, the National Property Fund could be asked to participate in financing the liabilities of privatized firms in case of their bankruptcy. While this legislation was recently amended to phase out these legal obligations of the National Property Fund, Consolidation Bank should provide an option. According to the introduced scheme, the creditors involved in the bankruptcy proceedings are entitled to sell their claims at a price below face value to Consolidation Bank (the standard price suggested was 60 per cent of the face value). This procedure should alleviate the negative impact on creditors of the anticipated prolonged time horizon of bankruptcy proceedings.

Recapitalization of commercial banks

Though discussed from the start of transition, the decision to recapitalize the big commercial banks which took over their portfolios from the former monobank system was taken by the authorities only in October 1991, i.e., almost two years after the introduction of the two-tier system. Financed from privatization proceeds, the amount of CSK 50 bn (i.e., equal to about 8 per cent of all bank credits to enterprises) was allocated for banks' recapitalization and write-offs through debt-for-bond swaps. The bonds allocated for the swap were to be repaid from privatization revenues or, alternatively, exchanged for equities in the privatized companies.

Part of this sum (CSK 12 bn) was earmarked to increase the banks' own capital, and the major part (CSK 38 bn) was allocated for write-offs of non-performing loans. The path the banks were expected to follow was to write off liabilities of such firms which, according to the banks' appraisal, had a good chance to survive given the bail-out, and the bank would be ready to extend them new credits.

Netting out companies' bilateral and multilateral arrears

Commercial Bank, and later on specialized institutions including private ones, took the initiative to net out mutual overdue obligations of enterprises. Though having some success, the netting activities also had their constraints. They could address only the symptoms of the problem, not its causes. Moreover, they increasingly interfered with companies' policies and preferences. With regard to these drawbacks, obligatory netting of mutual overdue obligations was discontinued in the second half of 1993.

The impact of the above steps aimed to cope with inherited bad loans and payments arrears appeared to be rather ambiguous. The measures taken were only resorted to under growing pressure and targeted simply to alleviate the worst problems.[4] Moreover, they were adopted and executed as an induced deviation from the government's policy stance[5] which linked the principal solution to privatization only.

Not solving the problem completely, the stock continued to be a constraint, and its impact on flows materialized in the follow-up period. Being fed-in by the side-effects of the stabilization policies and by both external and domestic shocks, credit contract failures and inter-enterprise arrears persisted on a mass scale, and their volumes increased further.[6]

From the stock approach point of view, the measures taken were only a compromise and were moreover delayed. To avoid a moral hazard problem, the banks' recapitalization should be a one-off action. As only a partial solution was effected, there was a risk that recapitalization would have to be repeated.

On the other hand, the steps to correct the legacy of the past were taken at an earlier stage compared to other EMEs and, while not solving the problem, they evidently alleviated its intensity. This seemed to be important particularly in the case of former Czechoslovakia where, unlike some other transition economies, relatively lower inflation rates had not eroded the weight of past debts significantly.

However controversial, the measures effected may well be one of the reasons for the relatively smooth development of the Czech banking system. Despite deep economic recession and the shocks and discontinuities experienced, there has as yet been no banking crisis, no case of a major bank evidently heading for bankruptcy, no dramatic decrease or discontinuity in bank lending.

Nevertheless, due to the factors generated in the course of transition, the intensity of the bad debt problem has been increasing. This would evidently be the case even if a more radical clean-up of banks' portfolios and an entire cancellation of all past debts were effected.

As follows from Table 10.2, the volume of so-called risk credits, i.e., classified, non-standard loans, amounted in 1993 in the Czech Republic to more than one-fifth of total banks' credits extended to firms and households in domestic currency. This share increased further in the course of the year.

According to available information, in the early stage of the stabilization and liberalization programme in former Czechoslovakia in 1991 about one-fourth of the outstanding loans were estimated to be either bad, non-performing or loans with considerable risk involved (Hrnčíř, 1992 and 1993). Such a share, i.e., in the range of one-fifth to one-fourth of total bank credits, was often referred to by external observers as the figure representing the volume of non-performing loans in Czechoslovakia. Blommenstein and Lange (1993) in a recent study quoted 21 per cent.

Certainly, an assessment of the real extent of bad, non-performing loans in transition economies could hardly be precise and unambiguous, given all the qualifications of data classification and evaluation. Nevertheless, the concept of risk credits, as used in the Czech banking statistics, should cover all the types of classified loans, of which bad, non-performing loans are only one, the worst sub-category.

According to the data in Table 10.2, the share of non-performing loans in total bank credits increased from 4 per cent at the end of 1992 to 6 per cent at the end of September 1993. However, comparing the relative changes in the same period, total banks' credits increased by 14 per cent, risk credits by 35 per cent and non-performing loans by 90 per cent.

Besides the policies already adopted, the range of options to cope with the bad debt problem could be extended by some other approaches, in particular by debt for equity swaps. Law No. 21/1992 on Banks provides for the capitalization of banks' credits to non-banking institutions. In accordance with this law, commercial banks are entitled to acquire stakes amounting to up to 10 per cent of the capital of a non-banking institution. The total volume of their stakes in non-banking firms should not, however, exceed 25 per cent of their own capital and reserves. To hold stakes exceeding these norms, the prior consent of the Central Bank is required.

However, the identified limits of banks' equity holdings did not seem to be an effective constraints. Rather, banks were discouraged by the non-transparent situation of companies and by the unsettled, fluctuating ratios of share prices. In the circumstances, the risk of trading bad debt for bad equity was relatively high. Besides, when co-owners of firms which turn bankrupt, banks were and are in a much less favourable position *vis-à-vis* other creditors to recover their assets. It follows that the time for debt for equity swaps is still to come.

A specific feature of ex-Czechoslovakia was the relatively high share of bad loans incurred in foreign trade deals. In accordance with the existing legislation, only claims on domestic debtors could be written off, given their liquidation or completed bankruptcy proceedings. To cope with this constraint, the amended procedure should also permit parallel write-offs in the case of foreign debtors. Moreover, a specialized consolidation agency for management of bad foreign loans and frozen claims, the counterpart of the domestic Consolidation Bank, appears to be on the agenda.

4   Restructuring the banking system: the causal factors and policies

4.1   Institutional developments and competitive environment

Identifying the institutional developments in the Czech banking system compared to other countries, the question is to what extent the adopted policies contributed to an enhanced competitive environment and, on the other hand, what might hold back the desired outcomes in reality.

Introduction of a two-tier system

Czechoslovak banks were restructured at the beginning of 1990 into a two-tier system comprising the Central Bank, the State Bank of Czechoslovakia, and mostly newly-created commercial and savings banks.[7] The change, though planned before this date, only began with the start of radical transition. Both Hungary and Poland effected this change earlier, in 1987 and 1988 respectively.

This difference was apparently of some importance for the institutional developments and behaviour characteristics in the banking sphere. On the one hand, being a late-comer to institution building, Czechoslovakia faced considerable constraints at the start of transition compared to Hungary and Poland: unlike these countries, it was not possible to draw on the already established two-tier banking institutions and the legislation and prudential regulations already in force.

However, being a late-comer also meant that big banks were installed as separate entities only with the start of radical political and economic reforms.[8] Thus most big 'old' banks were not much older than the 'new' small private ones. Besides, starting reform activities with the prospect of being included in the forthcoming first wave of voucher privatization, with changed incentives and mostly newly-recruited management, the behaviour pattern, policies and preferences of old banks did not diverge in principle from those of new banks.

Certainly, the old banks' network staff were involved in the past developments and their personal ties with 'traditional' clients implied the risk of biased decisions at the cost of new entrants. However, the other side of the coin was the asset of their expertise and information on enterprises with which they had been dealing. Given the changed incentives and environment both outside and inside banks, this asset was likely to outweigh the risk implied.

As experience showed, in the course of transition the dividing line among Czech banking institutions could be increasingly identified not between old and new ones, but rather between the well and badly managed banks.

Changes in the size and composition of the banking sector

As in other transition economies, the introduction of a two-tier framework marked the start of a dramatic increase in bank and also non-bank financial intermediaries. From only seven commercial and savings banks operating in January 1990, numbers have steadily grown, amounting to 50 in the Czech Republic alone in mid-1993 (compare Table 10.3).

While all operating banks were state-owned at the beginning of 1990,[9] at the beginning of 1993 there was only one bank in the Czech Republic, Consolidation Bank, entirely state-owned, apart from the Central Bank. As follows from Table 10.3, most banks acquired the form of joint-stock companies. However, via the shares held by National Property Fund the state has retained a significant stake of around 43 per cent in most old banks (the 'big four') privatized through a voucher scheme.[10] The other banks, newly created, are owned by either domestic and/or foreign capital.

The Law on Banks (No. 21/1992) provided a liberal regime for the entry of foreign banks and at mid-1993 just half of all licensed banks in the Czech Republic were either partly or wholly foreign-owned. In accordance with the law, foreign banks can establish not only joint-venture banks and wholly-owned subsidiaries as before, but also branches. Full national treatment is accorded to all licensed foreign banks in the country.

The Law on Banks (No 21/1992) provided for a universal type of banking, integrating both commercial and investment banking activities. In accordance with the law, most banks developed as universal banks. This trend resembled the Polish solution, while the Hungarian legislation seemed to opt for a more pronounced distinction and separation of commercial and investment banking. Along with universal banks, a number of specialized banking institutions started their activities, including Czech-Moravian Guarantee and Development Bank (targeted to promote small and medium firms), savings banks for housing construction as well as banks dealing in mortgages.

Despite the rapidly increasing number of banking institutions, the credit and deposit markets continued to reflect their infancy stage: a limited range of products, low competitive pressure and serious market imperfections. Nevertheless, compared to the initial stage of reform in 1990, the rate of change proved to be significant. The combined share of six big, i.e. old banks in total credits extended by the banking sector in former Czechoslovakia was as high as 98 per cent and their share of deposits was even higher, more than 99 per cent at the end of 1990 (see Table 10.4). A relatively sharp drop to a 77 per cent share in total credits only a year later was mostly due to the transfer of a substantial part of perpetual credits for inventories from the balance sheets of big commercial banks to the newly-established Consolidation Bank. Then, however, the process of changes in the market structure accelerated.

Though the degree of concentration in both credit and deposit markets remained relatively high and the share of newly-established banks, including foreign-owned ones, has been increasing only gradually, a tendency to a more equal distribution and more competitive setting in both credit and deposit markets has been clearly developing since 1990.[11] Table 10.5 identifies this tendency in the Czech credit and deposit markets in 1993.

Credit market developments

Compared with the almost negligible credit activities at the end of 1990, the newly-founded small banks managed to increase their share to 22 per cent in total bank credits, to almost 29 per cent in short-term credits and to more than 30 per cent in medium-term credits by the end of September 1993, i.e., within a period of less than three years. In contrast, in the long-term market segment the role of big banks (plus Consolidation Bank) continued to be rather high.[12] Such an outcome could, however, be expected. Given the shortage of domestically generated long-term savings, coupled with considerable risk in tying up the resources in an unstable environment, the new entrants into banking industry, mostly with a rather limited capital base, could hardly afford to lend extensively long term.

The development of banks with dominant positions in individual market segments diverged: the share of Commercial Bank and Czech Savings Bank in short-term and medium-term credit markets declined steadily, while the opposite tendency could be identified for Investment Bank and Czech Savings Bank in long-term credits.

The related data on sectors' proportions reveal that the share of private sector (non-financial corporate and non-corporate businesses) on total banks' credits continued to grow in the course of 1993, reaching 48 per cent at the end of September 1993. The shares of credits to state companies and households correspondingly declined.

Deposit market developments

Though the role of new banks in deposit markets has been increasing as well, the degree of concentration and the big banks' share continued to be considerably higher compared to credit markets. At the end of September 1993 this share still amounted to about 80 per cent of total deposits (see Table 10.5), while for long-term deposits it was as high as 97 per cent.

The newly-founded banks mostly lacked branch networks in the initial period of their existence and, consequently, their opportunities to collect primary deposits were rather limited. As a result, they appeared much more dependent on Central Bank refinancing credits than big banks. While these credits amounted to only 5—10 per cent of big banks' resources, they were as high as 60 per cent in the case of small banks.

Though declining, the share of Czech Saving Bank in deposit markets remained dominant in 1993 (45 per cent in September), in particular in long-term deposits (60 per cent). This high share is linked with the role of households' savings (46 per cent of total) which were traditionally collected by savings banks. Two major banks with established networks, Czech Savings Bank and Commercial Bank together accounted for 67 per cent of total deposits, 65 per cent of short-term, 76 per cent of medium-term and 67 per cent of long-term deposits in September 1993. This reveals the continued rather high degree of concentration in all segments of deposit markets.

Nevertheless, the data on deposit and credit market developments in the Czech Republic showed that a process of de-specialization and integration of previously traditionally separated financial circuits had been taking place. Commercial banks were increasingly engaged in deposit markets, including household savings, while savings banks developed their lending activities and services to enterprises.

The interbank money and foreign exchange markets

Though still underdeveloped and constrained by a number of imperfections, the instalment of interbank money and foreign exchange markets contributed to the promotion of a competitive environment. The former quantity constraints in fund and credit allocations could be gradually phased out and market clearing functions of interest rates enhanced.

4.2　Trends in regulation and deregulation

In the 1970s and early 1980s, on the other hand, the OECD countries in particular effected a wide-ranging process of domestic deregulation and external liberalization in the financial sector. The view started to dominate that the increasingly complex process of allocation of financial and real resources could hardly be met by over-protected and over-regulated financial and banking systems, particularly in an environment of increased internationalization. As a consequence, interest rate controls were largely, or entirely, dismantled, cartel agreements on interest rates and commission prohibited, controls on the setting up of new banks were lifted or eased, regulations limiting the range of permissible activities of banks were relaxed, and financial systems were more intensively opened to foreign banks and foreign competition.

The situation in the EMEs was specific and challenging in the requirement to build up simultaneously the institutional, legal and operational conditions for a market-type system and to advance in a parallel way with both efficiency and stability targets. The issue faced by policy makers was to decide what could and should be the pace of reform to liberalize and restructure the financial and banking systems (enhancing their functional efficiency) and, at the same time, to reconcile the objective of functional efficiency with that of stability and soundness in each transition stage. On the whole, the monetary authorities in individual EMEs responded in different ways. What were the characteristics of the approach adopted in former Czechoslovakia and in the Czech republic?

Deregulation policies

While departing from the totally regulated system of a centrally-planned economy, Czechoslovak monetary authorities installed ceilings for credit volume and interest rates to help implement their monetary and credit policies, given the constraints and imperfections of the existing environment.

The Central Bank set individual credit volume limits for all major banks in the context of its strictly restrictive monetary and credit policies at the start of transition. Though formally lifted only in October 1992, these upper limits of credit activities in fact did not prove to be binding constraints as the commercial banks concerned were rather cautious in extending new credits.

Given the existing non-competitive environment, the Central Bank imposed obligatory interest rate ceilings on commercial banks' credits, to avoid interest rates unduly surging. These ceilings, introduced in October 1990, were gradually modified and phased out entirely on 1 April 1992.

The extent and the speed of interest rate deregulation was remarkable, even compared to the postwar experience of developed economies, and represented a clear signal of the determination of the monetary authorities to move to a market-type environment. Though the phasing out of interest rate regulation seemed to be to some extent substituted by 'window guidance' by the Central Bank,[13] in principle commercial banks were free since then to set their lending and borrowing rates. This gave them the leeway to develop their own interest rate policies, to react to market conditions and to reflect the differences in creditworthiness and riskiness of their clients and projects.

The only regulated rates, apart from Consolidation Bank with its special mission to manage the state's long-term assets, remained in special subsidized schemes of households' loans (in particular for housing construction), which were kept afloat from the past. Housing loans in the Czech Republic amounted to about one-tenth of long-term bank credits. Though a much lower share than in Hungary, for example, both their volume and interest rates were nevertheless important for the corresponding aggregates.[14]

The introduction of prudential regulation

The more competitive and liberalized the environment, the more banks and other financial institutions are exposed to risk and, consequently, the more necessary are the prudential rules and guidelines of their behaviour. The policies of deregulation, aimed at increasing the functional efficiency of banking institutions, phased out such forms of intervention which can be summarized as anti-competitive. Such examples were ceilings on credit volume and interest rates. Prudential regulation, on the other hand, should cope with the implied systemic risk by protecting clients and investors and securing the stability and credibility of the banking institutions and of the entire financial system.

It follows that the effected deregulation steps and the introduction of various rules of prudential regulation were related to different dimensions of banking activities. Deregulation and the simultaneous introduction of new regulatory measures were thus not contradictory, but rather complementary. In accordance with Law No. 22/1992 and its amendment No. 6/1993, establishing the Czech National Bank, the setting of guidelines, supervision of banks and prudential regulation of the whole banking system were vested with the Central Bank.

Supervising the banks was a priority from the very start of transition. A special department of the Central Bank being made responsible, all banks incorporated in the Czech Republic were subject to both on-side and off-side examinations. A similar priority was attached to the development of auditing, obliging banks to have their books scrutinized by external auditors too.

The setting of entry regulations for the banking industry reflected a trade-off between the dual objective of promoting a competitive environment and the soundness and stability of banking institutions. Though principally maintaining the policy stance supporting the new entries, the Central Bank set a relatively demanding standard for the granting of new bank licences.[15] The interaction of the constraints inherited from the past with the risk generated in the course of transition made the banking system and individual institutions vulnerable. In the circumstances, the priority given to the building up of a credible and stable system of financial intermediation, which found its expression in entry conditions, proved entirely warranted.

The corresponding argument refers to the scrutiny imposed on foreign exchange activities. Reflecting the underdevelopment of domestic foreign exchange markets, the limited supply of qualified personnel, technical know-how and other resources available to individual banks, licences for foreign exchange transactions were graded into five categories, thus regulating the foreign exchange engagement of individual banks as well as their access to the interbank foreign exchange market.

As elsewhere, the introduced rules of prudential regulation followed the standards recommended by the Basle Committee for Banking Supervision and Practices. However, in their targeting and in setting the time profile, the Central Bank had to account for the constraining factors, in particular for the heritage of the past. Consequently, a step-wise approach was mostly adopted.

In implementing the standard capital/assets ratio, the required target of eight per cent, risk weighted, was only made obligatory for new entrants, i.e. for those starting banking activities after 1 January 1991. The old banks were granted a transitional adjustment period with the following interim targets: at least 4.5 per cent by the end of 1991; 6.25 per cent by the end of 1993; and the final target of 8 per cent not later than the end of 1996. In a parallel way, the banks' liquidity ratios, rules for credit exposures and for open foreign exchange positions also provided for gradual stages of adjustment.

Since 1 June 1993 the banks incorporated in the Czech Republic were obliged not to exceed their net credit exposure as follows:

— to one client (or an integrated group): not more than 40 per cent of bank's capital by the end of 1993, and 25 per cent by the end of 1995;
— to a bank in the Czech Republic and in the OECD countries (or an integrated group of these banks): not more than 80 per cent of bank's capital by the end of 1995;
— to legal persons, equity capital of which the bank owns in the amount of 10 per cent and more, or controls them: not more than 20 per cent of bank's capital by the end of 1993;
— to the ten largest debtors (combined): (the total amount of credit) not more than 230 per cent of bank's capital by the end of 1995.

5 Policy options in developing efficiency and stability of the banking system

5.1 Developments and policies in the transition years

At the very start of transition, former Czechoslovakia adopted a type of shock approach to macroeconomic stabilization and to price, foreign trade and foreign exchange liberalization. At the same time, it launched a programme of mass privatization, including privatization of banking institutions. Though delayed compared to initial aspirations, the steps implemented by this programme pushed the country well ahead in the process of institutional and ownership changes, both in 'real' and financial spheres. However, after passing from the initial stage of macroeconomic stabilization to the next adjustment and consolidation stage with its dominant institutional and micro-economic developments, the policies followed a more gradual pattern.

As discussed above, a relatively wide time scope was set for meeting the norms of prudential regulation. In principle, an evolutionary approach was also followed in coping with the inherited problems and in working out the bad debt problem. Old and new banking institutions coexisted, and a solution was seen in their privatization and internal restructuring, coupled with increasing competitive pressure from both foreign and newly-created banks, rather than in some form of dismantling or discontinuity.

A step-by-step approach was also adopted in implementing bankruptcy legislation.[16] The bankruptcy law approved by the Parliament of former Czechoslovakia in the autumn of 1991 was to come into force on 1 October 1991. The extent of its enforcement was, however, constrained by an article effectively preventing bankruptcy procedures from starting except in the special case of 'overindebtedness'. Though scheduled for full applicability from the autumn of 1992, it was once more postponed until April 1993 and, at the same time, its provisions were amended by a new reading in the Czech Parliament at the beginning of 1993. These amendments introduced a number of safeguards, including the institution of a three-months' grace period, aimed at avoiding a domino effect and an uncontrolled chain of bankruptcies.

The reasoning behind such a cautious approach was to reconcile the intensity of the given law's impact with the underlying institutional and economic conditions of the particular development stage. In the given period, the constraining factors were seen in particular in the delayed implementation of the first wave of voucher privatization and in the still underdeveloped infrastructure, including the courts. That was why the amendments to the bankruptcy law provided for, among other things, outside court solutions. The intention was to permit bankruptcies to occur, but at the same time to avoid their unnecessarily high costs.

The aim of both government and Central Bank was to maintain the balanced course and links of their policies with the advance in privatization and in micro-economic and institutional adjustment. As it turned out that, unlike macroeconomic stabilization and liberalization, institutional and ownership changes required longer to be effective, policies also had to become more evolutionary and gradual.

A number of positive features in the financial and banking developments in the Czech Republic can be linked to the policies adopted. There were no discontinuities in bank lending to enterprises and households, and old banks were in a substantially better shape compared to the initial stage when they were all technically bankrupt. Provided with sufficient time for adjustment, they could improve their capital/assets ratios and create previously lacking reserves and loan-loss provisions, to be better equipped to handle more extensive clients' bankruptcies. Moreover, the spread between lending and borrowing interest rates could be maintained at a relatively moderate level.

The extent and consequences of this borrowing-lending margin proved to be a controversial transition issue (Begg and Portes, 1992). On the one hand, the drawbacks of the large spreads were evident: a tax was in fact imposed on both savings and investment at a time when incentives to increase savings were vital for restructuring and economic recovery. This argument therefore called for as small margins as possible, excluding their use as a means of coping with the stock problem.

However, the other side of the coin was the stability and credibility of the entire banking system. This applied in particular to old banks, undercapitalized and lacking adequate reserves and loan-loss provisions. They had inherited a substantial share of bad loans and faced considerable uncertainty about the real performance of their portfolio once the wave of bankruptcies started. However, their potential competitors faced the same constraints and the still low competitive pressure in the domestic market allowed them to make use of a wider interest rate margin. This became a feasible way out for commercial banks.

Thus, the Central Bank found itself in a contradictory position: on the one hand, in the interests of the credibility of the banking system it motivated commercial banks to build up reserves and channel a large part of their profits into loan-loss provisions. At the same time it used forms of moral persuasion and 'window guidance' to make the large banks gradually narrow their spreads.

An acceptable compromise seemed to develop, avoiding both dramatic increases in spreads and the failure of the banks. As follows from Table 10.1, the average spread increased to 5—6 per cent in 1991 and 1992 and fluctuated at around 7 per cent in the second half of 1992 and in 1993. Though higher than in most developed market economies, it was, however, significantly lower and more stabilized than in other transition economies, including Hungary and Poland, and also lower than elsewhere in periods of economic reform (as demonstrated, for example, in Chile). To make such an international comparison of the margins consistent, the nominal data should be corrected for differentiated inflation rates in individual countries. Though to a lesser extent, in real terms also the average margin appeared relatively narrower compared to other EMEs.

Though evidently to some extent still the price to pay for persisting low efficiency, the interest rate margins enabled the banks' reserves and loan-loss provisions to grow to a more satisfactory level (see Table 10.2). Nevertheless, extensive debt contract failures and the implied bank risk made the price of credit higher than it might otherwise have been. The burden was thus shared by those debtors who did pay and honour their obligations, and also by those who would contract credits provided their cost were lower.

Due to this gradual approach in institutional and micro-economic policies, the adjustment costs, including the costs of debt contract failures and payment arrears, were widely spread, both in time and across individual types of economic agents. The sources drawn upon to cover the costs included: proceeds from privatization; state assets and budgetary means; and Central Bank funds. At the same time, a substantial part of the costs was met through negative real interest rates and wide borrowing-lending margins. It followed that the costs were distributed among a wide range of agents: households as savers, general public as tax-payers and recipients of privatization proceeds, and firms which were duly meeting the terms of their debt contracts and other obligations.

The spreading of costs made them easier to cope with and allowed gradual adjustment to take place. The disadvantage may have been a slower pace of restructuring, as defaulters only paid to a minor extent (as yet there have been no major cases of bankruptcy).

5.2   Pros and cons of alternative strategies

The apparent pros of any policies must be confronted with the cons. The often highlighted symbiosis of old banks and state enterprises (Dittus, 1994; Phelps *et al.*, 1993), the continued unsatisfactory level of competitive pressure and only slowly increasing role of new banks in the financial markets also generally apply to the Czech case. They can be interpreted as interrelated by-products of the adopted policies or as a consequence of the fact that other policies were not followed. Hence, what alternatives are there?

The options suggested in the literature include:

— dismantling the big old banks to make smaller units;
— importing the banking system from the West (Schmieding and Buch, 1992); and
— expanding new banks and shrinking old ones, e.g., via recapitalization of new instead of old (Phelps *et al.*, 1993).

The proposal to dismantle the big banking institutions in order to secure a more competitive environment was circulating especially in the initial stage of transition when the process of secession from the former monobank system was under way. Though attractive as a concept, its applicability was constrained by a number of arguments:

— the mere continuation of financial intermediation and payments flows at the initial stage of transition was only feasible through existing institutions with established networks;
— in the circumstances, the only viable option could have been to divide operations along regional lines. But such a solution could provide hardly any improvement, as the Polish experience with the

establishment of nine regional banks clearly demonstrated (Mullineux and Belka, 1993);
— any economy needs big banks, on both domestic and international grounds.

The entire take-over of the domestic banking sector by Western institutions took place only in the specific case of German unification. The main West German banks indeed rushed in and within a relatively short period effectively transformed the banking system in the 'Neuen Ländern' to the Western standard. However, even under intra-Germany conditions, these banks remained far behind expectations regarding their role in restructuring East German firms and providing new investments and fresh funds (Griffin, 1993).

In the Czech case, as well as in other transition economies, despite the favourable legal regime and a rapidly growing number of foreign banks and banks with foreign participation, their real engagement and the implied competitive pressure remained limited for some time. They have developed their activities rather cautiously, mostly confining themselves to specialized services in foreign exchange transactions for multinationals and joint-ventures, not yet moving into retail banking to a substantial extent. Under the existing conditions, the implied costs and risk associated with an early move into retail banking were evidently considered too high compared to the potential gains. However, with the increasing engagement of their clients in the Czech Republic, the incentives for 'moving in' became stronger, as suggested, for example, by the decision of Creditanstalt to establish several branches in the country. Nonetheless, if not due to other reasons, the mass take-over by foreign banks did not appear to be a viable option in the early stage of transition.

The drawbacks of existing institutions, slow emergence of new ones and hence lack of real competitive pressure, led to other attempts to encourage and help new entrants. One of the alternatives put forward was the recapitalization of the new, rather than the old banks. This scheme assumed the removal of a portion of depository accounts from existing banks and its transfer to new institutions (Phelps *et al.*, 1993, pp. 28—29); thus depleting the former and creating new large banks to provide healthy competition for the old institutions.

This line of reasoning deviates from the traditional approach and as such it certainly deserves in-depth discussion and evaluation. Due to the different progress in banking reform and conditions in individual transition economies, the potential gains and constraints of this alternative are likely to vary in each particular case.

There may, however, be several general qualifications to this approach. While the argument for the old banks' recapitalization was to compensate for the previous institutional past which was hardly related to current developments, on what grounds would some new banks be selected for recapitalization? This seems to imply to 'pick up winners' (for example, in the Czech Republic there are about 50 acting banks). However, such forms of 'industrial policy' are rather controversial. The approach is based on the assumption that there is a clear-cut dividing line between old and new banks regarding their behaviour patterns, incentives and efficiency.

The authors do not expect the existing banking institutions to play any positive role, expressing doubts about both the feasibility and rationale of their restructuring and privatization. The actual role of these banks is interpreted by the authors as the '... main tool in the state enterprises' strategy of resistance to significant departures from the status quo' (Phelps *et al.*, 1993, p. 25).

It appears, however, to be an open issue as to what extent these conclusions reflect the common characteristics and current state of affairs of all EMEs. Confronted with the evidence and experience from the Czech developments, the above line of reasoning seems to underestimate the adjustments taking place both within the existing banks and in their environment. Nevertheless, the Czech case may be specific in the sense that most old banks developed their activities only with the start of transition and shortly afterwards they were privatized in the framework of the voucher scheme. As a result, the dividing line runs between well and badly managed banks rather than between old and new ones. At the same time, the spontaneous development of Investment Privatization Funds and Investment Funds and Societies, along with the increasing involvement of foreign banks and the growing market share of new banks, seems to be imposing a more competitive environment for the big old banks too.

5.3   Trends in the sectors' shares of credit allocation

It has been often asserted that one of the main drawbacks, if not the single most damaging one, to banking intermediation in the EMEs is the continued flow of available funds to the wrong clients, in particular to the large, loss-making state firms, at the expense of prospective clients especially of the emerging private sector. A number of reasons have been cited in this respect, including:

— the continued symbiosis of state firms and their traditional creditors, exacerbated by the 'locked in' effect on banks;
— the availability of collateral;
— the too high level of interest rates constraining new entrants in particular;

—   the lack of expertise in assessing the creditworthiness and the degree of risk of individual clients and projects.

The potential misallocation of a considerable part of savings is an issue of key importance for all EMEs. In response to it, Begg and Portes (1992) suggested instituting selective credit policies as the first corrective step.

The main alleged culprit, the symbiotic relationship between the old banks and state enterprises, was in the past hardly avoidable. This was especially true for ex-Czechoslovakia, where there was virtually no private sector as late as 1990. However, as follows from Table 10.6, a remarkably increased volume of bank credits was earmarked for the private sector since then. For example, in the first half of 1993, credits to the private sector (including cooperatives) increased by more than 24 per cent, while to state firms they decreased in absolute terms. As a result, the share of the private sector of total bank credits in the Czech Republic surpassed 40 per cent in mid-1993, compared to 10 per cent at the end of 1991 (plus a further 10 per cent allocated at that time to cooperatives, which have since mostly been transformed). On the other hand, the share of state firms decreased in the same period from 67 per cent to 42 per cent. Consequently, the private sector's share of total bank credits (40 per cent) has considerably outrun its share of the GDP, estimated at 30 per cent in the first quarter of 1993.

The presented data on the private sector's share do not distinguish between the newly-emerging private businesses, firms sold to domestic and foreign investors and firms privatized through the voucher scheme. Accordingly, the resulting shift in the sectors' shares may appear less persuasive. Nevertheless, the available evidence on new credits extended by individual banks supports the conclusion that a significant reallocation of credits was going on in favour of the private sector.[17] This also applied to the old banks, as the share of newly-extended credits they lent to the private sector was not very much lower than the share to the group of new private banks, including foreign-owned ones.

The data on sectors' shares refer to only one dimension of the complex issue of credit allocation. Accordingly, this data can neither support nor reject the assertion that a considerable part of savings continued to be misallocated. The evidence presented should, however, contribute to some qualification of the conventional wisdom which seemed to develop, as if the once identified drawbacks of banking practices, including the symbiotic relationship between the old banks and old state firms, were inevitable phenomena persisting in the course of transition.

6   In conclusion: what type of banking system for EMEs?

The common standard for the emerging financial markets and banking institutions in transition economies is (and should be) provided by the developed market economies. However, following Saunders and Walter (1991), three alternative modes of financial contracting and flows can be distinguished:

— credit institutions, i.e. savings/commercial banking and other traditional forms of intermediated finance;
— the public securities markets, i.e. investment banking and securitized intermediation;
— private placement, which channels finance directly from lenders to borrowers.

At the same time, these types of linkages were dominant characteristics of individual development stages in the world economy. While after World War II traditional bank intermediation prevailed, since then the financial systems of developed market economies have become more market-oriented.[18] This shift was promoted in particular by the process of financial markets' deregulation, accompanied by the widely spreading replacement of non-negotiable debts and loans by negotiable securities, i.e., by securitization. The trend towards disintermediation has been further intensified by the increasing weight of privately-issued securities and related products.

Reflecting these degrees of maturity, the relevant standard for the evolving financial systems in transition economies should be the postwar stage of developed market economies rather than their current systems. However speedy the process of catching up in the institutional spheres might be, the successive development stages cannot be avoided. It seems therefore both naive and counterproductive to try to imitate, without adequate learning and adjustment process, the present highly sophisticated financial markets and products of developed market economies.

Though some trends and initial expectations suggest otherwise, which prompted Corbett and Mayer (1991) to address them as 'progress with the wrong model', there has been a fairly general consensus that banks are the institutions which are in place and which must form the core of financial systems in the EMEs.

Discussion of the advantages and disadvantages of a universal type of banking versus separated commercial and investment banking is related to the strategic issue of what the role of banks should be in the real sector and in the corporate governance in EMEs. Though not necessarily implying the German model of the banks' role in the non-financial sector, the universal type of banks does create prerequisites for such an approach. Banks, while simultaneously extending credits and holding equity, are in a better position, due to intimate insider information, to manage the development of the firm, exercise control over projects and investments and, having an interest in long-term profitability, smooth periods of financial distress. Under the specific conditions of EMEs it seems to be particularly important for universal banks to be in a strong enough position to force the early restructuring of enterprises, short of bankruptcy.

However, there are also at least two classes of constraints. The first one is related to the risk inherent in such a solution in general. The arguments discussed in the literature include the moral hazard problem, potential conflict of interest and the monopoly position of conglomerate financial institutions in the economy. To cope with such risks, the EMEs need to develop adequate regulations, anti-monopoly procedures and banks' reputed standards, and to maintain an open financial system for the new entries and competition from abroad.

The second type of constraint is related to the existing conditions in EMEs. On the one hand, the given model could imply the risk of maintaining and even promoting the traditional pattern of keeping afloat non-viable firms. On the other hand, it is an open question whether and when the banks would be interested in such a solution and capable of effecting it.

Though with some limits, the legal framework in the Czech Republic made it possible for the banks to hold equities of non-banking companies. For a number of obvious reasons, in particular the still rather unstable share prices, banks were not yet particularly eager to hold their clients' equities. At the same time, however, the Investment Privatization Funds founded by banks and other financial institutions became owners of a substantial share of property privatized in the first wave of the voucher scheme (of the ten most successful, nine were funds founded by banks and other financial institutions). The bank-oriented model of corporate control may ultimately develop through this intermediation.

Notes

1. The views expressed in this chapter are mine and do not necessarily reflect those of the Czech National Bank. For helpful comments on an earlier draft I am particularly indebted to István P. Székely. I would also like to thank Werner Varga and the participants of the Vienna Conference for stimulating discussion.
2. As reported in *The Financial Times* (15 September 1993, p. 17) the joint study by the World Bank and the IMF on Hungarian banking concluded that a number of the country's banks, including the two largest, were technically insolvent according to internationally accepted accounting standards (IAS), and the financial system was unable to finance the transformation to a market economy.

3.   The term 'functional efficiency' is used as an integrating concept to cover allocative efficiency, availability, quality, costs and competitiveness of banking services and, in a dynamic setting, the capacity to innovate and to adjust to changing needs and requirements.

4.   The decision on the establishment of Consolidation Bank was taken only after the burdened banks, in particular Commercial Bank, were no longer ready at the beginning of 1991 to provide a special regime for the perpetual inventory credits and were about to charge the current rate of interest on them.

5.   Václav Klaus, the prime minister of the Czech government, claimed that the amount of CSK 50 bn assigned for the recapitalization of banks and for the write-off of their non-performing loans was already beyond the limit the state could afford to spend for this purpose. At the same time he raised doubts about the potential benefits of the move compared to other options (Klaus, 1992, p. 18.).

6.   For data on inter-enterprise arrears in ex-Czechoslovakia see Hrnčíř (1993).

7.   Signalling a departure from the traditional monobank system, two laws came into force on 1 January, 1990: Law No. 130/1989 on the State Bank of Czechoslovakia, and Law No. 158/1989 on Banks and Savings Banks. However, within two years both the laws were substituted by new ones, reflecting the rapidly changing requirements in the institutional field as well as the determination to adjust the legal framework to European standards in connection with the EC Association Agreements. Effective 1 February 1992, Law No. 21/1992 on Banks provided for a universal type of banks. Law No. 22/1992 on the State Bank of Czechoslovakia set the legal basis for its operation as a standard central bank, independent from the state's executive authorities. The latter law had to be amended again with the split of the Czechoslovak Federation into two states, the Czech Republic and the Slovak Republic. Law No. 6/1993 established the Czech National Bank, the central bank of the Czech Republic, as of 1 January 1993.

8.   However, this does not fully apply to Savings Bank, Czechoslovak Trade Bank and Živnostenská Bank, the institutional continuity of which was in principle maintained.

9.   Except for the Czechoslovak Trade Bank which was constituted as a joint-stock company, with 51 per cent of its shares owned by the State Bank and the remainder by specialized foreign trade corporations.

10.   Živnostenská Bank, also an old bank but a small one, was entirely privatized. A minor part of the share was sold through the voucher scheme, the dominant part by direct sale to foreign investors.

11.   With the enactment of the Competition Law (Law No. 63/1991) defining market monopoly and dominant positions, the banks' credit and deposit market shares also became subject to the provisions of this law. To comply with them no bank should exceed a 30 per cent share on the respective market. Though obligatory only in a three-year period after adoption, its impact on the behaviour of the potential offenders can already be identified. However, even if this limit is met in aggregate (for total credits or deposits), the particular segments of these markets may remain rather non-competitive.

12.   Chapters 12 and 13 report a similar tendency in Hungary.

13.   The apparent divergence between market interest rate developments and implied policies in a number of instances during 1993 suggested that the potential impact of this window guidance was rapidly diminishing.

14. Based on the adopted legislation, only in the course of 1993 did the new framework and banking institutions specializing in savings for housing construction and mortgage loans start to develop. Accordingly, the volume of mortgage loans was rather low prior to this development.

15. The standard to be met for granting a banking licence was corrected upwards after 1989. Among others, the minimum level of initial bank's capital was increased from CSK 50 mn to 300 mn, equal to USD 10 mn. The argument was that universal banks, developing in accordance with the adopted legislation, were likely to be exposed to increased risk.

16. For a detailed discussion of the issue of bankruptcy in transition economies, see also Chapter 6.

17. Begg and Portes (1992, p. 16) cited evidence from the survey by Webster (World Bank) on the access of private manufacturing firms to bank credit, and concluded: 'The CSFR has very high private sector dealings with the banking system. 80 per cent of respondents had a bank loan, many had several loans ... To date, new private business borrowing has perhaps been impeded less in the CSFR than in Poland, and especially Hungary.'

18. In France, for example, net borrowing in the form of securities amounted to an average of 27 per cent of the total in the period 1972—1980, but increased to 53 per cent from 1980—1987. Though debt contracts continued to dominate as a means of raising funds in Germany and Japan, in these countries the use of securities has been steadily increasing.

References

Begg, D. and Portes, R. (1992), 'Enterprise debt and economic transformation: financial restructuring of the state sector in Central and Eastern Europe', Discussion Paper No. 695, Centre for Economic Policy Research, London.

Blommenstein, H.J. and Lange, J.R. (1993), 'Balance sheet restructuring and privatization of the banks', in *Transforming of the Banking System: Portfolio Restructuring, Privatization and the Payment System*, Paris, OECD.

Brainard, L. (1991), 'Strategies for economic transformation in Central and Eastern Europe: the role of financial market reform', in Blommenstein, H. and Marrese, M. (eds), *Transformation of Planned Economies: Property Rights Reform and Macroeconomic Stability*, Paris, OECD.

Corbett, J. and Mayer, C. (1991), 'Financial reform in Eastern Europe: progress with the wrong model', *Oxford Review of Economic Policy* 7(4), 57—75.

Dittus, P. (1994), 'Finance and corporate governance in Eastern Europe', in Fischer, B. (ed.), *Investment and Financing in Developing Countries*, Baden-Baden, Nomos Verlagsgesellschaft, (forthcoming).

Griffin, J.R. (1993), 'Privatization and financial capitalism in East Germany', (mimeo).

Hare, P. (1992), 'The assessment: micro-economics of transition in Eastern Europe', *Oxford Review of Economic Policy* 8(4).

Herr, H., Tober, S., and Westphal, A. (1991), 'A strategy for economic transformation and development in Eastern Europe', *De Pecunia* 3(3).

Hinds, M. (1990), 'Issues in the introduction of market forces in Eastern European Socialist economies', World Bank Seminar Paper, IIASA, Laxenburg.

Hrnčíř, M. (1992), 'Money and credit in the transition of the Czechoslovak economy', in Siebert, H. (ed.), *The Transformation of Socialist Economies*, Kiel, Kiel Symposium.

Hrnčíř, M. (1993), 'Financial intermediation — progress evaluation and lessons from the former Czechoslovakia', (mimeo), Institute of Economics, Czech National Bank, Prague.

Klaus, V. (1992), 'Interview', *Ekonom* 32.

Lampe, J.R. (ed.) (1992), *Creating Capital Markets in Eastern Europe*, Baltimore, Johns Hopkins University Press.

Mullineux, A. and Belka, M. (1993), 'Hardening micro budget constraints: banks behaviour and corporate governance in Poland', (mimeo), University of Birmingham.

Nuti, D.M. and Portes, R. (1993), 'Central Europe: the way forward', in Portes, R. (ed.), *Economic Transformation in Central Europe: A Progress Report*, London, Centre for Economic Policy Research.

Nyberg, P. and Vihriälä, V. (1993), 'The Finnish banking crisis and its handling', Discussion Papers No. 8, Bank of Finland, Helsinki.

OECD (1991), *Economic Survey, Czech and Slovak Federal Republic*.

Phelps, E.S., Frydman, R., Rapaczynski, A., and Shleifer, A., (1993), 'Needed mechanism of corporate governance and finance in Eastern Europe', Working Paper No. 1, EBRD, London.

Saunders, A. and Walter, I. (1991), 'Reconfiguration of banking and capital markets in Eastern Europe', *The Journal of International Securities Markets* Autumn.

Schmieding, H., and Buch, C. (1992), 'Better banks for Eastern Europe', Kiel Discussion Paper No. 197, Kiel.

Table 10.1 Average lending and borrowing interest rates of commercial banks

Czechoslovakia	1989	1990				1991				1992			
		I.	II.	III.	IV.	I.	II.	III.	IV.	I.	II.	III.	IV.
Credits (lending rates)	5.7	5.4	5.4	5.6	7.6	14.7	15.1	14.2	13.9	13.4	13.7	13.6	13.3
Deposits (borrowing rates)	2.5	2.6	2.6	2.8	3.3	7.6	8.2	8.6	8.0	8.6	6.9	6.6	6.6
Margin	3.2	2.8	2.8	2.8	4.3	7.1	6.9	5.6	5.9	4.8	6.8	7.0	6.7

Czech Republic	1992				1993					
	I.	II.	III.	IV.	1	2	3	4	5	6
Credits (lending rates)	13.9	13.4	13.4	13.2	13.7	14.2	14.4	14.6	14.8	14.8
Deposits (borrowing rates)	7.9	6.7	6.1	6.3	6.8	6.9	7.2	7.3	7.5	7.0
Margin	6.0	6.7	7.3	6.9	6.9	7.3	7.2	7.3	7.3	7.8

Source: Czech National Bank; Financial Statistical Information

Table 10.2 Risk credits, reserves and provisions of the banking institutions in the Czech Republic

	12/92	3/93	6/93	9/93
Credits total[a]	571.4	597.9	631.8	654.4
Risk credits total	110.0	133.8	139.7	149.4
of which				
temporary illiquid claims	62.5	70.0	24.2[b]	28.1
- temporary tied claims	0.3	..	2.7	0.1
- clients in deteriorated				
situation	51.0	51.2	13.7	10.9
- credits not paid out on				
maturity	11.2	18.8	7.8	17.1
sub-standard and				
non-performing loans	47.5	63.8	115.5[b]	121.3
- sub-standard loans	..	27.7	37.1	46.3
- doubtful loans	26.1	22.1	43.2	34.2
- non-performing loans	21.4	14.0	35.2	40.8
share of risk credits on total credits (%)	19.3	22.4	22.1	22.8
Reserves and loan-loss provisions total	56.7	61.4	65.9	72.5
Reserves	45.3	49.9	54.5	61.1
- reserves against losses	16.5	19.6	23.7	28.8
- banks reserve funds (from profits)	28.8	30.3	30.8	32.3
Loan-loss provisions	11.5	11.5	11.4	11.4
share of reserves and provisions on risk credits (%)	51.5	45.9	47.1	48.5

Notes: a) Bank credits to firms and households extended in domestic currency, in CK bn

b) The shift in the relative weight between the first and second sub-category of risk credits in the second quarter of 1993 was due to the changed classification.

Source: Czech National Bank, own calculations

*Table 10.3 Banking institutions in ex-Czechoslovakia and in the Czech Republic**

| | 1990 | | 1991 | | 1992 | | 1993 |
	1.1	31.12	31.3	31.12	31.3	31.12	30.6
Czechoslovakia - total	7	23	30	39	43	61	
state financial institutions	6	6	7	8	4	3	
JSC without foreign participation	1	11	13	16	22	33	
CS banks partly foreign-owned	-	5	5	6	8	11	
CS banks entirely foreign-owned	-	1	5	9	9	9	
branches of foreign banks in the CSFR	-	-	-	-	-	5	
Czech Republic total	5	21	27	33	35	46	50
state financial institutions	4	4	5	5	1	1	1
JSC without foreign participation	1	11	12	15	19	25	24
CZ banks partly foreign-owned	-	5	5	5	7	7	8
CZ banks entirely foreign-owned	-	1	5	8	8	9	11
branches of foreign banks in the CR	-	-	-	-	-	4	6

Notes: JSC = Joint Stock Company
CS = Czechoslovak
CZ = Czech
* Licensed commercial banks, including branches of foreign banks
Source: Czech National Bank

Table 10.4   The structure of credit and deposit markets in ex-Czechoslovakia

(at the end of the year, in per cent)

	1990		1991		1992[a]	
	Credits	Deposits	Credits	Deposits	Credits	Deposits
1. Big ('old') banks, total	97.9	99.3	77.1	93.3	77.0	91.2
Commercial Bank Praha	47.8	17.5	26.4	17.8	24.7	18.4
General Credit Bank Bratislava	20.1	7.9	14.5	8.0	14.7	6.5
Investment Bank Praha[b]	14.6	8.9	14.8	7.0	10.5	5.1
Investment Bank Bratislava	–	–	–	–	5.0	2.3
Czechoslovak Trade Bank	5.1	2.7	7.9	4.1	7.0	4.4
Czech Saving Bank	6.7	42.3	9.2	39.0	10.2	37.8
Slovak Saving Bank	3.6	20.0	4.3	17.4	4.9	16.7
2. Small ('new') banks, total	2.1	0.7	7.2	3.5	10.6	6.6
Agrobank	1.6	0.4	2.9	0.9	3.1	1.6
Other small banks	0.5	0.3	4.3	2.6	7.5	5.0
3. Consolidation Bank	–	–	15.7	3.2	12.4	2.2

Notes: a) For 1992, figures are for the end of July.
b) In 1992 the Investment Bank was split into Investment Bank, Praha and Investment Bank, Bratislava

Source: Czech National Bank

Table 10.5 The structure of credit and deposit markets in the Czech Republic

(in per cent)

	Credit markets*			Deposit markets		
	12/92	6/93	9/93	12/92	6/93	9/93
1. Big ('old') banks total	68.4	67.3	66.6	88.8	83.9	79.9
Commercial Bank	31.5	31.3	31.0	25.9	22.0	22.1
Investment Bank	13.0	11.9	11.8	6.7	8.7	8.4
Czechoslovak Trade Bank	8.1	8.4	8.2	5.2	4.9	4.2
Czech Saving Bank	15.8	15.7	15.6	50.2	47.4	45.2
2. Small ('new') banks total	17.5	20.8	22.1	10.3	15.3	18.6
Agrobank Praha	4.6	5.0	5.3	3.0	4.1	4.8
Bohemia Bank	0.8	1.1	1.3	0.8	1.6	1.9
Credit Bank Plzeň	0.9	1.0	1.2	0.2	0.7	0.8
Moravia Bank	0.2	0.5	0.6	0.2	0.4	0.6
Post Bank	0.3	0.5	0.6	0.3	0.6	0.7
3. Consolidation Bank	14.1	11.9	11.3	1.7	1.7	1.5

Sectors' Shares on Total

	Credit markets*			Deposit markets		
Non-financial corporate sector of which	83.7	80.8	81.9	27.0	21.8	22.4
State-owned	49.0	44.2	40.2	13.6	10.2	9.0
Private	32.0	34.1	38.4	11.4	10.1	11.5
Foreign controlled	2.6	2.4	3.2	2.0	1.5	1.9
Non-corporate private businesses	4.6	6.4	6.5	3.9	3.6	4.3
Households	8.0	7.1	6.8	46.3	47.4	45.9

Note: * Banks' credits to enterprises and households in domestic currency
Source: Czech National Bank, own calculations

Table 10.6 Sector's shares on bank credits in the Czech Republic

| | 12/91 | | 12/92 | | 3/93 | | 6/93 | |
	CK bn	in %	CK bn	in %	CK bn	in %	CK bn	in %
state firms	333.7	66.89	283.7	47.71	279.1	45.42	280.0	42.53
cooperatives[a]	49.9	10.00	45.9	7.72	-	-	-	-
private sector	48.8	9.78	166.6	28.02	230.4	37.49	264.0	40.10
foreign exchange credits to								
residents	3.5	0.70	16.0	2.69	16.2	2.64	20.8	3.16
households	36.3	7.28	46.5	7.82	45.5	7.40	45.2	6.87
other[b]	26.7	5.35	35.9	6.04	43.3	7.05	48.3	7.34
total credits	498.9	100.00	594.6	100.00	614.5	100.00	658.3	100.00

Notes: a) Since the beginning of 1993 the credits extended to cooperatives are included in the private sector's share.

b) Other are mostly unidentified cases, in the process of change in their status, i.e. especially where privatization was under way.

Source: Own calculations based on CNB data

11 Money and Capital Market Reforms in Poland

Ryszard Kokoszczyński

1 Introduction[1]

Poland in the 1980s was already a long way from the textbook version of a centrally-planned economy. Numerous attempts at decentralizing the economy had had some effect, though they had almost no impact on the financial sphere. The National Bank of Poland (NBP) fulfilled the functions of both a central bank and a commercial bank responsible for financing state-owned industry; other, so-called specialized banks had a formal monopoly in various fields (e.g. Bank Handlowy was responsible for all foreign operations of enterprises and the state itself; Bank PeKaO S.A. was responsible for foreign currency operations in the household sector).

This legal segmentation resulted in the lack of any choice for potential customers — there was no need even for a credit market.[2] All financing being in the form of classic debt made a money market impossible; the capital market was substituted by the plan mechanism, as is typical for central planning.

Some of these things started to change in 1987, and in 1988 a new bill on bonds was passed, but it was really in 1989 that foundations were laid for financial markets in the true meaning of this word.

2 Two-tier banking system as a precondition for existence of a money market

2.1 Interbank deposits

In the 1980s further attempts to decentralize the economy led to the lowering of some entry barriers allowing the private sector to engage in economic activities on a broader scale. This in turn led to important changes in the institutional structure of the banking system. In January 1989 the new banking law and the law on the NBP established a two-tier banking system in Poland.

New commercial banks were established shortly after that: some of them state-owned, formed on the basis of operations (and substance) previously conducted by the NBP, some of them brand new, established as joint stock companies with private or mixed capital. The quantitative dimension of this process is summarized in Table 11.1.

The increasing number of banks and the new institutional framework, providing, for example, new access rules to central bank refinancing, made it possible and meaningful to develop interbank transactions. This was the very beginning of the money market in Poland.[3]

The very first segment of the money market was hence the development of interbank deposits; until early 1989 excess reserves of other banks were located in the NBP. At the same time, the NBP satisfied in a relatively automatic way all the refinancing needs of other banks implied by the credit plan. In 1988 the NBP's refinancing amounted to zloty (zl) 3.3 bn, and banks' deposits with the NBP were zl 2.5 bn; in 1989 these figures were zl 20.1 bn and zl 3.4 bn, respectively.

March 1989 saw the first interbank deposit of zl 10 bn with both sides of this transaction being commercial banks. The growth of this market was quite dramatic and the volume of interbank deposits went up to zl 1775 bn at the end of December 1989. Further development of this market had somewhat slower rates of growth, but already in 1990 it started to play an important role in adjusting the structure of banks' supply of loanable funds to that of their customers' demand.

Table 11.2 clearly shows the importance of this market for the state banks. With the exception of the State Savings Bank (PKO BP) and cooperative banks, most of them concentrated their business within the enterprise sector. Polish enterprises up to the early 1990s usually had negligible deposits, so state banks previously had quite large credit portfolios refinanced with the central bank's credit. When the central bank started its transformation the need arose to find another source of loanable funds. Household savings behaviour, being relatively difficult and expensive to change, meant that interbank deposits became an important source of funding needed to balance to some extent the asymmetry of the state commercial banks' balance sheets.

The nature of the demand for interbank deposits is indicated by the relatively long maturity of deposits (see Figure 11.1).

2.2 Development of a proper money market

In 1990 a huge surplus in the Polish trade balance, combined with the convertibility of domestic currency being limited to current accounts, started to undermine monetary policy based on the control of money supply. No short-term securities existed, which could be used for sterilizing this growth of money reflecting the growth in foreign reserves.[4] The State budget showed a large surplus, so the government, because of its still low credibility, was reluctant to issue any kind of Treasury securities. This led to the issue of the central bank's own bills around mid-1990 with maturity of 30 days. They were sold at weekly auctions as zero-coupon securities.

This was the beginning of an open money market, because NBP bills could be bought by all economic agents, households included.[5] The bills were used primarily to control the liquidity of the banking system, and in 1990 approximately 86 per cent of them circulated within the banking system.

In May 1991 Treasury bills (T-bills), typical instruments creating the most important segment of a money market, were introduced. During the months after that the NBP and the Polish Ministry of Finance coordinated their policies by offering securities with different maturity periods. Due to the budget deficit — which from spring 1991 seemed to become a permanent feature of the Polish economy — and legal constraints on possible ways of financing it, the T-bills market developed quite rapidly. Up to mid-1992 weekly primary market auctions of zero-coupon bonds were open to all economic agents, but then the NBP, as a government agent, limited the access to the primary market, nominating some commercial banks as money-market dealers. This event took place at a time when the secondary market, due to the past efforts of the central bank and some big commercial banks, was already well-developed.

Other money market instruments started to be used in 1991 or 1992, but their importance is still negligible compared to the T-bills market. Commercial papers, certificates of deposit and similar financial instruments exist in Poland, and there is a limited market for them, but they will probably be more important in the future.

It can be said, nevertheless, that the money market as a whole started to play an important role. Its two major parts, interbank deposits and T-bills, were roughly equal to more than 50 per cent of total assets of the banking system at the end of 1992.

Another important aspect of money market development is the increasing reliance on this market to achieve short-term monetary policy targets. In 1990, this market's existence was not enough to sterilize, via NBP bills, the increase in money supply resulting from a surplus in the trade balance. Some administrative measures (such as credit ceilings) were needed in the last instance to keep the money supply under control. However, the development of the money market led to the introduction of repos and reverse repos in late 1992. The NBP increased the volume of open market operations in 1993, when they started to be the major tool of short-term monetary policy.

The information role of the money market is another important feature. The Warsaw Interbank Bid and Offered Rate started to be quoted daily, and the T-bills yield curve was an interesting and useful indicator of expectations that helped both the central bank in designing and implementing monetary policy, and economic agents in building their own plans for future financial transactions. Figures 11.2 through 11.4 show the basic interest rates and yields for NBP and T-bills.

3   Capital market

The development of the capital market was defined far more by legal changes. As mentioned above, a bill on bonds was issued as far back as 1988, but it was adjusted to the needs of economic agents in a centrally-planned economy. A new bill on securities, the Act on Public Trading and Trust Funds, only came into force in 1991. It created a market, though a heavily regulated, or even overregulated one.

Nevertheless, it provided the basis for the main components of a capital market — brokerage houses, securities exchanges and trust funds — with the Securities Commission being the government agency responsible for the control, supervision and development of the capital market.

The Warsaw Stock Exchange was established in April 1991 and its first trading session took place on 16 April, when five privatized companies' stock was traded by seven bank-owned brokerage houses. The turnover was approximately USD 2000.

Some people felt that conditions for the admission of securities to public trading were harsh. The Exchange Board grants permission for this admission based on the following criteria:

— formal approval from the Securities Commission;
— unlimited transferability of shares;
— total value of shares introduced to the market to be not less than ECU 1 mn;
— information to be made available to investors allowing them to assess the financial conditions of the issuer, its legal obligations, etc.;
— dispersion of shares to ensure proper liquidity of the market.[6]

However, the development of the Warsaw Stock Exchange seems to show that there is a trade-off between the safety of a market like this and its rapid growth in the first period of existence. A company which intends to go public has to satisfy quite harsh conditions and the number of existing companies which have made use of a capital market to increase their capital or to broaden their stockholders' base is still very small. The vast majority of the companies listed at the Warsaw Stock Exchange are privatized companies.

The most important factor influencing the development of this segment of the capital market seems to be the interest rate policy. After the last decline in interest rates in February 1993 there was an unprecedented period of rapid growth for both prices and turnover of stocks traded publicly. The average turnover per session in 1992 was approximately zl 23 bn (which was equal to USD 1.7 mn at the then prevailing exchange rate); in August 1993 average turnover reached zl 1000 bn (approximately USD 52 mn), although the number of sessions per week increased. The market capitalization of companies listed rose from USD 100 mn at the beginning of 1992 to USD 1.5 bn around mid-1993. The development of Warsaw Stock Exchange Index WIG and P/E ratio are shown in Figures 11.5 and 11.6.

This impressive development has, alas, psychological and systemic rather than economic importance. If one compares the data quoted above with the total volume of credit extended by commercial banks to the non-financial sector (which is approximately 10 times higher than the market capitalization of publicly traded companies), it is easy to show that the equities market is still of secondary importance for resource allocation in Poland. What is even more important, the stock exchange is used to raise new capital only to a very limited extent.

High inflation and interest rates make it difficult for the bond market to develop rapidly.[7] The credit market is the dominant form of capital allocation. However, the average maturity of loans extended in the 1990s is relatively short — housing and central investment are the only areas with a large volume of long-term loans, but legal and systemic constraints make them difficult to be analysed in a purely economic way.

To summarize, the modern part of a capital market is quite well organized, its legal and institutional framework (Securities Commission as a control body, Stock Exchange, etc.) does not require any major changes, but the market itself is rather thin and dominated by equity. This is in part due to some political obstacles to fast and mass privatization; however, the current tendency in this respect may result in some positive feedback.

The debt market in Poland really means the credit market, where some activities are still influenced by the past (housing and central investment); and government subsidies (agriculture and housing again).

4   Conclusions and prospects for the future

Some German economists have coined a new term to describe the processes taking place in Eastern Europe. They call these economies not market, but money ones. This is — in a nutshell — the conclusion of this text.

The first obstacle to creating a market economy from a planned one, which F. Holzman called commodity inconvertibility of money in a centrally-planned economy,[8] is already a matter of the far and forgotten past in Poland. The domestic currency is freely convertible into any product, its external convertibility, though formally limited, seems to satisfy the needs of most economic agents. Money, as opposed to capital, is already allocated more or less in a market way. However, a major portion of capital is still distributed in a mixed manner. Economic reasoning is an important factor in making these decisions, but it is not the only one.

Important changes fostering this development are being elaborated and partly implemented. The most important one in my opinion is the reform of ex-NBP state-owned commercial banks.[9] Their privatization is a long-term goal, but various reasons make it impossible to achieve quickly. First of all, privatization was to be a way to increase their efficiency — which requires investors not only with enough capital, but also with some professional experience in banking. Investors of that kind require detailed information based on Western accounting standards, a stable legal framework (prudential regulations, tax system etc.), and reliable auditing, already in place. On the other hand, the money needed for buying at least a significant part of any Polish bank's stock is not negligible — since they have a vast branch network, with a brand name well-known to domestic customers, and the largest ones have funds in the range of several hundred million dollars.

In 1991, the starting point on the road to privatization was thus reshaping the commercial banks into joint stock companies,[10] which gave them some degree of independence from government bureaucracy in daily management. At the same time, these banks were being ranked according to their quality, and two of the best ones started to prepare for privatization. The first, Wielkopolski Bank Kredytowy, was publicly offered in the first half of 1993; the strategic investor being the EBRD. The second, Bank Śląski, was to be sold around November 1993; according to rumours some commercial banks were interested in buying a significant part of its stock.

The Treasury retains part of the stock in the privatized banks, but it is only a minority shareholder. Hence, it might be assumed that these banks' choice of how to allocate their funds will now be governed by economic factors. Another important factor is the increasing share of (generic) private banks in the banking sector. Both factors taken together justify the opinion that the Polish capital market (banks' brokerage houses play a dominant role at the stock exchange too) will soon be fully controlled by economic factors.

Notes

1. I am grateful to John P. Bonin for his comments and suggestions. The opinions expressed in this chapter are those of the author and not necessarily those of the National Bank of Poland.
2. There was one exception, however; foreign currency, traded in some periods only on the black market, fulfilled some functions of a financial instrument.
3. Another important feature of the banking reform of 1989 was that all existing banks were granted universal licences, small cooperative banks included. The expansion of these banks (there were approximately 1600) was one of the important factors for the development of the interbank deposits market.
4. The bill of exchange was formally a legally valid financial instrument through the whole period after World War II, but it was virtually non-existent in the domestic financial markets. Some attempts to revive its circulation by promotion of discount and rediscount crediting with interest rates significantly below the market level took place in 1990, but after promising initial results, they stabilized at a rather low level.
5. However, the lowest bill had a face value of zl 100 mn, which was equal then to almost 100 average monthly wages or 11 times the average households savings in the form of bank deposits.
6. Warsaw Stock Exchange (1993), 'Organization and operation', Warsaw, May.
7. The exception being the Treasury bonds market; these bonds, however, are indexed.
8. As far as I know he coined the term in *Foreign Trade under Central Planning*, published in 1964.
9. These nine banks still dominate in industrial credits.
10. Other state-owned banks (Bank Handlowy, PKO SA or Export Development Bank) had this form from the very beginning. One of them, Export Development Bank (BRE SA), was privatized in 1992 through a public offering of the shares that were owned by government agencies (approximately 40 per cent).

Table 11.1   The number of banks in Poland

(end of year)

	1988	1989	1990	1991	1992
Number of banks[a]	5	17	43	89	94
of which					
state banks	2	11	12	3	3
banks with state					
as a major shareholder	3	3	3	12	12
private domestic banks[b]	-	3	27	67	77
private foreign banks[c]	-	-	1	7	11

Notes: a) without cooperative banks — their number was relatively
stable, on average around 1600;
b) banks with shareholders from both private and public sector;
c) legally Polish companies with a major share of foreign capital; the figure for 1992 includes one branch of a foreign bank.

Source: National Bank of Poland

Table 11.2   Interbank deposits in Poland

(zl bn)

	net deposits of 14 state banks	net 14 plus cooperative banks	gross deposits of new banks
December 1990	-771	126	842
March 1991	-1387	633	1420
June 1991	-416	1620	2448
September 1991	-1124	1165	2066
December 1991	-1963	18	1203
March 1992	-2034	454	1497
June 1992	-1985	1111	2026
September 1992	-3053	1927	2129
December 1992	-2616	2874	3598
March 1993	-4204	2302	2987
June 1993	-2102	3870	3942
September 1993	-3533	3327	3226

Source: National Bank of Poland

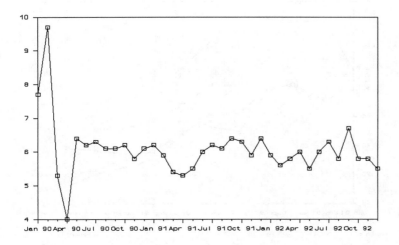

Figure 11.1 Weighted average maturity of interbank deposits (months)

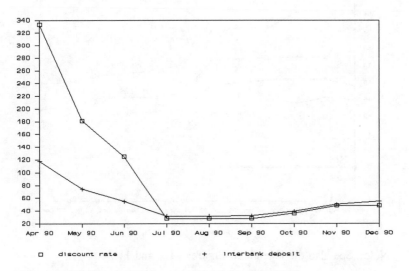

Figure 11.2 Basic interest rates in Poland in 1990

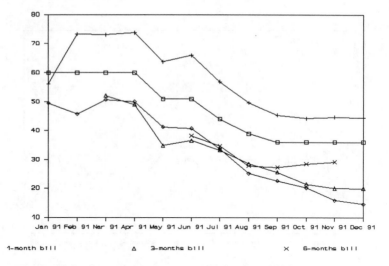

Figure 11.3 Basic interest rates in Poland in 1991

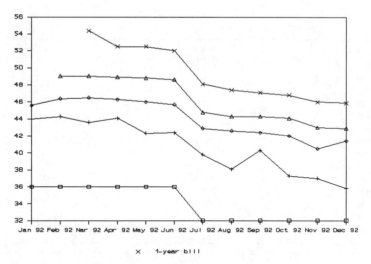

Note: See also the legends in Figures 11.2 and 11.3

Figure 11.4 Basic interest rates in Poland in 1992

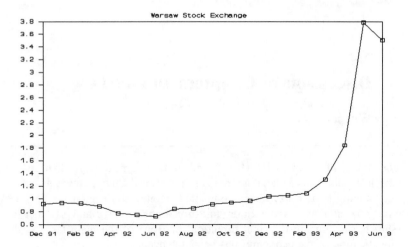

Figure 11.5 The values of the Warsaw Stock Exchange Index (WIG)

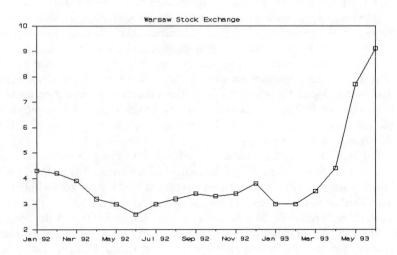

Figure 11.6 The P/E ratio at the Warsaw Stock Exchange

Discussion of Chapters 10 and 11

Werner Varga

The excellent chapters by Hrnčíř and Kokoszczyński show that in the Czech Republic and Poland the basic organizational changes towards a two-tier banking system have been completed, money and capital markets are emerging, so that — from an organizational angle — we may say that the 'ship is steaming in the right direction' and one of the main targets, the monetization of the economy, has been achieved.

Therefore, further development is closely interrelated with achievements in the transformation of the economic system and economic development. So from the organizational side, there is nothing left to do: the rules are set, evolution may continue, and the system will develop itself. Macroeconomics may leave the scene and industrial economics may take the floor.

However, some questions concerning the present stage as well as the further development of the reforming countries' banking system are still of interest, from the practical as well as the academic point of view.

The Visegrád countries' (the Czech Republic, Hungary, Poland and Slovakia) banking systems are already closer to a market-type framework than in the case of the other transformation countries, as Hrnčíř points out in his chapter. Following this statement I tried to check how far the region's banking system had developed, by making a rough comparison with the Austrian banking industry.

For this comparison I took as a yardstick the aggregate total assets of banks in relation to the GNP of the individual countries. The ratio of total banking assets to GNP shows the importance of banking services within the individual countries. Poland's ratio, at 58 per cent, is the lowest, followed by the Czech Republic with 80 per cent and Hungary with 105 per cent.

The ratio for Hungary indicates that its banking system offers a wider range of services than the other reforming countries do. Compared with the Austrian banking system on the basis of this indicator, we find Poland at the level the Austrian banking system reached in 1960, the Czech Republic between 1965 and 1970 (this ratio for the period 1960/1970 was 93.7 per cent for Austria) and Hungary between 1970 and 1975 (in 1975, the value of this ratio for Austria was 127.5 per cent; in 1980, 1985, and 1990, they were 187, 228, and 225 per cent, respectively).

Hrnčíř claims that '... the characteristics of a banking system which appeared satisfactory in the given conditions of a particular country and/or transition stage may prove entirely deficient in others'. If so, we have to ask the following question: what is the 'standard' provided by Western developed market economies? Is it the American or European standard? And is it a flexible pattern that may lead to a country's own development within this framework, a development oriented towards the needs of the reforming countries?

In the first wave, the reforms were oriented more towards the US system. New banks mushroomed in these countries, especially in Poland. The US-type division between commercial and investment banking was in vogue. The ideology of a free market where the creation of banks depends on nothing but the entrepreneurial spirit, gained ground. However, all the Visegrád countries today have a universal banking system — the European system, but with a certain difference — the restriction of banking activities in the field of investment banking. This approach, different from Germany or Austria, may be regarded as a pragmatic touch, a search for a system meeting the countries' individual needs.

Within the Visegrád countries we can now distinguish between:

— 'old' banking institutions, e.g., Foreign Trade Bank;
— new banks resulting from a spin-off from the Central Bank;
— newly-founded private banks;
— foreign banks.

'The ex-National Bank', state-owned commercial banks, as Kokoszczyński calls them, with their bad loan portfolios, are not to be privatized overnight. However, the reform process led to a change in banking practice in every country, and especially in the Czech Republic where, as Hrnčíř pointed out, the banks resisted the pressure to provide a 'special regime' for the perpetual inventory credits and were about to charge them at the current rate of interest. This led to the establishment of the Consolidation Bank.

It should be mentioned that the Czechs were the forerunners in creating the recovery agency called Consolidation Bank, founded in March 1991, whereas in Hungary the loan consolidation scheme was established in March 1993. This fact is probably one of the main reasons for 'the alarming weakness of a number of Hungarian banks', as Hrnčíř puts it.

The question is: how was it possible? How could the Czech banks resist government pressure, and where did this entrepreneurial behaviour come from? There was no privatization at that time!

Regarding bad loan management, three basic methods are mentioned:

— exchanging irrevocable loans for claims on the public sector;
— allowing banks to outgrow their undercapitalization and provisioning requirements;
— currency reform.

However, the first two actions may be implemented together, one does not exclude the other. The problem can be resolved by establishing a consolidation bank and the 'takeover of the non-performing loans' as well as by giving banks a chance to grow out the problems associated with their old burdens by means of large spreads.

Both ways have their problems, such as what should be done with a consolidation bank afterwards. One proposal might be to transform it into a semi-official institution such as an export finance agency. The other solution, however, produced windfall profits for private (foreign) banks.

The controversial 'interim pragmatic measures' (Hrnčíř) in the Czech Republic were not planned but resulted from the programme of rapid mass privatization that needed more time than initially thought. The evolving situation required pragmatic approaches and led to a 'gradualistic' policy.

It is interesting to see the gradual application of bankruptcy legislation in the Czech Republic, which Hrnčíř mentions. During the first reform stage Hungary, too, feared a domino effect and a long, uncontrolled trail of bankruptcies. However, I believe the Hungarian authorities thought that inter-enterprise indebtedness forced them to apply strict bankruptcy legislation. They feared that unusually high lending amongst enterprises would undermine or at least seriously disturb the monetary policy. However, as Schaffer tries to show in his discussion (see Chapter 6), this may be an unjustified panic, as compared with Western economies no exceptionally high inter-enterprise indebtedness seems to exist.

The ability, and to a certain extent even the need, to look for and live with compromises — see Hrnčíř quoting Klaus — may be a further important requirement for a successful way towards transition.

Compromises are never theoretical, never 'pure or clean'; they create a new reality and system. In this sense, all our so-called economic systems are mixed. There are many examples of targets set just to get closer to a more ideal economic system, such as a yearly reduction of the budget deficit in the reforming countries, without regard to social costs or adverse effects on social cohesion.

The Czech Republic, as Hrnčíř says, financed the costs caused by the 'contract failures' in a pragmatic way out of a wide range of sources including state assets and budget means, Central Bank funds, wide interest rate margins on lending, etc. This approach to burden-sharing may be one of the secrets of the success of the Czech Republic.

Finally, the intellectual as well as the cultural ability not just to follow Western standards, but to adopt and change, if necessary, certain parts of them, enables these countries to establish an economic system in accordance with their needs. The Western developed market economies are not one homogeneous system; there are many models on which further reforms can be based. The Visegrád countries, therefore, need to find their own ways and, as we can see, they are beginning to do so.

12 Market Structures and Competition in the Hungarian Banking System

István Ábel and István P. Székely

1 Introduction[1]

This chapter investigates the conditions for and degree of competitiveness in the Hungarian banking system during the period between 1987 and 1991. The beginning of this period was marked by the first major reform of the Hungarian financial system which established a two-tier banking system and set out the institutional framework for integrating the two formerly segregated financial circuits for households and enterprises (Balassa, 1992; Székely, 1990). Though by now the figures for 1992 have become available, the major changes in the way balance sheets of Hungarian banks were compiled made it impossible for us to extend our analysis to include the year 1992 without the risk of arriving at erroneous conclusions.

The Hungarian banking industry underwent substantial changes resulting in tangible improvements in the conditions for competition and in the degree of competitiveness (Balassa, 1992; Blejer and Sagari, 1991; Estrin *et al.*, 1992). Banks expanded their supply of financial services at a fairly rapid pace. In the analysis that follows, we try to assess the direction and the extent of changes, the degree of competitiveness in the Hungarian banking system, and the differences in this respect among the various segments of the banking market.

Although no reform of the financial system in itself can solve the enormous problems involved in the process of transition to a market economy, a well-functioning financial system can facilitate economic restructuring and produce new financial instruments for sharing the risk inherent in economic transformation. Therefore, the success of economic transformation in the economies of Central and Eastern Europe (CEE), in particular in Hungary, depends to a large extent on how competitive and innovative their financial services industries are and will become (Brainard, 1991; Calvo and Fenkel, 1991; Caprio and Levine, 1992; Fisher and Gelb, 1991; Kemme and Rudka, 1992; Székely, 1993).

The access to capital markets and the cost of capital for the producers of the region is to a large extent determined by the efficiency of the capital allocation in these countries. The degree of competitiveness of this industry has a direct impact on financial markets. For financial investors, competition and innovation brings about financial products that meet their time and risk preference, and a structure and level of yield that ensure the correspondence between the liability and asset portfolios of financial firms, and between demand for and supply of direct finance by non-financial firms.

Several factors are investigated in other chapters that have a significant impact on the degree of competitiveness in the Hungarian banking system. Chapter 5 is devoted to the issue of bank privatization, while the issues of 'bad loans' and loan consolidation schemes are discussed in detail in Chapters 5 and 13. Therefore, though these aspects are very important in analysing changes in competitiveness, we do not explicitly deal with these issues in our analysis. Moreover, mainly due to space limitation, we do not touch upon the issue of legal regulations. Finally, as Chapter 13 deals extensively with future reforms in the Hungarian banking system, we focus our attention on analysing the actual development and leave the policy implications to Chapter 13 to discuss.

2   Market structures in banking

Though the number of banks in itself is not a particularly good indicator of the competitiveness of the market place, in a country just departing from an economic system characterized by a repressed financial system, like Hungary, the number of business units is an important indicator of the direction of overall development. The number of banks given in Table 12.1 shows that the system remained more or less unchanged until the end of 1989, but it showed a spectacular growth in the group of mid-sized banks in 1990 and 1991. While in 1990 this was almost entirely of domestic origin, in 1991 foreign participation was very substantial among new entrants.

1991 marked the end of this spectacular growth in terms of the number of units. Now there is an urgent need for strengthening the mid-sized banks, so further development will be characterized by important intra- and inter-group movements. The first mid-sized bank expected to enter the group of large banks is Postbank, which already in 1991 was on the verge of becoming a true large commercial bank.

Though commercial banks are licensed to collect non-corporate deposits and lend to and provide financial services for non-corporate clients, the non-corporate market was dominated by the two banks classified as household banks in Hungarian terminology (National Savings Bank, NSB and Hungarian Savings Cooperative Bank, HSCB). The number of foreign banks, which is already fairly high, is also expected to further increase, though mainly through privatization and by acquiring equity stakes in existing banks.

The figures in Table 12.1 also show that until the end of 1991, the Hungarian banking industry had not really witnessed exits. Though in 1991 one of the saving cooperatives was liquidated, and there was an almost open failure of a bank (Ingatlan Bank), the first real case was in the summer of 1992 when two banks (Ybl Bank and General Bank for Venture Finance) and one saving cooperative, mainly due to massive insider lending activities, became insolvent.

In analysing market structures, the ideal solution is to go down to the product level and analyse markets for (more or less standard) products. The proper level of disaggregation is important because the nature of the factors determining the static and dynamic characteristics of markets can be rather different for different products. In the analysis that follows we use a disaggregation far from the best, but still more detailed than usually used. We consider the following typical products: long- and short-term corporate loans, bills of exchange, (underwriting of) corporate bond, corporate deposits, long- and short-term non-corporate loans, and non-corporate deposits. Since the Financial Institution Act allows for direct investment by banks, we also consider the banks' activities in the equity market.

A general picture can, however, be gained from investigating the overall market structure in banking based on balance sheet totals. Table 12.2 provides these figures and reveals the main tendency of gradual increase in the market shares of mid-sized banks, from 4.7 per cent in 1987 to 22.1 per cent in 1991, that is, an almost fivefold increase.[2] Table 12.2 also reveals the fact that most of the increase took place in the last two years of the period under investigation.

2.1 Corporate deposit and loan markets

The relative importance of deposits as sources of loanable funds for banks increased gradually during the period under investigation. This was equally true for large and mid-sized commercial banks.[3] The share of deposits in total assets of household (retail) banks showed a reverse tendency. This was, however, natural because the NSB and savings cooperatives (SCs) were there to collect private savings and channel the (strictly planned) excess liquidity to the central bank. As this function of the NSB and SCs gradually ceased to exist and the NSB obtained a full commercial bank licence, and the joint bank of the SCs (HSCB) was established also with a commercial bank licence, the relative importance of deposits started to decline in this group as well. The final outcome is that the relative importance of deposits (their shares in total liabilities) is becoming rather uniform across the different groups of banks.

If we further disaggregate the deposit market and concentrate on corporate deposits, we can find more empirical evidence supporting our general finding that the degree of concentration in banking declined significantly in Hungary during the period under investigation. Table 12.3 reveals the fact that the market share of the large commercial banks declined substantially in this segment of the banking market, from 84 per cent in 1987 to slightly below 55 per cent in 1991. The winners are the mid-sized banks, increasing their market share from 6.1 per cent to 29.7 per cent;[4] and the household (retail) banks, increasing their share from 8.5 per cent to 15.1 per cent. These changes took place in a fairly gradual manner over time, though in the case of the mid-sized banks the increase in 1991 is outstanding.

A very similar tendency can be observed in the corporate loan market, though the extent to which mid-sized banks and household (retail) banks increased their market shares is somewhat smaller (see Table 12.4). However, if we take short-term corporate loans separately[5] (see Figure 12.1), we find that the increase in the market share of the mid-sized banks was spectacular. This finding is further corroborated by the figures for bills of exchange given in Table 12.5, showing a very substantial gain in market shares by mid-sized banks.

Financing economic restructuring: long-term loans

Relatively fast and substantial restructuring of these economies is necessary for successful economic transformation and long-term development. However, restructuring requires a reallocation of capital, increased investment activity, and an economic environment within which successful private enterprises can expand their activities at a much faster pace than before.

In practice, at least during the period under investigation in Hungary, the banking system was able to provide long-term finance for economic restructuring only to a very moderate extent. The real value of outstanding long-term corporate loans was continuously declining, with a cumulative decline of 38.5 per cent between 1987 and 1991. This market was the least contested by the mid-sized banks. The only group which showed a real appetite for this business was the group of household (retail) banks. These banks rapidly increased their long-term corporate lending until 1990, but this tendency was reversed in 1991. Though in principle it was a positive development, what is somewhat questionable is the ability of these banks to pursue corporate lending in a prudent manner, because the amount of non-standard loans in their loan portfolios increased dramatically.

Figure 12.2 shows another aspect of this development. The relative size of long-term corporate loans in the asset portfolios, again with the exception of household (retail) banks until 1990, decreased continuously. That is, commercial banks were increasingly unable and unwilling to assume the risk involved in holding long-term corporate loans in their asset portfolios. Put differently, banks gradually moved towards less risky, short-term instruments and also towards instruments issued by the state (T-bills, state bonds). As we shall see below, besides the increased risk attached to long-term (investment) corporate loans, the term structure of the liabilities was another very important factor which forced banks in this direction.

Whatever the reasons were, the outcome was that it became increasingly difficult and expensive for the corporate sector to secure banking finance for investment purposes, or indeed any long-term finance. Enterprises experienced similar development in the markets for direct finance (bond and equity), thus as far as finance is concerned, the chances for a relatively smooth and fast economic restructuring are not particularly good. The Hungarian experience lends some empirical support to the theoretical finding of McKinnon (1991) concerning the likely nature of corporate finance during economic transformation. Retained earnings and foreign direct investment will for quite some time be the major sources for long-term finance in Hungary. Banks are moving increasingly towards narrow banking without any regulation imposed on them.

3   The characteristics of the behaviour of mid-sized commercial banks

The group of mid-sized banks consists of fully foreign-owned subsidiaries, joint ventures, subsidiaries of large Hungarian commercial banks, joint ventures of other Hungarian financial institutions and other independent mid-sized private banks. The characteristics of the behaviour of banks in the group of mid-sized banks are of particular importance for several reasons. First, though at present the banking market as a whole is still dominated by the four large, directly and indirectly state-owned banks, there is no doubt that the future belongs to some of the currently small or mid-sized banks, 'the winners'. It is safe to say that the 'banks of the future' have the 'enterprises of the future' as their clients and always expand their activities in the most dynamic and profitable segments of the market. As a consequence, some of them, and thus together as a group as well, are growing at a spectacular pace (see Tables 12.1 to 12.5).

Second, in this group, private ownership is absolutely dominant, which as pointed out above is not the case in the group of the large commercial banks. Moreover, due to their sizes, corporate structures and forms of ownership, these banks have easily identifiable owners, and thus no problem with management control. On the other hand, they are clearly not 'too big to fail', in fact they can be ideal cases for the authorities to use as examples of how to handle open failure or exit through merger or acquisition, and also how to make the industry understand that not every bank will always be bailed out, should any of them get into serious trouble. Third, as also pointed out above, these banks are expanding their activities in fairly competitive and dynamic markets of mainly (in Hungary) newly-emerging products. Therefore, one would expect these banks to be competitive, to behave like 'real banks'; that is, the observable characteristics of these banks can in principle be taken as an indication of how a profit-oriented enterprise behaves under the given circumstances.

The latter is very important for several reasons. Many of the characteristics of the banking market in CEE can sometimes mistakenly be attributed to market imperfections, the dominance of state ownership and other factors characterizing the banking industry in this region. Some of these 'distortions' are, however, outcomes of rational business strategies of competitive enterprises designed to suit the given business environment. That is, one has to make a distinction between what is caused by factors within and beyond the control of an enterprise. It is very likely, for example, that the lack of long-term finance for enterprises is much more due to the excessive level of uncertainty in the economy than to the lack of competition in the marketplace. On the other hand, the fact that the spreads for mid-sized banks, basically free from inherited bad loans, have caught up with those of the large commercial banks, laden with such debts, is most likely a sign of market imperfection.

Figure 12.1 gives a very good picture of the relative importance of mid-sized banks as a group in the Hungarian banking industry, the main characteristics of their business strategy, and the way they developed during the period under investigation. It shows that business strategies of mid-sized banks are very much geared towards markets for short-term, and thus less risky financial instruments. As we proceed towards longer-term and/or more risky instruments (from the left to the right in the figure) so the market share of these banks declines. The figure also reveals that these banks are more active in deposit collecting than their overall share (as measured by balance sheet size) would suggest. This indicates their quite active involvement in interbank markets, where they were indeed major players mainly lending to large commercial banks and to each other in the short term. The market shares of large commercial banks do not reveal a similar pattern.

Mid-sized banks moved towards shorter-term, less risky instruments gradually, most likely as a reaction to changes taking place in the internal and external economic environment of the country and in the economic policy of the administration. Figure 12.3 indicates that mid-sized banks followed the pricing policies of large banks, in spite of the fact that, with the exception of the subsidiaries and joint ventures of the large commercial banks in this group, they had very little non-standard loans. This shows that mid-sized banks mostly competed on the quality of products and services and very moderately, if at all, on prices.

4   Product pricing and cost structure

The level of disaggregation is perhaps even more important in investigating product pricing. If products are not standard it is very difficult, if at all possible, to interpret prices. Moreover, if markets are imperfect, information is asymmetrically distributed and information is slow and costly to gather, it is not at all clear what a recorded price reflects. In the case of a newly-emerging market, such as the Hungarian one, each of the above factors is undoubtedly present, making the analysis of pricing behaviour of financial firms rather difficult. Consequently, one should be very cautious in interpreting any data or finding in this respect. Due to the underdeveloped nature of the Hungarian financial system, more sophisticated products which make possible the rebundling of the different sorts of risk involved in traditional financial products (e.g., corporate loans of different sorts) are not yet available. Thus, the way the market prices different kinds of risk is not directly observable. Moreover, the classification of borrowers according to their riskiness is far from being readily available and obvious for a bank. On the contrary, in most cases they have to conduct their own research in this respect.

4.1   Interest rate spread

One of the standard indicators of pricing behaviour and competitiveness is the interest rate spread. Though it is a widely used concept, it is a rather controversial one. In investigating economies in transition, one should be even more cautious with interpreting figures on spreads, especially when comparing them across countries, different types of banks and over time, for several reasons:

— The liability structures of commercial banks in CEE have special characteristics. Deposits (mainly enterprise deposits) are neither the only nor sometimes even the most important source of loanable funds for commercial banks, thus comparing deposit rates to lending rates might be misleading, especially as far as dynamics is concerned.

Refinance credit is an important source, especially for those banks which are crammed with bad loans, and in fact a considerable part of these bad loans were originally transferred into their portfolios together with the corresponding refinance credits. The rate on refinance credit is determined by the central bank, and its dynamics can again be rather different from that of deposit rates. The point is that the shares of the above elements, and their costs (level and dynamics) are rather different for different financial institutions, for financial institutions in different CEE countries, and over time. Consequently spreads are informative indicators only if and to the extent they take the above characteristics into account.

— Regulations on obligatory reserves (on different types of liabilities) are frequently changing over time. Moreover, the opportunity cost of these reserves (depending on the rate the central bank pays on them) is also changing. They may even be different on different types of liabilities (e.g., on deposits denominated in domestic currency and in foreign currencies, and naturally may well depend on maturity).

— The corporate loan market is imperfect. Therefore, loan rates are far from being uniform across the economy. Though this is also true for developed market economies, the extent of this in an economy where the costs of monitoring or gathering information are extremely high, and in a period of very high volatility (due to stabilization, trade reorientations, etc.) is much greater.

— The treasury is a dominating borrower. The extent of crowding-out by the state is one of the factors explaining the level and dynamics of spreads at the macro level. (In fact the regulations on reserves are probably strongly influenced by the desire for seigniorage.)

It is important to follow more closely how the damaging effects of wide spreads work. Bad loans force the banks concerned to maintain wide spreads. This can, however, be attained in several different ways.

First, banks can be provided with cheap refinance. If so, their lending rates are not pushed up (at least not to the same extent as in other cases discussed below). Their customers do not pay for credit failures, but the costs are spread through the (consequently) high costs of other sources (e.g., auctioned refinance, refinance for hard currency denominated deposits, etc.). That is, the costs are paid by those firms which are the clients of banks that have to rely on these sources, because for them the cheap (normative) refinance is not available, or not to the same extent as for the banks with bad loans. Cheap refinance also tends to result in more stringent regulations on reserves (a higher level and a lower rate paid by the central bank). This again means that the clients of the banks who rely more on deposits will foot the bill. To some extent, the price is paid by depositors, or alternatively this source can dry up and move into securities (e.g., CDs), with straightforward consequences for banks of a different sort.

Second, if no cheap refinance is available, or if this source is drying up, banks that have accumulated bad loans have to push up their lending rates. As the empirical evidence shows, these banks are price leaders on corporate loan markets, which in turn pushes up corporate loan rates across the whole economy. In this case, each firm pays for the wide spreads (irrespective of whose client it is).

The actual figures for interest rate margins[6] in Hungary are given in Figure 12.3. As this figure shows, absolute margins increased rapidly, in particular for mid-sized banks. By 1991, average interest rate spread reached 8 percentage points, which is fairly high. That is, capital costs for borrowers were undoubtedly increasing significantly throughout the whole period. As pointed out above, this in itself cannot be regarded as a sign of a decreasing degree of competitiveness in the market place. However, what seems to be a sign of the lack of really strong competition is the fact that mid-sized banks caught up fast with large banks in this respect, though some of the reasons which may explain widening spreads for large banks were not relevant to this group.

4.2   Earning ratios

Earning ratios are another standard way of measuring competitiveness and efficiency. Naturally, due to accounting standards not being in line with Western standards, it is very difficult to judge the level of these ratios. However, their dynamics provide useful information, as well as their relative size for the different groups of banks. The figures on nominal return-on-assets ratios (ROAs) presented in Table 12.6 reveal that until 1989, ROAs in each group increased rapidly, stagnated in 1990 and dropped substantially in 1991. The relatively low figures for retail banks are to a large extent explained by their liability structures. A higher degree of dependence on a large number of smaller deposits naturally results in lower ROAs (because of the higher costs attached to maintaining retail deposits).

The higher ROAs for mid-sized banks can be explained, on the one hand, by their higher level of efficiency and, on the other hand, by the fact that mid-sized banks captured the upper end of the banking market and engaged in retail businesses only to a moderate extent. The sudden drop in 1991 clearly reflects the large increase in the stock of low quality assets and the changes in the regulation on loan classification. That is, the large drop in 1991 is mainly the result of the substantial provisioning by the financial institutions. If profit figures from balance sheets and the amount of risk reserves generated in 1991 had been added up (that is if banks had not generated risk reserves to the extent they actually did), the tendency of stagnation characterizing 1990 would have continued. This also explains why the drop for mid-sized banks is significantly lower than that for the industry as a whole.

Notwithstanding these problems related to the interpretation of the ROAs and to the comparison of these figures with international ones, we ought to point out that even the figures for 1991 are fairly high by international standards. This is a clear indicator of the limited extent to which the market place was competitive in Hungary.

Table 12.6 further corroborates our general finding that the degree of concentration in banking has decreased substantially. The share of the profit of mid-sized banks in the industry total increased rapidly and by 1991, partly due to the substantial fall in the profitability of large banks, mid-sized banks as a group overtook the large banks. In 1991, mid-sized banks realized more than 40 per cent of profits in the industry.

Another standard measure of the level of profitability and efficiency is the nominal return-on-equity ratio. The nominal ROEs are given in Table 12.7. The difference between the absolute levels for the different groups is partly explained by the differences in leverage. The extremely high values for household (retail) banks reflect the fact that these banks were seriously undercapitalized until 1991. The figures are again very high by international standards even in 1991, though in this respect one should take into account the fact that inflation was high and accelerating during the period under investigation. However, even if adjustment is made for inflationary losses on financial assets, the real ROE turns out to be 20.1 per cent for the industry as a whole in 1990 (the corresponding figures for 1988 and 1989 are 30.6 and 32.4 per cent respectively). These figures are well above the ones for countries with competitive banking industries. Similar figures can be observed in economies with underdeveloped and highly protected banking industries.

5   State influence in banking

The most visible and obvious channel through which the state can exert control over banks is equity ownership. As the detailed discussion in Chapter 13 shows, state ownership was dominant in the Hungarian banking industry. However, as far as dynamics is concerned, state ownership was much less important. New developments and major changes, especially in the corporate market, were almost exclusively attributable to mid-sized banks where state ownership is insignificant. That is, the dynamics of the industry comes from the private sector, and therefore the directions of changes and developments are determined by the behavioral characteristics of private (to a significant extent foreign-owned) banks.

Another, perhaps less visible channel of state influence was refinance credit provided by the central bank. For reasons spelled out in Király (1993), one should make a clear distinction between long-term and short-term refinance credit. Normative schemes for providing short-term refinance credit gradually lost their importance and were replaced by schemes based on competitive bids. The latter ones gave no preferences to banks based on their size or ownership. Therefore, these schemes could not and did not serve as vehicles for exerting state influence on banks.

Long-term refinance credit was a different story, and on the whole it can be taken as a channel through which the state could exert some influence. In addition, the ways in which these credits were granted were anything but competitive and sector neutral. Figure 12.4 plots the ratios of long-term refinance credit to total long-term corporate loans extended by banks to corporate lenders and also to total assets of banks for the period under investigation. These ratios show that the overall share of refinance credit was relatively moderate and gradually decreasing. The importance of refinance credit as a source enabling banks to extend long-term corporate loans was, however, overwhelming and not declining at all. That is, through refinance credit the state preserved a relatively important mechanism through which it could exert direct influence over the banking industry.

However, it should also be mentioned that, as pointed out earlier, long-term finance available for the corporate sector gradually diminished. Thus this influence of the state was rather static, largely confined to the policy of not forcing the large, directly or indirectly state-owned commercial banks to withdraw long-term finance from the large SOEs pushing these enterprises into insolvency. That is, this was basically an element of the policy to maintain the status quo in the economy.

No mandatory deposit insurance scheme (deposit protection fund) was set up during the period under investigation. However, it was set up later on. Deposit insurance may be another form through which the state can exert influence over the banking system. Therefore, a lot will depend on the actual working of this institution.

6   Conclusions

The Hungarian banking industry underwent major changes in the period 1987—1991. The overwhelming dominance of the large directly or indirectly state-owned four commercial banks decreased tangibly, and in certain niches of the banking market (e.g., discounting of bills of exchange, or providing certain financial services related to foreign payments) it even disappeared altogether. The number of mid-sized, including the partly or fully foreign-owned banks increased substantially. All these changes made the market place more competitive.

Naturally, these changes (and the consequent increase in the degree of competitiveness) were not evenly distributed across the different segments of the market. This unevenness of development is due to several reasons. First, the newly-emerging banks are rather small units by any standard. Consequently, they have to adopt a very cautious business strategy. Their capacity to assume risk in a prudent manner, a consideration of utmost importance in an economy just undergoing economic transformation, is rather limited. Thus, even without any market imperfection, or lack of contestability of markets, it is fairly reasonable for these banks to vigorously contest markets with products carrying limited risk, and to concentrate on financial services where they are best suited to provide high quality service. That is, to some extent it is only rational for these banks to be very cautious in entering the market of long-term corporate loans.

The orientation towards products with short(er) maturity is also easily explainable by the portfolio preferences of financial investors and by the inherent risk in long-term financial instruments with fixed rates for both ends of these markets.

Regarding future development, successful mid-sized banks can be expected to follow more or less the natural life cycle of a bank, mainly capitalizing on profits, and, to some extent, relying on the capital strength of the foreign partner (if any). The number of commercial banks is probably near its peak, and through mergers and acquisitions, it can be expected to eventually decrease. This is again a rather general tendency in European banking, especially in countries with small domestic markets. The number of open failures will depend, to a large extent, on the policies adopted by the State Banking Supervision and the deposit insurance agency. If they have a policy of trying to avoid open failure and arrange (and financially support) quick mergers for banks in trouble, we can expect the main form of decrease to be through mergers and acquisitions.

The increase in foreign participation will also most likely be closely linked to this process. Established mid-sized banks in trouble but with a well-developed client base are natural targets for foreign investors, for this way set-up costs and consequently risk can be lowered substantially. Another possible and important channel for an increase in foreign participation is the privatization of the four large commercial banks, though progress in this regard is at best very modest. This development can be explained by several factors. First of all, by the inability of the administration to come up with any workable idea as to what to do with the bad loans in these banks. The administration chose perhaps the most harmful option: doing always too little, too late.

Without a solution to this problem, the large commercial banks are ventures just too risky even for investors with sizeable capital strength and a strong position in foreign markets. Moreover, dealing with a major part of the corporate sector and maintaining a fairly large branch network requires a very good understanding of local market conditions.

Though the number of commercial banks will most likely start to decrease in the near future, the degree of concentration will further decrease in banking. Whatever happens to the large commercial banks, their absolute sizes and market shares will most likely further decrease, making more room for the successful mid-sized banks, some of them entering the league of large banks fairly soon.

The analysis above detected sizeable increases in the degree of competitiveness in almost all product markets in banking. Although for reasons mentioned above, the development was rather uneven, the overall result was that during the period under investigation the market place became much more competitive than it was at the start in 1987. The changes gathered momentum gradually. The relatively large number of foreign banks participating in joint ventures, or having subsidiaries in Hungary is another proof of the overall positive development.[7] With further easing of restrictions on cross-border capital movements this process can be expected to continue in the future.

As a result of the previous reform steps and the changes during the period under investigation, the Hungarian banking sector became perhaps the most sophisticated one in CEE. This gives a relative advantage to the Hungarian economy over other CEE economies, and partly explains why foreign direct investment is concentrated so much in Hungary. However, in order to maintain this relative advantage, Hungary has to remain in the forefront of financial reforms aimed at the opening up of financial markets and the further increase of competitiveness.

Notes

1.   The research reported in this chapter was conducted under the auspices of the Centre for Economic Policy Research research programme on Economic Transformation in Eastern Europe. The views expressed are those of the authors and do not necessarily reflect the views that any of the institutions the authors are affiliated with might hold.
2.   One could suggest combining the shares of mid-sized banks and specialized financial institutions (SFIs) for the purpose of the present argument, as many of the SFIs obtained full commercial bank licence during the period under investigation. If we take the combined shares, the increase reduces to three and a half times, still an impressive number.
3.   The mirror image of this is the decline in the importance of refinance credit (as measured, for example, by its share in total liabilities).

4. It may again be advisable to regard mid-sized banks and SFIs together for the sake of this argument. However, this regrouping does not change the nature of our finding.
5. Unfortunately, due to the lack of proper disaggregation of the available data, we can provide shares only for 1991 and for the whole short-term loan market, including non-corporate loans as well.
6. Calculated as the difference between the average rates on deposits and on loans for the group of banks concerned, expressed in percentage points.
7. The number of participating foreign banks is most likely the highest in Hungary in CEE, and, much higher than, for example, in Finland, though there, unlike in Hungary, practically all restrictions on foreign banks have been lifted.

References

Balassa, Á. (1992), 'The transformation and development of the Hungarian banking system', in Kemme and Rudka (1992).

Blejer, M.I. and Sagari, S.B. (1991), 'Hungary: financial sector reform in a socialist economy', Working Paper WPS 595, The World Bank, Washington, D.C.

Brainard, L.J. (1991), 'Strategies for economic transition in Central and Eastern Europe: role of financial market reform', in Blommenstein, H. and Marrese, M. (eds), *Transformation of Planned Economies: Property Rights Reform and Macroeconomic Stability*, Paris, OECD.

Calvo, G.A. and Fenkel, J.A. (1991), 'Obstacles to transforming centrally-planned economies: the role of the capital markets', Working Papers Series No. 3776, NBER.

Caprio, G. and Levine, R. (1992), 'Reforming finance in transitional socialist economies', Working Paper WPS 898, The World Bank, Washington, D.C.

Estrin, S., Hare, P., and Surányi, M. (1992), 'Banking in transition: development and current problems in Hungary', *Soviet Studies* 44(5), 785—808.

Fisher, S. and Gelb, A. (1991), 'The process of socialist economic transformation', *Journal of Economic Perspectives* 5(4), 91—106.

Kemme, D. and Rudka, A. (eds) (1992), *Monetary and Banking Reform in Postcommunist Economies*, New York, Institute for EastWest Studies.

Király, J (1993), 'A short run money market model of Hungary', in Székely, I.P. and Newbery, D.M.G. (eds), *Hungary: An Economy in Transition*, Cambridge, Cambridge University Press.

McKinnon, R. (1991), *The Order of Economic Liberalization*, Baltimore, Johns Hopkins University Press.

Székely, I.P. (1990), 'The reform of the Hungarian financial system', *European Economy* No. 43 March, 107—123.
Székely, I.P. (1993), 'Economic transformation and the reform of the financial system in Central and Eastern Europe', Discussion Paper Series No. 816, Centre for Economic Policy Research, London.

Table 12.1 The number of banks in Hungary

	1987	1988	1989	1990	1991
Commercial banks	15	16	16	23	32
large	5	5	5	4	4
mid-sized	9	10	9	17	26
household	1	1	2	2	2
Spec. Fin. Inst's	6	8	8	8	5
Total	21	24	24	31	37
out of which joint ventures or foreign-owned	3	3	8	9	15

(end of year)

Notes: In addition to the banks above there was a special state financial institution, the Pénzintézeti Központ, which is not taken into account here. Thus, the total number of financial institutions was 38 in 1991.

In 1991, the group of large commercial banks (called 'large banks' hereafter) included Hungarian Credit Bank, Commercial and Credit Bank, Budapest Bank, and Hungarian Foreign Trade Bank. Until 1990, this group also included General Banking and Trust. In 1991, the group of household banks consisted of National Savings Bank and Hungarian Savings Cooperative Bank. The latter one was formed in 1989.

Table 12.2 Market shares of groups of banks in Hungary as measured by the size of total balance sheet

				(percentage of industry total)	
	1987	1988	1989	1990	1991
Large banks	58.2	53.3	52.0	48.2	42.4
Mid-sized banks	4.7	6.1	7.2	13.7	22.1
Household banks	35.6	38.1	37.8	36.0	34.8
Commercial banks total	98.4	97.5	97.1	97.9	99.3
SFIs	1.6	2.5	2.9	2.1	0.7
Total	100.0	100.0	100.0	100.0	100.0

Note: The figures above are based on the balance sheets of banks (Pénzintézeti Központ and CIB excluded).
Source: National Bank of Hungary

Table 12.3 Market shares of groups of banks in the corporate deposit market in Hungary

				(percentage of total corporate deposits)	
	1987	1988	1989	1990	1991
Large banks	84.0	77.3	68.4	66.9	54.9
Mid-sized banks	6.1	5.8	7.7	18.0	29.7
Household banks	8.5	13.0	21.4	14.6	15.1
Commercial banks total	98.6	96.1	97.5	99.5	99.7
SFIs	1.4	3.9	2.5	0.5	0.3
Total	100.0	100.0	100.0	100.0	100.0

Note: The figures above are based on the balance sheets of banks (Pénzintézeti Központ and CIB excluded).
Source: National Bank of Hungary

Table 12.4 Market shares of groups of banks in the corporate loan market in Hungary

	(percentage of total corporate loans)				
	1987	1988	1989	1990	1991
Large banks	91.6	85.7	79.2	68.6	62.9
Mid-sized banks	6.9	8.4	11.1	18.5	26.8
Household banks	0.0	2.5	5.4	11.1	10.1
Commercial banks total	98.5	96.6	95.7	98.2	99.8
SFIs	1.5	3.4	4.3	1.8	0.2
Total	100.0	100.0	100.0	100.0	100.0

Note: The figures above are based on the balance sheets of banks
         (Pénzintézeti Központ and CIB excluded).
Source: National Bank of Hungary

Table 12.5 Market shares of groups of banks in the bills of exchange market in Hungary

	(percentage of industry total)				
	1987	1988	1989	1990	1991
Large banks	90.3	79.5	64.4	26.9	20.3
Mid-sized banks	6.7	13.2	16.0	38.0	43.9
Household banks	0.0	0.0	1.3	24.2	34.1
Commercial banks total	97.0	92.7	81.7	89.1	98.3
SFIs	3.0	7.3	18.3	10.9	1.7
Total	100.0	100.0	100.0	100.0	100.0

Note: The figures above are based on the balance sheets of banks
         (Pénzintézeti Központ and CIB excluded).
Source: National Bank of Hungary

Table 12.6 Nominal return-on-assets ratios (ROAs) for groups of banks and shares of groups of banks in total profit

(in percentage of industry total profit)

| | 1987 | | 1988 | | 1989 | | 1990 | | 1991 | |
	ROA %	% of total	ROA %	% of total	ROA %	% of total	ROA %	% of total	ROA %	% of total
Large banks	3.16	64.7	3.91	60.7	4.04	52.6	3.93	48.6	1.40	36.4
Mid-sized banks	4.93	8.1	6.25	11.3	5.76	10.4	5.03	17.7	3.18	41.8
Household banks	2.09	26.1	2.15	24.0	3.45	32.9	3.35	30.8	1.02	21.2
Commercial banks total	2.85	98.9	3.37	96.0	3.94	95.9	3.87	97.0	1.68	99.4
SFIs	1.93	1.1	5.41	4.0	5.53	4.1	5.64	3.0	1.26	0.6
Total	2.84	100.0	3.42	100.0	3.98	100.0	3.91	100.0	1.68	100.0

Notes: ROA stands for nominal return-on-assets ratio, expressed in per cent. Shares are expressed in per cent and are the ratio of profit in the given group to total profit of financial institutions in the given year. The data are based on the unaudited balance sheets and profit and loss statements of 36 Hungarian banks (Pénzintézeti Központ and CIB excluded) for 1991.

Source: National Bank of Hungary

Table 12.7 Nominal return-on-equity ratios (ROEs) for groups of banks

	1987	1988	1989	1990	1991
Large banks	50.7	44.7	45.1	50.5	12.3
Mid-sized banks	20.2	28.8	32.9	33.2	25.8
Household banks	151.0	182.9	161.6	108.6	17.9
Commercial banks total	53.4	51.0	56.9	54.7	17.3
SFIs	3.9	14.7	20.3	18.6	4.2
Total	47.2	46.4	53.0	51.7	16.9

Notes: ROE is calculated as the ratio between return and equity and expressed in per cent.
The figures above are based on the balance sheets of banks (Pénzintézeti Központ and CIB excluded).

Source: National Bank of Hungary

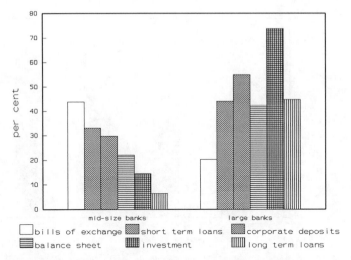

Figure 12.1 Market shares of mid-sized and large banks in Hungary in 1991

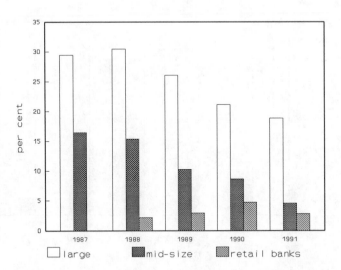

Note: Loans to corporate borrowers with maturity over one year.

Figure 12.2 Long-term corporate lending as a share of total assets of Hungarian banks

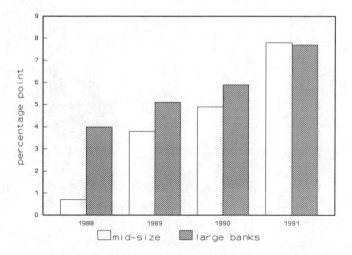

Note: Calculated as the difference between average deposit and loan
rates.

Figure 12.3 Interest rate spreads in Hungary

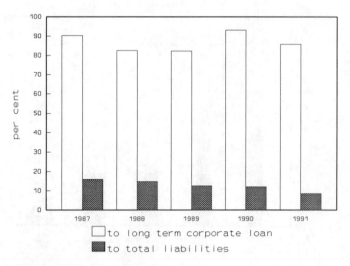

Note: With maturity over one year.

*Figure 12.4 The ratios of long-term refinance credit to long-term
corporate loans and to total bank liabilities*

13 The 'Second' Reform of the Hungarian Banking System

Éva Várhegyi

1 Introduction

The Hungarian banking system is in a much more severe situation than anybody expected. Though previous reforms created an institutional and legal framework that is rather similar to those prevailing in developed market economies, a major part of the banking system is still locked into the situation inherited from the past. Privatization has not yet started and bad loans have not yet been seriously tackled. The repercussions of economic transformation have further aggravated the situation, as many large enterprises with sizeable loans have suddenly lost their export and domestic markets. It seems that market forces in themselves will not be able to solve this problem: they are likely to destroy the state-owned commercial banks currently in trouble faster than they could create new banks strong enough to assume the roles of these banks. That is, a market solution, one that does not entail any intervention by the state, would result in the collapse of the payment and financial intermediation system, an outcome hardly acceptable to any government. Put differently, in our opinion, the present situation necessitates the active involvement of the state (government) in order to create banks that are fit for privatization and competition. Such a solution should entail the cleaning up of the loan portfolios of commercial banks, a more advanced system of banking regulation and supervision, and an eventual privatization of the large state-owned commercial banks.[1]

The present chapter first discusses the banking reforms that have been carried out until now in Hungary. It is followed by an investigation of surviving and newly-emerging problems serving as the basis for developing a comprehensive reform package which we shall call the 'second' reform of the banking system. Section 4 is devoted to the loan consolidation programme which is regarded as a key element of this package. Finally, the remaining part of the chapter deals with further specific elements of this package. Throughout the chapter, we shall argue that policy makers need to reconsider their views regarding the desirable direction of development in the Hungarian banking sector.

2   The first phase of banking reforms

The first phase of the reforms of the banking system in Hungary created an institutional and legal framework in line with European banking legislation. The first important step was the dismantling of the monobank system by setting up a two-tier banking system which is a key element of any market economy. In the new system, which started to operate on 1 January 1987, the National Bank of Hungary (NBH) performed mostly central bank functions, while the separated new commercial banks assumed the classical functions of merchant banks. This separation made it formally possible for the NBH to conduct monetary policy by using the traditional tools, and for the commercial banks to allocate credit on a commercial basis.

The central bank, however, remained under strong pressure by the administration to unconditionally finance budget expenditures of different kinds (Várhegyi, 1993a). On the other hand, the nature of credit allocation carried out by the newly-created commercial banks was not radically different from the one that was prevailing under the monobank system (Spéder, 1991), mainly because the direct and indirect state ownership of these banks was preserved (Nyers and Pap, 1992). The banks which inherited the corporate loans made by the monobank did not manage to get rid of the 'dowry' of the monobank system (Spéder and Várhegyi, 1992). Even in 1992, a considerable part of the outstanding bad loans of the three commercial banks separated from the NBH was directly or indirectly linked to the inherited loans. In addition to the inherited bad loans, the lack of necessary changes in business policy and enterprise performance monitoring also contributed to the fact that the efficiency of banking system did not improve tangibly (Székely, 1993; Várhegyi, 1993a).

The second important step towards the modernization of the banking system was the creation of a legal framework which almost fully conforms to European legislation, consisting of the Act on the National Bank of Hungary and the Act on Financial Institutions and Financial Institutional Activities (Acts No. LX. and No. LXIX. of 1991). These laws protect banks from political pressure and support a development that eventually leads to the integration of Hungarian financial markets and financial institutions into the highly integrated financial systems of developed market economies.

The Act on the National Bank of Hungary gave the central bank the autonomy which is essential to keep the value of national currency (the basic task of the NBH). According to the law, the NBH, which became independent from the government, has the obligation to support in general, but not in an unqualified manner, the economic policy of the government. From 1993 onwards, the central bank is no longer obliged to provide unlimited finance for the budget deficit.

The Act on Financial Institutions sets requirements for banks that can only be satisfied by pursuing prudent business policy and giving preference to investments where the risk involved is foreseeable and can be controlled. These include a minimum capital adequacy requirement, the requirement to accumulate an adequate level of reserve funds, restrictions on the equity share any single owner can hold in a bank, and on the sizes of loans a bank can grant to any single client ('large loans').

Regarding financial discipline, two other acts must be mentioned. According to the Act on Accounting (Act No. XLIII. of 1991), proper reserves should be generated against doubtful claims. Previously these claims were parts of the 'false' income shown in the balance sheets of companies. The Act on Bankruptcy (Act No. IL. of 1991) does not allow major delays in payments without serious consequences. These laws contribute to the strengthening of payment discipline and, through this, the hardening of the budget constraint of companies (Kornai, 1993).

As pointed out above in Chapter 5, the problem these (otherwise undoubtedly rational) acts created stems from the fact that neither companies nor banks had been prepared for the writing-off of doubtful claims. It was only after the introduction of the new accounting, tax and banking acts that banks and companies could accumulate proper risk reserves from their pre-tax incomes (previously, they could accumulate these reserves only from their after-tax incomes). Furthermore, as discussed in detail in Chapter 6, the ill-designed act on bankruptcy which was introduced at the wrong time aggravated the shock due to the collapse of Eastern European markets and led to an excessively large increase in loan losses, endangering the stability of the whole banking system.

3   Surviving and newly-emerging problems of the banking system

In spite of the reforms described above, the large state-owned commercial banks and thus the whole banking system remained trapped by its inherited clients, owners and distorted market relations. Moreover, the unsolved old problems were accompanied by newly-emerging ones.

3.1   The dominance of state ownership

In spite of the relatively large number of newly-established private banks, direct and indirect, through state-owned enterprises (SOEs), state ownership has remained dominant in the Hungarian banking system. At the end of 1991, the proportion of direct state ownership reached 38 per cent in the whole banking system, and 64 per cent in the group of five largest banks.

The combined share of (direct and indirect) state equity was much higher: it amounted to 66 per cent in the whole sector and 86 per cent in the group of largest banks (see Table 13.1). Since then the situation has not improved. Moreover, in the case of some large commercial banks, direct state ownership has further increased due to the seizure of bank equities held by the SOEs which were transformed into joint stock companies.

The state (or the government) is not a suitable owner of business ventures, especially in banking, for several reasons. First, it is interested in collecting the highest possible tax receipts and dividends from banks. Second, the government is responsible for economic policy. This role may well conflict with the requirements of efficient and prudent banking. Under the pressure of different interest groups, the Hungarian government is inclined to hold the 'inadequate' credit policies of banks responsible for the decline of 'national' industry and agriculture, the failures of certain branches of industry or companies, or the unfavourable trends in inflation, investments and unemployment.

Experiences so far show that the dominance of state ownership is a factor which hinders rather than improves the efficiency of banks, and, thus, the overall efficiency of capital allocation. This fact is recognized by the banking act when it stipulates that the direct and indirect equity share of the state in each individual bank should be reduced to 25 per cent by 1997.[2] Until now, however, the high share of state ownership has not diminished.

3.2   Market distortions and competition

Since the establishment of a two-tier banking system in 1987, favourable as well as unfavourable changes have taken place. There were two major groups of favourable changes. First, market segmentation characterizing the early period became less rigid. Second, the number of agents in the market increased and competition became stronger.

In the relaxing of market segmentation, an important factor was that commercial banks were allowed to offer retail services from 1989 onward. In the beginning, banks entered this market only to collect savings. However, later on, mainly due to the increasing extent of enterprise insolvency, the banks were increasingly forced to turn to the retail market by offering a more complete spectrum of services. This was, however, hindered by the significant costs of investments needed for developing a suitable branch network.

The number of banks increased for several reasons. Most specialized financial institutions operating in 1987 were transformed into commercial banks (State Banking Supervision, 1990). The degree of competition was also increased by the newly-established foreign and joint venture banks, as well as by the banks that were founded by large banks. The number of financial institutions thus grew from 20 in 1987 to 37 by the end of 1991, and then decreased to 35 after the failure of two small banks at the end of 1992. During the same period, the combined market share of the four largest commercial banks financing a decisive part of the enterprise sector decreased from 58 to 39 per cent, while that of the group of mid-sized financial institutions increased from 5 to 20 per cent.[3]

Besides these favourable changes, some adverse trends could also be observed. First, a new segmentation of the market started to take place. Second, certain very important forms of enterprise finance became extremely scarce.

The new segmentation of the market developed as the result of 'imperfect competition' between large banks burdened with inherited bad loans and mid-sized banks bearing less of this kind of burden (Ábel and Székely, 1992). As discussed in more detail in Chapter 12, mid-sized banks increased their market shares in profitable markets (of less risky products, such as short-term credits and interbank lending) to the detriment of large banks. On the other hand, large banks were caught up in less profitable (or even loss-making) and riskier markets, such as medium- and long-term enterprise (investment) credits. As refinance credit became more scarce, this situation became increasingly disadvantageous for large banks.

The tax allowance granted to foreign and joint venture banks was another distorting factor in the banking market. Moreover, most of these banks had access to cheap sources of finance and could attract a fast-growing number of joint ventures and domestic subsidiaries of foreign firms, the best clients in the Hungarian banking market, through their foreign parent-banks.

There were two major types of enterprise finance where commercial banks were less willing or able to supply sources, investment loan and long-term direct (equity and bond) finance. While in the former case it was mainly due to the substantially increased level of risk, in the latter case commercial banks were restricted by legal regulations.

Moreover, there were several other factors reducing the supply of long-term finance. First, as a consequence of high inflation and uncertain prospects, the share of long-term deposits was decreasing in the balance sheets of banks.[4] Second, credit risk increased substantially due to the growing number of insolvent enterprises. Third, low quality loan portfolios also hindered banks from granting new investment loans or investing directly in enterprises. Finally, the huge and fast increasing level of budget deficit crowded out private investment. The low levels of investment finance and investment banking activities slowed down industrial restructuring and privatization.

The stock exchange could not provide enterprises with substantial amounts of long-term finance either. An overwhelming majority of

Hungarian enterprises, most of all the newly-established ones, have no access to the stock market as a source of new capital, because of the lack of correctly audited balance sheets. On the demand side, the development of the Hungarian Stock Exchange is restricted by the low level of liquidity of shares. According to the Act on Securities and Stock Exchange (Act No. VI. of 1990), banks are allowed to trade on the stock exchange only through broker companies. Private pension funds and insurance funds that could increase the demand for equity shares are not yet in place.[5] Though the legislation makes it possible to create investment funds, and tax allowances encourage individuals to invest in them, high inflationary expectations and decreasing real incomes lead to low levels of long-term savings.

To sum up, the significant increase in the number of the participants neither tangibly improved the quality and supply of bank services nor reduced their prices. At the same time, an increasing number of financial institutions became unstable due to liquidity problems and deteriorating bank portfolios. Therefore, we can conclude that a substantial improvement in the banking market cannot be expected merely from liberalization and growing competition.

3.3   Problems of the bank portfolios

As pointed out above, an important factor that contributed to the inefficient and unsatisfactory operating of the banking system was the low quality of banks' loan portfolios. Before the loan consolidation (at the end of September of 1992), the non-performing (qualified) loans of the Hungarian banking sector reached 17 per cent of the total loans (see Table 13.2). According to the estimate given by Szalkai (1993), the amount of qualified corporate loans represented nearly 30 per cent of the total claims on enterprises.

The deteriorating position of banks regarding their capital strength was reflected by the increasing gap between the required and generated risk reserves against qualified assets. At the end of 1991, the generated risk reserve was HUF 51 bn, while the requirement (according to the Hungarian regulation) was HUF 83 bn. By the end of 1992 (before the loan consolidation was launched) risk reserves grew to HUF 89 bn, while the requirement, due to the huge increase in the amount of qualified assets, increased to some HUF 220 bn. Thus, the reserve shortfall became greater than the total adjusted capital[6] of banks; that is, the Hungarian banking system had practically lost its capital base by that time.

The low levels of capital adequacy also demonstrated the structural problems of banks' balance sheets. Most banks, in particular the large commercial banks, did not reach the 8 per cent capital adequacy ratio stipulated by the law. According to the International Accounting System (IAS), the capital adequacy ratio of some large banks became negative. This situation seriously endangered the secure operation of the banking system.

The accumulation of reserve funds required by the regulations played a significant role in the deteriorating profitability of banks. In 1991, 55 per cent of the operating profit of the whole banking sector and 68 per cent of the operating profit of the five largest banks was used for this purpose. In 1992, risk reserve formation required more funds than the entire operating profit, reflecting the fast deterioration of loan portfolios mentioned above. Consequently, Hungarian banks produced a total loss of HUF 8.7 bn, resulting in an average ROE of -5 per cent for the banking sector as a whole.

4   Loan consolidation attempts

Though the necessity of a loan consolidation scheme aimed at cleaning the banks' balance sheets was not questioned, policy makers faced several dilemmas.[7] One of them was about who should bear the burden of the scheme. In a normal situation, the banks' owners should bear the losses. In the case of the Hungarian banks, however, this matter was somewhat more complicated. Between 1988 and 1991, that is, until the implementation of the Act on Financial Institutions, the state received substantial tax and dividend revenues from the 'paper profits' of banks that existed because of inadequate accounting standards and tax regulations and the lack of a bankruptcy law and proper control over bank management. Besides the state's apparent responsibility for the situation, it also had certain motivations for implementing a loan consolidation scheme. The most important ones were the expected increase in revenues from bank privatization and the increasing future capacity of banks to pay taxes.

The other dilemma was related to the method for improving the quality of the banks' balance sheets. The simplest solution would have been an injection of new capital to assure appropriate capital adequacy ratios. This solution, however, had to be ruled out at the outset, because it would have required immediate massive budgetary expenditures, and the budget deficit was already dangerously high. Therefore, policy makers had to opt for a solution which spread the costs of the operation for both the budget and the other owners of the banks over time.

The first step of the cleaning-up of balance sheets was taken at the end of 1992. Under the so-called 1992 Loan Consolidation Scheme, under-capitalised banks had the opportunity to swap loans classified as 'bad' in 1991 and 1992 for 20-year state bonds in an amount equal to 50, 80, or 100 per cent of face value depending on certain characteristics of the loans. A total of HUF 102 bn in loans was transferred from the banks to the Hungarian Investment and Development Ltd. in exchange for HUF 80 bn in state bonds which yielded market rates of the three-month T-bills against loan principal, and 50 per cent of this rate against accrued interests.

The 1992 loan consolidation scheme improved the quality of bank portfolios and, thus, the capital adequacy ratios. According to the original arrangements, the banks should have paid annual loan consolidation fees proportional to the amount of state bonds received for the swapped loans. This solution was chosen to minimize the burden on the state budget. However, international auditors dealing with the Hungarian banks, soon after introducing the system, called the government's attention to the accounting problems created by this method, namely that it reduced the market value of the received state bonds. Following revision of the original conditions, consolidation fees were cancelled and low-yield state bonds were exchanged for 'normal' securities issued under more favourable conditions. These changes tangibly improved the position of the banks concerned.

At the same time, government hesitation increased the precariousness of the banking system which in turn had an undesirable impact on both bank managers and potential investors. The protraction of loan consolidation and the lack of a clear government policy made bank managers interested in improving their bargaining position *vis-à-vis* the government rather than in improving the banks' operations. On the other hand, the faltering of the government greatly increased the uncertainty regarding the market values of (future income flows generated by) the banks up for privatization. This is the reason why it is important to develop and announce a clear-cut government programme for stabilizing and privatizing the banking system.

The solution promising the best results would be to allow banks to participate, at their own risk, in the reorganization of the companies involved by acquiring equity shares. However, the law on financial institutions allows for this method to a very limited extent. Without firms having the necessary capital strength for and interest in the reorganization of indebted companies, the state itself must take on most of the losses.

The improvement of the still poor balance sheets should be the next step of loan consolidation. Since the new wave of enterprise bankruptcies and liquidation rendered an additional massive amount of corporate loans qualified (doubtful or bad), the improvement in the quality of bank portfolios brought about by the 1992 loan consolidation scheme quickly diminished. However, unless the government makes it clear that this scheme will be the ultimate one, the moral hazard issue may become unmanageable.

Based on suggestions made by international bank experts, the Hungarian government is trying to deal with the issue by injecting additional capital into the banks concerned. As a result of this capital injection, their capital adequacy ratios will improve. Achieving capital adequacy ratios[8] of 0 per cent in each bank concerned would require a capital injection of HUF 120 bn (this sum exceeds the total registered capital of the banking sector). Since the current state budget cannot afford such a burden, the banks will be given government bonds. In 1993, this solution requires no (current) budget expenditure. However, from 1994 onward, the interests paid on these bonds will appear as a current budget expenditure.

In contrast to the 1992 scheme, the burdens of the 1993 loan consolidation scheme will have to be borne by all owners of the banks, since credit losses will reduce the value of bank shares. Therefore, for certain banks the level of direct state ownership will greatly increase. In the course of the 1993 loan consolidation, the bad assets (and investments) will remain in the banks' portfolios. Hence, the banks will have to manage these outstanding debts, or sell them (for example, to their own subsidiaries or other firms).

5   The 'second' reform of the banking system: conditions and possible methods for stable consolidation

The 1993 loan consolidation scheme may be a good starting point for a longer-term solution to the problems of the banking system. However, providing the banks with adequate capital is a necessary but limited condition. A successful longer-term solution requires further steps to be taken by the government. First, state-owned commercial banks have to be privatized in order to improve management. Second, the playing field has to be levelled so that the position of large banks financing a decisive part of the Hungarian economy becomes more favourable than that of other banks. Third, regulations have to be changed in order to allow the major commercial banks to more actively participate in the reorganization of companies. Finally, the regulatory and institutional environment has to be changed in order to reduce the risk attached to bank loans.

5.1 Privatization

As pointed out above, the large state-owned commercial banks, financing the major part of the enterprise sector, are directly dependent on the government. The 1993 loan consolidation scheme, also pointed out above, will further increase the influence of the state as a shareholder. This dependency distorts the operation of the banks even if those representing the state as a majority shareholder are not politicians but experts. The 'success index' of the bank managers is not only linked to the efficiency of bank operations but also includes certain elements related to economic policy preferences that may very well work against efficiency. This situation can only be broken up by privatizing the large banks.

The present situation of the state budget simply does not allow the State Property Agency to clean up bank portfolios prior to privatization. Therefore, it is important to find, as soon as possible, investors with sufficient capital strength to take equity shares in these banks and embark upon their reorganization. There are three possible groups of owners to choose from: foreign strategic (professional) investors, primarily financial institutions; Hungarian and foreign institutional (portfolio) investors; and small investors.

The choice of strategic investors consisting mainly of foreign banks as shareholders would have several advantages. Through the increase of capital they are expected to make after acquiring equity shares, the large Hungarian banks may conform to the capital adequacy requirement. Strategic investors can also be expected to have a long-term interest, because their main motivation is probably to gain a market share in Hungary. Therefore, they would make sure that sufficient reserves are generated in order to ensure safety and soundness. Moreover, they would be able to modernize banks and improve management. Finally, the international business contacts these banks have would make it possible for Hungarian banks to get access to foreign capital markets.

It is important to investigate to what extent and under what conditions new owners are prepared to take part in the privatization of Hungarian banks. One of the conditions is that the investment should provide a substantial market share in the Hungarian banking sector. Ownership of the large Hungarian commercial banks provides this opportunity, though only if investors are allowed to get the controlling package.

Institutional (portfolio) investors (pension funds, insurance companies, investment funds) would be interested in the stable development of banks. Moreover, they take a long-term view which is advantageous for the banks. Their interest is, however, conditional on the expected price-earnings ratios in the short to medium run. They would invest and accept low dividends in the beginning necessary to generate sufficient risk reserves only if returns are promising within their planning horizon. For this reason they are better brought into the process of bank privatization after cleaning up the balance sheets and recapitalizing the banks. Otherwise, bank equities can be sold to them only at a very high discount. In addition to private portfolio investors, international portfolio investors such as the EBRD or IFC might also be interested in taking part in the privatization of large Hungarian commercial banks. Their involvement would increase the confidence of private investors.

Given the current situation, small investors cannot be expected to take part in the process of privatization in large numbers. This source of finance will most likely be available in later phases. Until now, employee's ownership has only emerged in the large banks, but it may become more widespread in the future.

The introduction of bank equities to the stock exchange would also be an important condition for attracting Hungarian small and institutional investors. This is however hardly possible precisely because of the large banks' current situation. Therefore, the process of increasing the capital of the large banks and privatizing them can be carried out in two steps: first the bank equities should be made marketable by bringing in professional strategic investors, and then a further increase in capital can be realized through public issues.

Given the situation analysed so far, the government has two options. First, to keep the controlling packages, and thus the influence over large banks. This means however that the equity up for sale can only be sold to portfolio investors at a low enough price to ensure an attractive yield for these investors. Second, to sell the controlling packages to strategic investors. This means basically selling market shares to these investors. The state must however make sure in this case that the strategic investors make commitments for further investments in these banks. The small size of the Hungarian banking market, however, raises some doubts as to whether it would be a really lucrative market for foreign banks.

5.2 Changing the conditions of competition

The large commercial banks financing the major part of the enterprise sector have several disadvantages that make it difficult for them to compete with some of the mid-sized banks, in particular foreign and joint venture banks. First, as pointed out above, the large state-owned commercial banks are locked into risky markets (products) generating low profits, mainly due to the way their portfolios were created. Second, foreign and joint venture banks in many cases enjoy tax holidays. Moreover, they have better access to cheaper foreign funds.

Finally, most mid-sized banks are new entrants. Therefore, they have more freedom in choosing their clients. If, as a result of strong competition, the large banks are forced to abandon their troubled clients, a sizeable part of the Hungarian economy may experience serious problems regarding finance and financial services. This, in turn, may aggravate the already difficult situation for these firms. In fact, there is a danger that this development will touch upon even those firms with relatively solid prospects which temporarily experience difficulties due to their need for financial restructuring.

Therefore, the government should consider certain measures to temporarily improve the position of large banks. First, it could temporarily tighten the licensing system. This may involve more strict conditions for establishing banks (e.g., by imposing requirements on opening a certain number of branches or keeping a certain number of accounts). Raising the entry barriers would also encourage investors to acquire an equity share in existing Hungarian banks, thereby facilitating the process of privatization and recapitalization. Second, it could level the playing field by abolishing those previously granted advantages that are unjustified under the current circumstances. This would first of all mean the withdrawal of tax allowances. Another possibility is a transitory re-establishment of an interest rate control mechanism (Sándor and Spéder, 1993).

Though these temporary measures would undoubtedly be against the present fairly liberal regulations, the costs of the alternative packages that could be implemented while fully preserving the present regulations would most likely be considerably higher.

Altering the regulatory environment would lead to a predictable environment for both present and future participants in the market. It would make it possible to avoid improvised ad hoc rescue operations that might result in an increased level of undesired state (government) influence on financial institutions. Tightening banking regulations would only reflect the fact that the Hungarian economy is not yet in a situation comparable to that achieved by advanced economies when introducing liberal financial regulations. The 1991 Act on Financial Institutions was, in many respects, prepared to follow the uniform European regulation that came into force from 1993. Since the integration of the Hungarian economy in the EC economy is a very important aspect of economic development, this was a proper choice in the long run. However, in the current fairly difficult process of transition into a market economy, Hungary is now justified in departing from the liberal regime in the short run.

5.3   Banks involvement in enterprise reorganization

A modification of banking regulations that would allow (German-type) universal banking would reflect the same recognition. The transformation process the Hungarian economy now faces is rather similar to the one that postwar Germany faced. As the financial institutions which could assume key roles in the necessary reorganization of the companies are either missing or too weak, it is obvious that this activity should, at least temporarily, be carried out by the banks financing the enterprise sector.

On the one hand, industrial restructuring and quick privatization is required to increase economic efficiency, and, as a result, the sources of long-term savings. On the other hand, these sources are required to accelerate the process of restructuring and privatization of the inefficient state industry. We are convinced that only a further reform of the financial system can solve this contradiction. Making financial institutions stronger and more efficient in collecting domestic and foreign savings could help industrial restructuring by providing sufficient finance. Agreeing with Corbett and Mayer (1991) in that substantial restructuring of SOEs can only be expected by strong control groups, we can identify the existing large commercial banks as the suitable candidates for this role, provided that they are recapitalized and their balance sheets are cleaned up.

The current Act on Financial Institutions sets, however, a strict limit on equity investments by commercial banks.[9] This severely limits debt/equity swaps. Moreover, in contrast to the EC legislation, the Act on Securities and Stock Exchange excludes banks from trading in securities, which is an inherent element of universal banking. By being allowed to be involved in this market and to hold equities, banks could have a certain control over companies.

A significant part of Hungarian enterprises is at present in need of capital and is therefore not creditworthy. If recapitalization took place together with a loosening of restrictions on equity investment by banks, the reorganization of a large number of companies could be carried out through the active participation of banks. Such a solution would result in less burden for the budget than other methods (such as directly cancelling enterprise loans, or allocating some capital by the state); at the same time the chances for successful reorganization would be enhanced by the fact that the process is carried out by market participants who know the firms involved well.

Letting the banks enter the stock exchange would at the same time help to generate long-term (equity) finance for enterprises. These temporary amendments of the act would not impede the ten-year programme of joining the European Community, neither would they hinder the development of institutions that could, later on, assume investment banking functions.

5.4 Reduction of banking risks

Due to their characteristics, commercial banks are not interested in making loans to start up ventures. Whatever the outcome of the consolidation schemes may be, interest rate spreads and thus lending rates will remain large due to the costs of building up the necessary reserves in banks. Therefore, provided banks have prudent policies, even enterprises with proper track records and good prospects will experience difficulties with obtaining bank loans. The start up ventures will be in a much more difficult position due to the fact that they have hardly any collateral to offer and lack an adequate track record. The kind of risk premium they will have to pay will scare away the solid and reliable entrepreneurs, thus increasing the proportion of gamblers among loan applicants. Therefore, both the stabilization of banks as well as the financing of new enterprises requires the establishment of institutions which are able to assume a significant part of the risks, rendering creditworthy those new enterprises with good prospects. Since private investors are not willing to assume this kind of risk, the state has to assume this role and put up the capital for credit insurance institutions that can take on part of this risk.

Notes

1. On these issues see Chapter 5 in this volume.
2. During the preparation of the bill, there was sharp debate on state ownership (see, e.g., Bokros, 1990; Nyers and Pap, 1992; Várhegyi, 1991).
3. For a more detailed discussion of competition in the Hungarian banking system see Chapter 12.
4. At the end of 1992 the share of deposits with maturity of at least a year amounted to 19 per cent of the total, while in 1987 it was 27 per cent.
5. The act on mutual insurance funds is expected to be passed in 1993.
6. According to the Act on Financial Institutions, adjusted capital consists of registered capital, capital reserves, retained earnings, profit (loss) for the year, general provisions and subordinated debt.
7. An overview of the goals and problems of the 1992 Loan Consolidation Scheme can be found in Ministry of Finance (1993), containing the views of ministry officials and top ranked bankers. Independent researchers also made their contributions to the debate (see, e.g., Ábel and Bonin, 1992; Székely, 1993; Várhegyi, 1993b).
8. The present (IAS-based) Hungarian rules that were introduced at the end of 1993, unlike the previous ones, require banks to form risk reserves against bad (equity) investments and guarantees, as well.
9. Though this regulation was to some extent relaxed at the end of 1993.

References

Ábel, I. and Bonin, J.P. (1992), 'Capital markets in Eastern Europe: the financial black hole', *Connecticut Journal of International Law* 8(1), 1—17.

Ábel, I. and Székely, I.P. (1992), 'The conditions for competition and innovation in the Hungarian banking system', (mimeo), Centre for Economic Policy Research, London.

Bokros, L. (1990), 'Gondolatok a pénzintézetek tulajdonviszonyainak reformjához' (Ideas on the ownership reform of financial institutions),

Bank Szemle 36(8).
Corbett, J. and Mayer, C. (1991), 'Financial reform in Eastern Europe: progress with the wrong model', *Oxford Review of Economic Policy* 7(4), 57—75.
Kornai, J. (1993), 'A pénzügyi fegyelem evolúciója a posztszocialista rendszerben' (The evolution of financial discipline under the post-socialist system), *Közgazdasági Szemle* 40(5).
Ministry of Finance (1993), 'The Hungarian credit consolidation (1992)', Public Finance in Hungary No. 118.
National Bank of Hungary (1990), 'Annual Report 1990'.
National Bank of Hungary (1992), 'Annual Report 1992'.
Nyers, R. and Lutz, E. (1992), 'A bankrendszer föbb jellemzöi az 1987—1991. évi mérlegbeszámolók alapján' (The main features of the Hungarian banking system on the basis of balance sheets of 1987—1991), *Bank Szemle* 36(8).
Nyers, R. and Pap, J. (1992), 'Privatizáció a magyar bankrendszerben' (Privatization in the Hungarian banking system), *Bank Szemle* 36(3—4).
Sándor, L. and Spéder, Z. (1993), 'Szabályozással a bankokért' (With regulation for the banks), *Bank & Tözsde* 1(5—7).
Spéder, Z. (1991), 'The characteristic behaviour of Hungarian commercial banks', *Acta Oeconomica* 43(1—2).
Spéder, Z. and Várhegyi, É. (1992), 'On the eve of the second banking reform', *Acta Oeconomica* 44(1—2).
State Banking Supervision of Hungary (1990), 'State Banking Supervision and Banks in Hungary', Occasional Paper.
State Banking Supervision of Hungary (1993), 'The financial institution system in 1992'.
Szalkai, I. (1993), 'Hungarian credit consolidation from the point of view of large banks', in Ministry of Finance (1993).
Székely, I.P. (1993), 'Economic transformation and the reform of the financial system in Central and Eastern Europe', Discussion Paper Series No. 816, Centre for Economic Policy Research, London.
Tözsde Kurír (1992), 'The banks: balance sheet data of 1991 in Hungary', Bank Letter 20, August.
Várhegyi, É. (1991), 'Unified Europe and the Hungarian banking system' (Az egységes Európa kihívásai és a magyar bankrendszer), *Európa Fórum* 1(2).
Várhegyi, É. (1993a), 'The modernization of the Hungarian banking sector', in Székely, I.P. and Newbery, D.M.G. (eds), *Hungary: An Economy in Transition*, Cambridge, Cambridge University Press.
Várhegyi, É. (1993b), 'Key elements of the reform of the Hungarian banking system: privatization and portfolio cleaning', Discussion Paper Series No. 826, Centre for Economic Policy Research, London.

Table 13.1   *Share of state ownership in the Hungarian banking sector[a] at the end of 1991*

Groups of banks	Share capital HUF mn	Direct state ownership[b] %	Indirect state ownership[c] %	Total state ownership %
National Savings and Commercial Bank	23 000	100.0	0.0	100.0
Large commercial banks[d]	43 093	44.2	30.7	74.9
Mid-sized banks	36 343	3.7	36.8	40.5
Total	117 172	38.0	28.0	66.0

Notes: a) Saving cooperatives are excluded.
　　　　b) Owned by government bodies (such as State Property Agency, or ministries).
　　　　c) Directly owned by state-owned enterprises.
　　　　d) Hungarian Credit Bank, Commercial and Credit Bank, Hungarian Foreign Trade Bank.
Source: Tözsde Kurír (1992).

Table 13.2   *Non-performing loans in the Hungarian banking sector[a]*

	1987	1990	1991	September 1992[b]	December 1992[c]
Non-performing loans, HUF mn	3	43	88	262	173
Total loans HUF mn	787	994	1230	1523	1611
Non-performing loans as percentage of total loans	0.4	4.3	7.1	17.2	10.7

Notes: a) Saving cooperatives are excluded.
　　　　b) Before loan consolidation.
　　　　c) After loan consolidation (which reduced the stock of non-performing loans by HUF 102 bn).
Source: Nyers and Lutz (1992), National Bank of Hungary (1990) and (1992), and State Banking Supervision (1993).

Discussion of Chapters 12 and 13

Peter Backé

Both of the chapters on the Hungarian banking system are of excellent quality, create awareness for the issues involved and provide a wide variety of ideas for further consideration. They contain comprehensive and, at the same time, concise analyses of the development of the Hungarian banking system since 1987 and its current problems. In addition, Chapter 13 lists a series of measures which should be undertaken in order to put the banking system on a sound footing or, in other words, to enable the financial system to finance the transformation to a market economy. Chapter 12, conversely, takes a closer look at a specific aspect of financial sector development in Hungary, namely the evolution of competition and changes in the market structure of the banking system. Let me first discuss this latter issue and then shift to the more general questions of banking sector reform.

Chapter 12 presents a series of pieces of evidence regarding the development of competition and changes in the market structure of the Hungarian banking sector. They carefully interpret the data used and are well aware of the limitations of their findings, e.g., when comparing prices for products which are most likely not homogeneous. The authors' findings about the degree of change may also be distorted by their distinction between large banks on the one hand and mid-sized ones on the other. As the latter group of banks is a very heterogeneous one (and there are also substantial differences in several respects between the large banks), it would arguably be more appropriate to distinguish between 'good' and 'bad' banks. Such an approach would admittedly encounter two difficulties. First, one would have to come up with sensible criteria for categorizing the banks (perhaps along the lines of ownership structure, profits and/or quality of bank management) and, second, the respective data must be accessible.

Citing major regulatory changes at the turn of 1991/92 and thus limited comparability between data before and after this point in time, Chapter 12 only covers the period up to 1991. Still, bearing in mind the rapid pace of the developments in the Hungarian banking system in 1992 and 1993, it would undoubtedly be worthwhile to analyse the changes in the recent past.

As to the question whether, with respect to the size of the Hungarian banks, small is beautiful, one should bear in mind that financial intermediation entails economies of scale. Thus, small banks may be beautiful from the competitive viewpoint but they may also prove to be costly. This being so, there appears to be room for an 'industrial policy for banks' (an issue raised by István P. Székely) to facilitate mergers.

Let me now move on to the general issues of banking sector reform. As the synopses of the evolution of the banking system until 1991 seem to be non-controversial, I will restrict my remarks to the most pressing present task of reform, namely to bank consolidation and to measures which should complement bank consolidation.

I agree with Éva Várhegyi that the 1993 bank consolidation exercise should ideally be the ultimate one, or else there is no chance left for strengthening the crediting responsibility of the banks. However, looking at the consolidation attempts so far does not bode well for arriving at a solution to the problems by the end of this year. Nor does the discussion about the 1993 consolidation scheme — at least to an outside observer — suggest that economic policy makers are coming to grips with the challenges of banking sector reforms.

Although this debate has been going on for well over half a year, not much progress has been achieved. As for the method of consolidation, there seemed to be widespread agreement in the early phases of the discussion on recapitalizing the banks while leaving the bad loans in their portfolios. During the past months, an alternative proposal has gained ground, namely that the consolidation of the banking sector should be preceded and, in fact, largely be substituted for by a comprehensive consolidation of the enterprise sector, i.e., a restructuring of state-owned 'problem enterprises' (debtor consolidation). Possibly, there will be a compromise on implementing bank and debtor consolidation simultaneously. Nevertheless, for the time being, the relative weight of bank consolidation on the one hand and of debtor consolidation on the other remains in the dark.

So far, a loan consolidation scheme for a dozen large state-owned enterprises has been initiated. Furthermore, the Hungarian authorities appear to plan or consider additional debtor consolidation schemes which are at least partly in contradiction with each other: according to the State Secretary responsible for privatization, a scheme for 40 state enterprises with debt above HUF 1 bn each is in preparation. The Ministry for Industry and Trade, however, is planning to extend the already existing loan consolidation scheme to another 80 firms. Eligibility for inclusion in this programme is to depend not only upon the quality of the reorganization plan but also upon other (e.g., employment) considerations. The State Property Agency, conversely, is working on a list of some hundred enterprises for the choice of firms for consolidation based on which firms cover operating costs excluding debt service. In addition, there are plans for debtor consolidation in the agricultural sector and intentions to bail out major export-oriented enterprises.

Furthermore, it is not yet clear what capital adequacy ratios in the banking sector the 1993 consolidation exercise intends to achieve. Some months ago, the authorities had a capital-to-asset ratio of 3 to 4 per cent as their goal. Lately however, ratios of 0 per cent by the end of 1993 (for the Budapest Bank: 4 per cent) and of 4 per cent by the end of 1994 (for the Budapest Bank: 6 per cent) have been mentioned. This shift seems to be a reaction to both the deepening fiscal crisis and a higher-than-expected volume of non-performing loans: according to the Secretary General of the Hungarian Banking Association, the banks' respective reports from September 1993 suggest a need to build risk reserves of more than HUF 200 bn if the rules of the International Accounting System are observed. Due to the depressed profits or even losses of virtually all bad-debt-ridden banks, only a small fraction of these reserves will be built up in the near future.

At least two further issues have not been resolved yet. Namely, who should conclude the recapitalization agreements with the banks? And in what way and to what degree should the supervision of the banks participating in the consolidation scheme be strengthened?

To sum up, it is hard to see how, in such a setting, the basic features of an adequate solution to the problem can be agreed upon until the end of 1993. If a package along the lines of the most recent statements of the authorities is agreed upon, there is an imminent danger that the bad debt problem will reoccur in 1994, as the scheme will most likely not provide for a fully-fledged solution to the flow problem of the non-performing loans. This is the case because, for the majority of the larger enterprises, there are no comprehensive restructuring plans at hand. Due to the enormous time constraint and against the background of state-guided enterprise restructuring to date (which has, apart from a few individual firms, not shown tangible results), most debtor consolidation programmes designed now will most likely not include a thorough restructuring package, but rather amount to mere debt relief. At the same time, banks will not be in a position to take an active part in the restructuring of the enterprises due to the intended recapitalization to a mere 0 per cent capital-to-asset ratio, even if legal obstacles to such undertakings are loosened or removed (as proposed by Várhegyi). As there is virtually no alternative source of finance for most state enterprises, pressure on the banks will mount to continue lending. Banks will likely yield to this pressure, all the more so, as — again — the intended low capital-to-asset ratio, in conjunction with the non-calculable costs resulting from future enterprise losses, will forestall their swift privatization and thus hamper, as it has to date, a fully-fledged adherence to sound business policies.

What is more, it is even questionable whether the 1993 loan consolidation, as it is in the offing right now, will solve the stock problem of the non-performing loans. The main reason is, once more, the insufficient degree of re-capitalization: a capital injection to a level of a 0 per cent capital-to-assets ratio would most likely inhibit the intended write-off of the non-performing loans by the banks.

All this strongly suggests that the final step of the consolidation of the banking sector will fall on that Hungarian government which is to be formed after next spring's elections, whereas the consolidation scheme which is currently being formulated will (like the 1992 exercise) most probably amount to another emergency bank rescue operation.

In order to meet the expectations, i.e., to solve both the stock and the flow aspects of the bad debt problem, the 1994 scheme will have to fulfil three sets of conditions. First, bank consolidation should be effected by a *recapitalization* of the banks which then would take over the leading role in enterprise restructuring. Undoubtedly, there is a strong case for doing so in Hungary because — as is argued in both chapters — banks generally have a thorough knowledge of the enterprises and their actual financial situation. To this end, work-out capabilities of the banks would have to be strengthened (be they located departments within the banks or in subsidiaries), particularly as the number of work-out specialists in Hungary is very small at the moment. Furthermore, in order to successfully cope with the moral hazard problem, the consolidation exercise should be done in one leap; it should be clearly signaled that it is of a once-and-for-all nature.

Second, the authorities should, despite budgetary restraints, aim at a sufficient degree of bank recapitalization. The adverse effects of an insufficient bank consolidation, i.e., of a malfunctioning of financial intermediation, on the economy as a whole and on the budget in particular clearly outweigh the additional expenditure resulting from a comprehensive bank consolidation.

Third, bank consolidation needs to be complemented by strong flanking policies. In Section 5 of her chapter, Várhegyi deals with these policies and proposes a set of measures, a 'second' reform of the Hungarian banking system, as she calls it, to be undertaken in conjunction with bank consolidation. While broadly subscribing to her well-devised proposals, I would be very cautious when assessing the chances for the — undoubtedly indispensable — privatization of the large banks and, in particular, the finding of foreign strategic investors for them, as establishing a new bank or buying into existing mid-size banks is much less costly and risky. Furthermore, as long as the latter possibility exists, temporarily restricting the establishment of new banks (as Várhegyi suggests) would not seem to provide an impetus to the privatization of large banks. If the privatization of banks (and especially of large banks) is stalled for this or other reasons, there may be a case for proceeding in an unorthodox way, namely temporarily laying the management of the state's ownership rights of banks in private hands — perhaps along the lines of (admittedly more general) proposals made by the Agenda Group or the Blue Ribbon Commission.

In addition to the measures Várhegyi proposes, actions in two further policy fields are needed to make bank consolidation a success. On the one hand, a critical mass of state enterprise restructuring has to be achieved. This means that reorganization plans for most of the 'problem enterprises' must be ready and the needed financial support schemes must be in place. On the other hand, a further strengthening of banking supervision, in addition to the efforts so far, and perhaps a concentration of banking supervisory skills is necessary.

Discussion of Chapters 12 and 13

Rosemary Piper

Chapter 12 by Ábel and Székely makes an extremely valuable contribution to the literature on the Hungarian banking system. It gives a needed and pointed description of the dramatic decline in market position of the large, state-dominated banks and the impressive growth of the mid-sized banks. Few other sources analyse the competitive situation of the banking system on a product-by-product basis as thoroughly. The chapter's discussion of the mid-sized banks and their behavioral characteristics is enlightening precisely because, as the authors point out, these banks represent the banks of the future.

The extreme importance of the information provided by the chapter makes this reader eager for more detail. The lack of 1992 data on any subject is disappointing. In certain cases, such as the number of banks or market share comparisons, its inclusion would not have been misleading. Even considering the 1992 figures on their own and describing the ways in which balance sheet changes have distorted any comparison would have been useful. In addition, including other assessment categories could have been very informative such as degree of branching, reliance on fee-service business, products divided by size and ownership profile of the client (private vs. state, domestic or foreign).

Likewise, the very interesting discussion of the behaviour of mid-sized banks suggests that much more could be learned by separating foreign wholly-owned and joint venture banks from the Hungarian-owned banks, were the data available. Given the variety of strategies, capital and profitability profile, and market position of these mid-sized banks, further disaggregation most likely would reveal quite distinct behavioral patterns. For example, it is difficult to conclude that the behaviour of foreign joint venture banks necessarily reveals how a Hungarian bank would act if it were profit-oriented.

The paper could state more emphatically the competition paradox, that despite the increasing market presence of the mid-sized banks offering clients more competitive financing alternatives to the large, state-owned banks, there is a lack of real competition in most segments. Banks continue to act in an oligopolistic manner in setting interest rates. The large banks appear to withdraw from markets rather than compete with the mid-sized

314

banks. The logical conclusion is that these large banks are then left with the very riskiest segments of the market — whatever the mid-sized banks do not want.

The reason the large banks are not really competing for market share with the mid-sized banks is unanswered. It could reflect their poor financial condition or the fact that they are not operating under profit-driven criteria. The lack of real competition begs for an analysis of why the mid-sized banks are not challenging the large banks in more areas.

Two final comments. The authors do not mention strongly enough the fact that the high profits prior to 1991 reflect inadequate provisioning. This income was recorded with no account taken of the assumed risk in the assets. Hence in 1992 the banks reported very low profits because they were making up for years of not provisioning enough for non-performing loans. Second, the authors too readily dismiss the potential power the state has over the banks because of its ownership stake. Arguably, the most promising avenue for the state to improve the position of those large banks that remain in state hands is through its direct influence; by making the board of directors, supervisory board and management of the banks more accountable for performance.

The authors deserve to be commended for a very provocative, informative and carefully-documented paper. The hope is that these comments will steer more research in the direction of those questions that remain unanswered.

Éva Várhegyi's chapter will be particularly useful to the reader unfamiliar with developments in policy initiatives in Hungary's financial sector. Várhegyi accurately portrays the dominance of state ownership and the resulting weaknesses in the banking system. She forcefully argues for what is becoming a growing consensus that the Hungarian government must take a more active role in improving the financial position of the banks. Indeed, the broad-scale 1993 bank recapitalization effort is a reflection of this consensus.

Várhegyi's conclusion that to date competition has not improved the quantity or quality of banking services or reduced prices appears to directly contradict the prior chapter on the expanding market position of mid-sized banks. Perhaps the reconciliation can be found in the fact that, as mentioned above, the large state-dominated banks are not really competing and therefore the overall market cannot be described as fully competitive.

Unfortunately, as is inevitable with papers on these topics, they rapidly become out of date. The paper would benefit from a full description of new developments in Hungary's banking system. To name a few: tax advantages for joint venture banks will be phased out in 1995; new categories have been developed for qualifying problem loans; and equity limitations on shares held by banks acquired through debt-equity swaps have been waived for 18 months.

I wholeheartedly agree with many of the central recommendations made by the author. In particular, the need for speedy privatization and for some assessment of investor interest in the banks; the importance of linking recapitalization to privatization; and the central role to be played by foreign strategic partners. However, the chapter does not address the controversial issue that foreigners are likely to require a controlling stake in these banks. Moreover, the chapter does not answer the question of what happens to those banks that foreign investors have no interest in purchasing. Finally, the author ambitiously makes three recommendations on raising equity requirements, eliminating tax advantages and introducing universal banking. All three topics would benefit from a more thorough analysis of the costs and benefits and a more detailed description of what these reforms would entail. (For example: how high should equity stakes be raised? What priority should be given to these recommendations? Do they promise more than a marginal improvement in the situation of financial intermediation in Hungary?)

In conclusion, this chapter serves an important role in providing a background assessment of the Hungarian banking system. Many of the recommendations made here have been seriously considered by the Hungarian authorities and some indeed have been adopted. However, as the chapter argues, the core to improving the banking system lies in privatizing the banks with the utmost speed. This important message should not go unheard.

14 Reform of the Financial System in Bulgaria

Rumen Dobrinsky

1 Introduction

Monetary and financial policy used to be a neglected issue in the practice of central planning and, accordingly, almost nothing was done to establish a modern institutional infrastructure for their implementation. Most Central and Eastern European (CEE) countries inherited from the communist period a rudimentary banking sector which was merely an appendix to the system of central planning, whose single function was to channel central-planning decisions into financial variables (Ábel and Bonin, 1992; Thorne, 1992b). Most of the countries in the region (Hungary being the exception) started developing such a system only during the economic transformation process after 1989 (Thorne, 1992b).

Many of the inherited structural economic problems in the CEEs are closely associated with the misallocation of resources (especially investment) which was partly due to the lack an efficient banking sector. On the other hand, financial institutions in the region in general have neither the experience nor the expertise to perform the intermediation functions typical of a market economy (Miller, 1993).

Thus the establishment of a modern and efficient financial system is a key element of the economic transformation in CEE countries. This problem is the focus both of the current agenda of legislative and institutional reforms in these countries and of research on the transformation process (Ábel and Bonin, 1992; Ábel and Székely, 1992; Corbett and Mayer, 1991; Estrin et al., 1992; Rybczynski, 1991; Székely, 1993).

The analysis of financial reforms in the CEEs so far reveals both similarities and differences due to different initial conditions and past practices (Thorne, 1992b). Nonetheless, the lessons which can be drawn from each country's experience can undoubtedly be shared by all of them.

The economic transition in Bulgaria up till now is proceeding at a slower rate than that in the front-running countries of Central Europe (Dobrinsky et al., 1992; Wyzan, 1992). In spite of this the process of financial reform in Bulgaria has also its unique features (Miller, 1992, 1993; Mladenov, 1992; Ravicz, 1992; Thorne, 1992a). This chapter is an attempt to analyse some features of the reform process in the Bulgarian financial system.

317

2   The Bulgarian financial system before 1990

In the pre-war period Bulgaria used to have a quite advanced banking system by the standards of the time. The Bulgarian National Bank (BNB), the central bank of the country, was established in 1883, immediately after the country regained its independence as a sovereign state (BNB, 1993). Almost since the beginning of its operations BNB has acted as a typical central bank responsible for currency emission and state budget servicing. At the same time, it used to perform some limited commercial activities but gradually these diminished and starting from 1926 its functions were restricted to purely central banking operations (BNB, 1993).

The commercial banking system consisted of a fairly large number of state-owned, cooperative and private banks of relatively small size. Before the Great Depression of 1929 the number of banks hit a record of 129 then in the 1930s it decreased to 34 (BNB, 1991). Immediately before World War II Bulgaria was considered to have the most sophisticated and well-functioning banking system in the Balkan region.

The postwar period was marked by a rapid degradation of the financial system. The Law on Banks of 1947 made the way for establishing a Soviet type of banking system in accordance with the norms of a centrally-planned economy (BNB, 1993). This law introduced the so-called 'state monopoly over banking activities'. Practically all private banks were nationalized and incorporated into the structure of BNB which took over the current accounts of enterprises and the short-term financial facilities dealing with commercial activity. A new institution — the Bulgarian Investment Bank — was established to accommodate long-term credit, whereas all retail banking was concentrated in the Post Credit Bank. In 1951 the latter was dissolved and its business was taken over by the newly-established State Saving Bank (SSB). The Bulgarian Investment Bank also existed only until 1967 when its operations were transferred to BNB and SSB. The Bulgarian Foreign Trade Bank (BFTB) was established in 1964 and incorporated all foreign exchange operations and transactions abroad. Thus a banking system typical of a centrally-planned economy was formed consisting of three banking institutions: BNB which combined the functions of as a quasi central and a commercial bank, BFTB and SSB.

The banking system existed in this shape until the beginning of the 1980s when some modest attempts to reform it were initiated. First of all a new banking institution, MineralBank was established in 1981 which was supposed to allocate credit resources to new small and medium size enterprises (including investment credit). The process of decentralization of the banking system was continued in 1987 when seven new 'sectoral' banks were formed with the purpose of reallocating the long-term financing of enterprises (Economic Bank, Biochim Bank, BalkanBank, Construction

Bank, Elektronika Bank, Agrocooperative Bank and Transport Bank). These banks were strictly specialized in specific industrial branches ('sectoral' banks); besides long-term financing they performed some other limited commercial activities. MineralBank became one of these 'sectoral' banks.

A further step was taken in 1989 after the adoption of Decree No. 56 on Economic Activity (Decree, 1989)[1] which set forth some modern regulations on economic associations (among other things, allowing for the first time the establishment of private businesses). Under this decree in 1989 the government adopted Ordinance No. 19 (Rules, 1989) with the so-called Rules for Banks which for the first time made a clear though incomplete distinction between the functions of BNB as a central bank and the commercial banks in the country. Under these rules BNB was assigned such typical central bank functions as 'regulation of the money circulation' and 'regulation of the activities of commercial banks'. At the same time it was defined as 'a body with a functional competence under the direct guidance of the Council of Ministers' (its task was to coordinate the so-called financial plan). Some limited commercial activities related to public services still remained in BNB.

The ordinance contained a prescription that commercial banks were to be established as joint stock companies (under Decree 56), performing as universal wholesale banks which were to 'self-finance their activities'. Their activities were to be closely scrutinized by BNB.

On the basis of Decree 56 and Ordinance 19, a substantial restructuring of the Bulgarian banking system was carried out in 1989. Most of the commercial activities of BNB were withdrawn from the central bank and were transferred to the newly-established, mainly regional, commercial banks, which were formed on the basis of the regional branch offices of the BNB. All in all, 59 new commercial banks were established in 1989 following this procedure, most of them rather small in size and scope of activity.

By 1990 BNB started to perform as a central bank, although not independent of the executive power in the country. The commercial banking system consisted of the old BFTB, SSB, the eight 'sectoral' banks and the 59 new 'regional' commercial banks.

In the beginning, the equity of commercial banks was held by BNB. After the adoption of Decree 56 in 1989 part of the stock of the commercial banks was purchased by state-owned enterprises and, later, by private companies and individuals. At the same time (before the adoption of the new Law on Banks and Credit Activity in 1992 which regulated this aspect in more restrictive terms) some banks acquired stakes in SOEs, creating a somewhat confused state-owned cross-shareholding on the eve of the transition period.

Summarizing, we can conclude that the Bulgarian banking system of the socialist period was typical of a centrally-planned economy. The changes which were introduced in the banking system in the 1980s were rather similar to the changes in the Polish banking system of that period, following with some lag the Hungarian model (Corbett and Mayer, 1991; Estrin *et al.*, 1992; Rudka, 1992; Thorne, 1992b). Similarly to Poland, the break-up of the monobank system was introduced shortly before the revolutionary political changes in the country, unlike in Czechoslovakia and Romania where the sequence of events was in reverse. Also similarly to Poland, the establishment of a two-tier system was accompanied by the formation of a large number of small-sized banking institutions, unlike the transformation of the banking systems in Hungary, Czechoslovakia and Romania where a relatively small number of new institutions emerged directly from the old system (Balassa, 1992; Jindra, 1992; Ghizari, 1992).

3   The reform process in the transition period

The process of financial reform was accelerated after 1990. In 1991 the Parliament passed some important economic legislation such as the Law on the Bulgarian National Bank (LBNB), the Commercial Law (regulating the establishment of economic entities), and the Law on Foreign Investment. In 1992 parliament continued this process by voting the Law on Banks and Credit Activity (LBCA), the Law on Privatization as well as a number of other bills making way for economic transformation. As regards the reform of the financial system, the most important systemic changes were introduced through the two banking laws — LBNB and LBCA.

3.1   The Law on the Bulgarian National Bank

The LBNB (voted on 6 June 1991) institutionalized the first part of the major banking reform in Bulgaria by clearly establishing a two-tier banking system based on an independent central bank — BNB, with clear and autonomous powers. Most of the provisions in this law were a novelty in the banking regulation and practice in Bulgaria.

According to this law the main functions of the central bank are defined as: maintenance of the internal and external stability of the national currency (the BGL); exclusive right of issuing banknotes in the country; and regulation and supervision of other banks' activities, aimed at ensuring the stability of the banking system (LBNB, 1991).

In implementing its functions, BNB is independent of the government and its bodies. The central bank reports to the parliament twice a year on its activities. In these reports BNB is supposed to review and assess monetary policy in the previous six-month period, give a statement on monetary policy in the following six-month period and define the principles of the intended medium-term monetary policy.

BNB is responsible for the foreign exchange reserves of Bulgaria and compiles the balance-of-payments. Another important function of the central bank is the 'fixing' of the central exchange rate of the national currency.[2] It is also the official depositor of the state and organizes the cash management of the state budget operations through the commercial banks.

The supervision of commercial banks was also mandated to the central bank (rather than creating a separate institution). BNB is empowered to set rules regulating different banking operations (including issuing of licences for banking activities) as well as 'to take all necessary actions for ensuring the stability of the banking system'. In implementing these functions the central bank has wide-ranging authority.

3.2 The Law on Banks and Credit Activity

The LBCA was voted by parliament on 18 March 1992, almost a year after the LBNB (LBCA, 1992). Many of the legislative provisions of the LBCA were borrowed from similar legislation in developed European countries such as Germany, Austria, Switzerland, France, etc.; besides it was attempted to make the law compatible (as far as it was possible at this stage) with the recommendations of the Basle Committee on Banking Supervision and those of the EC (Stratev, 1992, 1993).

According to the provisions of the law, commercial banks should be either joint-stock companies or cooperatives. Permits (licences) for conducting banking operations are granted by the central bank (BNB) under specified conditions. The operations of the bank should follow strictly the scope of the permit granted by the central bank.

The LBCA favours small shareholding in commercial banks: acquiring more than five per cent of the total voting shares in a bank by a single person (individual or legal person) can only be done with the central bank's permission. The law does not contain inhibitive restrictions on foreign participation in local banks; banks can be 100 per cent foreign owned, but they must follow the general prescriptions on banking activity (including the structure of the bank's equity).

The law stipulates that banks are managed and represented jointly by at least two persons, who should have the necessary qualifications and expertise. The BNB is authorized to remove from office top executive bank managers who do not meet the explicit requirements of the law.

For the first time in recent Bulgarian history the LBCA addressed the issues of capital adequacy, liquidity as well as some other requirements of banking activity. However, these issues were treated in the law in very broad terms which made further regulation necessary (see Section 3.3).

According to the prescriptions of the LBCA, banks are required to form two types of reserves:

—   a general 'reserve' fund, by allocating at least one-fifth of their after-tax profit until this fund reaches 1.25 per cent of their total assets;
—   provisions against substandard or non-performing loans, which the banks are entitled to deduct from their before-tax profit; however, the law does not contain practical details.

The LBCA also treats the problem of 'large' bank loans (defined as exceeding 15 per cent of the shareholders' equity). A single large loan cannot exceed 25 per cent of the bank's equity and the total amount of such loans cannot exceed eight times the bank's equity.

The law does not make a specific distinction between commercial, savings or investment banks, i.e. it creates the conditions for banks to develop as universal banks. Besides, it sets quite generous limits to bank investments: the total amount of a bank's investments in real estate, equipment and stakes in non-financial companies can be as large as the total bank's equity (but a single investment should not exceed 10 per cent of the non-financial enterprise equity). These limits can be temporarily exceeded if stakes are acquired as a result of foreclosures; in this case the bank has a three-year period to transfer the excess investments.

The LBCA extended the supervision regulations assigning additional authorities to the central bank. It empowers BNB to perform on-site inspections of commercial banks' operations as well as to apply court procedures and administrative measures in cases of inflicted damages.

In general the LBCA laid the foundations for the development of a modern commercial banking system in Bulgaria. However, in many aspects this law was a compromise between the urgent necessity for new regulation and the lack of banking experience in a market environment. Many aspects of banking regulation were left open in the LBCA and/or were delegated to be regulated by the central bank. In this sense the LBCA is not a codification law (Stratev, 1992). The rationale behind such a solution was that this would provide greater flexibility in a fast-changing economic environment.

The general philosophy of the Bulgarian LBCA is closer to the German model of the banking system based on universal banking institutions and providing the possibility for banks to participate in the control and management of the corporate sector (Thorne, 1992b). It could be mentioned that most of the CEEs followed a similar philosophy, Hungary being the main exception with a clear distinction between commercial, investment and saving banks (Ábel and Székely, 1992).

3.3 Further development of banking regulations

The LBNB and LBCA were not elaborated to the extent of providing the full scope of comprehensive regulatory norms necessary for the efficient performance of the banking system. The most serious gaps were to be found in the field of prudential banking regulations.[3] The closing of this gap was set by the World Bank as one of the preconditions for the successful implementation of the SAL agreement of 1991.[4]

However, it was not until the middle of 1993 that this task was finalized. It took the form of six ordinances adopted by the Managing Board[5] of BNB:

— No. 2 on the Permits (Licences) Granted by the BNB (11 February);
— No. 7 on Large and Internal Loans of Banks (28 January);
— No. 8 on the Capital Adequacy of the Banks (18 March);
— No. 9 on Loan Classification and the Formation of Mandatory Special Reserves (Statutory Provisions) by the Banks (31 May);
— No. 10 on Internal Control in the Banks (3 June);
— No. 11 on Liquidity of the Banks (18 June).

We shall comment briefly on three of these ordinances — Nos. 8, 9 and 11 which are probably the most important ones in terms of their novelty for the banking practice of the country.

The Ordinance on the Capital Adequacy of the Banks contains several important norms:

— A minimum capital base requirement: BGL 200 mn (roughly USD 8 mn at that time) to perform domestic banking operations and BGL 500 mn (about USD 20 mn) to perform external banking operations.[6]
— Rules for defining the value of the capital base. Primary capital consists of shareholders' equity and general capital reserves. The capital base is defined as the sum of primary capital, current year after-tax profit and other additional reserves.
— Rules for classifying the bank's assets according to their riskiness. Four types of assets are introduced here: risk-free assets; low-risk assets; average risk assets; and high-risk assets. The risky component of the bank's assets is calculated as a weighted average of the three latter categories.

— Rules regarding the capital adequacy ratios:
core capital adequacy ratio (the core capital as a percentage of the risky component of the bank's assets), which should not be lower than 4 per cent;
general capital adequacy ratio (the capital base as a percentage of the risky component of the bank's assets), which should not be lower than 8 per cent.
— Supervision of the capital adequacy of commercial banks by BNB.

A grace period of two years is granted to commercial banks to conform fully with the requirements of the ordinance.

The Ordinance on Loan Classification and the Formation of Mandatory Special Reserves (Statutory Provisions) sets rules for classifying the credit portfolio of the commercial banks and for provisioning against substandard and non-performing loans. Commercial banks are required to classify their credit portfolio into four main groups:

— regular (standard) loans;
— dubious (substandard) loans - type A: overdues up to 30 days (or other specified conditions);
— dubious (substandard) loans - type B: overdues up to 90 days (or other specified conditions);
— uncollectible (non-performing) loans: overdues over 90 days (or cases of bankruptcy or liquidation of the credit holder).

Banks allocate provisions (from their before-tax profit or from their general reserves) against sub-standard and non-performing loans as follows:

— substandard loans type A: 20 per cent of the principal;
— substandard loans type B: 50 per cent of the principal;
— non-performing loans: 100 per cent of the principal.

Commercial banks are required to report the state of their credit portfolio and their provisioning policy to the BNB.

The Ordinance on Liquidity of the Banks sets rules and guidelines for the control and management of the liquidity position of the commercial banks.

Commercial banks are to classify their liquid assets and liabilities (with maturity up to one year) into six categories depending on the maturity of the asset (liability). On the basis of this classification banks calculate a number of liquidity and coverage ratios which have to fit the ranges fixed by the central bank.

Commercial banks are required to adopt internal rules for the management of their liquidity and to report their liquidity position to the central bank. The Supervision Division of BNB is authorized to monitor the liquidity position of the commercial banks and in case of necessity to act in accordance with the provisions of the LBCA.

A grace period of six months is provided for commercial banks to meet the requirements of this ordinance.

With the adoption of the six new BNB ordinances the regulatory framework for the reform of the Bulgarian banking system is nearly complete; this framework is to a large degree consistent with the recommendations of the Basle Committee for Banking Supervision and those of the Commission of the EC.

Among other important innovations in the Bulgarian banking system it is worth mentioning the following. Since 1991, a new Banking Integrated System for Electronic Transfer (BISERA) is gradually being introduced which is supposed to cover all interbank payments replacing the previous paper-based system. In 1992 BNB adopted unified banking standards (standardized banking technologies), most of which were based on BISERA. These standards have been applied since October 1992 and are a major innovation in Bulgarian banking practice.

At the same time a new system of settlement was introduced at BNB (also based on BISERA) which considerably raised the efficiency of the transaction clearing system (one of the bottlenecks in the Bulgarian banking system in the past). In principle the new settlement system should allow all clearing transactions to take place within a maximum of three days (Miller, 1993) whereas in the past this process could take weeks.

Another innovation which is still being developed is a banking system based on bank cards, or the so-called BORICA: Banking Organization for Payments Initiated by Cards (Matrozov, 1993). The first project planned under BORICA is the introduction of national debit cards as well as the installation of automated teller machines.

On the other hand, among the important fundamentals of a modern banking system which are still missing in Bulgaria one should point out the lack of a deposit insurance system. Currently only deposits at the State Saving Bank are insured 100 per cent (by virtue of the old Law on SSB), whereas no deposits at commercial banks are covered by any type of insurance. Although the LBCA prescribes the development of such a system its practical implementation has been delayed.

4 Monetary policy and development of financial markets

A new type of monetary policy was needed in the transition process and this was also an area where Bulgaria had no relevant experience. A detailed analysis of monetary policy in the transition period is beyond the scope of this chapter; the reader can refer on this subject to the studies of Genov (1993), Gueorguiev and Gospodinov (1992) as well as to the annual reports of BNB (BNB, 1991, 1992, 1993). Here we shall only try to outline those aspects of monetary policy which had a more direct impact on the functioning of the financial system and, hence, on the process of its transformation.

4.1 Monetary policy tools

The primary objective of the central bank, as stipulated in the LBNB, is to maintain a stable (both internally and externally) domestic currency. To do this BNB is entitled to regulate the money supply by formulating and implementing the national monetary and credit policy. It is a completely new function which the central bank started to implement since 1991, after the definite establishment of the two-tier system. As this was practically building a new system from scratch the monetary policy instruments of BNB are still limited in scope (Filipov, 1992).

At this stage the instruments of direct monetary control still prevail over market-based instruments (Coats, 1992). Open-market operations (one of the main monetary policy tools in developed market economies) are just being introduced by BNB and still play a very minor role in the monetary policy system. In any case, monetary policy in this period of turbulent change exerts a fundamental impact on the financial system.

Credit ceilings

Currently the most important monetary policy instrument in Bulgaria is credit ceilings. Credit ceilings, an instrument of direct control over money supply, have been applied by BNB since 1991 to control the credit expansion of commercial banks. They were introduced as part of the stabilization programme of 1991 and provided an easy-to-handle means of controlling the growth of money supply. The ceilings set an upper limit to the commercial loans denominated in national currency, which are allocated by the bank during a certain time span. Credit ceilings do not apply to loans denominated in convertible currencies.

Credit ceilings are determined individually for each commercial bank on a quarterly basis (since April 1992, on a monthly basis), using a complex formula which takes into account the track record of the bank and the money supply targets of the central bank (BNB, 1993). When a bank exceeds its credit ceiling a penalty is imposed on it in the form of higher reserve requirements.

The aggregate credit ceilings which were set by the central bank on the total commercial credit expansion in the economy amounted to a growth rate of 52 per cent in 1991 and 29 per cent in 1992 (BNB, 1992, 1993). As compared to the inflation rate in this period such targets speak of a rather restrictive monetary policy, and in 1991 especially they made it possible to bring money supply under control in the face of three-digit inflation.[7] So credit ceilings had an important, positive impact at the start of the transformation process; however, later on their efficiency started to erode.

Reserve requirements

BNB used minimum reserves requirements as a means to control the money supply since its establishment as a central bank in 1990. At first the level of the reserve requirements was fixed at 5 per cent but by the end of 1990 it was increased to 7 per cent and has not been changed since that time (BNB, 1992, 1993).

Reserves are kept in the form of non-interest-bearing deposits of commercial banks with BNB. Their regulation is not very sophisticated: reserves are monitored once a month on the basis of the monthly balance sheets which commercial banks have to submit to the central bank (Filipov, 1992).

The introduction of the payment clearing system in October 1992 made it possible to modernize the handling of reserves by unifying the banks' reserve account with the current account used for settlement. Moreover, banks have access to an overdraft facility on their current account amounting to the value of their reserve requirements.

Refinancing

Recent changes in the central bank's refinancing policy played an important role in the evolution of the whole financial system. Until 1991 BNB refinanced the commercial banks by direct allocation of uncollateralized credits. The main source of such refinancing were the 'excess' deposits of SSB which the latter was mandated to hold with BNB.

The first new type of refinancing introduced by BNB in 1991 were the so-called interbank deposit auctions. Commercial banks can offer some of their deposits to be auctioned by the central bank in the form of monthly deposits. Banks which need additional resources make their bids and those which offer the highest interest get the deposits. Interbank deposit auctions have been conducted twice a month since September 1991. The main supplier of deposits to these auctions is SSB which still holds a substantial share of the retail market; however, lately other commercial banks also entered this market as suppliers of monthly deposits for auctioning.

Another innovation in the national banking practice, introduced in 1991, were the Lombard loans advanced by the central bank to commercial banks against collateral. Commercial banks were very responsive to this innovation especially due to the fact that government securities were accepted as collateral for the Lombard facility.[8]

In the same year the central bank also started to discount bills of exchange, but its share in total refinancing is still low. At the same time the refinancing balance sheet of BNB still contains some uncollateralized refinancing, mainly balances of old long-term refinancing.

Interest rate policy

BNB has another very strong monetary policy tool — the central interest rate. Until November 1991 the central interest rate was applied to all refinancing transactions of the central bank. Since that time it applies only to the Lombard facility whereas all other types of refinancing require a premium over this rate.

Currently the central interest rate is a much more powerful tool in Bulgaria than the central bank discount rate usually is, because almost all prices in the banking sector are directly linked to the central interest rate. Accordingly, a change in the central interest rate has a very profound impact both on the banking system and on the whole economy.

Together with the credit ceilings the central interest rate is one of the most important monetary policy tools of BNB. In 1991/1992 the central bank implemented a flexible interest rate policy in an attempt to match its sometimes conflicting monetary policy goals regarding money supply, inflation and exchange rate.

The comparison of interest rates dynamics with inflation in this period reveals a somewhat controversial picture. In 1991 real interest rates were highly negative due to the large price adjustment jump at the beginning of the stabilization programme. If inflation is measured by CPI or by the GDP deflator real interest rates continued to be negative in 1992 also; however, in terms of the producers' price index the average real lending rate of commercial banks in 1992 was highly positive. So it was mainly producers who were hit by restrictive monetary policy in this period, which added to the overall depressed economic performance.

As to individuals, interest rates continued to be negative in 1992 but this did not discourage them to save, in spite of the obvious losses they incurred; on the contrary, personal savings in 1992 more than doubled. One explanation of this phenomenon is the lack of other investment alternatives.

Exchange rate policy

Since 1991 Bulgaria introduced a floating exchange rate over which the central bank has no direct control (see note 2). After 'overshooting' in 1991 (a result of the accumulated monetary overhang) the nominal exchange rate was fairly stable in 1992 (meaning appreciation in real terms due to the high inflation). This made deposits in domestic currency attractive and was another factor for the boosting of personal savings in 1992.

4.2 The impact of monetary policy on the banking system

The analysis of current monetary policy and the figures on refinancing reveal a substantial change in the behaviour of the banking industry in recent years. Banks now have alternatives for refinancing and can conduct their own policy; they also have a number of new opportunities thanks to the development of financial markets. These changes are starting to create the institutional environment and infrastructure which, though far from being complete, force commercial banks to behave in a more market-oriented manner.

At the same time, some of the current monetary policy tools are rather archaic and contradictory in their application. Among these the most debated are credit ceilings, regarding both their efficiency as a means to control the growth of money supply and their controversial impact on the financial system.

Coats (1992) argues that by administratively determining the growth in individual banks, their incentive to work harder to deliver better services at lower costs is greatly diminished. There is sufficient evidence that such symptoms are present in the Bulgarian banking system (see Section 5).

On the other hand, credit ceilings are an efficient means to control money supply only if commercial loans (plus cash in the vault and deposits with the central bank) were the only possible bank assets and the banks had no alternatives to diversify their portfolios (Miller, 1993). However, when such alternatives are available, as is the case of Bulgaria (e.g., government securities or investments), the efficiency of credit ceilings as a means to control money supply starts to erode due to the possibilities for the banks to reallocate their credit portfolio.

Moreover, under the current penalty system, banks may decide to deliberately violate the credit ceilings in cases where they have a chance to allocate resources in projects which (due to high enough efficiency) may enable them to offset the negative impact of the penalty. Actually, evidence from the performance of the Bulgarian banking system shows that in the aggregate credit ceilings have been persistently violated: on a quarterly basis the ratios between the allocated total commercial credit in BGL and the aggregate credit ceilings for the four quarters of 1992 have been 103.2, 107.2, 111.6, and 114.3 per cent, respectively (Genov, 1993).[9]

Another negative impact of credit ceilings is the possible reinforcing of the crowding-out effect. If a bank manages its credit portfolio by minimizing its risk exposure, and having alternatives to allocate limited resources, it is likely to increase the relative share of the less risky government securities and decrease that of commercial credits, thus directly creating a crowding-out effect. The actual data confirm that crowding-out increased in recent years: the government's share in total borrowing denominated in BGL increased from 19.1 per cent in 1991 to 27.8 per cent in 1992 (BNB, 1993). Of course the additional incentives for the banks to buy government securities (the access to Lombard loans collateralized by securities) also contributed to such a development.

Though the different negative impacts of credit ceilings mentioned above would presume mutually exclusive types of individual banks' policies, there is evidence that all of them were present, in varying degrees, in the Bulgarian banking system. This would suggest gradually reducing the use of credit ceilings as a tool of direct monetary control and substituting them with other, more modern and efficient tools of indirect control. Moreover, the new set of prudential banking regulations creates the basic conditions for such a change.

The interest rate policy also had a profound impact on the banking system. First of all, the high interest rates (as already mentioned, high also in real terms for some sectors of economic activity) create the conditions for the Stiglitz effect (driving the commercial banks to finance the more profitable but riskier business projects), increasing the general risk exposure of the banking system. This increases the chances for borrowers to default adding to the problem of 'bad' loans (discussed in Section 5). The growing volume of bad loans, in its turn, forces the banking system to operate with larger spreads in order to be able to provision. These two aspects in fact create a positive feedback loop which endangers the stability of the whole financial system.

The exchange rate policy adds another dimension of risk to the performance of the banking system. Due to the floating exchange rate and the lack of a medium-term exchange rate policy the foreign exchange risk in Bulgaria is currently extremely high. The commercial banks are completely unprotected against this type of risk and have to be ready to accommodate it in full.

Of course this brief analysis reveals only some aspects of the impact of current monetary (and economic) policy on the banking system. However, it is indicative of some of the important (and high) risks of current banking in Bulgaria.

4.3 Development of financial markets

Financial markets in Bulgaria started to emerge only after 1991. They are still underdeveloped and their coverage is very small. On the other hand, they are one of the most dynamic parts of the Bulgarian financial system.

Interbank money market

The interbank money market which has operated since the beginning of 1991 (BNB, 1993) consists of direct interbank deposit trading (82 per cent of the volume of deals in 1992) and interbank loans (18 per cent of the volume in 1992). There is also an interbank market for credit ceilings but its performance is not well-documented (Miller, 1993).

The interbank money market is already the biggest source of liquidity for commercial banks. Most of the trading on this market is with short-term resources: 87.3 per cent of the deals in 1992 had maturity up to one month of which 12.2 per cent had up to one week (BNB, 1993).

The interbank money market turned out to be rather attractive for commercial banks due to the fact that it offered a relatively cheap source of financing (the average interest rate on the interbank money market in 1992 was four percentage points lower than the average interest rate at the interbank deposit auctions in the same year, see BNB, 1993).

Government securities

The government securities market exists in a very rudimentary form. Firstly, the choice of such securities is rather limited (see note 8) and, secondly, up till now there exists only a primary market with limited participants.

This market functions in the following way. The securities (mostly short-term Treasury bills) are issued by the Ministry of Finance and are auctioned by the central bank. The only buyers of these securities are the commercial banks; later on, they either keep some of the securities in their portfolio or resubmit them to BNB as a collateral for Lombard loans.

No well-defined secondary market for government securities exists yet. Only recently the central bank started some limited open-market operations, by buying back some securities from the commercial banks (Filipov, 1992). However, one can expect that a normal secondary market will develop only after the appearance of longer-term government securities.

Foreign exchange market

The foreign exchange market is perhaps the most active financial market in Bulgaria. It consists of a wholesale (interbank) market and a retail market (exchange bureaus). Within the wholesale market the most important segment consists of 16 so-called market-maker banks whose transactions are monitored by the central bank and serve as the basis for 'fixing' the central exchange rate. The retail market grew very rapidly since 1991: up till now[10] the central bank has granted 964 licences for operating exchange bureaus. Accordingly, it is a very competitive market.

Stock market

The stock market scarcely exists yet. Two 'stock exchanges' pretend to operate in Sofia (and several others in other cities) but in fact they are simple financial houses performing very limited over-the-counter trading (there is no law on stock exchanges yet).

To summarize, one can say that Bulgaria has made some progress in the development of money markets whereas there is still a long way to go for the development of normal capital markets. This situation poses serious limits and restrictions on the performance of the banking system which is forced to restrain itself in a limited market.

5   Evolution and performance of the commercial banking sector

Currently the Bulgarian banking sector is undergoing substantial restructuring. Many new private banks are entering the market while the old state-owned ones are in a process of consolidation. These changes are taking place in a very depressed economy which also exerts an important impact on the behaviour and performance of the banking sector.

5.1   The evolution of the Bulgarian banking system after 1990

As already mentioned, at the start of the transformation process the Bulgarian commercial banking sector consisted of a relatively large number of mainly small-sized banks which inherited the commercial activity of BNB from the monobank period (see Table 14.1).

In 1991 a very important decision was taken (the World Bank and the IMF actively advocated it) to consolidate the state-owned commercial banks. The main goals of process of consolidation were (Mombru, 1992):

— To restructure the state-owned banks by concentrating their activity into a smaller number[11] of relatively larger commercial banks. It was considered that this would also increase the overall efficiency of the banking sector.
— To facilitate the process of privatization of the state-owned banks.

By that time the stock of the state-owned banks was already quite dispersed, though most of it still remained on the balance sheets of BNB and BFTB. Thus, a specific solution was needed to perform the process of consolidation and it was found in the establishment of the Bank Consolidation Company (BCC).

BCC was registered as a joint-stock company in February 1992 with the mission to perform the process of consolidation and privatization of the banking sector. The formal founders (and owners) of BCC are BNB and BFTB which transferred to BCC all the stakes in state-owned banks which they previously held. Further, according to a government resolution all state-owned enterprises were obliged to exchange their commercial bank common stock for BCC's common stock.

The implementation of this resolution continued throughout 1992 and by the end of the year BCC formally held most of the common stock in state-owned commercial banks and thus became their formal proprietor. In this way it could enforce its decisions regarding the restructuring of the banking system, including mergers and acquisitions. At the same time banks were advised to negotiate among themselves possible consolidation strategies in order to reach mutually acceptable solutions for the consolidation process.

In the second half of 1992 the first consolidation project was finalized and the first consolidated bank 'United Bulgarian Bank' was licensed by BNB and registered in court. It was formed by merging 22 banks focused around two Sofia-based banks: the Doverie and Construction Banks (see Table 14.2). This first project was to a great extent inspired by bank managers themselves.

In the first half of 1993 decisions were taken on four other projects and they are in being implemented: BalkanBank, HebrosBank, ExpressBank and SofiaBank (Table 14.2). Unlike the first one, these projects were orchestrated by BCC.

A sixth project (Biochim Bank) is still being discussed and there are no clear intentions yet for several banks. Probably two large banks — MineralBank and Economic Bank (they are also the most burdened with bad loans) will remain in their current form; a possible merger of BFTB with PostBank (the latter having a well-developed branching network) is being discussed as well as the possible merger of SirBank (very specialized in financial services) with another financial institution. There is no final decision either on the troubled Yambol bank.

In this way, within less than two years the number of state-owned banks decreased to about ten medium-sized banks (see Tables 14.1 and 14.2).

As pointed out, it was thought that the consolidation process would be closely connected with the privatization of state-owned banks. The intention was (and still is) to perform large-scale privatization of the consolidated banks by selling stakes to strategic, presumably foreign, investors. This should be done by BCC and after it has sold all the shares it should be dissolved (the enterprises holding BCC shares would be compensated by interest-bearing government securities).

However, up till now no large-scale privatization deal has been completed. The European Bank for Reconstruction and Development has just started investigating the possibility of acquiring an interest in the new United Bulgarian Bank. The current financial situation of the state-owned banks means they are not very attractive to foreign investors and the overall success of the planned privatization strategy is questionable.

At the same time, in a period of unclear legislative norms a wave of spontaneous bank privatization took place in 1990/1991. Although formal selling of common stock to private companies and individuals was banned there was no ban on issuing new stock. Many banks in this period increased their capital in this manner and sold new stock mainly to private persons. After the voting of the Law on privatization in 1992 such deals were restricted but the results of the preceding years are impressive.

Four regional banks — First East International Bank (former Kremikovtzi), CrystalBank (former Madan), BusinessBank (former Petrich) and Dobrich, where the new emissions constituted a control interest — went into private hands through such spontaneous privatization. In many other state-owned banks private ownership of common stock became substantial. All in all, by the end of 1992 19.4 per cent of the common stock of state-owned commercial banks (excluding the four banks mentioned above) was in private hands (see Table 14.1).

Even more impressive is the process of emerging of new private commercial banks. The first private bank in the country was established at the end of 1990 (symbolically named First Private Bank); immediately after it followed the Bank for Agricultural Credit (with the participation of an Austrian bank, Raiffeisen Zentralbank).

In 1991 six new private banks were registered: Central Cooperative Bank, Credit Bank, AgrobusinessBank, TouristsportBank, International Trade and Development Bank and International Investment and Development Bank (the last two with foreign participation). Five more new private banks have been licensed since that time and several more are being surveyed for licensing by BNB (BNB, 1992, 1993).[12]

This boom led to a significant expansion of the private commercial banking sector in Bulgaria: currently private banks account for about a quarter of the commercial bank common stock and for about 10 per cent of commercial bank assets in the country (see also Table 14.4).

5.2 Performance of the banking sector

The current performance of the Bulgarian commercial banking sector is influenced by several major factors among which we could mention the legacies of the past (especially the bad loans); the deep general economic crisis in the country; the current economic policy; and the implications of transformation process. Here we shall only touch on some aspects of the Bulgarian banking industry's current performance on the basis of the available statistical data.

Like most of the CEEs the Bulgarian financial system inherited from the socialist period a formidable problem in the form of the bad loans of state-owned enterprises (Ábel and Bonin, 1993; Thorne, 1992b). Most of the inherited bad loans in Bulgaria resulted from investment decisions when decision makers chose loan instead of equity financing (see Székely, 1993 for a discussion on this issue).

However, in spite of the acuteness of the problem no radical solution was sought till now. Instead, a partial 'cleaning' of bad loans was attempted in 1991 by replacing some BGL 5 bn of enterprise debt with government bonds (in line with the Begg and Portes (1992) approach but applied with limited scope). The outcome of this move was more than disappointing: it only created an expectation that all old enterprise debt would be undertaken by the state. In the absence of proper bankruptcy legislation state-owned enterprises started to default extensively on their old loans. As a result the volume of bad loans snowballed in 1991/1992 (Table 14.3). The situation deteriorated especially in 1992 when the deepening of the economic crisis worsened financial discipline considerably.

By mid-1992 the amount of bad loans reached over BGL 111 bn; almost 38 per cent of them were credits allocated after 1991 (see Table 14.3).[13] To assess the magnitude of these figures we shall mention that Bulgarian GDP in 1992 amounted to BGL 195 bn in current prices.

Only in 1993 did the government start to discuss a general solution to the bad loans problem. Most probably, the solution will be of a similar type (taking over the old enterprise debt by the state[14] and recapitalizing the banks with government bonds) but it is suggested that these bonds would carry below-market interest.

The impact of the bad loans on the banking system was really devastating.[15] In fact a large share of the bad loans is concentrated in a small number of banks — the 'sectoral' and some of the regional state-owned banks. However, due to its magnitude the problem reverberates throughout the whole financial system.

The first important implication for the economy was that the banks burdened with bad loans were forced to work with high interest spreads in order to be able to provision. In a competitive market environment the outcome of this is that these banks would be gradually priced out of the market. This is not what is happening in the Bulgarian banking system, at least up till now. Instead, the banks which are not burdened with bad loans simply follow the pricing policy of the first who become the market makers.

The reason for this type of behaviour is the existence of credit ceilings which effectively set limits on the market expansion of individual banks. Accordingly, the 'clean' banks have no incentives to deviate from the pricing policy of the market makers as the demand for credit generally exceeds the supply restricted by the credit ceilings. Under such circumstances the whole commercial banking sector operates in essence as one huge cartel.

There are winners and losers in this situation. In spite of the large interest spread[16] the banks burdened with bad loans are unable to allocate sufficient provisions due to the very depressed economy and the snowballing of the bad loans themselves. In fact, by the middle of 1992 the commercial banks had been able to provision only about 5 per cent of the total outstanding bad loans (Table 14.3). At the same time they allocated for this purpose most of their net income (as well as some of their general purpose reserves) or even finished the year at a loss (see Table 14.1). On the other hand, the 'clean' banks (these are mainly the new private ones) have the chance to cash in windfall profits from this situation.

The data on the current performance of the Bulgarian commercial banking sector (Tables 14.4 and 14.5) confirm this controversial picture.

Due to the lack of data on bad loans in individual banks we have used a simplified breakdown: state-owned (bad-loan burdened) and private ('clean') banks. The comparison of performance indicators gives a clear notion of the distinctively different situation in these two groups (to a large extent driven by the bad loans problem). In 1992 the private banks which held 23.2 per cent of the banking stock and accounted for 9.8 per cent of the total assets of the banking system reported 82.6 per cent of the aggregate after-tax profit of the industry.

The most important reason for this was not an increased profitability in the private banks (actually they also experienced a fall in their returns in 1992) but a catastrophic drop in the (after-tax, i.e, after-provision) profit margins of the state-owned banks (Table 14.5). A comparison of the weighted averages and the medians within the group of state-owned banks indicates that the smaller-sized banks perform better than the larger ones, which can also be attributed to their lighter burden of bad loans.

The figures in Table 14.5 also reveal that in terms of capital adequacy (here measured roughly by the unadjusted capital/asset ratio), on average the private banks are better prepared to face the realities of the market economy than the state-owned ones. However, the banking system as a whole is extremely undercapitalized and the situation can be improved only by an injection of fresh capital into the system.

From this brief analysis we can conclude that the current situation in the Bulgarian banking industry is still characterized by oligopolistic rather than competitive market behaviour. This is an outcome of the combined effect of two factors: legacies of the past (bad loans) and monetary policy (credit ceilings). The breaking of this link is a necessary (though insufficient) condition for the creation of a competitive market environment. Thus both the resolution of the bad loans problem and the replacement of credit ceilings with indirect, market-based policy tools will be crucially important for the future of the banking sector.

It could be mentioned that the growth of new market entries, or new private banks, works in the same direction even in the presence of credit ceilings as each new bank augments the relative share and therefore the importance of the 'clean' banks. So the encouragement of new market entries will have a positive impact on the market in terms of increased competitiveness and efficiency. This would also improve the aggregate capital adequacy of the banking system.

6 Conclusions

The Bulgarian banking system is undergoing a process of fundamental changes. It is still only starting out on the road to market transformation. The legislative reform and the new regulations for prudential banking have laid a relatively good basis for the continuation of the reform process.

However, the general delay in implementing reforms in Bulgaria as well as the delays in solving some of the most acute problems such as bad loans have contributed to the deterioration of the banking sector's performance. The situation has reached a point where the stability of the whole financial system is in danger. This situation requires decisive and comprehensive economic policy measures and acceleration of the reform process.

Notes

1.   Since that time numerous further amendments to this important decree have been adopted; in 1991 its most significant part regarding the institutionalizing of economic entities was replaced by the new Commercial Law, but it is still partly

in force in the areas of taxation of business activity.

2.   Currently Bulgaria has introduced a floating exchange rate regime and the BNB 'fixing' merely reflects the weighted average of the operations of the main market makers on the foreign exchange market (16 large banks). Of course the central bank can also intervene on this market.

3.   This immediately became a serious problem for Bulgaria especially due to the general lack of experience of banking staff in the country. In 1992 two commercial banks (Yambol and Bobovdol) went bankrupt due to violation of the norms of prudential banking.

4.   In fact, Bulgaria did not meet the deadlines of this part of the agreement. Subsequently the final tranches of the SAL were suspended in 1992 so the whole agreement was not brought to a successful end. It should be noted that the change of government in 1992 also contributed to this negative development.

5.   It should be noted that the LBCA delegated far reaching regulatory powers to the central bank (a consequence of the gaps in the law itself) in areas which are usually subject to legislative treatment. Apart from the possible conflict of interest which may arise under such circumstances, this creates a danger of instability of the BNB regulations (as compared to the law).

6.   This is a repetition of the requirement which had actually been introduced by a separate decision of BNB in May 1992 in a move to try to enforce the bank consolidation process.

7.   The discrepancy between the inflation rate and the rate of money supply in 1991 is also an indication of the magnitude of the monetary overhang at the start of the stabilization programme.

8.   Currently government securities in Bulgaria are also rather limited — mainly short-term Treasury bills with maturity from 3—9 months. Only in the middle of 1993 did bills with maturity up to 2 years appear on the market.

9.   It should be noted that these figures are an estimate of the Agency for Economic Coordination and Development. The BNB estimate of this ratio for 1992 as a whole is 105.4 per cent (BNB, 1993).

10.   Until the end of June 1993.

11.   Different numbers have been quoted as goals of the process of consolidation ranging from 6 to 10.

12.   New state-owned banks were also established in this period, such as PostBank and SirBank.

13.   As Table 14.3 shows, a large share of those loans were denominated in convertible currencies. Therefore, the high domestic inflation in 1991—1992 could not erode them.

14.   31 December 1990 is suggested as the deadline to define 'old' debt.

15.   A rough estimate based on the aggregated balance sheet of commercial banks (News Bulletin of the BNB) indicates that bad loans account for over half of their total outstanding credit.

16.   There are no systematic data on individual bank interest spread but it has been reported that in 1991/1992 it reached up to 15—20 percentage points.

References

Ábel, I. and Bonin, J.P. (1992), 'Capital markets in Eastern Europe: the financial black hole', *Connecticut Journal of International Law* 8(1), 1—17.

Ábel, I. and Bonin, J.P. (1993), 'Crippled monetary policy: Hungary's financial legacies', in Siklos, P.L. (ed.), *Varieties of Monetary Reform: Lessons and Experiences on the Road to Monetary Union*, Dordrecht, Kluwer Academic Publishers, (forthcoming).

Ábel, I. and Székely, I.P. (1992), 'The conditions for competition and innovation in the Hungarian banking system', (mimeo), Centre for Economic Policy Research, London.

Balassa, Á. (1992), 'The transformation and development of the Hungarian banking system', in Kemme and Rudka (1992).

Begg, D. and Portes, R. (1992), 'Enterprise debt and economic transformation: financial restructuring of the state sector in Central and Eastern Europe', Discussion Paper Series No. 695, Centre for Economic Policy Research, London,

BNB (1991), 'Bulgarian National Bank Annual Report, 1990', Sofia.

BNB (1992), 'Bulgarian National Bank Annual Report, 1991', Sofia.

BNB (1993), 'Bulgarian National Bank Annual Report, 1992', Sofia.

Coats, W. (1992), 'Bulgaria: market based monetary control', Central Banking Department, International Monetary Fund, Washington, D.C.

Corbett, J. and Mayer, C. (1991), 'Financial reform in Eastern Europe: progress with the wrong model', *Oxford Review of Economic Policy* 7(4), 57—75.

Decree (1989), 'Decree No. 56 on Economic Activity', State Gazette No.4.

Dobrinsky, R., Markov, N., Nikolov, B., and Yalnazov, D. (1992),'Economic transition and industrial restructuring in Bulgaria', paper presented at the workshop on 'Industrial Restructuring and Reorientation of Trade in Eastern Europe', Prague, 2—5 April.

Estrin, S., Hare, P., and Surányi, M. (1992), 'Banking in transition: development and current problems in Hungary', *Soviet Studies* 44(5), 785—808.

Filipov, L. (1992), 'Monetary policy instruments of the Bulgarian National Bank', *Bank Review* 4, 13—18.

Genov, K. (1993), 'Monetary policy in 1992: instruments and results', *Bank Review* 1, 7—17.

Ghizari, E.I. (1992), 'Banking reform in Romania', in Kemme and Rudka (1992).

Gueorguiev, N. and Gospodinov, N. (1992), 'The monetary policy: mechanisms and results', Agency for Economic Coordination and Development, Sofia.

Jindra, V. (1992), 'Problems in Czechoslovak banking reform', in Kemme and Rudka (1992).

Kemme, D.M. and Rudka, A. (eds) (1992), *Monetary and Banking Reform in Postcommunist Economies*, New York, Institute for EastWest Studies.

LBCA (1992), 'Law on Banks and Credit Activity', Bulgarian National Bank, Sofia.

LBNB (1991), 'Law on the Bulgarian National Bank', Bulgarian National Bank, Sofia.

Matrozov, A. (1993), 'BORICA: banking organization for payments initiated by cards', *Bank Review* 1, 18—23.

Miller, J. (1992), 'Financial institutions, risk and resource allocation in Bulgaria', *Bank Review* 2, 51—56.

Miller, J. (1993), 'The Bulgarian banking system' Bulgarian National Bank, Sofia.

Mladenov, M. (1992), 'Money, banking and credit: the case of Bulgaria', in Kemme and Rudka (1992).

Mombru, J.L. (1992), 'Banking consolidation in Bulgaria: a few ideas and suggestions from an international view', *Bank Review* 4, 19—31.

Ravicz, R.M. (1992), 'The Bulgarian banking system', *Bank Review* 2, 28—45.

Rudka, A. (1992), 'Reform of the banking system in Poland', in Kemme and Rudka (1992).

Rules (1989), 'Ordinance No. 19 of May 19, 1989 for adoption of rules for banks', Bulgarian National Bank.

Rybczynski, T. (1991), 'The sequencing of reform', *Oxford Review of Economic Policy* 7(4), 26—34.

Stratev, B. (1992), 'The law on banks and credit activity as the legal framework for commercial banking', *Bank Review* 2, 46—50.

Stratev, B. (1993), 'The regulations and the implementation of the law on banks and credit activity', *Bank Review* 2, 15—24.

Székely, I.P. (1993), 'Economic transformation and the reform of the financial system in Central and Eastern Europe', Discussion Paper Series No. 816, Centre for Economic Policy Research, London.

Thorne, A. (1992a), 'Issues in reforming financial systems in Eastern Europe. The case of Bulgaria', WPS 882, The World Bank, Washington, D.C.

Thorne, A. (1992b), 'The role of banks in the transition: lessons from Eastern European countries' experience', ECA/MENA Technical Department, The World Bank, Washington, D.C.

Wyzan, M. (1992), 'Stabilization policy in post-communist Bulgaria: the search for a basis of comparison', paper presented at the Arne Ryde Symposium on the 'Transition Problem', Rungsted Kyst, Denmark, June 11—12.

Table 14.1 Bulgarian commercial banks in 1992

(ranked by total equity, values in BGL mn)

No	Commercial Bank	Common stock	of which state-held	Reserves	Total equity	Total assets	After-tax profit
I.	State-owned banks						
1	Bulg. Foreign Trade Bank	1200.00	1179.70	3658.62	4858.62	72500.00	1114.82
2	MineralBank	291.78	130.05	3183.45	3475.23	27547.05	-682.52
3	State Saving Bank	800.00	800.00	2100.00	2900.00	n.a.	n.a.
4	United Bulgarian Bank	679.47	298.00	368.70	1048.17	25965.94	0.02
5	Biochim Bank	160.00	80.59	358.78	518.78	8610.54	20.43
6	Vazrazhdane Bank	26.69	15.90	486.94	513.63	873.17	0.87
7	Sofija Bank	200.00	200.00	153.31	353.31	5467.72	301.07
8	BalkanBank	200.00	117.69	152.53	352.53	14383.51	0.00
9	Agrocooperative Bank	90.00	63.25	110.31	200.30	7980.34	-4.38
10	Plovdiv	62.47	53.23	83.53	146.00	4091.26	5.83
11	Elektronika Bank	68.35	65.12	58.35	126.70	4958.43	-418.99
12	Transport Bank	47.40	46.46	78.93	126.33	3203.37	74.42
13	Varna	36.50	36.01	84.68	121.18	2032.09	40.50
14	Economic Bank	100.00	63.53	0.00	100.00	37872.59	-159.60
15	Burgas	24.95	22.19	65.34	90.29	2402.81	12.32
16	Blagoevgrad	18.00	17.04	66.29	84.29	1577.03	5.39
17	Stara Zagora	35.43	33.84	38.97	74.40	1791.97	3.59
18	Hemus Bank	35.60	23.99	34.77	70.37	1005.12	9.28
19	Sredetz Bank	13.69	12.10	55.55	69.24	1944.82	6.92
20	PostBank	60.00	60.00	9.14	69.14	2543.73	23.66
21	SirBank	44.25	41.45	10.32	54.57	1107.51	8.42
22	Veliko Tarnovo	21.10	19.40	32.71	53.81	1181.91	8.62
23	Razgrad	12.67	10.99	36.37	49.04	730.07	0.00
24	Vidin	12.17	11.32	30.69	42.86	899.51	1.02
25	Kazanlak	21.00	20.22	14.21	35.21	1045.96	0.00
26	Vitosha Bank	9.60	9.26	25.10	34.70	810.04	0.00
27	Kyustendil	18.40	18.19	13.53	31.93	393.85	6.03
28	Karlovo	21.79	21.03	6.58	28.37	1039.34	-59.57
29	Trakia Bank	16.90	15.47	8.87	25.77	860.99	0.00
30	Troian	7.00	5.34	17.36	24.36	282.19	4.58
31	Rila Bank	7.00	5.72	16.37	23.37	532.76	0.00
32	Gorna Oriahovitza	9.51	8.80	11.51	21.02	619.85	4.47
33	Smolian	7.00	4.39	12.27	19.27	574.18	4.95
34	Yambol	13.09	9.39	4.53	17.62	3352.08	-244.70
35	Silistra	13.13	11.65	3.07	16.20	736.34	0.02
36	Asenovgrad	7.00	4.97	8.46	15.46	299.72	6.53
37	Cherven Briag	7.00	6.78	7.46	14.46	340.46	0.11
38	Provadija	7.00	5.49	6.03	13.03	279.47	-1.71
39	Devin	7.00	6.63	4.70	11.70	88.41	1.51
40	Parvomai	7.00	5.13	3.99	10.99	153.28	0.80
41	Elin Pelin	7.00	6.30	3.45	10.45	128.32	0.20
42	Lyaskovetz	7.00	6.15	1.85	8.85	141.76	0.72
43	Gotze Delchev	7.00	6.85	0.92	7.92	290.57	0.00
44	Chepelare	7.00	6.43	0.83	7.83	115.04	4.78
45	Mezdra	7.00	6.26	0.43	7.43	260.46	0.00
	Subtotal	4454.93	3592.28	11429.78	15884.71	243015.53	100.43

Table 14.1 Bulgarian commercial banks in 1992 (continued)

(ranked by total equity, values in BGL mn)

No	Commercial Bank	Common stock	of which state-held	Reserves	Total equity	Total assets	After-tax profit
II.	Private banks						
1	First Private Bank	337.01	0.00	7.43	344.44	8406.43	79.70
2	Central Coop. Bank	223.32	0.00	41.56	264.88	1284.84	8.13
3	Bank for Agric. Credit	150.00	63.35	109.61	259.61	6354.50	271.81
4	First East Int. Bank	200.00	3.15	30.38	230.38	1825.51	8.64
5	Dobrich	30.00	3.49	139.42	169.42	2007.15	44.81
6	TouristsportBank	150.00	11.28	0.00	150.00	3201.94	32.26
7	Private Agro Inv. Bank	110.00	0.00	10.00	120.00	500.59	0.04
8	CreditBank	61.20	0.00	0.00	61.20	1647.40	2.19
9	CrystalBank	20.42	4.93	18.29	38.71	406.74	17.18
10	BusinessBank	27.55	4.66	3.88	31.43	402.28	8.68
11	AgrobusinessBank	22.00	0.46	0.08	22.08	246.37	1.96
12	Int. Trade&Dev. Bank	14.30	0.00	0.00	14.30	n.a.	n.a.
	Subtotal	1345.81	91.32	360.64	1706.45	26283.75	475.39
	Total	5800.74	3683.60	11790.42	17591.16	269299.28	575.82

Source:

Bulgarian Business, 22, 1993;

Balance sheets of commercial banks (various publications).

Table 14.2   Consolidation of Bulgarian state-owned commercial banks, 1992-1993

No	Consolidated bank	Incorporates following banks
I.	*Consolidation completed or under way*	
1	United Bulgarian Bank	Doverie Bank, Construction Bank, Rousse, Pleven, Vratza, Shoumen, Haskovo, Gabrovo, Kardjali, Lovech, Montana, Pazardzik, Peshtera, Sliven, Nova Zagora, Iskar, Elhovo, Botevgrad, Samokov, Targovishte, Pernik, Popovo
2	BalkanBank	Balkanbank, Vidin, Gorna Oriahovitza, Lyaskotetz
3	HebrosBank	Agrocooperative Bank, Plovdiv, Veliko Tarnovo, Blagoevgrad Vitosha Bank, Mezdra, Troian, Chepelare
4	ExpressBank	Transport Bank, Varna, Vazrazhdane Bank, Kyustendil, Silistra, Razgrad, Smolian, Cherven Briag, Rila Bank, Gotze Delchev, Provadija, Devin
5	SofiaBank	Sofia Bank, Hemus Bank, Elektronika Bank, Kazanlak
II.	*Planned consolidations*	
6	Biochim Bank	Biochim Bank, Sredetz Bank, Burgas, Stara Zagora, Karlovo, Trakia Bank, Asenovgrad, Parvomai, Elin Pelin
III.	*Undecided*	
7	Bulgarian Foreign Trade Bank	
8	MinaralBank	
9	Economic Bank	
10	PostBank	
11	SirBank	
12	Yambol	

Source: Bank Consolidation Company

Table 14.3   Substandard and non-performing loans of Bulgarian commercial banks on 30 May 1992

Denomination	Total amount of the outstanding loans	Sum of overdues by term					Total amount of allocated reserves
		Total	From 30 to 90 days	From 90 days to 1 year	From 1 to 3 years	Over 3 years	
I. Values in millions of BGL							
A. Allocated before 31 December 1990							
In BGL	34742	11904	2528	3023	5722	631	1551
In convertible currencies	34428	12665	913	3963	4475	3314	2731
Subtotal	69170	24569	3441	6986	10197	3945	4282
B. Allocated after 1 January 1991							
In BGL	37793	9512	4580	4298	626	8	1096
In convertible currencies	4171	575	316	233	27	-	13
Subtotal	41964	10087	4896	4531	653	8	1109
Total	111134	34656	8337	11517	10850	3952	5391
II. In percentage to the outstanding loans							
A. Allocated before 31 December 1990							
In BGL	100.0	34.3	7.3	8.7	16.5	1.8	4.5
In convertible currencies	100.0	36.8	2.7	11.5	13.0	9.6	7.9
Subtotal	100.0	35.5	5.0	10.1	14.7	5.7	6.2
B. Allocated after 1 January 1991							
In BGL	100.0	25.2	12.1	11.4	1.7	0.0	2.9
In convertible currencies	100.0	13.8	7.6	5.6	0.6	0.0	0.3
Subtotal	100.0	24.0	11.7	10.8	1.6	0.0	2.6
Total	100.0	31.2	7.5	10.4	9.8	3.6	4.9

Source: Annual Report of the Bulgarian National Bank, 1992.

Table 14.4   Market shares of state-owned and private banks in Bulgaria

	Common stock	Total equity	Total assets	After-tax profit*
1991				
State-owned banks	81.1	94.3	96.0	90.4
Private banks	18.9	5.7	4.0	9.6
1992				
State-owned banks	76.8	90.3	90.2	17.4
Private banks	23.2	9.7	9.8	82.6

Note: * Excluding State Saving Bank
Source: Author's own calculations

*Table 14.5   Performance of the Bulgarian banking sector: financial ratios**

(in per cent)

	State-owned banks		Private banks		All banks	
	Weighted average	Median	Weighted average	Median	Weighted average	Median
1991						
Return on equity	34.54	58.96	50.19	66.88	35.60	60.04
Return on assets	1.80	2.76	3.79	3.04	1.89	2.79
Capital/asset ratio	5.20	4.40	7.55	7.56	5.32	4.51
1992						
Return on equity	0.77	3.96	28.09	21.50	3.92	4.83
Return on assets	0.04	0.18	1.81	0.95	0.21	0.36
Capital/asset ratio	5.34	4.33	6.44	8.44	5.45	4.66

Note: * Excluding State Saving Bank
Source: Author's own calculations

Discussion
Lyubomir Filipov

When economic reform began in Bulgaria early in 1991 there were two main peculiarities in comparison with other Central and East European countries. The first one — a structural peculiarity — was the fact that at that time almost 70 commercial banks already existed in the country. The second peculiarity was a macroeconomic one, consisting of the enormous monetary overhang represented by money supply equal to 106 per cent of the GDP for 1990. Let us consider the roots of these peculiarities and the ways of surmounting them.

In early 1989, there were 11 banks in Bulgaria — eight commercial banks, specializing mainly in investment credits; the Bulgarian Foreign Trade Bank; the State Savings Bank; and the Bulgarian National Bank, which at that time was not only the central bank of the country but also the biggest commercial bank in short-term credit activity for working capital lending.

Among other attempts to improve and thus preserve the system of the centrally-planned economy (CPE) through introducing some modest market-oriented instruments was the decision, taken in August 1989, that the Bulgarian National Bank (BNB) was to be transformed into a normal central bank, and a system of commercial banks was to be created on the basis of its 145 or so branches. As a result of the implementation of this decision, an additional 59 new commercial banks were established by the end of 1989 when the changes in the Bulgarian political and economic system began. The minimum capital of these banks was BGL 7 mn, equal to almost USD 9 mn according to the official exchange rate at that time.

From the point of view of the present transitional period of rapid economic reform, the decision to establish a system of more than 60 commercial banks was certainly wrong.

But let us remember the situation in Bulgaria in mid-1989, when this decision was taken. At that time, nobody believed that only half a year later the country would be on the threshold of a real market economy. So the concept was to artificially introduce competition on the money and credit markets as another effort to increase the efficiency of central planning.

Of course, at that time, the already existing eight specialized commercial banks wanted to obtain the BNB branches. The BNB management deliberately rejected the proposal for the following reasons. Each of the eight commercial banks was under the strong influence or even indirect rule of a particular politically strong member of the Government or even a member of the Politburo of the Central Committee of the Communist Party. Those commercial banks were almost beyond the control of the BNB — the Bank was subordinated to the Council of Ministers and from 1984 the

Bank's Governor was no longer even a member of the Government. Therefore, if the proposal had been accepted, it would have led virtually to an absolute loss of control by the central bank over the monetary and credit situation in the country. Being politically dependent and weak at that time, the central bank could not afford a system of practically uncontrollable commercial banks and was forced to permit those former branches of the BNB, which wished to form commercial banks other than the eight specialized banks, to do so.

Since the beginning of 1991, the situation changed drastically. Many of the old credits given to the state-owned enterprises which had been guaranteed in the past by the government turned into bad loans. After the liberalization of the exchange rate regime, the fast initial devaluation of the domestic currency made the minimum commercial bank capital equal to only USD 0.25 mn, far from any international standards.

In mid-1991, it was already absolutely clear that a reform of the financial sector was necessary on the basis of the consolidation of the banking sector and cleaning up of the commercial banks' credit portfolios. The outlines of these two topics are comprehensively discussed in the chapter.

Let us discuss the second issue — the sources of the large money overhang in Bulgaria at the end of 1990 and the steps for overcoming it. The transition from a CPE to a market economy was characterized by large imbalances. The monetary imbalance in Bulgaria was considerable at the end of 1990 with a huge volume of money supply ('broad money') exceeding the size of the GDP.

Let us note the main groups of factors which led to the 'overcrediting' of the economy and respectively to the enormous money supply growth. The first group was related to the growing state budget deficit (explicit and hidden) which included: direct credits; substitution of working capital by bank credit after working capital (inventory) evaluation; and mandatory crediting of investment projects (these to be normally financed by budget funds), as well as subsidies in raw materials and energy industries, etc.

The second group of factors was related to the overestimation of the bank's capacity to increase economic efficiency through credit allocation, which led to an unnecessary credit expansion. A typical example of this was the introduction in the 1970s of financing unfinished construction completely through bank credits.

Under these circumstances, in February 1991 when the share of liberalized prices increased, the basic goal of the monetary policy was to achieve a money supply growth definitely lower than the inflation rate during the first months of the liberalization. This would limit purchasing power, but, at the same time, reduce monetary overhang to a large extent.

The actual development since the beginning of the economic reform shows that the BNB had reached the targets of the monetary policy.

Monetary overhang had been successfully eliminated, the money supply (broad money) to GDP ratio decreased from 109 per cent at the end of 1990 to 85 per cent at the end of 1991, and remained at this level in 1992.

Finally, I would also like to discuss some features of the development of the BNB's monetary policy instruments in the framework of reform. The first feature was the effort to avoid some mistakes by using the developed countries' historical experience in this area. For example, since the beginning of reform the BNB had never tried to impose any restrictions on interest rates applied by the commercial banks, either on deposits or on credits. In the same respect, no automatic overdraft facility had ever been permitted for the state budget.

Another feature was the central bank's policy to decrease the share of refinancing commercial banks' credits through the BNB. Consequently, the share of the central bank's credits and deposits granted to banks as opposed to commercial banks' credits decreased from 53 per cent at the end of 1990 to 10 per cent in September 1993. At the same time the share of the interbank market increased from virtual zero to 41 per cent.

The third characteristic was the continuous growth of the securitization of loans granted by the central bank. In the beginning of 1991, all credits and deposits granted to commercial banks were not secured, whereas by the end of 1993 the proportion of collateralized loans of the central bank was about two-thirds. Consequently, the BNB was in a position to begin open market operations in 1993, and it intends to make them the main instrument for liquidity control in 1994.

As a fourth feature we could mention the BNB's interest rate policy for maintaining credit rates at zero level in real terms with slightly negative real deposit rates. This has been helping to slow the growth of inflation without substantially increasing the bad debt problem.

There are some unsolved problems of financial reform in Bulgaria. First, there is the continuing delay in the cleaning up of commercial banks' credit portfolios by a substitution of the old bad loans inherited from central planning for long-term government securities. A draft of an appropriate law has been waiting in Parliament for several months.

The second problem is the almost total monetization of the fast-growing state debt. Household deposits doubled last year but enough incentives have not yet been introduced to draw them into the capital market for privatization and financing government debt.

Last but not least, is the problem of implementing the BNB's recently released prudential and supervisory regulations for commercial banks. To take an example: the core capital/risk assets ratio of 8 per cent was postponed by Parliament until the second half of 1995, which will perhaps force the central bank to preserve credit ceilings for two more years.

Finally, some words about the central bank's independence. According to the Bulgarian Constitution and the Law on the Bulgarian National Bank, passed in 1991, the central bank is independent and is accountable only to the Parliament. But in an environment of deep recession and a poorly educated banking and non-banking public, it is very difficult and sometimes even risky to act independently.

Modern speakers usually begin with a story — I am going to finish with one. At a seminar, organized by the Bank for International Settlements, the representative of the Deutsche Bundesbank, following his comments on the central bank's independence, was asked by the representative of the Bank of Norway: 'Sir, can you imagine our esteemed Bank, with your law and your personnel, but in Brazil?'

Discussion
Eduard Hochreiter

Dobrinsky's chapter is very informative, full of useful technical detail and covers a lot of ground. It starts with an overview of the development of the Bulgarian banking system from the pre-war period, when Bulgaria had a rather modern, market-based banking system, the establishment of the monobank system during communist rule, to its break-up shortly before the revolution and the subsequent (re)establishment of a Western-style central bank and commercial banking system. It also covers the important issues of banking supervision and the clearing system as well as surveying the performance of the Bulgarian banking sector including the burning issue of bad debt. Ample space is devoted to the discussion of monetary policy, its instruments and the development of financial markets.

As I am in broad agreement with Dobrinsky's views, and do not have much to add to the technical part, I will only touch on one factual topic and highlight a few issues brought up in the more analytical part.

I would like to start by focusing on the Bulgarian National Bank Act. With regard to the statutes, the following points deserve particular mention:

— The Bulgarian National Bank (BNB) today is a central bank in the Western sense.
— Its prime responsibility is to maintain internal and external stability of the national currency.
— There exist very strict limitations on fiscal financing.
— The BNB enjoys a high degree of independence with regard to the implementation of monetary policy.
— The BNB Act provides for the fiscal agent function of the BNB.
— The BNB also exercises regulatory and banking supervisory powers.

The Bulgarian National Bank Act has, along with others (for example, the Czech National Bank Act) been compared to the Bundesbank Act. In this context, it has to be mentioned that the mandate to maintain price stability in the Bulgarian National Bank Act is formulated in much stricter terms than in the Bundesbank Act. In this respect it resembles more the Austrian National Bank Act. The paper is unclear as to the responsibilities with regard to the setting of the exchange rate regime. According to Dobrinsky, the BNB only 'fixes' the central exchange rate of the national currency (Section 3.1). Moreover, it is still too early to say how the legal provisions are being dealt with in practice; for example, in the problems related to adhering to limitations on financing the government. The paper needs to clarify what happens if the Bank does not adhere to the law.

I would like to commend the author for the detailed discussion of the Law on Banks and Credit Activity, including the clear description of the still existing gaps, which are — to a large extent — the result of a trade-off between the need for rapid legislation and detailed examination of regulatory requirements.

I will now turn to a discussion of monetary policy issues. The paper argues that the instruments of monetary policy are still in their infancy and that direct controls still dominate market-based instruments. This should not be surprising given the fact that the entire financial system, its institutions as well as its instruments had to be designed from scratch. Since their first use hardly four years have passed. Apart from credit ceilings, reserve requirements have been applied since 1990. For refinancing, traditional instruments, i.e., discount and Lombard financing, have been in use.

I fully agree with the author that credit ceilings can only be regarded as a stop-gap measure, that their effectiveness declines over time and that they tend to 'petrify' the banking structure. Nonetheless, they serve their purpose while markets are in development. Moreover, I also support the use of traditional instruments in countries such as Bulgaria, as they are simple and can be readily understood. The introduction of very sophisticated instruments should be postponed until the respective markets are sufficiently developed and until market participants are able to understand them.

I have some problem with the discussion of the ceiling-induced crowding-out. It is argued (Section 4.2) that risk-aversion on the part of banks leads them to acquire low-risk government securities at the expense of high-risk commercial credit. Indeed, the share of the government in total borrowing rose from 19.1 per cent in 1991 to 27.8 per cent in 1992. It is then argued that high real interest rates for some commercial borrowers (nominal interest rates deflated by producer prices) induce banks to finance riskier business and, thereby, add to the bad debt problem. Both statements tend to be contradictory and therefore need clarification. While it is conceivable that the risk distribution is two-humped, i.e., centred at low as well as high risk, I feel that the sharp increase of government debt in the portfolio of banks indicates risk-aversion.

The final point I would like to raise is related to the role foreign banks can play in the development of money and capital markets. There is, I believe, unanimous agreement that a functioning financial system and financial markets are essential for a successful transition. It is also true that, as the paper correctly points out, financial transition in Bulgaria has been relatively slow but is advancing. The immediate problem — apart from legal issues — is who supplies capital and financial expertise. The fastest way, to my mind, is to invite foreign banks to take part in this process. There are, however, a number of problems.

First, there is widespread resentment in many countries (also in the West) about allowing foreign banks to take over domestic banks. It is noteworthy that the minimum capital requirement according to Bulgarian banking law is, calculated at current exchange rates, higher than the corresponding EC guidelines (in Bulgaria around USD 7.3 mn for domestic operations and USD 18.3 mn for international operations; in the EC around USD 6.3 mn for both). While, in the case of Bulgaria, this stipulation cannot be interpreted as discrimination against foreign banks, it is certainly not an incentive to set up shop in Bulgaria.

Second, and more important: privatization has been delayed and, up to now, no bank has been privatized although some spontaneous privatization occurred. Without clearing up this issue, foreign banks will be very reluctant to participate in the development of the Bulgarian banking sector.

Third, and, perhaps, most pressing: so far the bad debt issue has not been decisively settled. The overall bad debt of banks in Bulgaria is estimated to be 57 per cent of GDP.

Summing up, I would once again like to commend Dobrinsky for his very useful and detailed paper.

Index

Ábel, I.
  and banking sector reform 221, 226
  and central bank independence 81, 82,
    86, 87
  and financial sector reform 109–26,
    127–31
  and financial system reform 323, 335
  and market structures and competition
    214–16, 272–85, 286–92, 297,
    306, 309–13, 317
  and system change 3, 4, 36, 37
Abrams, R.K. 88, 210
accounting see international
Accounting Act 295
after-tax lending rates 213
Agenda Group 313
Âkerholm, J. 210
Alesina, A. 72, 74, 81, 85, 99
Alexandrowicz, A. 37
Antall government 142
arrears, bilateral and multilateral 230–2
Arrow-Debreu type 215
asset prices 171
Aufricht, H. 74, 85, 86
Austria 4, 5, 191
  central bank independence 74, 101, 106
  financial reform 131, 321
  money and capital market reforms 268
  National Bank 106, 181
  see also financial liberalization

Bacchetta, P. 170
Backé, P. 309–13
bad loans 117–21
Bade, R. 72
Balassa, Á. 38, 74, 272, 320
Balcerowicz, L. 13, 138
Balicka, M. 150
Banaian, K. 72
Bank of Canada Act 75
Bank Consolidation Company (BCC) 21,
    333, 334

Bank of Finland 199, 200, 202, 209, 210,
    213
Bank for International Settlements (BIS)
    standards 2, 44, 77, 349
Bank of Norway 349
banking
  sector problems 203
  sector reform see Czech Republic
Banking acts 111, 118, 185–6, 191
Banking Integrated System for Electronic
    Transfer (BISERA) 325
Banking Law 248
Banking Organization for Payments
    Initiated by Cards (BORICA) 325
banking sector 190–1
  size and composition changes 233–4
  see also banking sector reform
banking sector reform in Czech Republic
    221–49, 251–6, 268–71
  average lending and borrowing interest
    rates of commercial banks 251
  banking institutions 253
  banking system type 246–7
  credit and deposit markets 254, 255
  functional efficiency and stability 223–
    5
  institutional developments and competi-
    tive environment 232
    banking sector size and composition
      changes 233–4
    deposit market developments 235–6
    interbank money and foreign ex-
      change markets 236
    two-tier system introduction 232–3
  policy options for efficiency and stabil-
    ity 239–45
    alternative strategies 242–4
    credit allocation 244–5
    transition years 239–42
  regulation and deregulation trends 236–
    9
    deregulation policies 237

353